Sacred SYMBOLS

Other books by Alonzo L. Gaskill

The Lost Language of Symbolism—An Essential Guide for
Recognizing and Interpreting Symbols of the Gospel

Odds Are You're Going to Be Exalted—
Evidence that the Plan of Salvation Works!

Paradise Lost—Understanding the
Symbolic Message of the Fall

Know Your Religions, Volume 1—A Comparative
Look at Mormonism and Catholicism

Nativity

The Savior and the Serpent—
Unlocking the Doctrine of the Fall

Sacred SYMBOLS

FINDING MEANING IN RITES, RITUALS, & ORDINANCES

Alonzo L. Gaskill

CFI
An imprint of Cedar Fort, Inc.
Springville, Utah

ISBN 13: 978-1-59955-965-0

Published by CFI, an imprint of Cedar Fort, Inc.
2373 W. 700 S., Springville, UT 84663
Distributed by Cedar Fort, Inc., www.cedarfort.com

The Library of Congress has cataloged the softcover edition as follows:

Gaskill, Alonzo L., author.
  Sacred symbols / Alonzo L. Gaskill.
     pages cm
  Includes bibliographical references and index.
  ISBN 978-1-59955-988-9 (alk. paper)
  1. Rites and ceremonies. 2. Ritual. I. Title.
  BL600.G35 2011
  261.2--dc23
                        2011032181

Cover design by Rebecca Jensen
Cover design © 2011 by Lyle Mortimer
Edited and typeset by Heidi Doxey

Printed in the United States of America

10 9 8 7 6 5 4 3 2 1

Printed on acid-free paper

For my mission president,
Ed Jolley Pinegar,
Who loves the Lord and His Holy House.

Table of Contents

Acknowledgments

A number of individuals deserve my acknowledgment and sincere expression of gratitude for their contributions to this volume.

First and foremost, I wish to recognize the invaluable work of my research assistant, Judson Burton, whose countless hours of scouring the library shelves for sources have been a tremendous boon to this project. He has winnowed thousands of pages down to hundreds, and in so doing, made this project manageable. His research skills, insights, and suggestions have greatly improved the manuscript.

To my friend Lori Denning, I express my appreciation for her selfless contributions. She gave freely of her time to read potentially germane sources, and to point me to texts and quotes applicable to my study. Her contributions exemplify consecration.

I also offer my heartfelt thanks to Dr. Richard Moore, Matthew Christensen, and Richard and Charlotte Lowary for their review of the text and their helpful suggestions. Knowing personally what it takes to do a thorough review of a manuscript of this length, I feel deeply indebted to each for their sacrifice.

As always, I express my heartfelt thanks to Jan Nyholm, who for many years now has edited my manuscripts, and thereby greatly improved my work. Her willingness to serve and sacrifice knows no bounds.

Finally, in the preface to his book, *The Temple: Where Heaven Meets Earth*, Truman G. Madsen wrote: "Clearly I have not written officially but only as a 'layman enthralled.'"[1] I must admit, I too only write from the perspective of an enthralled layman. This work is not a publication of The Church of Jesus Christ of Latter-day Saints nor of my employer, Brigham Young University. I bear sole responsibility for the content of this book.

Notes
1. Madsen, Truman G. *The Temple: Where Heaven Meets Earth* (Salt Lake City: Deseret Book, 2008), x.

Introduction

The French philosopher, Paul Ricoeur, wisely noted that symbols are specifically designed to be provocative—to give rise to, or provoke, thought![1] As a professor of world religions and Christian history, I've always been curious about the rites and rituals of the ancients, as well as those of faiths other than my own. Symbolism possesses me; it *absolutely* provokes me! And, as the language of ritual is specifically symbolism, I crave a knowledge of what symbolic acts, gestures, covenants, and clothing mean—in my own faith, as well as in the faiths of others.[2]

As the reader will shortly discover, this book is somewhat unique in its approach and content. Its audience is primarily practicing Latter-day Saints, and yet its focus is essentially ceremonies that are non-LDS in their origin and practice. Indeed, gathered together between the covers of this book are a variety of rites, rituals, ceremonies, and sacraments that hail primarily from ancient and modern Judaism and Christianity.[3] I have intentionally avoided much discussion of rituals that are uniquely LDS, primarily because it seemed wise to keep the sacred ceremonies of the Restoration "secret."[4] This is not to say that the rites that will be discussed are somehow void of sacral content—or that we should respect our own rites but not those of another's faith. On

1

the contrary, that which is sacred to the participants of a given faith should be treated as such by those outside of that faith. However, the rituals and ceremonies that will be discussed herein are published rites,[5] which, I believe, are illustrative of symbols Latter-day Saints would do well to understand.

Mormons are traditionally not an extremely ritualistic people—at least not in their Sunday worship, nor in their day-to-day lives.[6] Consequently, some find very little meaning in liturgy or ritual. Indeed, some Saints struggle to "see symbolically," per se. One LDS scholar suggested that we Latter-day Saints "have become an asymbolic society, and, as a result, we do not understand the power of our own rites of passage." This same source added that most of us make little effort "to understand the meanings of our own rituals or what ritual behavior implies." Consequently, we fail "to comprehend or internalize the messages contained in ritual symbols."[7] In support of this sad claim, I recently delivered a lecture at a university on the subject of interpreting symbols in art. Immediately following the lecture I was approached by one of the attendees who expressed concern that she had always seen things quite literally and thus had ever struggled to find symbolic meaning in the ceremonies and symbols of the Church and its ordinances or rituals. Almost in a spirit of pleading, she asked "How can I get myself to see the symbols, and find meaning in them?" The pages of this book are devoted specifically to the task of helping that sister, and others like her, to more successfully see symbolically, and thereby find personal application in the rites and rituals of the restored gospel.

We too often assume God will just give us the meaning of the symbols that overlay the rites and rituals we participate in. Like Oliver Cowdery, we naively 'take no thought save it were to ask Him' for understanding (D&C 9:7). However, if we expect to learn and understand the symbols of the ceremonies, like Oliver in his efforts to translate, we too must "study it out" (D&C 9:8). We should put more time and effort into understanding what we experience in rituals—time contemplating those rites both before and after we participate in them. Rather than just participating in the ordinances, we should engage in study and contemplation over their message and their meaning. Then God will be able to teach us from on high. But to assume God will reveal the meaning of the symbols without a concerted effort on our part is to be naive. Only after paying a personal price can we expect God to open the windows of heaven and pour out understanding beyond our own.

I must make a rather important point germane to this particular work and its intended purpose. Over the years Deseret Book and the Foundation for Ancient Research and Mormon Studies have produced a number of popular apologetic[8] texts, such as Donald W. Parry's *Temples of the Ancient World*[9] or Hugh Nibley's *Mormonism and Early Christianity*.[10] As a follow-up to Parry's book, he and Stephen D. Ricks edited a volume entitled *The Temple in Time and Eternity*.[11] And Nibley produced other similar works on the temple, such as *The Message of the Joseph Smith Papyri—An Egyptian Endowment*[12] and *Temple and Cosmos*.[13] These are but a few of the plethora of works that Latter-day Saint scholars have produced in recent decades, each highlighting parallels between ancient Christian or Jewish rites and Latter-day restored temple rites. Each of these aforementioned works are apologetic in their focus. Though this text may have a seemingly familiar style, it is decidedly *not* apologetic in its purpose! This book is about symbolism, and each of the examples offered herein have been presented, not for any apologetic value, but for their symbolic merit only. I ask that the reader keep this in mind as he or she reads, lest any misunderstanding of intent arise and the reader inadvertently slide into the practice of "parallelomania"—a danger ever present in the field of apologetics.[14]

As a matter of approach, where possible I have sought to be non-dogmatic about the symbolic meaning of the various rites and rituals discussed in this book. Indeed, in most cases I have offered several interpretations of the symbolism—or suggested several layers of symbolism in a singular rite—as the published accounts of the rites and the practitioners thereof have seen many symbolic meanings.[15] As one non-LDS scholar of the ancient temple wrote: "There are enormous problems for anyone attempting to write about the temple and I am only too well aware of them. There are few certainties and many possibilities."[16] Another author noted that "symbols rarely have a single meaning."[17] Such is likely true of *any* ordinance of the gospel—or *any* ceremony of *any* religious tradition. What a rite or ritual means to one participant may not be what it means to another. Additionally, what the symbolic ceremonies performed in the restored gospel mean to you at one time in your life will likely be different than what they mean at a different time—contingent upon your spiritual maturity and your personal needs at any given stage of your life. The gospel's symbols tend to grow and evolve with us and our needs. I'm drawn to Elder David B. Haight's counsel: "allow the Spirit to teach you by revelation what the symbols can mean *to you*."[18] Thus, in this text the reader is left to decide for himself which symbolic interpretations to embrace and which to leave upon the shelf. After all, the ultimate goal of this volume is *not* to convince the reader of a particular interpretation of a given ordinance. Rather, this volume simply seeks to *encourage* its readers to be more attentive and think more symbolically about rites and rituals when they participate in those sacred acts.

Notes

1. See Paul Ricoeur, *The Symbolism of Evil* (Boston: Beacon Press, 1967), 348.

2. Though we will use the terms somewhat interchangeably herein, it seems appropriate up-front to define and distinguish between the terms "liturgy," "rite," "ritual," and "ceremony." In its traditional sense, the word "liturgy" means: "Prescribed forms or ritual for public worship in any of various Christian churches." ("Liturgy," Jean L. McKechnie, ed., *Webster's New Twentieth Century Dictionary of the English Language, Unabridged*, second edition [Collins World, 1978], 1058.) The word "rite," on the other hand, is usually defined as: "A ceremonial or formal, solemn act, observance, or procedure in accordance with prescribed rule or custom, as in religious use." "A prescribed form or particular system of ceremonial procedure, religious or otherwise." ("Rite," ibid., 1565.) The term "ritual" means: "A set form or system of rites, religious or otherwise." ("Ritual,"

ibid.) And, finally, the word "ceremony" is defined as: "A formal act or set of formal acts established by custom or authority as proper to a special occasion, such as a wedding, religious rite, etc." ("Ceremony," ibid., 296.) Again, these are general definitions, and our usage will blur these lines, particularly since our focus will be on religious (non-secular) rites, rituals, and ceremonies.

3.   A few supplementary examples have been gleaned from Islam, Hinduism, and the rites of ancient Egypt.

4.   The few references I make to LDS practices focus on that which the average Latter-day Saint would be comfortable discussing outside of an LDS temple.

5.   I have intentionally avoided exposés or published texts written with the goal of demeaning, mocking, or treating lightly the faith or practices of others. For the most part, I have used texts published by practitioners of the faiths whose rituals I will herein discuss.

6.   Latter-day Saints don't always like symbols. Truman Madsen noted this of his own initial encounter with the symbols of the temple: "I had a built-in hostility to ritual and to symbolism. I was taught by people both in and out of the Church—with good intention, I have no doubt—that we don't believe in pagan ceremony: we don't believe in all these procedures and routines; that's what they did in the ancient apostate church; we've outgrown all of that." (Madsen [2008], 12.)

7.   Suzanne E. Lundquist, "Native American Rites of Passage: Implications for Latter-day Saints," in John M. Lundquist and Stephen D. Ricks, eds., *By Study and Also By Faith*, 2 vols. (Provo, UT: Foundation for Ancient Research and Mormon Studies, 1990), 1:441–43. We all first engage in ceremonies when our level of spiritual maturity is such that we cannot possibly understand even a small percentage of the symbolic or spiritual implications of the ordinance. Participation in rites and ordinances is good and important, even when we don't fully grasp their meaning or implications. However, over time, our degree or depth of understanding can and must change. We necessarily must seek to find meaning in the rituals and ordinances of the gospel or they will never have significant power to change our lives. If one cannot be absorbed *by* the ritual, one will never find significant meaning *in* the ritual. One scholar of world religions noted: "Highly ceremonial religions say that one best transcends oneself to make contact with the divine by losing oneself in the drama and aesthetic stimulation of a mighty liturgy, or religious ceremony." Robert S. Ellwood, *Many Peoples, Many Faiths*, fourth edition (New Jersey: Prentice Hall, 1992), 10.

8.   The word "apologetics" comes from the Greek word, meaning "to defend." Thus, apologetics is a branch of theology focused on defending one's faith. It is sometimes defined as a systematic defense of a principle or doctrine, or as a branch of theology devoted to the defense of the divine origin and authority of a given denomination or faith.

9.   Donald W. Parry, ed., *Temples of the Ancient World* (Salt Lake City and Provo, UT: Deseret Book and Foundation for Ancient Research and Mormon Studies, 1994).

10.   Hugh Nibley, *Mormonism and Early Christianity* (Salt Lake City and Provo, UT: Deseret Book and Foundation for Ancient Research and Mormon Studies, 1987).

11.   Donald W. Parry and Stephen D. Ricks, eds., *The Temple in Time and Eternity* (Provo, UT: Foundation for Ancient Research and Mormon Studies, 1999).

12.   Hugh Nibley, *The Message of the Joseph Smith Papyri—An Egyptian Endowment*, second edition (Salt Lake City and Provo, UT: Deseret Book and Foundation for Ancient Research and Mormon Studies, 2005).

13.   Hugh Nibley, *Temple and Cosmos: Beyond This Ignorant Present* (Salt Lake City and Provo, UT: Deseret Book and Foundation for Ancient Research and Mormon Studies, 1992).

14.   In writing apologetic texts one must always be conscious of the dangers of "parallelomania," or "that extravagance among scholars which first overdoes the *supposed* similarity in passages and then proceeds to describe source and derivation as if implying literary connection flowing in an inevitable or predetermined direction." (Samuel Sandmel, "Parallelomania," *Journal of Biblical Literature* 81 [1962]: 1. See also James L. Kugel, *Traditions of the Bible: A Guide to the Bible as it Was at the Start of the Common Era* [Cambridge, MA: Harvard University Press, 1998], 38, n. 31; emphasis added.] In other words, when writing an apologetic text—particularly one about the rites and rituals of the temple in antiquity in comparison to those of the temples of the Restoration—there can be what one scholar referred to as the "disease" of making connections between texts, cultures, rites, and rituals, which *do not* legitimately exist, or of ignoring context all together, often because there is some apologetic value in so doing. (See Sandmel [1962], 13.) Though I accuse none of the aforementioned authors and eds. of so doing, I acknowledge this is a real danger that Latter-day Saint authors must be aware of, and cautious about, when writing apologetic works associated with early Christianity: its doctrines and rituals. Because this book is about symbolism, the concern of "parallelomania" seems less germane, as the examples presented herein

have *not* been offered for their apologetic value, but rather simply for their symbolic merit—and with the full acknowledgment that in many cases there may be *no* connection whatsoever to the restored gospel or the ancient Church. But the symbolic value and instructive nature of the symbolism inherent in the rite justified its inclusion in this text. Thus, if the reader chooses to engage in "parallelomania," he or she will first misunderstand the content and meaning of the ancient rite, and second will miss the purpose and intent of this book.

15.   While throughout the text I have offered interpretations of various rituals proposed by members of the faiths in which those rituals are found, nevertheless, I wish the reader to be aware that, in many cases, I have also offered my own interpretation, or that of LDS scholars who have commented on these—or similar—rites or rituals. I in no way wish to imply that each and every interpretation offered herein would be accepted or embraced by all members of a given faith whose rituals are under examination in this book. Indeed, in some cases it seems fair to say that the interpretations offered would be foreign to non-Mormons who actually participate in the rites under examination. However, as the symbolism seemed germane to temple-attending Latter-day Saints—who comprise the bulk of my audience—I have taken liberty to view these sacred ceremonies through LDS lenses. In so doing, I mean no disrespect to those whose rites I have discussed. On the contrary, it is the beauty and applicability of those rites that have provoked their discussion herein, and it is out of respect for those rites (and the faiths that practice them) that I, in a spirit of admiration, have written.

16.   Margaret Barker, *The Gate of Heaven: The History and Symbolism of the Temple in Jerusalem* (Sheffield, England: Sheffield Phoenix Press, 2008), 1.

17.   John D. Charles, *Endowed From On High: Understanding the Symbols of the Endowment* (Bountiful, UT: Horizon Publishers, 1997), 38.

18.   David B. Haight, "Come to the House of the Lord," in *Ensign*, May 1992, 16; emphasis added.

One

People in Ritual

In ritual, people can function as patrons, as principle players or actors in the drama, or as officiators in and over the rites being enacted. No matter what one's role, some symbolic meaning is intended by the position occupied. The focus of this chapter will be to examine a few figures that have played a symbolic role in certain rites, rituals, or ceremonies of the Judeo-Christian tradition.

Our first symbolic figure is the Roman Catholic "porter,"[1] which has traditionally played a preliminary role leading up to the Mass.[2] While the position or "order" was officially dropped from the Catholic Church in 1972, from at least the sixteenth century onward porters were men whose vocation or calling was to stand as a guard at the doors of the church to insure that none who were unauthorized or unworthy entered.[3] In the Eastern Georgian rite church[4] this same position of guarding the entrance of the sanctuary from those unworthy to enter was held by a subdeacon.[5] A portion of the setting apart ritual of one serving as a subdeacon (or porter) reads as follows: "God and Father of our Lord Jesus Christ, . . . look upon this your servant _____ , who is sealed as [a] subdeacon [or porter], . . . to the end that he may serve unabashed the door of your holy Church . . ."[6] In the Melkite[7] ordination rite of this same order, the significant portion of the ordination blessing is as follows: "God and Father of our Lord Jesus Christ, . . . look upon this your servant who is now being appointed subdeacon [or porter], and make him worthy of the ordination to service which he will serve with boldness at the door of your Church . . ."[8] This is followed by a second prayer, which adds: "Call this your servant . . . by ordination to service, and make him worthy, that, loving the beauty of your house, he may also stand in fear before the door of the holy Church."[9]

Symbolically speaking, the point of a porter was to have a guard or sentinel, of sorts, to insure that only the worthy entered holy or sacred ground. The church was considered God's realm. It represented His presence; His abode. It was a symbol for heaven, or (in the LDS vernacular) the celestial kingdom. Thus, in a sense, the porter's role was symbolically foreshadowed by Elohim's command to Jehovah to place "cherubim and a flaming sword" (Moses 4:31) to guard the way. For some the porter symbolizes the notion that those holding the priesthood protect the sacred precincts of God—here and beyond. And the porter can thus be a representation of angels or priesthood powers that will ascertain if those seeking entrance into God's presence should, indeed, obtain it.[10] On a related note, as part of the initiation process of the Roman Catholic Knights of Columbus, there has traditionally been a questioning procedure, which would probe into the soon-to-be initiated Catholic's faith in God, the Church, and so on. This serves as a sort of recommend interview by which the interviewer is enabled to know if the individual seeking initiation has the requisite testimony of the faith that, among other things, qualifies him for initiation.[11] One text notes: "All candidates must have signed an application" to participate in the rites of the Knights of Columbus. "These certificates dispense with all examination in the ante-room," or, in other words, by having such a certificate before one arrives at the place of the ritual, one need not be interviewed there to ascertain one's worthiness to participate.[12] While the Knights of Columbus do not use a "porter," in the official sense of the word, the individual at the hall who asks to see one's signed certificate functions in a similar vein as did the church porter. The "recommend" or "certificate" presented to the guardian of the door acts as a testament to the holder's worthiness and faith—and it also attests to the fact that the holder has recently been thoroughly interviewed by one qualified to judge the initiate's fitness to attend to the rites or ordinances.

Porters were symbols of God's presence in the world through His servants, and symbols of the coming day of judgment. Their interaction with those seeking entrance mirrored worthiness interviews with priesthood leaders, and also our ultimate interview with the Lord "before the pleasing bar of God, which bar striketh the wicked with awful dread and fear" (Jacob 6:13). Porters were symbols of our obligation to give an account of our worthiness—the regular bearing of our own testimonies regarding our cleanliness and faithfulness to God's commands. Indeed, each time one approached a porter, one was testifying of one's worthiness to be in God's presence or, as the case may be, lying to God about that same thing.

We now turn our attention to patrons and priests, and their symbolic place in religious rites. One's role in liturgy or ritual determines what one symbolizes. Speaking in general terms, most Christian ordinances or rites place a priestly figure at the center of ceremony. The priest may not be the focus, but his presence is often highlighted by presiding over, performing, or authorizing the ordinance or ritual. One commentator noted: "The first Christians thought of themselves as . . . the new generation of the sons of God, angels upon earth living the life of eternity whilst still in this world."[13] In large measure, this explains the symbolism of the general participant in sacred ceremonies. He is a symbol of a son of God—indeed, he is a symbol of *the* Son of God. The patron—a holder of God's holy priesthood—functions as God's emissary; His workman. He represents the fact that angels sent from God's abode have their place, and accomplish their work, in this fallen, telestial world. Those angels may be divine beings, or divinely inspired mortals; but they are God's emissaries either way. Thus, the second century BC Testament of Levi suggests that the washed, anointed, and clad priest was both a representative and substitute for the Lord.[14] He symbolically represents God upon the earth, and his works and rites are symbols for that which God Himself would do were He present. Significantly, then, in the case of salvific rites or rituals, we see the symbolic message that God desires the salvation of all—and would perform such exalting rites on behalf of all in an effort to save them. The priest, therefore, is a mediator; a servant. He is a "[savior] on mount Zion," per se (Obadiah 1:21).[15] Significantly, in the Merkabah branch of Jewish mysticism the ritually performed "ascent to heaven" is "repeated many times over" during one's life.[16] Some benefit was perceived as coming through repeating the same rite over and over again. This idea is not foreign in ancient sources. Indeed, the *Pistis Sophia*[17] indicates that the "mysteries" were first entered into by the faithful for themselves. Then, having received those saving rites in their own lives, they would "celebrate the mystery" on behalf of those who had "passed from the body without" having "received the mystery during their lifetime."[18] This practice of performing for the deceased rites one previously performed for himself explains the symbolism of the priest and patron in the sacred ceremonies. They are symbols of the Savior—laying down their lives on behalf of others. This is in no way to suggest that the sacrifice of time, talents, energies, or money (by a priest or patron) is in any way comparable to Christ's sacrifice. But, symbolically speaking, the individual who performs rites of salvation for those who cannot do so for themselves functions on behalf of God, and in the image of God. Consequently, the high priest who worked in the ancient temple was perceived as an earthly representative of the divine.[19] And so it is with any priest or patron who officiates or serves others through sacred rites and rituals. Thus, according to Philo of Alexandria, the high priest of the ancient temple wore a golden band on his head covering, which had engraved on it "the four letters of the sacred name." "In other words, the high priest bore the name Yahweh." Thus, he stood as a representation of God when dressed in his temple clothing, and while serving in the temple.[20]

Priests and patrons engaging in sacred ceremonies represent God, His angels, and His servants. They are saviors in a micro sense, in that what they do is small in comparison to Jesus, nevertheless they do God's saving work on behalf of those who cannot do so for themselves.

Let us now turn our attention to another set of figures with symbolic merit. In ancient extra canonical religious literature—particularly apocalyptic literature—there was a common theme of the visitation to select mortals of tripartite (i.e., three) messengers who had been sent from God. The tripartite messengers also appear with some frequency in scripture and sparsely in liturgy. The noted symbologist, Erwin Goodenough, wrote that "the total number of scenes" in the Bible "which represent a group of three" divinely sent messengers seems "quite beyond coincidence." Goodenough acknowledges that the tripartite messengers are representations of God.[21] Indeed, the number three symbolically represents that which is of God, comes from God, or is authorized by God.[22] Thus, the repetitive appearance of three divine messengers to mortal man indicates both from whence these heavenly beings have come and whom they represent.

As an example of this prevalent theme, in Genesis 18:2 we read: "And [Abraham] lift up his eyes and looked, and, lo, three men stood by him: and when he saw them, he ran to meet them from the tent door, and bowed himself toward the ground." Though we do not know the identity of these "three men," the Joseph Smith Translation (JST) refers to them as "holy men . . . after the order of God" who were "angels" having been "sent forth" to teach Abraham.[23] Curiously, the English word "apostle" comes from a Greek word that means, literally, *"sent* one" or "one who is *sent forth*."[24] While the fact that Abraham's "messengers" had been "sent" to teach him in itself does not prove that these three were apostles, it certainly does make one wonder about the identity of these tripartite visitors. In the first century of the Common Era, Philo of Alexandria spoke of Abraham's three messengers as

13

symbols for the reality that it was God who ministered to the patriarch.[25] He called the three visitors "the ministers and lieutenants of the mighty God, by means of whom, as of ambassadors, he announces whatever predictions he condescends to imitate to our race."[26]

As noted, in intertestamental literature these tripartite figures are commonplace. For example, in reference to Satan, the *Apocalypse of Daniel* states: "Three men will go forth and will condemn him as a liar and a deceiver. And these three men, two from heaven [Peter and James?], and one from the earth [John?]" will expose him as the "Anti-Christ" and encourage all mankind to worship "Christ or Lord."[27] Likewise, in the book of 1 Enoch we read of three messengers "wearing snow-white clothes" who appeared to the prophet on numerous occasions, each time grasping him by the hand.[28] Enoch says of these three that the first time they appeared to him they descended "from heaven." The prophet indicates that these three messengers, when they first appeared, were accompanied by another "being" that appeared "in the form of a snow-white person." However, in subsequent appearances to Enoch, the three messengers were no longer accompanied by the "being in the form of a snow-white person."[29] In a similar vein, several extra-canonical sources speak of the visitation of the tripartite messengers to Adam and Eve.

Professor S. Kent Brown wrote: "According to the Apocalypse of Adam, . . . Adam's recovery of the knowledge of both his premortal existence and what was to happen in future ages of the earth was . . . learned from three messengers who revealed to him the history of the world from beginning to end. Adam then transmitted those secrets to his son Seth, who was said to transmit them to 'his seed,' that is, only to worthy initiates."[30]

Curiously, even in modern times these triple messengers have made their appearance. As an example, President Wilford Woodruff regularly told of how (in the winter of 1840) he was accosted by Satanic influences while serving a mission in London and that, in response to his prayer, "the door [of my room] opened and three messengers entered, and the room was filled with light equal to the blazing of the sun at mid-day. Those messengers were all dressed in robes of immortal beings. Who they were I do not know."[31] On another occasion President Woodruff, in speaking about the appearance of these three heavensent beings, noted that they were each "dressed in temple clothing."[32]

As we already suggested, the number three represents that which is of God, comes from God, or is authorized by God. Thus, the repetitive appearance of three messengers indicates both their origin and what they represent. More than any other number, three symbolizes God. Consequently, when the number is employed in scripture or ritual, it frequently serves to emphasize divine involvement, backing, or influence.[33] Whether appearing to Adam and Eve or serving as the head of a post-resurrection church, tripartite messengers (like Peter, James, and John), are simply symbols of something much greater than themselves; namely the Godhead.

Matthias F. Cowley of the Twelve wrote: "The offices of this priesthood consist of the First Presidency, a quorum of three, bearing the holy apostleship, and as the organization of the Church on earth typifies the heavenly, these three symbolize the Father, Son and Holy Ghost, and hold the keys of authority over all departments of the Church, on all matters, spiritual and temporal, even as the Godhead is the great ruling power of the universe, the heavens and the earth and all that in them is."[34]

All sets of tripartite messengers, and all presidencies, represent the Godhead—whether they are appearing in scripture, functioning in liturgy, or presiding over the Church. Using Peter, James, and John as examples of this—specifically because they are one of the few sets of tripartite messengers identified by name in scripture—we see how clearly and deeply this typology[35] has been established in ritual and scripture.

Peter	James	John
Peter, in his presidency, is a symbol of God the Father.	James was a symbol of Jesus the Christ.	John was the third member of the presidency and symbolized the Holy Ghost.
He possesses a resurrected, glorified, and perfected body.	He possesses a resurrected, glorified, and perfected body.	He is the only one of the three with a non-resurrected body, just as the Holy Ghost is the only member of the Godhead who does not have a physical, resurrected body.[36]
Peter was the presiding figure over the post-resurrection New Testament Church, and held and exercised all priesthood keys during that era.	James is a brother of John of Zebedee, just as Jesus is a brother of the Holy Ghost.[37]	John is a brother of James, just as the Holy Ghost is a brother of Jesus.

Peter	James	John
	James's surname (Zebedee) means "gift from God," just as Jesus is the ultimate Gift from God (John 3:16).[38]	John's surname (Zebedee) means "gift from God," just as the Holy Ghost is a gift to us from God (D&C 20:43).
	In holy precincts, it is James who leads us in prayer, just as Jesus taught His disciples how to properly pray in ancient times. The Lord's prayer was not just a corporate prayer; it was an ordinance of prayer.[39]	In his gospel, John leaves himself unnamed. Similarly, the name of the Holy Ghost is unknown.[40]

Symbolically speaking, when scripture, liturgy, or experience present before us the tripartite messengers, we are to see in them a representation of the Father, Son, and Holy Ghost. Just as Peter, James, and John were types for the Godhead, we must necessarily see in any presidency of three this same symbolism.[41] As it pertains to Latter-day Saints, the Lord declared: "Whether by mine own voice or by the voice of my servants, it is the same" (D&C 1:38). Thus, if members of The Church of Jesus Christ of Latter-day Saints heed the First Presidency's council as they would the Heavenly First Presidency's, they will indeed regain the presence of the Father and Son, and partake of eternal life with them in the celestial kingdom of God. If they do not, they have no such hope. Consequently, one author noted that we must "learn to hear and feel true messengers because they speak God's message with the power of the Holy Spirit as though God were speaking directly to us (see Matthew 10:40). Otherwise, if we reject true messengers and their heavenly gifts we will at the same time reject the Lord."[42] Our source continues: "It is God's will that we follow His true messengers . . . *These messengers are His prophet and counselors—the current Peter, James and John of His church.* As true messengers, they point the way through this mortal desert, leading us to the iron rod and the straight path up Mount Zion."[43]

Porters, priests, patrons, and prophets each, in slightly different ways, symbolize God. As a person interacts with them, or symbolically acts as one of them, he or she is taught about God and Christ, and about his or her relationship to and with Them.

Notes

1.   A porter was a minor office in the Catholic priesthood.

2.   The Mass is the Roman Catholic equivalent of the LDS sacrament meeting. It is the traditional name for the service in which the sacrament of the Eucharist (or Lord's Supper) is consecrated or blessed, and the suffering, death, and resurrection of Christ is celebrated as a saving gift to God's creations.

3.   See Richard P. McBrien, ed., *The Harper Collins Encyclopedia of Catholicism* (San Francisco: Harper San Francisco, 1995), 1034, S.v. "Porter." In the opinion of some, gargoyles served a purpose similar to porters or subdeacons, in that they "guard the doorways," acting as protectors from the profane. See David Adams Leeming, "Quests," in Mircea Eliade, ed., *The Encyclopedia of Religion*, 16 vols. (New York: Macmillian, 1987), 12:149.

4.   The Georgian Byzantine Catholic Church is a small faith with its origins in the country of Georgia, on the eastern shore of the Black Sea. It was formed by missionaries working in that region, beginning in the thirteenth century—though Christianity in that region existed by at least the beginning of the fourth century. The Georgian Christians are affiliated with the Roman Catholic church; however, they are Byzantine in their liturgical practices. See McBrien (1995), 557, S.v. "Georgian Byzantine Catholics"; Paul F. Bradshaw, *Ordination Rites of the Ancient*

Churches of the East and West (New York: Pueblo Publishing Company, 1990), 10.

5. Bradshaw (1990), 99.

6. Bradshaw (1990), 167–168.

7. The Melkites are a "Byzantine Catholic counterpart to the Orthodox patriarchate of Antioch, concentrated in Lebanon and Syria"—though today they are found throughout the world. Their origins can be traced back to the fifth century, when they expressed a belief in the doctrines espoused by Chalcedon (AD 451). An eighteenth century schism within the patriarchate of Antioch appears to be responsible for their existence as a formal denomination within Roman Catholicism. In liturgy they are very Eastern Orthodox in appearance, but, strictly speaking, they are formally affiliated with the Roman Catholic branch of Christianity. See Ronald G. Roberson, "Melkite Catholic Church," in Richard P. McBrien, ed., *The Harper Collins Encyclopedia of Catholicism* (San Francisco: Harper San Francisco, 1995), 851–852; Bradshaw (1990), 13.

8. Bradshaw (1990), 204.

9. Ibid.

10. Like Catholics, Latter-day Saints have also occasionally used the term "porter" for an office associated with ritual. In early LDS practice the individual who stood on the celestial side of the temple veil, representing the Father, was sometimes referred to as a "porter." (See, for example, Brigham Young, discourse given August 8, 1844, in Richard S. Van Wagoner, ed., *The Complete Discourses of Brigham Young*, 5 vols. [Salt Lake City: The Smith-Pettit Foundation, 2009], 1:43; Brigham Young, discourse given July 6, 1851, in Van Wagoner [2009], 1:444. See also Brigham Young, in Joseph Smith, *History of the Church of Jesus Christ of Latter-day Saints*, 7 vols. [Salt Lake City: Deseret Book, 1978], 7:240.) This LDS "veil porter" must be distinguished from the aforementioned Catholic porter who would be more akin to the Mormon priesthood holder who occupies a position at the temple recommend desk. Nevertheless, the symbolism of guarding God's abode—whether at the door of the church/temple or at the veil—is clearly a related motif.

11. Thomas C. Knight, *The Knights of Columbus—Illustrated* (Chicago: Ezra A. Cook, 1920), 45.

12. Knight (1920), 41.

13. Barker (2008), 103.

14. See Barker (2008), 162. The "Testament of Levi" is found in a larger work by the name of the "Testaments of the Twelve Patriarchs," which purports to be the final words of Jacob's twelve sons uttered shortly

before each of their deaths. The document is pseudepigraphical in nature (meaning we do not know for certain who authored it), and it likely originated in Syria in the third century before the common era, though there is some debate regarding its date. The text is historically important because it established the diversity in Jewish thought that existed in the years prior to the Maccabean revolt. See H. C. Kee, "Testaments of the Twelve Patriarchs—A New Translation and Introduction," in James H. Charlesworth, ed., *The Old Testament Pseudepigrapha*, 2 vols. (New York: Doubleday, 1983, 1985), 1:775–781.

15.   Margaret Barker wrote: "Those who passed through the veil were the mediators, divine and human, who functioned in both worlds bringing the prayers and penitence of the people to God." Barker (2008), 105.

16.   See P. Alexander, "Introduction" to "3 (Hebrew Apocalypse of) Enoch—A New Translation and Introduction," in Charlesworth (1983, 1985), 1:238. Merkabah Mysticism is a branch of Jewish Mysticism that dates roughly from the first through tenth centuries of the Common Era.

17.   The *Pistis Sophia* is an important Gnostic Christian text that purports to record the teachings of Jesus to a group of His most intimate disciples, among whom is found Mary (His mother), Martha, and Mary Magdalene. It has been dated as late as the 6th century, but as early as the 3rd century of the Common Era. Its importance is to be found in its record of the development of gnostic thinking and also for its text of the psalms. See Kurt Rudolph, *Gnosis: The Nature & History of Gnosticism* (San Francisco: Harper San Francisco, 1987), 27.

18.   For example, the *Pistis Sophia* records: "And Mary [Magdalene] came forward, [and] she threw herself at the feet of Jesus and worshipped them [i.e., His feet], saying: . . . 'O Master, supposing a righteous man, who hath accomplished all the mysteries, and he hath a kinsman, in a word some dear one, and this one . . . hath passed from the body, . . . what, then, shall we do to save him from the torments . . . , and have him carried into a righteous body which shall find the mysteries of the kingdom of light, that he may continue righteous and enter into the height and inherit the kingdom of light?' The Savior answered and said unto Mary: '[You should] . . . celebrate [or participate in] the one and only mystery [or rite] of that ineffable which ever remitteth sins, and when ye have finished the celebration of that mystery, say, 'May the soul of such a man of whom I think [upon] in my heart [or mind] . . . be taken out of these torments' . . ." Jesus then informs Mary that the light can "seal [the deceased individual] with the seal of the ineffable . . . that it may become good, and enter into the height, and inherit the kingdom of light." Then He adds that those

divinely authorized can "baptize that soul, and seal it with the sign of the kingdom of that ineffable, and bring it into the orders of the light." Finally, the *Pistis Sophia* adds: "When [individuals] have received the mystery during their lifetime, and have passed from the body, they will become flames of light . . . But if they be sinners who have passed from the body without repentance, and if ye celebrate the mystery of that ineffable for them, to have them taken out of every punishment, . . . the receivers of Melchisedec [sic] shall come to find them, and shall bring them unto the . . . light." See "Second Book of Pistis Sophia," #325–27, 329, in G. R. S. Mead, *Pistis Sophia* (London: The Theological Publishing Society, 1896), 325–27, 329–30.

19. See Barker (2008), 116–17.

20. See Barker (2008), 117, 120; Truman G. Madsen, " 'Putting on the Names': A Jewish-Christian Legacy," in Lundquist and Ricks (1990), 1:465; Madsen (2008), 145.

21. See Erwin R. Goodenough, *Jewish Symbols in the Greco-Roman Period*, 6 vols. (New York: Pantheon Books, 1953–56), 1:26–27.

22. See, for example, John J. Davis, *Biblical Numerology* (Grand Rapids: Baker Book House, 2000), 121, 123; Kevin J. Todeschi, *The Encyclopedia of Symbolism* (New York: The Berkley Publishing Group, 1995), 185; David Fontana, *The Secret Language of Symbols* (San Francisco: Chronicle Books, 1993), 64; J. C. Cooper, *An Illustrated Encyclopaedia of Traditional Symbols* (London: Thames and Hudson, 1995), 114; William Henry Bennett, "Number," in James Hastings, ed., *Dictionary of the Bible* (Charles Scribner's Sons: New York, 1963), 703; Georges Ifrah, *The Universal History of Numbers: From Prehistory to the Invention of the Computer* (New York: John Wiley & Sons, 2000), 499; E. W. Bullinger, *Number in Scripture: Its Supernatural Design and Spiritual Significance* (Grand Rapids: Kregel Publications, 1967), 107–108, 122–23; Mick Smith, *The Book of Revelation: Plain, Pure, and Simple* (Salt Lake City: Bookcraft, 1998), 288; Robert D. Johnston, *Numbers in the Bible: God's Design in Biblical Numerology* (Grand Rapids: Kregel Publications, 1990), 39–40; Maurice H. Farbridge, *Studies in Biblical and Semitic Symbolism* (London: Kegan Paul, Trench, Trubner & Co, 1923), 144; Friedrich Rest, *Our Christian Symbols* (New York: The Pilgrim Press, 1987), 17–18, 60–61; J. E. Cirlot, *A Dictionary of Symbols*, second edition (New York: Philosophical Library, 1962), 232; Nadia Julien, *The Mammoth Dictionary of Symbols* (New York: Carroll & Graf Publishers, 1996), 448.

23. Not all are in agreement as to the nature of Abraham's three visitors. Some see them as divine beings (e.g., angels), and others as mortals sent

from God. (Compare, for example, Joseph Fielding Smith, *Doctrines of Salvation*, 3 vols. [Salt Lake City: Bookcraft, 1998], 1:16 and Ellis T. Rasmussen, *A Latter-day Commentary on the Old Testament* [Salt Lake City: Deseret Book, 1993], 47 with Hugh Nibley, *Teachings of the Book of Mormon—Semester 1* [Provo, UT: Foundation for Ancient Research and Mormon Studies, 1989–90], Lecture 13, Page 2 and Victor L. Ludlow, *Unlocking the Old Testament* [Salt Lake City: Deseret Book, 1981], 13.) Either way, their interactions place them appropriately among the tripartite messengers of old, and their symbolic meaning is not changed by their personal nature (i.e., mortal or angel).

24.   One LDS commentary on this passage referred to these "men" as "three divine messengers." (See Ludlow [1981], 13.) Some early Christians saw these three "messengers" as angels of God. For example, the fourth century church father, Ephrem the Syrian, suggested that the "men" who appeared to Abraham were no mere mortals, but, rather, beings sent from the Father. (Ephrem the Syrian, "Commentary on Genesis" 15:1, in Mark Sheridan, ed., *Ancient Christian Commentary on Scripture: Genesis 12–50* [Downers Grove, IL: InterVarsity Press, 2002], 63.) Ephrem's reasoning is based on the fact that these "three" clearly speak on behalf of the Lord during their interaction with Abraham. The Anchor Bible's commentary on the book of Genesis suggests that while the chapter begins intentionally vague (regarding the identity of the three), "gradually, however, it dawns on [Abraham] the host (vs. 10) that the *'ªdōnī* (approximately 'sir,' . . .) to whom he had been speaking is no mere mortal." See E. A. Speiser, *The Anchor Bible: Genesis* (New York: Doubleday, 1962), 131.

25.   See, for example, C. D. Yonge, trans., *The Works of Philo* (Peabody, MA: Hendrickson Publishers, 1997), 101, 421–23.

26.   See Yonge (1997), 421. Cyrus Gordon, a professor of Near Eastern Studies (at Brandeis University), highlighted the peculiar fascination in the Eastern Mediterranean (during the last half of the second millennium BCE) with presidencies of three among the military of the Greeks and the Hebrews. He refers to "triads of officers" and points out that it is "not unusual in both traditions to designate one officer in each triad as the chief. Much as Sarpedon is called superior to his two associates (Ilia 12:101–104), Abishai is honored in 2 Samuel 23:18 as 'chief of the triad' and as having won special 'fame among the three.' 1 Chronicles 11:21 states that of the three 'he was more honored than the other two and became their general.'" (See Cyrus Herzl Gordon, *Before the Bible: The Common Background of Greek and Hebrew Civilizations* [New York: Harper and Row, 1962], 16–17. Gordon points to biblical passages [e.g.,

2 Samuel 23, 9, 16–19, 22–23; 1 Chronicles 11:21] and also the writings of Homer [e.g., *The Iliad* 2:563–67, 12:85–107; *The Odyssey* 14:470–71] as evidence that among the Greeks and Hebrews of the second millennium BCE there was a commonality of a "triad of officers.") Related to this, in the Book of Daniel we read: "It pleased [King] Darius to set over the kingdom an hundred and twenty princes, which should be over the whole kingdom; And over these three presidents; of whom Daniel was first [or head]: that the princes might give accounts unto them, and the king should have no damage. Then this Daniel was preferred above the presidents and princes, because an excellent spirit was in him; and the king thought to set him over the whole realm" (Daniel 6:1–3). One commentator noted that Daniel "is recognized as one of the triumvirate of presidents responsible for the whole realm. . . . Because of an 'excellent spirit' (v. 3), he has been able to outstrip his colleagues" in the presidency. [Robert A. Anderson, *International Theological Commentary: Daniel—Signs and Wonders* (Grand Rapids: Eerdmans, 1984), 66.] King Darius is also known to have had "three youthful bodyguards who guarded the person of the king" (1 Esdras 3:4). In each case, the guards, presidents, or officers are set to protect. This may have some significance as it relates to presidencies. Presidencies are placed to protect those over whom they preside.

27. "The Apocalypse of Daniel" 14:1–2, in Charlesworth (1983, 1985), 1:755–70; See chapters 13–14 of the "Apocalypse" in their entirety. The Apocalypse of Daniel is an early ninth century apocalyptic text likely written in Greek in the city of Constantinople. Its authorship is unknown.

28. See 1 Enoch 90:31, in Charlesworth (1983, 1985), 1:71.

29. See 1 Enoch 87:2–3, in Charlesworth (1983, 1985), 1:63.

30. S. Kent Brown, "The Nag Hammadi Library: A Mormon Perspective" in *Apocryphal Writings and the Latter-day Saints*, C. Wilfred Griggs, ed. (Provo, UT: Religious Studies Center, Brigham Young University, 1986), 260. See "The Apocalypse of Adam," chapters 2–3, in Charlesworth (1983, 1985), 1:712–14; "The Apocalypse of Adam," 65:26–68:28, in James M. Robinson, ed., *The Nag Hammadi Library*, revised edition (San Francisco: Harper and Row, 1988), 279–80. Time and again Hugh Nibley makes reference to one Mandaean text (the *Ginza*) which speaks of three messengers who were sent to Adam and Eve to instruct them and supervise the work. These three angels were later to live on the earth as ordinary mortals and prophets. See Hugh Nibley, "The Expanding Gospel," in *BYU Studies,* vol. 7, no. 1 (Autumn 1965): 12; Hugh Nibley, *Ancient Documents and the Pearl of Great Price* (Provo, UT: Foundation for Ancient Research and Mormon Studies, 1989), Lecture 6, p. 9; Hugh Nibley, *Since Cumorah*

(Provo, UT: Foundation for Ancient Research and Mormon Studies, 1988), 155–56, 460–61, n. 47. In one of his books, Nibley suggests that the Berlin Papyrus depicts God's messengers (who were sent to teach Adam and Eve) as instructing our first parents in "the order of prayer." See Hugh Nibley, *Old Testament and Related Studies* (Provo, UT: Foundation for Ancient Research and Mormon Studies, 1987), 156, 158. As for other references made by Nibley to the "three messengers" or three "sent ones," see Nibley (2005), 322; Nibley, *Old Testament* (1987), 153–55, 158, and 201 n. 61–62; Nibley, *Mormonism* (1987), 64; Nibley (1992), 299–309.

31. Wilford Woodruff, discourse given October 5, 1896, in Brian H. Stuy, comp. and ed. *Collected Discourses Delivered by President Wilford Woodruff, His Two Counselors, the Twelve Apostles, and Others*, 5 vols. (Burbank, CA: B. H. S. Publishing, 1987–92), 5:199. On October 18, 1840, Elder Woodruff wrote the following in his journal: "We [Wilford Woodruff and George A. Smith] retired to rest in good season and I felt well in my mind and slept until 12 at night. I awoke and meditated upon the things of God until near 3 o'clock and while forming a determination to warn the people in London and overcome the powers of Darkness by the assistance of God; A person appeared unto me which I considered was the Prince of Darkness or the Devil. He made war with me and attempted to take my life. He caught me by the throat and choked me nearly to death. He wounded me in my forehead. I also wounded him in a number of places in the head. [The sentences "He wounded me in my forehead. I also wounded him in a number of places in the head" are written in the original but have been struck through with pencil by someone at a later date.] As he was about to overcome me I prayed to the father in the name of Jesus for help. I then had power over him and he left me though much wounded. Three personages dressed in white came to me and prayed with me and I was immediately healed and [they] delivered me from all my troubles. (Scott G. Kenney, ed., *Wilford Woodruff's Journal*, 9 vols. [Midvale, UT: Signature Books, 1983], 1:532.) Although he doesn't mention it in the foregoing account, on later occasions, Wilford indicated that Satan did physical harm to *both* him and George A. Smith—and had it not been for "three holy messengers" who gave them each a priesthood blessing, both of them would have been killed by Satan on that occasion. (See Wilford Woodruff, March 3, 1889, discourse in Stuy [1987–92], 1:218; Wilford Woodruff, *Leaves from My Journal* [Salt Lake City: Juvenile Instructor Office, 1881], 109–10; Wilford Woodruff, October 19, 1896, discourse in Stuy [1987–92], 5:236–37.)

32. See Wilford Woodruff, March 3, 1889, discourse in Stuy (1987–92),

1:218; Woodruff (1881), 109–10; Wilford Woodruff, October 19, 1896, discourse in Stuy (1987–92), 5:236–37.

33.   Bullinger (1967), 107; Davis (1968), 123; Cirlot (1971), 232; Johnston (1990), 55.

34.   Matthias F. Cowley, *Cowley's Talks On Doctrine* (Chattanooga, TN: Ben. E. Rich, 1902), 46; See also Rodney Turner, "The Doctrine of the Firstborn and Only Begotten" in *The Pearl of Great Price: Revelations From God* (Provo, UT: Religious Studies Center, Brigham Young University, 1989), 96; Lorenzo D. Young, October 25, 1857, in *Journal of Discourses* (Liverpool: Latter-day Saint's Book Depot, 1859), 6:224–25; Bruce R. McConkie, *Doctrinal New Testament Commentary*, 3 vols. (Salt Lake City: Bookcraft, 1987–88), 1:766; Bruce R. McConkie, *The Promised Messiah*, (Salt Lake City: Deseret Book, 1978), 114.

35.   Typology is a branch of symbolism where a symbol (i.e., the "type") is fulfilled in someone or something else (i.e., the "antitype"). So, for example, the lamb slain during the Passover recorded in the book of Exodus was a type, which found its fulfillment in the crucified Christ (the antitype). Most often the type points to a future antitype. However, sometimes the type can point back to its fulfillment—as with the sacrament of the Lord's Supper. It is a symbol fulfilled in a previous event, yet it is typological in nature.

36.   "The Father has a body of flesh and bones as tangible as man's; the Son also; but the Holy Ghost has not a body of flesh and bones, but is a personage of Spirit. Were it not so, the Holy Ghost could not dwell in us" (D&C 130:22).

> And the Lord said unto me: John, my beloved, what desirest thou? For if you shall ask what you will, it shall be granted unto you. And I said unto him: Lord, give unto me power over death, that I may live and bring souls unto thee. And the Lord said unto me: Verily, verily, I say unto thee, because thou desirest this thou shalt tarry until I come in my glory, and shalt prophesy before nations, kindreds, tongues and people. And for this cause the Lord said unto Peter: If I will that he tarry till I come, what is that to thee? For he desired of me that he might bring souls unto me, but thou desiredst that thou mightest speedily come unto me in my kingdom. I say unto thee, Peter, this was a good desire; but my beloved has desired that he might do more, or a greater work yet among men than what he has before done. Yea, he has undertaken a greater work; therefore I will make him as flaming fire and a ministering angel; he shall minister for those who shall be heirs of salvation who dwell on the earth.

And I will make thee to minister for him and for thy brother James; and unto you three I will give this power and the keys of this ministry until I come. Verily I say unto you, ye shall both have according to your desires, for ye both joy in that which ye have desired. (D&C 7:1–8)

37.   "Well, let me tell you, the Holy Ghost is a man; he is one of the sons of our Father and our God; and he is that man that stood next to Jesus Christ, just as I stand by brother Brigham." Heber C. Kimball, discourse given August 23, 1857, in *Journal of Discourses*, 5:179. "The Church of Jesus Christ of Latter-day Saints teaches that the Holy Ghost is a spirit man, a spirit son of God the Father." Joseph Fielding McConkie, "Holy Ghost," in Daniel H. Ludlow, ed., *The Encyclopedia of Mormonism*, 4 vols. (New York: Macmillian, 1992), 2:649. "The Father existed prior to the Son and the Holy Ghost. . . . They are his offspring." Stephen E. Robinson, "God the Father," in Ludlow (1992), 2:548.

38.   Joseph H. Thayer, *Thayer's Greek-English Lexicon of the New Testament* (Peabody, MA: Hendrickson Publishers, 1999), 270; Stelman Smith and Judson Cornwall, *The Exhaustive Dictionary of Bible Names* (North Brunswick, NJ: Bridge-Logos Publications, 1998), 257; *L. D. S. Bible Dictionary* (Salt Lake City: The Church of Jesus Christ of Latter-day Saints, 1986), 791.

39.   Luke records: "And it came to pass that, as he was *praying in a certain place*, when he ceased, one of his disciples said unto him, Lord, teach us to pray . . ." (Luke 11:1, emphasis added). This is followed by a version of the Lord's Prayer. One scholar has argued convincingly that the Lord's Prayer, which is part of the Sermon on the Mount, is itself a temple text. (John W. Welch, *The Sermon at the Temple, and the Sermon on the Mount* [Provo, UT: The Foundation for Ancient Research and Mormon Studies, 1990], 14–83.) Regarding the temple-oriented nature of Christ's prayer, Elder Bruce R. McConkie wrote: "Jesus himself 'was praying in a certain place.' Prayers may be offered in all places and at all times, but we are dealing here with a particular prayer . . . Clearly it was a prayer in marked contrast to those customarily offered by the Jews in general . . . Jesus now [taught] the true order of prayer . . . [as] he had done . . . in Galilee." (Bruce R. McConkie, *The Mortal Messiah*, 4 vols. [Salt Lake City: Deseret Book, 1979–81], 3:186–87. See also Nibley, *Mormonism* . . . [1987], 55.)

40.   In his gospel, John refers to himself by titles such as "the disciple whom Jesus loved" (John 13:23), or "another disciple" (John 18:15). By so doing, John has confused some scholars as to the identity of this

"other" disciple. (See, for example, Floyd V. Filson, "Who Was the Beloved Disciple?" in *Journal of Biblical Literature* 68 [June, 1949], 83–88; Merrill C. Tenney, "The Gospel of John," in Gaebelein [1976–92], 9:140; Eric L. Titus, "The Identity of the Beloved Disciple," in *Journal of Biblical Literature* 69 [December 1950], 323–28.)

41.   One text notes: "The calling of Peter, James, and John to act as holy angels, sent to declare the Gospel to Adam and Eve, portended their mortal calling as apostles of the Savior and portends their post-mortal calling as ministering angels (see D&C 7:5–7; 128:20). There have been many who have worked on both sides and between the veils as true messengers." Mark H. Green, III, *The Scriptural Temple* (Springville, UT: Cedar Fort, 2004), 124.

42.   Green (2004), 116.

43.   Ibid., 125. Emphasis in original.

Two

Initiation Rituals

M ost major world religions have some form of initiation ritual. The various denominations of Christianity are no exception to this rule. Practices, such as washing or baptizing, clothing or naming, covenanting or oath-swearing, are common-place among the world's faiths. One text on ritual initiation notes: "Rites of passage often reenact symbolically the separation of the initiates from their previous social condition and their reintegra-tion into a new position."[1] In other words, when one becomes "initiated" into a society, faith, or order, one becomes a new person, with a new position in the world because of his or her new position in the society or faith. Ritual initiation also separates the initiate from the fallen world, and potentially from the initiate's former allegiances.

BAPTISM

Baptism is a central rite in the Christian tradition—though it certainly predates Christianity, and is found in a number of faiths throughout the world.[2] As is commonly known, Paul indicated that the baptismal font is a symbol of the grave, and that its design is first and foremost to remind the participants in the ordinance of Christ's death and resurrection, which makes our salvation possible. Musing on baptism by immersion, one author suggested: "Ascension to God is a theme that appears often in the Church. For instance, at baptism, members descend into the water, symbolically burying their own selfish desires, witnessing that they have given up their will to God. The ascension out of the water symbolizes new life in Christ and begins the new journey upward to God."[3] Thus, associated with the aforementioned "separation" and "new position" which comes as part of initiation, we understand that being immersed in a baptismal font also symbolizes the death of the initiate's old, sinful self and his or her rebirth as a new creation in Christ (see Romans 6; D&C 128:12–13; 2 Corinthians 5:16–21).[4] Ritualistically speaking, those who are baptized are reborn, in part, through the ordinance of baptism; the water and the font being "symbolic not only of the tomb but also the womb."[5] One scholar noted:

> The Christian ritual of baptism . . . draws its meaning from women's work of giving birth. In some of the earliest baptismal rites, converts entered the waters naked, like the baby in the womb. After being immersed they came forth from the water as people who had been born again. The first food these "newborn" converts received was in fact made of milk and honey—an imitation of breast milk—signifying their entrance into the Christian community as babes.[6]

On a related note, one LDS text notes:

> In all births, three elements are present: water, blood, and spirit (Moses 6:59–60). These same three elements were present at the atonement of Christ: water (from his side), blood (from his sufferings), and spirit (the Father's presence, the Son's own spirit, and the Holy Ghost). These three elements are present at our spiritual rebirth: the water of baptism, the blood of Christ through the atonement, and the Spirit of God. And they are also present, or represented, as we remember Christ and our covenant to him in the sacrament.[7]

Thus, the Christian baptismal rite was a multi-faceted

symbolic ordinance. It reminded the participant of Christ's Atonement (including His Resurrection from the dead), along with our own eventual physical death and resurrection—which would be effected through Him. But the symbolism of being born again is also strongly associated with this ancient ordinance. The water was designed to remind the initiate of the spiritual grave in which his or her old and sinful person must die as to the things of this world. In addition, it also forcefully symbolized the womb and amniotic fluid through which physical birth takes place, highlighting the necessity of being "born again." Thus baptism is in many ways about death and rebirth, about rejection of old ways of life and the embracing of new ways, about leaving the world and coming unto Christ, about entrance into this fallen world and a conscious leaving of it behind. Of course, water is consistently the symbol of choice in this requisite ritual. We have already noted its symbolic association with the womb and birth. However, a more obvious symbol behind the use of water in baptism is that of cleansing—not just physical cleansing (often associated with water), but also spiritual sanctifying, which comes through the Atonement and via the Holy Spirit. Water, itself, is often a symbol of the Holy Ghost (John 7:37–39). Consequently, the way in which baptism has been performed in Christianity throughout its approximately two thousand years implies it is a vehicle to the receipt of the Holy Ghost. The reader will likely be aware of a comment made by the Prophet Joseph Smith: "You might as well baptize a bag of sand as a man, if not done in view of the remission of sins and getting of the Holy Ghost. Baptism by water is but half a baptism, and is good for nothing without the other half—that is, the baptism of the Holy Ghost. . . . The baptism of water, without the baptism of fire and the Holy Ghost attending it, is of no use; they are necessarily and inseparably connected."[8]

Thus, water's symbolic association with the Holy Ghost is not surprising since it is the Spirit that remits sins through the process of the ordinance, and in the days following—rather than the actual immersion in water.[9] Consequently, the utilization of the water during that holy rite teaches us of the need to keep our lives saturated in the Spirit in order to be clean. Indeed, one text notes: "Immersion in the water symbolizes the total commitment of our whole being, fully entering into covenant, fully being washed, fully being covered by the living water that is Christ. With immersion we follow Christ into a new birth. . . . We follow him with all our being."[10] The water of the baptismal rite reminds the Christian initiate that he or she must immerse himself or herself so fully in the Spirit that he or she cannot only be led by it, but also be constantly cleansed by it. To be immersed in the water is to commit to fully immerse one's self in the work of the kingdom, and, by default, in the Lord's sanctifying and cleansing Holy Spirit.

CLOTHING

It was common anciently, as it is today, for many Christians to dress in white clothing either before or after their baptism. One text states: "Changing out of street clothes into the white baptismal clothes . . . represents . . . newness of person."[11] The white clothing worn by the initiate is a reminder to all participating or viewing the rite of the purity that will come to the baptized through Christ's Atonement.[12] In other words, it is a testament to the role baptism plays in helping one apply the atoning blood of Christ and thereby gain an inheritance in God's eternal kingdom. Beyond its connections to Christ's atoning sacrifice, the color white is also associated with the concepts of purity, righteousness, holiness, innocence, victory, light, and revelation.[13] In addition, white is also occasionally equated with happiness, virginity, the presence of the Holy Ghost, and spiritual dedication or mastery.[14] Each of these ideas has obvious connections to the ordinance of baptism.

WASHING

We now turn our attention from baptism to other esoteric initiatory rites of the ancients.[15] As is well known, Solomon's temple housed a font or laver used for ritual washings. Of it, 1 Kings 7:23,

25 states: "And he made a molten sea. . . . It stood upon twelve oxen, three looking toward the north, and three looking toward the west, and three looking toward the south, and three looking toward the east: and the sea was set above upon them, and all their hinder parts were inward." Of this unique and very symbolic font, one text notes that it was "used for ablutions or ritual washings (Exodus 30:18: Hebrews 9:10; D&C 124:37). These washings symbolized the cleansing of the soul from sin and iniquity through the power of the Atonement (Ephesians 5:26; Isaiah 4:4)."[16] Because of the symbolism inherent in baptism, it will be no surprise to the reader that the washings of the Solomonic laver also represented cleansing through Christ's sacrifice. However, there are other elements in the font that seem significant. Whereas the ancient baptismal font spoke mostly of the grave and the womb, something entirely different seems referenced by this "molten sea" resting upon the backs of twelve oxen facing the four cardinal directions.

First of all we highlight the fact that the laver rested upon the backs of twelve oxen. Oxen are established types for God and His righteous followers. To the ancients they represented power, patience, and sacrifice, as well as Christ or deity.[17] They also suggest images of royalty, divinity, power, sacrifice, atonement, and Jehovah.[18] Thus, as the initiate was washed in the font or laver, symbolically he was taught who it was that supported him in this new relationship—namely God and His righteous disciples. Hence, one was not alone in his efforts to keep the covenants he was entering into at the laver or font. He would be supported by his God, and by those who were members of his covenant community. One LDS source states:

> The . . . font rests securely on the strong backs of twelve oxen. They represent the tribes of Israel, and we belong to those tribes. It is totally appropriate that the font should be so situated. The saving ordinances for the world rest on backs made strong by the blessings of the Restoration. That weight will not be removed until every child of God is found. With our heads directed to the four points of the compass, we desire and invite all to receive the

ordinances that open the sanctifying power of the Atonement.[19]

The number twelve typically symbolizes priesthood authority, including its power and right to govern.[20] Consequently, the twelve oxen can remind the initiate that the washing that takes place via the laver is a priesthood ordinance, which must be done by proper priesthood authority. Perhaps related is the fact that the way in which one becomes one of the twelve tribes of Israel, and a descendant of Abraham, is through a ritual washing or baptism. The number four symbolizes geographic completeness or totality.[21] In other words, if the number four is associated with an event or thing, the indication is that it will affect the entire earth and all its inhabitants, or that it is requisite for all.[22] Thus, the placement of the oxen under the laver or font, facing the four cardinal directions, implies that the cleansing that takes place therein is important for all mankind. All must be cleansed. All must receive the sanctification associated therewith. Related to the oxen facing four directions, one commentator suggested that in ancient times the thrones of kings often sat on the back of statues of oxen or lions, which pointed in the four cardinal directions.[23] Thus, the font's placement on the back of twelve oxen facing north, south, east, and west implies enthronement, and the promise that those who overcome all things will be given the right to preside over all things. Thus, symbolically speaking, the washing in the laver mirrors the initiate's entrance onto the path leading to enthronement, exaltation, and deification. By being washed one was also being offered enthronement—though, admittedly, that blessing was to be delayed. Oxen are "clean" or "kosher" animals and, as such, have a parted hoof (Leviticus 11:3; Deuteronomy 14:6). Anciently the parted hoof implied eternal opposition or, in other words, living in the world and yet looking forward to the world to come.[24] One modern source states: "Cloven-hoofed animals which part their hooves symbolize that all our actions must betray proper ethical distinction, and be directed toward righteousness."[25] The twelve oxen, upon whose backs the laver rested, parted the hoof, and therefore were an invitation to those washed therein to live a life of proper ethical and moral conduct. By being washed in the unique font, the initiate was, in a very real sense, saying he would live as God and His Christ would live—as faithful followers of the Messiah should live.

Beyond baptism and the priestly washings of the Hebrew Bible, a number of other ritual initiations take place in the various Christian communions. Ritual washings, anointings, investing with sacred articles of clothing, and naming rites have been found among branches of the ancient church. As a sort of summary of the interplay between these various initiatory ordinances, note the following rather curious account by Levi, the third son of Jacob and Leah, in which we learn that he saw in vision seven men dressed in white clothing who initiated him for priestly service. The account tells that, as part of that initiation, these men or angels whom he viewed in his vision "washed [Levi] with pure water," and "anointed [him] with holy oil." He also indicates that these ministers "put on [him] something made of linen" and spoke to him of "a new name." The beings "dressed in white" commanded Levi to "arise [and] put on the vestments of the priesthood." Among the articles of clothing he was commanded to don were "the robe of truth," a cap or miter for his head, a "girdle" or sash, and "the apron for prophetic power."[26] Thus, though we will discuss below these various rites—washing, anointing, clothing, and naming—as separate rituals, the reader should be aware that they were often practiced anciently, not in isolation of each other, but rather in concert with each other.

Some form of ritual washing has ever been part of the Judeo-Christian-Islamic tradition. Indeed, most of the world's faiths have some sort of cleansing ritual as part of their rites of transformation.[27] As an example, the *Bektashi*—an order of Sufi[28] Muslims—have an initiation ritual they go through associated with ablution or cleansing.[29] The initiate is taken into a room separate from the main assembly (where the previously initiated await his appearance). There he is ceremonially cleansed via water while a "guide" recites "the meaning of the purification" taking place.[30] One text describes the initiation as follows:

He washes his hands in order to be freed from all the prohibited things to which he has stretched his hands before; he rinses his mouth in order to cleanse it from all falsehood and fault that may have issued from it; he rinses his nose to cleanse it from whatever forbidden things he has smelt; he washes his face in order to be absolved from every shameful thing; his feet [are washed] in order to be cleansed from every instance of having walked in rebellious and mistaken paths; . . . he wipes his head and ears . . . to be absolved from every unreasonable thing which is counter to the religious law, and further, [he wipes] his face [that he may be cleansed] from all the acts of disobedience which he has committed. . . . This ablution differed from the ordinary ablutions in so far as it was effective forever. The meaning [of the ceremonial washing] is quite clear: it is the complete removal of all that is sinful and unclean and belongs to his former life.[31]

Once the initiate is washed and clothed in ceremonial clothing, he is considered "a member of the order and is taught their secrets."[32]

Related to this example of ritual washing among certain Muslims, in Judaism the law of Moses required ritual washing prior to service in the tabernacle or temple. These "ritual washings . . . were necessary before the high priest could enter the holy of holies"[33] One text noted that the "ablation [of Jewish priests] took place before the anointing and the putting on of sacred clothing."[34] Whereas among the Muslim *Bektashi* the washing was for membership in the society, in ancient Israel the tabernacle or temple washing was for the purification and qualification of one who was already a member of the society. It was, for the Jews, a rite of cleansing prior to service in the temple.

Christianity has had various washing or purification rites also—baptism being chief among them. Though the New Testament seems to suggest that baptism in the first century was most often (if not exclusively) by immersion,[35] apparently sometime during the second century the baptismal ritual merged with, or was replaced by, an alternate Christian rite of initiation, which consisted of a washing and anointing, but which began to be referred to (from the second century onward) as "baptism."[36]

When the early Christians were ceremonially washed, the act was less a real washing and more of a symbol. Thus, while a limited quantity of water was used, and a limited portion of the body was literally physically cleansed, nevertheless, symbolically the initiate's entire person was being washed. As the French philosopher Paul Ricoeur once noted: "The body itself is not only a literal body, so to speak, but also a symbolic body. It is the seat of everything that happens to me without my doing."[37] We know that many ancient initiation rituals were synecdoche, meaning they were a part which represents the whole. So, while one might preform a short washing ritual, that truncated rite traditionally represented a more thorough cleaning—a cleansing of the whole by washing only a part.

NUDITY

History indicates that the early Christians were typically nude when they participated in these aforementioned ritual washings. This custom of nudity was a symbol "of a return to the state of innocence that [was] obtained in paradise before the Fall of Man."[38] In so many words, when one was washed one overcame the Fall. One was returning to Eden, and the washing was symbolically removing one from the fallen state he or she was in. In the fourth century, in a lecture given to new converts to the Church, Cyril of Jerusalem[39] spoke of the symbolism of disrobing before being ceremonially cleansed.[40] He said: "Having stripped yourselves, ye were naked; in this also imitating Christ, who was stripped naked on the Cross, and by His nakedness *put off from Himself the principalities and powers, and openly triumphed over them on the tree.*" Cyril added that removing your garments symbolized removing your sinful self and "the adverse powers [which have] made their lair in your members [or the various parts of your body]." "May the soul which has once put [Satan] off, never again put him on." Finally, Cyril noted that in removing one's street clothes "truly ye bore the likeness of the first-formed Adam, who was naked in the garden, and was not ashamed."[41] Thus, according to this fourth century bishop, the removal of one's clothing prior to the Christian washing rite stood as a symbol of the rejection of Satan's influence and ways—including the ways of the world so aptly represented by mankind's worldly garb. By disrobing before being washed, one takes upon himself or herself the powers of Christ, by symbolically stripping off the sinful desires, practices, and characteristics consequent to mortality.

Related to the concept of purity and the removal of sins is the notion of separation from the world and its influences. Ritual washing, if understood by the initiate, implied exactly that—the initiate was making a conscious choice to separate himself or herself from the fallen world and its evil or harmful influences.[42] It was a covenant or commitment, of sorts, that one had decided to be different—inaccessible to Satan's work and worries. One text on ancient rites of passage suggested: "Initiation [is] a threshold through which an individual passes from one status to another."[43] Elsewhere we read: " 'Purifications' (washing, cleansing, etc.) constitute rites of separation from previous surroundings."[44] Thus, when one is "initiated" one becomes a new person; separated from the old self, the old ways, the old desires, and sometimes old relationships.[45]

As would be expected, washing rituals in Christianity cannot be separated (symbolically speaking) from the Atonement of Christ. It has been pointed out that initiation rituals—whether ancient or modern—are typically symbolic of death and rebirth, or death and resurrection.[46] Thus baptism, as noted above, is commonly associated with *both* the womb *and* the grave. One recent text points out that: "Ritual ablutions, or washings with water, are directly connected to the atonement, for they symbolically cleanse us from sin and iniquity, just as the atonement literally cleanses us from sin and iniquity."[47] Even the ritual washings required by the law of Moses (prior to service in the temple) were associated with the cleansing power of the Atonement.[48] Consequently, one author noted that being "symbolically washed" represents "the cleansing and covering power of the Atonement."[49] In the late second or early third century, Tertullian of Carthage[50] wrote: "The flesh,

ANOINTING

Nibley, in reference to ancient Egyptian initiation rites, wrote: "Purification, rather than being an end in itself, always prepares the way for things to follow, being part of a larger sequence of ordinances."[56] In other words, washing is a rite, in and of itself. However, anciently it tended to be connected to, or lead to, other ordinances or rituals. As it was with the Egyptians, so it apparently was with the ancient Christians. Sometime around the turn of the second to third century, Tertullian wrote:

> Not that *in* the waters we obtain the Holy Spirit; but in the water . . . we are cleansed, and prepared *for* the Holy Spirit . . . After this . . . we are thoroughly anointed with a blessed unction [or oil]—a practice derived from the old discipline, wherein on entering the priesthood, men were wont to be anointed with oil from a horn, ever since Aaron was anointed by Moses. Whence Aaron is called 'Christ,' from the "chrism," which is "the unction." . . . He was "anointed" with the Spirit by God the Father . . . Thus, too, in *our* case, the unction [or oil] runs carnally, (*i.e.* on the body,) but profits [us] spiritually . . . In the next place the hand is laid on us, invoking and inviting the Holy Spirit through benediction.[57]

Tertullian suggested that the washing with water cleansed the initiate, and prepared him or her to receive the Holy Spirit, which was typically symbolized among the ancients by the act of anointing with oil from a horn. He also informs the reader that the gestures of washing and then anointing parallel ancient priesthood ordinations wherein those thus anointed thereby became symbols of Christ, whose title means quite literally "anointed one." Hence, to be washed led to an anointing, and to be anointed suggested that one was God's representative. The rite was, in the very least, a commitment on the part of the initiate to live and minister as God would. Clearly washings and anointings were often connected among the early Christians.

Examples of anointing rituals are fairly common among the ancients. The Hebrew Bible speaks of various anointing rites. Lepers,[58] priests,[59] and kings[60] all had their individual anointing

indeed, is washed, in order that the soul may be cleansed
is anointed, that the soul may be consecrated; . . . the fles
owed with the imposition [or laying on] of hands, that
also may be illuminated by the Spirit; the flesh feeds on
and blood of Christ [in the sacrament of the Lord's Supp
the soul likewise may fatten on *its* God."[51] Tertullian's p
that what is done to the body is really done to the spirit.
body is washed, really it is the spirit that is being cleansed.
to wash the spirit (or, as Tertullian would call it, "the s
atonement imagery, and suggests the remitting of sins. Ma
similar point about atonement imagery in ritual washings
of Jerusalem noted that one does not enter the holy sanc
with the intent to "stand around God's altar," without wa
first. He notes that the act of ritual washing "is a symbo
ye ought to be pure from all sinful and unlawful deeds . .
washing therefore . . . is a symbol of immunity from sin."[52]
tions, or ceremonial washings, were believed by certain anc
to avert evil, give life and strength to the individual being wasl
and symbolize the rebirth of the initiate. Indeed, it was held
he who was washed was also "endowed with divine qualiti
Again, we see connections between the Atonement and wash

Atonement leads to cleansing, and cleansing leads to dei
tion. God cleanses His people in order to make them like F
He seeks to make them all kings and priests, just as He is a
and a priest. Margaret Barker, in one of her many publication
the temple, wrote: "What had formerly been the role of the
became that of the whole people or of the individual. All
chosen, all were the sons of God (e.g., Deuteronomy 14:1–2),
all were the holy priesthood (Exodus 19:6)."[54] Thus, one is wa
as a king was anciently washed. And just as the king, through
washing, was believed to be endowed with the authority and a
butes of the divine, all of the covenant people could be wa
and cleansed and endowed to be kings and priests or queens
priestesses.[55]

rituals—though each was for different purposes, and had different symbolic meanings.[61] It has been pointed out that the "priests in Old Testament times had to be anointed with oil before they were authorized to enter God's presence . . . (Exodus 29:7) . . . Kings were also anointed with oil, to indicate that they had been chosen and consecrated by God."[62] What seems most germane to our study here are the highly symbolic anointing rituals of the early Christians; namely those that followed the ceremonial washing, and that eventually became known as part of "baptism" or "chrism."[63] For example, in the fourth century Cyril of Jerusalem taught the following to those who were about to be washed with water[64] and anointed with oil:

> When you were stripped [of your street clothes], ye were anointed with . . . oil, from the very hairs of your head to your feet, and were [thereby] made partakers of the good olive-tree, Jesus Christ. For ye were cut off from the wild olive-tree, and grafted into the good one, and were made to share the fatness [or blessings] of the true olive-tree. The . . . oil therefore was a symbol of the participation of the fatness [or blessings] of Christ, being a charm [or power] to drive away every trace of hostile influence [in your life].[65]

Thus, Cyril suggests that the anointing with oil symbolically represented communion and oneness with Christ, along with receipt of (or a right to) the blessing of Christ. He also suggests that the anointing endowed the recipient with the power to limit Satan's influence in his or her life. Cyril then adds this:

> There was given [to you] an Unction [or anointing], the anti-type[66] of what wherewith Christ was anointed . . . And as Christ was . . . anointed with an . . . oil of gladness, because He is the author of spiritual gladness, so ye were anointed with ointment [or oil], having been made partakers and *fellows of Christ.* . . . Which ointment is symbolically applied to thy forehead and thy other senses [or sense organs]; and while the body is anointed with the visible ointment, thy soul is sanctified by the Holy and life-giving Spirit. Ye were first anointed on the forehead, that ye might . . . *reflect as a mirror the glory of the Lord.*[67] Then on your ears; that ye

might receive the ears which are quick to hear the Divine Mysteries, of which Esaias said, *The Lord gave me also an ear to hear* [Isaiah 1:4]; and the Lord Jesus in the Gospel, *He that hath ears to hear let him hear* [Mark 4:9]. Then on the nostrils; that receiving the sacred ointment ye may say, *We are to God a sweet [savor] of Christ, in them that are saved.* Afterwards on your breast; that having put on the *breastplate of righteousness, ye may stand against the wiles of the devil.*[68]

According to Cyril, when one is anointed with the consecrated olive oil, one becomes a symbol of Christ—the title Christ meaning literally "anointed one."[69] He also points out that anointing on each of the sense organs (e.g., the forehead, ears, eyes, mouth, nose, and so forth) symbolized a blessing of having the Holy Spirit work on and through those organs. In other words, for Cyril, such an anointing symbolized the power of the Holy Spirit in the life of the anointed. The Holy Ghost could act as a "breastplate" against the influence and temptations of Satan—for those who lived up to the covenants associated with the anointing. Thus, the anointing acted as a covenant, blessing, and protection. Hence, of the initiate receiving these anointing rites, one text suggests: "He is sealed with [anointing oil] . . . upon the organs of sense that they may not be entrances of sin. Again on the forehead that he may be terrifying to [evil spirits]. Again on the joints (members) that they may be instruments of righteousness"[70] As one allowed the Spirit to direct thoughts (forehead), words (mouth), what one viewed (eyes) or listened to (ears), one would be blessed with protection and inspiration. Similar to what Cyril recorded, near the beginning of the sixth century an obscure deacon in Rome, simply known as John, wrote a letter to a man by the name of Senaris (possibly a member of the Roman nobility[71]), who had requested of the deacon information on Christian initiatory rites of that period (circa AD 500). In John's response he explained some of the symbolism behind the rites then common within the Church. Among other things, John wrote that the ears are anointed with oil:

> because through them faith enters the mind . . . so that, the ears being as it were fortified by a kind of wall of sanctification,

may permit entrance to nothing harmful, nothing which might entice them back [into wicked ways]. When their nostrils are touched, they are thus without doubt admonished that for so long as they draw the breath of life through their nostrils they must abide in the service and the commandments of God . . . , that since the oil is blessed in the name of the Saviour [sic], they may be led unto his spiritual odour [sic] by the inner perception of a certain ineffable sweetness . . . And so the nostrils, being fortified by this mystery, can give no admittance to the pleasures of this world, nor anything which might weaken their minds.[72]

Like Cyril, John informs Senaris that the anointing of the ears symbolizes the need to insure that one rejects all harmful things he or she might hear in the course of the day. To so reject is to build and protect one's testimony and one's Christianity. John also speaks of the anointing of the nose as a reminder to the initiate of the importance of enduring to the end; of keeping all of God's commandments until one takes one's last mortal breath. John the Deacon also informed Senaris that: "The oil of consecration is used to anoint their breast [meaning the breast of the initiate], in which is the seat and dwelling place of the heart; so that they may understand that they promise with a firm mind and a pure heart eagerly to follow after the commandments of Christ."[73] In other words, the anointing of the breast reminds the initiate to only desire that which is pure and holy; that which is of God. Finally, the deacon informs his hearer that during the rite of anointing, the initiates "are commanded to go in naked even down to their feet" after which the one being anointed is

> arrayed in white vesture, and his head anointed with the unc-
> tion of the sacred chrism: that the baptized person may under-
> stand that in his person a kingdom and a priestly mystery have
> met . . . All the neophytes [or newly initiated] are arrayed in white
> vesture to symbolize the resurgent Church, just as our Lord and
> Saviour [sic] himself in the sight of certain disciples and proph-
> ets was thus transfigured on the mount. And so they wear white
> raiment so that though the ragged dress of ancient error [or past
> sins] has darkened the infancy of their first birth [or has tainted
> the early years of their lives], the costume [or dress] of their second

birth should display the raiment of glory, so that clad in a wedding garment [the initiate] may approach the table of the heavenly bridegroom as a new man.[74]

Because such anointings were, in ancient times, associated with priests and kings, John the Deacon suggests that one thus anointed becomes a king and priest unto God.[75] He also indicates that the receipt of the garments of white (after the anointing) serves as a reminder to the wearer of Christ's transfiguration, and consequently God's power to transfigure (or, in our case, transition) man from fallen person to exalted being. Thus the white garments donned after the ritual anointing symbolize God's forgiveness of the initiate's past shortcomings.

Like the rites common in the days of Cyril and John the Deacon, a sixth century Catholic "baptismal" or anointing rite depicts the officiating priest as touching the candidate on various parts of his or her body, while reciting the following:

> I sign [or anoint with oil in the sign of the cross] your forehead in the name of the Father, the Son and the Holy Spirit so that you may be a Christian. I sign your eyes so that you may see the glory of God. I sign your ears, so that you may hear the voice of the Lord. I sign your nostrils so that you may breathe the fragrance of Christ. I sign your lips, so that you may speak the words of life. I sign your heart so that you may believe in the Holy Trinity. I sign your shoulders so that you may bear the yoke of Christ's service. I sign your whole body, in the name of the Father, the Son and of the Holy Spirit, so that you may live for ever and ever.[76]

The forehead here appears to symbolize the whole person. Each of the anointing blessings pronounced symbolically highlight the need for the Spirit's influence upon and through that organ of the body. Each act of anointing implies a blessing and potential curse. The anointed eyes can enable one to "see the glory of God" if one is faithful to covenants. The unrighteous will be eternally cast from God's presence. The anointed ears enable one to "hear the voice of the Lord." However, he who is unfaithful will be left to himself; living a life void of personal revelation. The anointed nostrils endow one with the ability to "breathe the fragrance of Christ." The meaning of the symbol is not entirely clear here. The nose is sometimes a symbol for anger or temperament.[77] Thus, one source reasons, "excited breathing, with distensions of the nostrils when moved by indignation, led to the nose being used figuratively for anger."[78] This being the case, it is possible that the blessing upon the initiate is one of calm and peacefulness (as one might feel when inhaling the fragrance of fresh flowers). Conversely, the cursing upon the unfaithful would be to live a life filled with frustration, anger, and discontent.[79] The anointed lips endow the initiate with the power to speak the words of life to those to whom he or she ministers. The unrighteous, however, will enjoy no such gift of tongues.[80] The anointed heart is the recipient of a testimony of the reality of God. The curse to the erring initiate is a weakness of faith and all that entails for a life filled with doubt. The anointed shoulders, our Catholic initiatory rite informs us, are blessed with the power to bear the burdens of service in the kingdom. For the wayward, the cursing is that calls to serve *will* be a burden rather than a blessing. Finally, the totality of the blessing, we are told, is that the individual faithful to his or her covenants will "live forever and ever." In other words, he or she will inherit eternal life in God's presence.[81] For those who do not keep their covenants, no such blessing awaits.

Though much of the symbolism associated with this ancient rite has already been conveyed above, there are a few other points that may be worth noting. First of all, olive oil is a typical symbol of the Holy Ghost[82]—as can be water. Thus, anointing with oil not only cleanses (through the Spirit's sanctifying power), but also directs and inspires the anointed in a variety of ways (as is implied by the various body parts anointed by the ancients). In Roman Catholic ordination rites "God is asked . . . to sanctify [the anointed] with spiritual unction corresponding to the oil that was poured on the head of Aaron and [which] flowed over all his body. . . . God is asked to let the Holy Spirit be with the ordained so that he may exhibit the qualities requisite for the discharge of his office, in which teaching and the ministering of discipline seem to be major features."[83] Part of the prayer vocalized during this rite requests of God: "Complete the fullness of your mystery in your priests . . . Hallow them with the dew [or oil] of heavenly unction. May it flow down, O Lord, richly upon their head; may it run down . . . to the uttermost parts of the whole body, so that the power of your Spirit may both fill them within and surround them without."[84] Thus, in ordaining one a Catholic bishop, oil is used to symbolize the need of the ordained to be endowed with divine qualities, power, and guidance. It is suggested that the oil anointing will fill and protect its recipient. Nibley pointed out that the ritual anointing "of the brow, face, ears, nose, breast, etc." clothes the initiate "in the protective panoply of the Holy Spirit."[85]

Related to the symbolism of the Spirit's sanctifying power is the fact that to the ancients "anointing denoted consecration."[86] Consecration implied cleansing, but also setting apart from the world or the status quo.

> The object of anointing with olive oil was to sanctify . . . people, meaning to declare them to be in a state of holiness. That is to say that the recipient of the anointing became worthy to stand before God in sacred places and to interact with the other sacred persons and objects in a temple setting. The recipient, like the temple itself, was "set apart" and "wholly other" from the profaneness of the world. . . . Those who received the anointing were sanctified and set apart from the profane world and were thus required to adhere to certain responsibilities (Lev. 21:10–12), but they were also offered special privileges (Lev. 4:3–12; 6:20–22; 16:32–34; Nub. 4:16; 18:8). For instance, those who received the anointing were protected by God (1 Chr. 6:22; Ps. 105:15; 89:20–23; D&C 121:16), taught from on high (1 John 2:27), gained salvation (Ps. 20:6; 28:8; D&C 109:80), and received mercy from the Lord (2 Sam. 22:51; Ps. 18:50).[87]

Consequently, those accepting an anointing were also accepting an obligation to change their surroundings, their clothing, their associations, and their focus. Their life would no longer be about building their personal kingdom. Now it was to be entirely about God's kingdom. They, through their anointing, were consecrating themselves to God. They were setting themselves apart from the world.

As with almost all other Christian rites, others help the initiate to receive the rite. We are baptized by others; confirmed by others; ordained by others; married or sealed by others. As it is in Christianity, so it is in Judaism. One commentator noted of nineteenth and early twentieth century Jewish rites: "Newcomers were initiated into the *mysteries* . . . not by the educators, social workers, industrialists, and labor leaders commonly thought of as the primary agents of acculturation *but by each other*."[88] Thus, there is meaning in the fact that those engaging in ritual typically receive their initiation at the hands of a brother or a sister, rather than by some high-ranking official of the faith. It is a message of consecration. It is a message about equality in the kingdom (i.e., no Christian or Jew is more important than another in the eyes of God). It reminds us that our calling is to serve each other, as Christ served. And it is certainly representative of how we typically encapsulate our baptismal covenant (see Mosiah 18:8–10). The Apostle Paul taught the Saints at Galatia to "love [and] serve one another" (Galatians 5:13). King Benjamin reminded us that we "ought . . . to labor to serve one another" (Mosiah 2:18) because "when ye are in the service of your fellow beings ye are only in the service of your God" (Mosiah 2:17). The initiation by peers tends to symbolize the call for all to be holy—for all to be God's hands in the world, and especially in sacred things. Indeed, this is particularly significant specifically because of the fact that the hands of those who perform rites on our behalf function as God's hands. Their work is His work.

We are informed: "When priesthood brethren use their hands to anoint someone's head with consecrated oil, . . . their hands represent God's hands. The recipient's head represents the whole of his or her being. The olive oil represents the Holy Ghost (D&C 45:56–57). The oil also suggests the oil that came forth from the olive press at the olive garden at Gethsemane, which in turn represents the Savior's suffering there."[89]

Thus the anointing is symbolically from God. It is He who

anoints us, through one of His authorized servants. Through their hands, His hands are placed upon us. As noted above, though it may be that only a portion of the body is anointed, symbolically speaking, the whole of the person is being blessed. And the oil reminds us that the blessings we are receiving through the anointing were bought for us by Christ, and with His own blood.[90]

The oil for ancient anointings—specifically that of kings—was often carried in a horn.[91] Horns symbolize power or strength.[92] Thus, in an anointing, the use of a horn was suggestive of the power that the anointed was being endowed with. Some sources associate horns with an outpouring of the Holy Ghost.[93] Thus, the anointing of an individual with oil from a horn implied that the initiate should seek to be directed by God's Spirit, and would be empowered by it if he or she lived and served faithfully.

Related to the idea of kingly anointings—and in an effort to establish Jesus as the King of the Jews—the book of Hebrews (drawing on Psalm 45:7[94]) states: "Thou [Jesus] hast loved righteousness, and hated iniquity; therefore God, even thy God, hath anointed thee with the *oil of gladness* above thy fellows" (Hebrews 1:9, emphasis added). God anointed Jesus with the "oil of gladness," and thus He is called "the Christ" (literally, "the anointed one"). One scholar pointed out that this anointing of Jesus represents or symbolizes promised "exaltation"[95]—which surely brings "gladness" to its recipients. While the book of Hebrews appears to be referencing Christ's anointing as the Messiah, nevertheless (as we have noted above) the early Church saw all those who received an oil anointing as becoming "christs" in some sense (Obadiah 1:21)—and thus this reference to the "oil of gladness" may have a degree of applicability to all anointed Christians.[96] It appears that one interpretation of the rite or ritual of anointing may be that it is a symbol for the promise of exaltation (contingent upon faithfulness). Consequently, one encyclopedia of religion points out that anciently anointing with oil was "a sign that mourning was at an end."[97] So it is that those who obtain exaltation in the celestial kingdom of God will no longer have cause to mourn (Revelation 21:4).

ENTHRONEMENT

In previous centuries—before and after the Common Era—washings and anointings were often attached to, or associated with, the ritual act of enthronement. Indeed, those washed and anointed were often seated (or enthroned) during some portion of the rite. Whereas being washed and anointed *could* designate one a priest *or* a king,[98] enthronement was consistently associated with kingship or deification. Consequently, enthronement (as a symbol) suggested that the one anointed was to become a king, but it also implied the initiate would become a judge, a ruler, or a god.[99] One scholar informs us that the seated or enthroned man was a symbol of "the ancient kings" *and also* of "the Lord."[100] The common use of thrones in antiquity show how universally meaningful this symbol was, and how central it was to their liturgical practice, their symbology, and potentially their soteriology and theology.[101] Simply put, one washed, anointed, and then enthroned was symbolically being offered an opportunity to be a king and priest—even a god—contingent upon faithfulness![102] This rite was, perhaps, one of the ultimate rituals of the ancient Church, as it stated, as clearly as any other ceremony, the ultimate goal of the Father for each of His children: namely deification, which included (among other things) priestly and kingly power. One source informs us:

> The temple was both heaven and earth. The throne of the Lord was in heaven, but also in the temple: "A glorious throne set on high from the beginning is the place of our sanctuary" (Jer. 17:12). The king had been the earthly manifestation of the Lord in his temple; he had been addressed as the Lord's son (Pss. 2:7; 72:1) and he had sat upon the Lord's throne as king: "Then Solomon sat on the throne of the Lord as king . . ." (1 Chron. 29:23). The memory of these royal rituals persisted long after the [temple] cult itself had been transformed; there was often a human figure on the divine throne, and the ancient enthronement ceremony which had reenacted the triumph of the Lord over his enemies passed into the vision of the last judgement.[103]

In a sense, in the enthronement rite of ancient times, heaven and earth met. For a fleeting moment, as the initiate was seated, symbolically God was present—his temple throne was no longer vacant, but was filled by His son who sat thereon in God's stead.

In modern ordination rites, the theme of priest (or divine representative) and king is represented through an enthronement ritual. One commentator pointed out: "The bishop's chair was an important symbol of his presidential [or presiding] role in the community."[104] He presides over the congregation just as God presides over all His creations. The bishop is symbolically God's presence in the midst of the congregation. As with the church, so also in the temple. One commentator noted: "Whoever sat on [the throne in the temple] would have acted as the spokesman of the Lord."[105] The modern bishop (in the Roman Catholic and Eastern Orthodox traditions) is seated on a throne, and therefore is seen as God's spokesman. He is initially enthroned when he is ordained or installed as bishop. The enthronement reminds his parish that he now represents the divine. As God is judge, the bishop (on behalf of God) is to function as a judge in Israel (See D&C 58:17 and 107:72, 76).[106] His actions and efforts to battle Satan, who seeks a presence amid the bishop's flock symbolize (or reflect) Christ's actions and efforts to battle the adversary who seeks to gain access to His flock. As noted, the bishop's triumphs represented "the triumph of the Lord over his enemies."[107] So also, the triumphs of the enthroned today reflect upon the Lord. Our successfully fought battles are really His successfully fought battles—as our ordination and our enthronement are really His.

NAMING

The practice of ritual naming and renaming stems from the earliest of times. One text on the subject points out: "The phenomenon and religious significance of naming, as well as the practices of renaming and of giving secret or hidden names, are richly attested in the extant sources among the peoples of the ancient Near East, particularly in Israel and Egypt; but they are also found in chronologically and geographically contiguous societies in the ancient world."[108] Elsewhere we read: "The giving or possessing of a second name, to be kept hidden from others, is widely attested in antiquity among both mortals and divinities . . ."[109]

Though in modern Western culture names are typically selected based on current societal trends, or how good a "first name" sounds with the newborn's surname, such a practice was less prevalent in ancient times.[110] The average modern does not see the meaning and value in a name that their ancient counterparts would have.[111] Indeed, one text noted, "When contrasted with their general devaluation in the modern West, the significance of naming and the wide attestation of renaming and the giving of hidden names in the ancient world is astonishing."[112]

In antiquity, the giving of a name was a sacred, significant, and meaningful experience. But the invoking of one's name—or the name of another—also held a great deal of significance in ancient societies. The employment of one's name over something implied ownership, possession, or responsibility. Thus, when a Christian enters into the covenant of baptism, and in so doing takes upon him or her the name of Christ, that person becomes Christ's possession.[113] "The phrase 'in [so-and-so's] name' can indicate status (Mt. 10:41–42; Mk. 9:41), impersonation (Mt. 24:5), responsibility, (Esth. 2:22; Eph. 5:20) or purpose (Ps. 118:26; Mt. 18:20). Usually, however, it claims delegated authority."[114]

In the esoteric ordinances of many ancient societies, there was a belief that, if one were in possession of a secret name, that name would need to be guarded with the utmost care. "By wearing or bearing the name, one is placed under God's special protection."[115] According to the Doctrine and Covenants (130:10–11), the new name is a "key word." It serves to endow the possessor with power before God.[116] For another to discover your secret or esoteric name would, it was believed anciently, give the discoverer power over you.[117] In addition, in numerous ancient cultures, the knowledge of certain "secrets"—including the knowledge of "secret names"—was necessary for one to inherit "everlasting bliss" where the initiate would learn his or her own "True Name."[118] Thus, one source suggests that " . . . by proper use of the name or names, one does not speak *of* or *about* God. He speaks *to* or . . . *with* God."[119] The name is a key word—and means by which one has access to God, and through which one may solicit entrance into God's realm.

In ancient scripture, names were generally given in order to indicate something about the nature,[120] character,[121] experience,[122] or function of the person,[123] place, or nation named.[124] It was common in antiquity for a name to capture the essence or experience of a person.[125] Thus, in Hebrew society, parents would often choose a name, either in the hopes that the child would live up to the connotations of their name,[126] or because of some circumstance or event surrounding his or her birth.[127] So Rachel's son was named Benoni ("son of my sorrow") because her labor was so hard that in the end it cost her her life (Genesis 35:18). Hannah named her boy Samuel ("heard of God") because she believed the boy to be an answer to her prayers (1 Samuel 1:20). Hagar named her child Ishmael ("the Lord hears") because an angel commanded her to do so as a token of the fact that God had and would continue to hear her in her afflictions (Genesis 16:11). Upon hearing the tragic news that her husband had been killed, her nation had been defeated, the ark of the covenant had been captured, and her father-in-law had suddenly passed away, Phinehas' pregnant wife went into labor and delivered a son which, just before she died, she named Ichabod ("no glory" or "the glory has departed") in recognition of what had taken place in her life and nation (1 Samuel 4:21). Rachel named her firstborn son Joseph ("he shall add" or "increase") as a sign of her faith that God was not yet done blessing her (Gen. 30:24).[128]

A frequent occurrence in scripture is the practice of renaming an individual at some stage in his or her life.[129] Babylonian priests, upon being installed, received a new name.[130] The same practice exists in Roman Catholicism, where those entering into holy orders, becoming a priest or nun, take a new name (as does a new pope).[131] Kings in many nations traditionally take a new name upon their coronation.[132] One source states: "New names were frequently conferred upon individuals at the time of their enthronement." This same text points out: "The receipt of a new name by the monarch at the time of enthronement is a nearly universal phenomenon."[133] This tradition of giving a new name is common in many initiation rites, as it well represents a transition—including the death of the old and the birth of the new.[134] One dictionary of symbolism reminds us:

> Formal renamings register a change in personality and signal a new phase of one's life. Abram, Sarai, and Oshea have their names replaced (Genesis 17:5, 15; Numbers 13:16); Naomi in her sorrow thinks that she should (Ruth 1:20). Jacob, Gideon, and Solomon are given supplementary names, Israel, Jerubbaal, Jedediah—nicknames, in the old sense. So also, in the New Testament, are James and John (Boanerges), Simon (Cephas/Peter), the Cypriot Joseph (Barnabas) and Thomas /Didymus (Aramaic and Greek for "twin"; his true name was Judas, according to patristic tradition). . . . Daniel's new name, Beltesshazzar, contains the name of the god Bel (Dan 4:8).[135]

New names or titles are relatively common in modernity also. One potentially receives them at birth, at baptism, upon ordination, when making certain covenants, and, in some cases, when married.[136] Each of these events signals a new stage in one's life, as does the accompanying name.[137] One dictionary of scriptural names indicates that each "new name" has meaning. So much so, that sometimes when a person's nature changed, God changed his or her name also.[138] Elsewhere we read, "If naming constituted the giving of an identity, the giving of a new name gave a new identity to the recipient, and was frequently associated with an important transition in the recipient's life."[139] One recent LDS text states the following regarding the ancient practice of giving new names:

> Taking upon oneself a new name is a symbol of becoming a new person. . . . The new name is a token [that one] has been spiritually reborn, that his "old man is crucified with [Christ]," as Paul would say (Romans 6:6), and that he has over time become a new person. This sanctification journey . . . is the same journey of renewal described by King Benjamin . . . in chapters 2 through 4 of the book of Mosiah. . . . [He] teaches unequivocally that salvation can come to none except those who will repent and

accept Christ as their savior, take upon themselves His name, and become new people—be born again—through His Atonement (see Mosiah 3:17; 5:8). . . . Benjamin insists that accepting Christ's salvation means undergoing a change of heart and character . . .[140]

Elsewhere we read: "Because the initiate is continually overcoming ignorance by gaining new, more advanced, sacred knowledge, he often takes upon himself a new name. These are true names, sacred names, names which imply that the initiate has become transformed . . ."[141]

In mediaeval Jewish Mysticism there existed a "rite of initiation" through which the initiate was endowed with, or given, the sacred name by one already in possession of this key word.[142] One early thirteenth century document describes part of the Jewish ritual of giving the name as follows:

> The name is transmitted only to the reserved—this word can also be translated as "the initiate"—who are not prone to anger, who are humble and God-fearing, and carry out the commandments of their Creator. And [the name] is transmitted only over water. Before the master [or officiator] teaches it to his pupil [i.e., the initiate], they must both immerse themselves and bathe in . . . flowing water, then put on white garments and fast on the day of instruction.[143]

According to one commentator on this Jewish rite, the officiator then transmits to the new initiate "one among the secret names of God that the adept is permitted to hear."[144]

Much like the changing of clothes, or the washing and anointing of the body, the receipt of a "new name" functions in ancient and modern rituals as a transition away from the old and fallen, and toward the new and repentant. To take a "new name" was to make a covenant to seek to live as a new person, with a new identity. In Christian rites, that new identity was being a Christian, with all that holy title implies.

Notes

1.   Daniel Soyer, "Entering the 'Tent of Abraham': Fraternal Ritual and

American-Jewish Identity, 1880–1920," in *Religion and American Culture*, vol. 9, no. 2 (Summer, 1999): 161.

2.   "From the middle of the 2d century B.C. until *c.* A.D. 300 there was a great deal of baptismal activity in Syria and Palestine, especially along the upper Jordan, among many different groups." (H. Mueller, "Baptism," in *New Catholic Encyclopedia*, second edition, 15 vols. [Detroit: Gale, 2003], 2:57.) Thus, baptism did not start with Christianity—nor is it exclusively Judeo-Christian in origins. See Michel Meslin, "Baptism," in Eliade (1987), 2:59–63. See also Sidney Heath, *The Romance of Symbolism and Its Relation to Church Ornament and Architecture* (London: Francis Griffiths, 1909), 164.

3.   Gerald E. Hansen, Jr., *Sacred Walls: Learning From Temple Symbols* (American Fork, UT: Covenant Communications, 2009), 40. The ascension motif, as it relates to ritual—particularly temple ritual, is a common one. Hansen wrote: "The theme of the . . . temple is ascension to God . . . Scriptural examples of the ascension motif include Moses' climb to Mt. Sinai (see Exodus 3:1–6), Israel's exodus from bondage to the promised land (see Exodus 13:17–19:1; Numbers 10:10–36:13; Deuteronomy 34; Joshua 1–11), Ezekiel's heavenly council experience (see Ezekiel 1–3), the Mount of Transfiguration (see Matthew 17:1–7), John the Revelator's heavenly council experience (see Revelation 4–5), Joseph Smith's First Vision (see Joseph Smith—History 1:16–20), and Joseph Smith's vision of the three degrees of glory (see D&C 76)." He adds:

> Ascension to God is a theme that appears often in the Church. For instance, at baptism, members descend into the water, symbolically burying their own selfish desires, witnessing that they have given up their will to God. The ascension out of the water symbolizes new life in Christ and begins the new journey upward to God . . . Christ's literal descent into the despair of Gethsemane and then death on the cross, followed by His resurrection and ascent to the Father, shines as the preeminent symbol of ascension and represents our own occasional suffering in mortality, our eventual death, and our own certain, future immortality.

Finally, Hansen points out: "The two main, fundamental parts of the plan of exaltation—the Fall and Atonement—also act as an instructive metaphor for humanity's possible journey upward from a selfish and willful, fallen state to the sanctified and godly character achieved by all those who have chosen redemption through Christ." (Hansen [2009], 40.) Elsewhere we read: "A dominant theme (in scripture) is the representation of God's temple as a holy mountain. Mount Sinai was called 'the mountain of God' (Exodus 3:1). . . . The image of a holy mountain is important in symbolizing our fall and the need to climb back to the elevated level of God. It is in climbing this mountain that our nature changes in preparation to meet God. As we climb, we get glimpses of the great view to be seen at the summit." (Donald W. Parry, "Sinai as Sanctuary and Mountain of God," in Lundquist and Ricks [1990], 1:482.) See also Richard O. Cowan, "Sacred Temples Ancient and Modern," in Parry and Ricks (1999), 106–107, who stated: "Moving from room to room symbolized [the initiate's] increasing understanding and progress."

4.   "On the one hand, our own baptism . . . represents the 'death' of our disobedient, sinful selves and our spiritual 'resurrection' into a newness of life. On the other hand, our baptism symbolizes our physical death and resurrection." Donald W. Parry and Jay A. Parry, *Symbols & Shadows: Unlocking a Deeper Understanding of the Atonement* (Salt Lake City: Deseret Book, 2009), 259.

5.   Parry and Parry (2009), 15.

6.   Karen Jo Torjesen, *When Women Were Priests: Women's Leadership in the Early Church & the Scandal of their Subordination in the Rise of Christianity* (San Francisco: Harper San Francisco, 1993), 258.

7.   Parry and Parry (2009), 15.

8.   Joseph Smith, *Teachings of the Prophet Joseph Smith*, Joseph Fielding Smith, comp. (Salt Lake City: Deseret Book, 1976), 314, 360.

9.   "Sins are remitted *not* in the waters of baptism, as we say in speaking figuratively, but when we receive the Holy Ghost. It is the Holy Spirit of God that erases carnality and brings us into a state of righteousness. We become clean when we actually receive the fellowship and companionship of the Holy Ghost. It is then that sin and dross and evil are burned out of our souls as though by fire. The baptism of the Holy Ghost is the baptism of fire . . . And thus it is that we receive a remission of our sins through baptism and through the sacrament. The Spirit will not dwell in an unclean tabernacle, and when men receive the Spirit, they become clean and pure and spotless." Bruce R. McConkie, *A New Witness for the Articles of Faith* (Salt Lake City: Deseret Book, 1985), 290, 299; emphasis added.

10.   Parry and Parry (2009), 15.

11.   Hansen (2009), 40.

12.   See Parry and Parry (2009), 14.

13.   Kevin J. Conner, *Interpreting the Symbols and Types* (Portland, OR: City Bible Publishing, 1992), 61; Harold Bayley, *The Lost Language of Symbolism*, 2 vols. (New York: Carol Publishing Group, 1990–93),

2:38; Farbridge (1923), 277–78; Smith (1998), 289; Allen C. Myers, *The Eerdmans Bible Dictionary* (Grand Rapids: Eerdmans, 1987), 227; Merrill F. Unger, *Unger's Bible Dictionary* (Chicago: Moody Press, 1966), 212–14; Joseph Fielding McConkie and Donald W. Parry, *A Guide to Scriptural Symbols* (Salt Lake City: Bookcraft, 1990), 33; Joseph Fielding McConkie, *Gospel Symbolism* (Salt Lake City: Bookcraft, 1985), 105, 256–57; Jay A. Parry and Donald W. Parry, *Understanding the Book of Revelation* (Salt Lake City: Deseret Book, 1998), 59, 278.

14. Todeschi (1995), 73; Hugh T. Henry, *Catholic Customs and Symbols* (New York: Benziger Brothers, 1925), 80–81; Fontana (1994), 67; Rest (1987), 46.

15. The term esoteric has reference to things that would only be understood by those initiated into the rite, the secret, or the mystery. Thus, esoteric knowledge is hidden or guarded knowledge understood only by those invited to be part of the select few to whom this knowledge has been revealed.

16. Parry and Parry (2009), 126.

17. Cirlot (1962), 34, 150–51; Cooper (1995), 124; Patrick Fairbairn, *The Typology of Scripture* (Grand Rapids: Kregel Publications, 1989),1:220; James Hall, *Dictionary of Subjects and Symbols in Art* (New York: Harper and Row, 1979), 231; Julien (1996), 309; Todeschi (1995), 25, 192. See also 2 Corinthians 6:14–17.

18. Cirlot (1962), 34, 66, 82–84, 104, 196, 331; Cooper (1995), 26–27; Fontana (1994), 92, 167; Hall (1979), 54; Julien (1996), 49–50; Todeschi (1995), 52.

19. S. Michael Wilcox, *House of Glory: Finding Personal Meaning in the Temple* (Salt Lake City: Deseret Book, 1995), 124.

82. Richard D. Draper, *Opening the Seven Seals* (Salt Lake City: Deseret Book, 1991), 24, 46, 56, 83; Parry and Parry (1998), 295; Bullinger (1967), 2–3, 107; Smith (1998), 288–89; Johnston (1990), 39, 83; Davis (2000), 122.

20. Draper (1991), 24, 77, 94; Smith (1998), 288; Johnston (1990), 61; Farbridge (1923), 115; Rest (1987), 61; Ifrah (2000), 499; Cirlot (1971), 232; Julien (1996), 167; Todeschi (1995), 186; Fontana (1993), 64; Davis (1968), 122–23; Cooper (1995), 115; Bennett, in Hastings (1963), 703; Smith (1979), 263; Carol L. Meyers and Eric M. Meyers, *The Anchor Bible: Haggai, Zechariah 1–8* (New York: Doubleday, 1987), 317.

21. "The number four always has reference to all that is created." Bullinger (1967), 123–24.

22. Hugh Nibley, "Facsimile No. 1, By the Figures (Part 8)," in *Improvement Era*, July 1969, 104.

23.   See "The Epistle of Barnabas," Chapter 8, in Alexander Roberts and James Donaldson, eds., *The Ante-Nicene Fathers*, 10 vols. (Peabody, MA: Hendrickson Publishers, 1994), 1:144.

24.   Mary Douglas, *Purity and Danger: An Analysis of Concepts of Pollution and Taboo* (Binghampton, NY: Vail-Ballou Press, 1980), 47.

25.   See "The Testaments of the Twelve Patriarchs—Testament of Levi," 8:1–19, in Charlesworth (1983, 1985), 1:790–91. Like the Testament of Levi, the book of Second Enoch gives a similar account of anointing and investiture among the ancients. "And the Lord said to Michael, 'Go, and extract [or remove] Enoch from his earthly clothing. And anoint him with my delightful oil, and put him into the clothes of my glory.' And so Michael did, just as the Lord had said to him. He anointed me and he clothed me. . . . And I looked at myself, and I had become like one of his glorious ones [or angels], and there was no observable difference." 2 Enoch 22:8–10, in Charlesworth (1983, 1985), 1:138.

26.   These washing rituals may be associated with membership in a faith, reaching puberty, getting married, being ordained, engaging in prayer or sacrifice, or some other act of worship or transition.

27.   The Sufis are Muslim mystics who practice a very esoteric version of Islam. For a discussion of the development and beliefs of Sufism, see Cyril Glassé, *The Concise Encyclopedia of Islam* (San Francisco: Harper San Francisco, 1989), 375–80.

28.   The *Bektāshīyah* are a Sufi order of Islamic mystics once widespread throughout the Ottoman Empire—particularly rural Turkey. The faith is believed to date from the thirteenth century and is unique, among other reasons, for its initiation rites. "These rites are private [and] reserved for other initiated members . . ." Outsiders or uninitiated individuals are not allowed to participate or view them. See Frances Trix, "*Bektāshīyah*," in John L. Esposito, ed., *The Oxford Encyclopedia of the Modern Islamic World*, 4 vols. (New York: Oxford University Press, 1995), 1:213. The faith is said to have borrowed heavily from a number of pre-Islamic traditions, including Christianity. See Trix, in Esposito (1995), 1:213; Glassé (1989), 71; Ira M. Lapidus, *A History of Islamic Societies* (New York: Cambridge University Press, 1989), 309, 327; J. Spencer Trimingham, *The Sufi Orders in Islam* (New York: Oxford University Press, 1998), 2, 68–69, 81–82, 136, 194; Annemarie Schimmel, *Mystical Dimensions of Islam* (Chapel Hill, NC: University of North Carolina Press, 1986), 340; John Kingsley Birge, *The Bektashi Order of Dervishes* (Hartford: Hartford Seminary Press, 1937), 210, 215–16. Consequently, some of its rites may appear familiar to Christians—though it cannot be proved which rituals were specifically

borrowed from Christian liturgical practices pre-dating Islam.

29.   Helmer Ringgren, "Initiation Ceremony of the Bektashis," in *Studies in the History of Religions*, Supplement to Number X (1956), 203.

30.   Ringgren (1956), 203–204. One text on the Bektashi initiation describes it as follows: "The *talip*, Seeker, is being prepared by one appointed to be his *Rehber*, Guide . . . On behalf of the *talip* the *rehber* recites the following *terceman* (in Arabic)." At this point in the initiation a portion of the Qu'ran (Surah 11:43) is cited.

> While pouring water to wash the candidate's hands the *rehber* says: "It is the sacred custom of the Prophet of God to wash your hands in order to be free and absolved from all the divine prohibitions to which you have stretched your hand from eternity until now." While pouring water for his mouth: "It is the sacred custom of the glorious Prophet, our Master, to cleanse your mouth from whatever falsehood and fault may have issued from it until now." While pouring water for his nose: "It is the sacred custom of the Exalted the glory of the Universe, our Master, to cleanse your nose from whatever forbidden things you have smelt until now." While washing his face: "It is an obligation required by God the Great, the Glorious, to wash your face in order to be absolved from every shameful thing which has happened from eternity to this moment." While washing his arms: "It is an obligation required by God to cleanse of everything to which you have put forth your hand to do a forbidden thing." While wiping his head and ears: "The head is the greatest member, in which the intelligence and the mind must be kept. To be absolved from every unreasonable thing which is counter to the religious law until now is an obligation required by the Lord, the Gracious." While washing his feet: "It is an obligation required by the Merciful, the Compassionate to be cleansed of every instance of having walked in rebellious and mistaken paths." While wiping his face and arms: "Wipe thy face clean of the acts of disobedience which thou hast committed until now, and of the impure water of ungodliness with which thou hast been polluted."

After this ritual washing, a threshold ritual takes place. "The *rheber* standing on the left of the talip and facing the closed door, the *rehber* in a very solemn voice says, in Arabic, 'O opener of doors,' to which from within the *mürŌit* replies, 'Verily we have opened to thee a manifest victory.' Then the *rehber* leads the *talip* into the *meydan*" or "place of worship." Birge (1937), 182–84.

31. Ringgren (1956): 207. Ringgren points out that once one has participated in these initiatory rites a "transition" takes place. The initiate is no longer "an ordinary believer." He is now "separate" from "his old life" and is "integrated" into the class of "those who have attained." See Ringgren (1956): 208.

32. Barker (2008), 62. See also Parry and Parry (2009), 23.

33. Parry and Parry (2009), 23.

34. The *Encyclopedia of Catholicism* states that "baptism in the early Church was by immersion. Paul's reference in Rom 6:4 to being 'buried' with Christ implies immersion. The account of the Ethiopian eunuch also speaks of going down into the water and coming up out of the water (Acts 8:36–38)." Anthony Sherman, "Baptism," in McBrien (1995), 135. See also Everett Ferguson, "Baptism," in Everett Ferguson, ed., *Encyclopedia of Early Christianity* (New York: Garland Publishing, 1990), 131–33; Joseph Martos, "Sacraments," in John Bowden, ed., *Encyclopedia of Christianity* (New York: Oxford University Press, 2005), 1062; Heath (1909), 67–68.

35. See Rudolph (1987), 228.

36. Ricoeur (1967), 332.

37. See Aimé Georges Martimort, *Deaconesses: An Historical Study* (San Francisco: Ignatius Press, 1986), 131.

38. Cyril (circa AD 315–86) served as Archbishop of Jerusalem, starting in the mid-fourth century (circa AD 349). Over a six-week period of time (during Lent season of AD 348) he delivered a series of eighteen lectures to individuals about to be baptized into the Christian church of his day. Of these presentations to those requesting baptism, one commentator wrote: "The Lectures of S. Cyril have a peculiar value as being the first and only complete example of the course of instruction given in the early centuries to Candidates seeking admission to the full privileges of the Christian Church." See Edwin H. Gifford, "Introduction" to "The Catechetical Lectures of S. Cyril," in Philip Schaff and Henry Wace, eds., *Nicene and Post-Nicene Fathers—Second Series*, 14 vols. (Peabody, MA: Hendrickson Publishers, 1994), 7:xlvi.

39. As stated previously, though the fourth century Christians would have referred to this rite as "baptism," its form suggests that it is an adapted version of some first century initiatory washing which had, by Cyril's time, been lost—at least as to its original and complete meaning or intent.

40. Cyril of Jerusalem, "Catechetical Lectures," Lecture 20:2, in Schaff and Wace (2004), 7:147. Emphasis in the original.

41. See Charles (1997), 49.

42. Fritz West, *Scripture and Memory: The Ecumenical Hermeneutic of the*

Three-Year Lectionaries (Collegeville, MN: Liturgical Press, 1997), 90.

43. Arnold van Gennep, *The Rites of Passage*, translated by Monika B. Vizedom and Gabrielle L. Caffee (Chicago: The University of Chicago Press, 1960), 21.

44. In their book, *The Mormon Experience*, Leonard J. Arrington and Davis Bitton wrote:

> Mormon family life often included experiences not easily dis-regarded—actual life as opposed to beliefs. For one thing, there was the original conversion to Mormonism, which often meant the schism of families. In the sense that it was virtually impossible to bring all of one's extended family into the new faith, some kind of religious separation was inevitable. The tears and heartache that fol-lowed such division, especially when it occurred in the immediate family, are incalculable. In 1832 Orson Hyde traveled through New York State preaching to friends and family. One of his diary entries reads: "I called on sister Laura and her husband Mr. North. They disbelieved. We took our things and left them, and tears from all eyes freely ran, and we shook the dust of our feet against them, but it was like piercing my heart; and all I can say is 'The will of the Lord be done.'" Leonard J. Arrington and Davis Bitton, *The Mormon Experience: A History of the Latter-day Saints* (Boston: George Allen & Unwin, 1979), 193.

45. See Nibley, *Mormonism* . . . (1987), 363. Nibley is quoting Mikhail I. Rostovzeff, *Mystic Italy* (New York: Holt, 1927), 76–78.

46. Parry and Parry (2009), 22.

47. See ibid., 23.

48. Green (2004), 61.

49. Of Tertullian (circa AD 160–250), one text states that he was a "brilliant Carthaginian apologist and polemicist who laid the foundations of Christology [i.e., the doctrine of Christ] and trinitarian orthodoxy in the West." See William C. Weinrich, ed., *Ancient Christian Commentary on Scripture: Revelation* (Downers Grove, IL: InterVarsity Press, 2005), 424–25. The aforementioned comment by Tertullian appears in an anti-Gnostic text in which the author sought to respond to heretical teachings regarding the nature of Christ's body and the resurrection from the dead. See "On The Resurrection of the Flesh," in Roberts and Donaldson (1994), 3:545.

50. Tertullian, "On the Resurrection of the Flesh," VIII, in Roberts and Donaldson (1994), 3:551.

51. See Cyril of Jerusalem, "Catechetical Lectures," Lecture 23:1, in Schaff and Wace (2004), 7:153.

52. See Stephen D. Ricks and John J. Sroka, "King, Coronation, and Temple," in Parry (1994), 241. Ricks and Sroka's reference here was to coronation ceremonies and other rituals found in the ancient Near East—including ancient Egypt.

53. Barker (2008), 74–75.

54. According to Madsen, one who washes is symbolically subservient to he who is washed—he functions as a servant of the person being washed. Consequently, subservience and dominion are represented in the ritual act of washing another. This would be expected if the person being washed is representative of a king or priest—or representative of God. Thus, the act of being washed also suggests enthronement. See Madsen (2008), 127.

55. Nibley (2005), 143.

56. Tertullian, "On Baptism," chapters 6–8, in Roberts and Donaldson (1994), 3:672. Emphasis in the original.

57. As a singular example, as part of the proscribed ritual for cleansing a leper, we read: "And the priest shall take some of the log of oil, and pour it into the palm of his own left hand: And the priest shall dip his right finger in the oil that is in his left hand, and . . . the priest put upon the tip of the right ear of him that is to be cleansed, and upon the thumb of his right hand, and upon the great toe of his right foot . . . And the remnant of the oil that is in the priest's hand he shall pour upon the head of him that is to be cleansed . . ." (Leviticus 14:15–18).

58. Regarding the anointing of priests, the book of Exodus informs us: "And Aaron and his sons thou shalt bring unto the door of the tabernacle of the congregation, and shalt wash them with water . . . Then shalt thou take the anointing oil, and pour it upon his head, and anoint him. And thou shalt bring his sons, and put coats [or linen undergarments] upon them" (Exodus 29:4, 7–8).

59. Of David's anointing we read: "Then Samuel took the horn of oil, and anointed him . . . : and the Spirit of the LORD came upon David from that day forward" (1 Samuel 16:13). Of Solomon's anointing the following is stated: "And Zadok the priest took an horn of oil out of the tabernacle, and anointed Solomon" (1 Kings 1:39).

60. One commentator on the rite wrote: "The ritual was performed in order to give power or majesty, enthrone, sanctify or set apart, prepare an individual or object to enter the presence of God, endow with a quality of Deity, and establish and finalize office and vocation." Daniel Becerra, "Three Motifs of Early Christian Oil Anointing," in *BYU Religious*

Education 1009 Student Symposium (Provo, UT: Religious Studies Center, 2009), 5.

61. Charles (1997), 51. Parry and Parry point out: "In ancient times, both objects and certain persons were anointed with holy oil in order to sanctify them . . . Priests, kings (1 Sam. 10:1, 24; 2 Sam. 2:4; 16:16; 19:11, and so forth), and certain prophets (1 Kgs. 19:16; 1 Chr. 16:22; see also Ps. 105:15; D&C 124:57) were . . . ceremonially anointed with olive oil for sanctification. Priests were anointed with olive oil in an elaborate ceremony that took place at the 'door of the tabernacle of the congregation' (Ex. 40:12–15; 29:4–7)." Parry and Parry (2009), 24. Curiously, according to one source, at the coronation of the Russian Czar he was anointed on his forehead, eyes, nostrils, mouth, ears, breast, and hands as a symbol of the influence of the Holy Ghost that would need to be upon him as he led his nation. See R. M Woolley, *Coronation Rites* (Cambridge, MA: Cambridge University Press, 1915), 29, cited in Ricks and Sroka, in Parry (1994), 244.

62. The term "chrism" has reference to an anointing with consecrated or blessed olive oil (though since 1990 the Catholic Church has allowed the use of vegetable, seed, or coconut oil instead). In Catholicism the act of "chrism" or anointing takes place as a post-baptismal rite, during confirmation, as part of ordination to the priesthood (or office of bishop), and during the dedication of churches and altars. See McBrien (1995), 308.

63. This washing rite, though not by immersion, was referred to by Cyril and others of his day as "baptism;" however, it looked nothing like what the Latter-day Saints or Eastern Orthodox of today would consider a baptismal rite.

64. Cyril of Jerusalem, "Catechetical Lectures," Lecture 20:3, in Schaff and Wace (2004), 7:147.

65. An antitype is something that is foreshadowed by a type or symbol, such as a New Testament event prefigured in the Old Testament, or, in this case, our anointing being foreshadowed by Christ's anointing. However, in this case, it may be better to see our anointing as looking back to Christ's; we being anointed as symbols of Him and His anointing.

66. Nibley renders Cyril's phrase, "Ye were first anointed on the forehead, that ye might . . . reflect as a mirror the glory of the Lord," as "You were anointed on the brow . . . that you might clearly perceive the glory of the Lord with wide-opened mind." See Nibley (2005), 517. With that rendering, Nibley elsewhere makes an interesting comment that seems germane. He wrote: "Why do we call the temple a school? The initiatory ordinances make that clear. We begin there with the first requirement, that our brain

and intellect be clear and active—we are there to learn and to understand. Bring your brain with you and prepare to stay awake, to be alert and pay attention; also come often for frequent reviews repeating the lessons to refresh our memory, for you cannot leave without an examination—you have to show you have learned some things." Hugh Nibley, *Eloquent Witness: Nibley on Himself, Others, and the Temple* (Provo, UT: Foundation for Ancient Research and Mormon Studies, 2008), 460.

67. Cyril of Jerusalem, "Catechetical Lectures," Lecture 22:1, 2–4, in Schaff and Wace (2004), 7:149–50. Emphasis in the original.

68. Similarly, in the second century Theophilus of Antioch noted: "We are called Christians . . . because we are anointed with the oil of God." (Theophilus of Antioch, "Theophilus to Autolycus," Chapter 12, in Roberts and Donaldson [1994], 2:92.) Early Gnostic-Christians taught a similar idea: "From the anointing we were called 'anointed ones' (Christians), not because of the baptism. And Christ was also (so) named because of the anointing, for the Father anointed the son, and the son anointed the apostles, and the apostles anointed us. He (therefore) who has been anointed has the All. He has the resurrection, the light, the cross, the Holy Spirit . . ." ("The Gospel of Philip," cited in Rudolph [1987], 229.)

69. See Jacob Vellian, ed., *Studies on Syrian Baptismal Rites* (Kottayam, India: C.M.S. Press, 1973), 4. For Gnostic-Christians the anointing with oil "expelled demons and gave protection against them; correspondingly it cured and dispelled the 'sickness' of the soul and the body" just as anointing the physically sick with oil seeks to dispel physical sickness. "Often the anointing is taken as a 'sealing', the ointment [or oil] as a 'seal', i.e. it is a protective act and a declaration of property. The deity in this way assures the believers through the priests and they enjoy [God's] protection." (Rudolph [1987], 228.) In other words, the anointed are "owned" by God, and He will watch over and protect His own.

70. See Maxwell E. Johnson, *The Rites of Christian Initiation: Their Evolution and Interpretation*, revised and expanded edition (Collegeville, MN: Order of Saint Benedict, 2007), 165.

71. John the Deacon, Letter to Senaris, cited in J. D. C. Fisher, *Christian Initiation: Baptism in the Medieval West* (Chicago: Liturgy Training Publications, 2004), 10. See also Johnson (2007), 166.

72. John the Deacon, Letter to Senaris, cited in Johnson (2007), 166.

73. Ibid.

74. One Catholic text points out that the oil's "symbolism is both royal and priestly." McBrien (1995), 308. An LDS author wrote: "The anointing . . . sets us apart to become a kingdom of priests, a royal priesthood, a holy

nation, a chosen generation, a peculiar people (see 1 Peter 2:9). Therefore, the anointing symbolically introduces [the anointed] into the Holy Order of God, anointing them to become kings and queens, priest[s] and priestesses (see Revelation 1:5–6). The anointing not only sets us apart for this royalty, but also like King David's anointing (see 1 Samuel 16:13), it is symbolic of receiving the Holy Spirit with His powers to teach, reveal, and seal." Green (2004), 65.

75.   Arthur McCormack, *Christian Initiation* (New York: Hawthorn Publishers, 1969), 50. On a related note, initiates in some Navajo rites of passage are "sprinkled" with corn meal, after which the following parts of their bodies are "in succession touched with the sacra and sprinkled with corn meal"—the head, the shoulders, the collar bones, the breast, the forearms, the hands, and the feet. This is considered a rite of "incorporation into the community." See Van Gennep (1960), 79.

76.   See, for example, B. O. Banwell, "Nose," in J. D. Douglass, ed., *The New Bible Dictionary* (Grand Rapids: Eerdmans, 1971), 895. In scripture, although an infrequent symbol, there are a couple of references to the nose as a symbol for temperament or indignation. The proverb warns, "Surely the churning of milk bringeth forth butter, and the wringing of the nose bringeth forth blood: so the forcing of wrath bringeth forth strife" (Proverbs 30:33). When God is depicted as being angry, we read of smoke coming forth from his nostrils (2 Samuel 22:9; Psalm 18:8; See also Job 41:20). God even tells ungrateful Israel that she will get so sick of quail that it will come out of her nose (Numbers 11:12; See also 2 Samuel 10:6, 16:21; 1 Chronicles 19:6).

77.   W. Ewing, "Nose, Nostrils," in Hastings (1963), 701. See also John L. McKenzie, *Dictionary of the Bible* (Milwaukee: The Bruce Publishing Company, 1965), 620.

78.   Of course, as we noted earlier, John the Deacon suggested that the anointing of the nose as a reminder to the initiate of the importance of enduring to the end; of keeping all of God's commandments until one takes one's last mortal breath. Consequently, Cyril's promise to the faithful that they will "breathe the fragrance of Christ" may be a promise to dwell eternally in Christ's presence. The converse cursing would be to be banished from His locale and influence, symbolized by His "fragrance" or sweetness.

79.   It will be recalled that the Prophet Joseph Smith taught that the primary purpose of the "gift of tongues" is to teach the gospel to someone who either doesn't understand your language or who needs the message communicated in some special way which is beyond the natural skills of

the minister presenting it. In other words, the "gift of tongues" is a spiritual endowment designed primarily for the advancement of missionary work and spreading the gospel. See Smith (1978), 2:162, 3:379, 5:31–32. See also Larry E. Dahl and Donald Q. Cannon, *The Teachings of Joseph Smith* (Salt Lake City: Bookcraft, 1998), 670–71.

80. As one Latter-day Saint author put it: "The anointing reminds initiates of their obligation to carry out God's work in this life, with the promise that if they are faithful, they will be exalted so they can continue to carry out God's work (i.e., direct his kingdom) in the next life." Charles (1997), 54.

81. The association of olive oil with the Holy Spirit is common, as suggested by the following quotes: "The anointing oil, symbolic of the Holy Spirit" reminds us "of the blessings from heaven for those who seek the pure spiritual oil of the Holy Spirit and the Savior." Green (2004),

82. "Anointing with oil . . . symbolized anointing with the Holy Spirit." Ronald F. Youngblood, "1, 2 Samuel," in Frank E. Gaebelein, ed., *The Expositor's Bible Commentary*, 12 vols. (Grand Rapids: Zondervan, 1976–92), 3:686. "The gift of the 'Spirit of the Lord' is here associated with the act of anointing." Gnana Robinson, *International Theological Commentary: 1 & 2 Samuel: Let Us Be Like The Nations* (Grand Rapids: Eerdmans, 1993), 96. Being "anointed with oil" symbolizes "a setting apart to holiness by reception of the Holy Spirit, whose power directs . . . and sanctifies" the anointed. Green (2004), 61. The oil used in anointing rites represents "the presence of the Holy Spirit." McBrien (1995), 308. "Oil [typifies] the effects of the Spirit or the Holy Ghost." J. F. McConkie (1985), 97. "The olive oil . . . may have been associated with the Holy Ghost and the light and truth which guides and directs (see D&C 45:56–57)." Richard Neitzel Holzapfel and David Roth Seely, *My Father's House: Temple Worship and Symbolism in the New Testament* (Salt Lake City: Bookcraft, 1994), 32.

83. Bradshaw (1990), 55–56.

84. Ibid., 216.

85. Nibley, *Mormonism* . . . (1987), 364. Nibley is drawing on the teachings of Cyril of Jerusalem.

86. Donald J. Wiseman, *Tyndale Old Testament Commentaries: 1 & 2 Kings* (Downers Grove, IL: InterVarsity Press, 1993), 73.

87. Parry and Parry (2009), 24–25.

88. Soyer (1999): 160; emphasis added.

89. Parry and Parry (2009), 13.

90. One scholar of Gnostic-Christianity pointed out that anointings among that group were associated with redemption. "The gift of

immortality . . . is transmitted by anointing. It was closely bound up with the paradisiacal 'olive tree' which . . . [was] the origin of the anointing oil . . . The Gospel of Philip says the same: 'But the tree of life is in the midst of paradise and [is] the olive tree from which the oil of anointing (*chrisma*) comes; through it came the resurrection." Rudolph (1987), 228–29. On a related note, Richard O. Cowan pointed out: "Many ancient peoples associated the olive tree with the 'tree of life.'" See Cowan, in Parry and Ricks (1999), 106.

91.   In scripture it is only kings who are specifically said to have been anointed from a horn. See 1 Samuel 16:1, 13; 1 Kings 1:39; the Hebrew of Isaiah 5:1. See also Youngblood, in Gaebelein (1976–92), 3:686–87, n. 1.

92.   See Mordechai Cogan, *The Anchor Bible: 1 Kings* (New York: Doubleday, 2001), 164; Wilson (1999), 231; Conner (1992), 25, 1149; J. F. McConkie (1985), 103, 262; Cooper (1995), 84; Leland Ryken, James C. Wilhoit, and Tremper Longman, III, eds., *Dictionary of Biblical Imagery* (Downers Grove, IL: InterVarsity Press, 1998), 400; Farbridge (1923), 191–92.

93.   See Bayley (1990, 1993), 1:119.

94.   The first and second chapters of the book of Hebrews cite some eight successive passages from the Hebrew Bible in order to prove that Jesus is the Messiah and King Israel had been waiting for. See Hebrews 1:5 through 2:8. See also D. Kelly Ogden and Andrew C. Skinner, *Verse by Verse: Acts Through Revelation* (Salt Lake City: Deseret Book, 1998), 247.

95.   See Harold W. Attridge, *Hermeneia—A Critical and Historical Commentary on the Bible: Hebrews* (Philadelphia: Fortress Press, 1998), 60. Attridge's reasoning is this: were the "anointing with the oil of gladness" a literal anointing then some tradition or record would exist. But, since none does, clearly the author of Hebrews is drawing on the symbolism behind the anointing, which he apparently feels his readers will know or understand. John of Damascus suggested that the anointing with "the oil of gladness" symbolized being "anointed with the Spirit." See John of Damascus, "Orthodox Faith," 4:6, in Erik M. Heen and Philip D. W. Krey, eds., *Ancient Christian Commentary on Scripture: Hebrews* (Downers Grove, IL: InterVarsity Press, 2005), 25. Cyril of Jerusalem made a similar claim. See Cyril of Jerusalem, "Catechetical Lectures," 21:2, in Schaff and Wace (2004), 7:149. Basil the Great also suggests that the anointing with the "oil of gladness" was an anointing with the Holy Spirit. See Basil the Great, "Homilies on the Psalms," 17:8 in Craig A. Blaising and Carmen S. Hardin, eds., *Ancient Christian Commentary on Scripture: Psalms 1–50* (Downers Grove, IL: InterVarsity Press, 2008), 349.

96. "By the pouring of the consecrated oil upon the head (see 1 K 93), there was thought to be effected a transference to the person anointed . . . part of the essential holiness and virtue of the deity in whose name and by whose representative the rite was performed. By the Hebrews the rite was also believed to impart a special endowment of the spirit of [Yahweh]." A. R. S. Kennedy and James Barr, "Anointing, Anointed," in Hastings (1963), 35.

97. Ibid.

98. The mention in ancient ordination rites of priests and princes or kings is an indication of the dual nature of the ordination. (See Bradshaw [1990], 47.) One text notes that "the association of the anointing of Christians with the anointing of priests and kings in the Old Testament recurs continually in liturgical and theological writings." (Leonel L. Mitchell, *Baptismal Anointing* [South Bend, IN: University of Notre Dame Press, 1978], 6.) This same source notes that: "The anointing of kings was . . . similar to the anointing of priests in meaning. It was an essentially theocratic act, by which the king became the 'Anointed of Yahweh.' It was more than a ceremony and actually conveyed the power for the exercise of regal authority." Mitchell (1978), 23.

99. "The dominant theme of the apocalypses is, as we should expect, the divine throne . . . From the time of Isaiah right through until the Book of Revelation, there was a continuous tradition of throne visions; a divine figure in human form sat on the throne and brought judgement." Barker (2008), 154.

100. Ibid., 133, 176.

101. Soteriology is the branch of Christian theology focused on salvation and how one obtains it.

102. In some cases the initiate was seated while he was washed and anointed. In such cases the symbolism of kingship is the same. The chair or seat represents the throne.

103. Barker (2008), 134.

104. Bradshaw (1990), 56. Elsewhere in this same text we read: "The typology of prophets, kings, and high priests has been imported [into the rite of ordaining a Catholic bishop] from the blessing of the oil in the rites of Christian initiation . . ." Bradshaw (1990), 52.

105. Barker (2008), 140.

106. This view is as present in ancient times as it is in modernity. For example, in the Melkite ordination rite for a subdeacon, God is acknowledged as anointing "priests and kings" to be His "servants" in his "house." See Bradshaw (1990), 204. The Melkites here referred to are Christians (from

the fifth century onward) who fell under the jurisdiction of the Antiochene patriarchate, and who remained faithful to the theological position of the council of Chalcedon (AD 451), in that they rejected Monophysitism (or the idea that Jesus was only divine, and therefore had no human side). See Frank L. Cross, ed., *The Oxford Dictionary of the Christian Church*, second edition (New York: Oxford University Press, 1990), 899, S.v., "Melchites"; Bradshaw (1990), 13. Scholars theorize that there was an ancient ritual in the autumn of each year, "at the time of their New Year," wherein "the Lord was enthroned as King, having triumphed over evil and his enemies. The question is: Did someone represent the Lord in these ceremonies? The most likely answer is that it was the king. Kingship was inseparable from Judgement; this is an important key to understanding much of the later use of the throne imagery." Barker (2008), 147.

107. Barker (2008), 134.

108. Bruce H. Porter and Stephen D. Ricks, "Names in Antiquity: Old, New, and Hidden," in Lundquist and Ricks (1990), 1:501.

109. Ibid., 1:508.

110. True, some people today select "family names" in order to honor someone from a previous generation. But this appears to be less common now than in previous generations. Truman Madsen wrote: "It is a standard view today that names, as well as concrete or abstract terms, are no more than a *flatus vocis*, a mere sound. This tendency to reduce language to whimsical convention without concern for more profound origins may be symptomatic of the secularization of men and even the trivialization of life itself. At any rate, it reflects a diminishing of the religious consciousness that some names were thought anciently to be of divine origin." Madsen, in Lundquist and Ricks (1990), 1:458. See also Madsen (2008), 138.

111. Gordon C. Thomasson, "What's in a Name? Book of Mormon Language, Names, and [Metonymic] Naming," in *Journal of Book of Mormon Studies,* vol. 3, no. 1 (Spring 1994): 8. In most civilizations of the past, a very high value was placed upon having one's name live on after one's death (Genesis 48:16; Numbers 27:4; Deuteronomy 25:6–7; Ruth 4:10; 1 Samuel 24:21; 2 Samuel 14:7, 18:18; Jeremiah 11:18; Psalm 41:5; Ecclesiastes 6:4; Isaiah 56:5). Similarly, scripture promised the wicked that their name would "rot," be "blotted out," or not have "honor" associated with it (Genesis 11:4, 8; Deuteronomy 25:10; Proverbs 10:7; Job 18:17; Psalm 34:16, 49:11–12, 83:4; Isaiah 14:22, 65:15; Zephaniah 1:4; Mosiah 1:12, 5:11, 26:36; Alma 1:24, 5:57, 6:3, Moroni 6:7; D&C 20:83).

112. Porter and Ricks, in Lundquist and Ricks (1990), 1:513.

113. Other examples include employing David's name over a city (see

2 Samuel 12:28), seven women seeking the name of a man to take away their reproach (see Isaiah 4:1), or the name of God being placed over the nations (see Amos 9:12) and over Israel (see Isaiah 63:19). McConkie & Parry (1990), 175.

114. Ryken, Wilhoit, and Longman (1998), 585. See also Myers (1987), 747. Note a few examples of using someone's name, whether in ministry (Deuteronomy 18:5; Matthew 18:5; Hebrews 6:10), battle (1 Samuel 17:45; 2 Chronicles 14:11; Psalm 20:5, 7, Psalm 118:10–12, 44:5), when acting as a representative by "investiture of authority" (John 5:43; Romans 1:5; Col 3:17), in a blessing or cursing (Deuteronomy 10:8; 2 Samuel 6:18; 2 Kings 2:24; Psalm 129:8; Isaiah 66:5), in commanding (2 Thessalonians 3:6), in speaking or prophesying (Exodus 5:23; 1 Kings 22:16; 1 Chronicles 21:19; Ezra 5:1; Jeremiah 20:9; Daniel 9:6; Acts 5:28, 9:29; James 5:10), in casting out evil spirits (Matthew 16:17; Luke 10:17; Acts 16:18), or in performing an ordinance (Matthew 28:19; Acts 2:38, 8:16, 10:48, 19:5).

115. Madsen, in Lundquist and Ricks (1990), 1:468; Madsen (2008), 148.

116. One source states: "In antiquity, several ideas about names recur, among which are the following: 1. In names, especially divine names, is concentrated divine power. 2. Through ritual processes one may gain access to these names and take them upon oneself. 3. These ritual processes are often explicitly temple-related." See Madsen, in Lundquist and Ricks (1990), 1:442. See also Madsen (2008), 138–39.

117. Porter and Ricks, in Lundquist and Ricks (1990), 512; James R. Harris, "The Book of Abraham Facsimiles," in Robert L. Millet and Kent P. Jackson, eds., *Studies in Scripture, Vol. 2: The Pearl of Great Price* (Salt Lake City: Randall Book, 1985), 270; Hugh Nibley, "On the Sacred and the Symbolic," in Parry (1994), 559; Ifrah (2000), 214; Derek Kidner, *Tyndale Old Testament Commentaries: Genesis* (Downers Grove, IL: 1967), 170; Richard J. Clifford and Roland E. Murphy, "Genesis," in Raymond E. Brown, Joseph A Fitzmmyer, and Roland E. Murphy, eds., *The New Jerome Biblical Commentary* (New Jersey: Prentice Hall, 1990), 34. Illustrative of this principle is a story found in the book of First Enoch, where we read of how an evil angel gave to Michael his "secret name" which he was to "memorize" and use in making an "oath." Michael is told that this oath and name would give him power. See 1 Enoch 69:14, in Charlesworth (1983, 1985), 1:48. In this passage of the Enoch text, along with chapter 68 of the same work, numerous angels come under fire for having revealed the "secrets" which were not supposed to be revealed. It appears evident from the text that the angel seeking to "reveal" secret things to Michael did so with an ulterior motive—namely to corrupt

Michael, or to get him to engage in evil. The book of First Enoch is the oldest of three pseudepigraphical books attributed to that mysterious ancient biblical figure. It is traditionally dated as early as 200 BCE and as late as AD 50. "This book has left its stamp upon many of the NT writers, especially the author of Revelation." Craig A. Evans, *Noncanonical Writings and New Testament Interpretation* (Peabody, MA: Hendrickson Publishers, 1992), 23. See also E. Isaac, "1 (Ethiopic Apocalypse of) Enoch—A New Translation and Introduction," in Charlesworth (1983, 1985), 1:5–12.

118. See Porter and Ricks, in Lundquist and Ricks (1990), 1:513. "The new name is associated, in [the Book of] Revelation, with the redeemed's permission to enter the celestial kingdom." Charles (1997), 63. For ancient Egyptians, "the name was used as a key to permit the initiate to enter into the true fold of God . . ." Porter and Ricks in Lundquist and Ricks (1990), 1:510.

119. Madsen, in Lundquist and Ricks (1990), 1:463; Madsen (2008), 143.

120. Names connected with a physical characteristic might include Esau ("hairy"), Adin ("dainty" or "delicate"), Amasai ("burdensome"), or Korah ("bald").

121. Names describing personality or temperament might include Nabal ("fool"), Achar ("one who causes trouble"), Hanan ("compassionate, merciful or gracious"), or Mithcah ("sweet").

122. "New names were frequently conferred upon individuals at the time of their enthronement . . . . In the Book of Mormon, all kings were to be called 'Nephi,' giving honor both to the original Nephi as well as to the new king (Jacob 1:11)." Porter & Ricks, in Lundquist and Ricks (1990), 1:507.

123. Names that indicate one's occupation might include Asa ("physician" or "healer"), Sophereth ("registrar" or "scribe"), or Machir ("salesman").

124. Frank E. Eakin, Jr., *The Religion and Culture of Israel: An Introduction to Old Testament Thought* (Boston: Allyn and Bacon, 1971), 70, 102; Conner (1992), 10. "Personal names served as miniature biographies, descriptions of character, testimonies or expressions of praise to God, reminders of significant events, and divine warning. In short, Bible names served as memorials, symbols, and prophecies." J. F. McConkie (1985), 173.

125. See, Ryken (1998), 583; See also Farbridge (1923), 239–44; McConkie & Parry (1990), 113, 175. "In the cultures of the ancient Near East . . . the name of someone (or something) was perceived not as a mere abstraction, but as a real entity, 'the audible and spoken image of a person, which was taken to be his spiritual essence.' According to Philo of Alexandria, the name 'is like a shadow which accompanies the body.' Similarly, Origen

viewed the name as the designation of the individual's essence." Porter & Ricks, in Lundquist and Ricks (1990), 1:501.

126. This is particularly the case with theophoric names. Israelite theophoric names are those which begin or end with some form of *Yah* or *Jah* (for Yahweh/Jehovah), or *El* (for Elohim). They are compound words composed of either a noun, pronoun, adjective, or verb, combined with a name of God. When given to a person, they represent declarations about or expressions of petition to the deity mentioned in the name. Parents would give their children theophoric names, both to honor their God, and in the hopes that the child would live a godly life.

127. Ryken (1998), 583; McConkie & Parry (1990), 113, 175. "The majority of Israelite names, and ancient Semitic names in general, had a readily understandable meaning. That parents consciously chose a child's name is implied by the content of these names, many of which are translatable sentences." Dana M. Pike, "Names," in Paul J. Achtemeier, ed., *Harper's Bible Dictionary* (San Francisco: Harper San Francisco, 1985), 682. See also John Taylor, "Name, Names," in Hastings (1963), 687. Names that indicated events surrounding the birth of a child would include Haggai ("born on a day of a festival"), or Peleg ("division") who was named such because he was born during the days when the earth was divided (1 Chronicles 1:19).

128. Kidner (1967), 162; E. Speiser (1962), 230. "Some children, such as Ishmael and Isaac, receive a name by divine command, usually one with prophetic meaning (Solomon, Jesus, John) or even direct prophetic purpose (Isaiah's children, Isaiah 7:3, 8:3, 18; Hosea's, Hos. 1:4, 6, 9). The name Jacob ('let God protect') was given punningly to a child who at birth seized his elder twin's 'heel,' and was later interpreted, by further wordplay, to explain his tendency to 'supplant' (Gen. 25:26, 27:36). When Jacob's name was extended to his posterity, these associations were not forgotten (Jer. 9:4; Hos 12:3). Abigail's similar joke about her husband's name, Nabal, meaning 'worthless' or 'good-for-nothing' (2 Sam 25:25), has been taken unsmilingly by generations of commentators." See Ryken (1998), 583; See also McConkie & Parry (1990), 175. Just as the names of people were highly significant in antiquity, so also were the names which the ancients assigned to their cities. Place names often commemorate events in history. For example, Babel ("confusion") was given in commemoration of the "confusion" of the languages as a result of the building of the pseudo-temple, tower of Babel (Genesis 11:9). Jacob was the recipient of a theophany (Genesis 32:30), for which he named the place at which the vision was received, Peniel ("the face of God"). After the barges had been prepared,

Mahonri Moriancumer is said to have ascended a mountain to which the "pilgrims" had given the name, "Shelem." "Zebach Shelem is the Hebrew for thank offering, wherefore we safely conclude that this mount had been set apart for sacred purposes (See Leviticus 7:12, 15; 22:27). Hence the name." (George Reynolds and Janne M. Sjodahl, *Commentary on the Book of Mormon*, 7 vols. [Salt Lake City: Deseret Book, 1955–61] 6:75.) In the book of Alma we read of the Lamanites being driven by the Nephites into a northern land that was "infested by wild and ravenous beasts" (Alma 2:36–37). The land had been called Hermounts by the people because of all of the ferocious animals that dwelt there. Hermonthis was the Egyptian god "of wild places" and "wild things." Bethlehem ("house of bread") was, appropriately so, the name of the city in which Jesus, the "Bread of Life," was born. Along with personal names, place names should not be ignored when reading scripture. (McConkie & Parry [1990], 113, 176.)

129. "The new name given to Abraham was intimately connected with the covenant he received from God. . . . Joseph of Egypt was renamed Zaphnath-paaneah . . . Eliakim and Mattaniah were respectively renamed Jehoiakim . . . and Zedekiah . . . Daniel was renamed Belteshazzar, and the three heroes of the fiery furnace—Shadrach, Meshach, and Abednego—were first known by their Hebrew names Hananiah, Mishael, and Azariah . . ." Porter and Ricks, in Lundquist and Ricks (1990), 1:505.

130. See E. Jan Wilson, "Inside a Sumerian Temple: The Ekishnugal at Ur," in Parry and Ricks (1999), 311.

131. See P. Rabikauskas, "Popes, Names Of," in *The New Catholic Encyclopedia*, second edition, 15 vols. (Detroit: Gale Group in association with the Catholic University of America, 2003), 11:506–507; Frederick Matthewson Denny, "Names and Naming," in Eliade (1987), 10:304.

132. See Ricks and Sroka, in Parry (1994), 244.

133. Porter and Ricks, in Lundquist and Ricks (1990), 1:507, 517, n. 32. Truman Madsen wrote: "In Egyptian initiation rites . . . prior to coronation, the candidate is presented to the gods . . . . In order to pass the obstacles, he recites the name of his god and thus is allowed to pass. If the candidate cannot produce the name, the gatekeepers are aggressive and unyielding." Madsen, in Lundquist and Ricks (1990), 1:459; Madsen (2008), 139.

134. Ricks and Sroka in Parry (1994), 246. "The name change or the receipt of a new name marks a turning point in the life of the initiate: he is 're-created,' so to speak, and becomes a new man." Receiving a new name symbolized "the 'determination to cut one's self off from one's worldly identification and one's former way of life.'" Porter and Ricks, in

Lundquist and Ricks (1990), 1:507. "In Egyptian initiation rites one puts off his former nature by discarding his name [given him at birth], after which he receives a new name." Madsen, in Lundquist and Ricks (1990), 1:459; Madsen (2008), 139.

135. Ryken (1998), 583; See also Porter and Ricks, in Lundquist and Ricks (1990), 1:504, 507. The word "patristic" means that which relates to the Church Fathers or their writings.

136. "The act of renaming is a sign that we will personally enter into a new covenant relationship. A married woman understands that taking upon her the name of her husband is the sign of a new relationship in her life. . . . We symbolically enact a 'marriage covenant' relationship with God when we receive a new name." Green (2004), 84–85.

137. One LDS author wrote: "People receive a new name, the name of Christ, as a symbol of their rebirth. . . . The new name is a powerful spiritual symbol that . . . people are determined to become like Christ." Hansen (2009), 48.

138. Smith and Cornwall (1998), vii. "This new name seems to symbolize the redeemed's new relationship with God." Charles (1997), 63.

139. Porter and Ricks, in Lundquist and Ricks (1990), 1:513.

140. Hansen (2009), 43.

141. Lundquist, in Lundquist and Ricks (1990), 1:440.

142. In Jewish Mysticism this rite was seen as requisite for any who sought to fathom God's mysteries. However, most Pietist German Jews—the mystics—never went so far in their initiation as to receive this higher level of initiation. See Ivan G. Marcus, *Piety and Society: The Jewish Priests of Medieval Germany* (Leiden, The Netherlands: E. J. Brill, 1981), 85.

143. See Gershom Scholem, "Kabbalistic Ritual and the Bride of God," in Jerome Rothenberg and Diane Rothenberg, *Symposium of the Whole: A Range of Discourse Toward an Ethnopoetics* (Berkeley, CA: University of California Press, 1983), 303–304. See also Marcus (1981), 85. The written source for this rite of initiation was Eliezer Ben Isaac of Worms (circa AD 1176–1238), a German Talmudic scholar who also dabbled heavily in Kabbalah (or Jewish mysticism). See *Encyclopaedia Judaica*, 17 vols. (Jerusalem: Keter Publishing House, 1972), 6:623–24. It is believed that the rite described predates Eliezer, having been transmitted orally for a significant amount of time prior to Eliezer's documentation of the ritual. See Scholem in Rothenberg and Rothenberg (1983), 303–304.

144. Scholem, in Rothenberg and Rothenberg (1983), 304.

Three

Ordination Rituals

Though Christianity has, in large measure, been influenced by what is commonly known as the "priesthood of all believers,"[1] nevertheless, for much of Christianity—and for many of the world's great religions—the concept of priesthood holders, or holy men, who are ordained or set apart to serve in some capacity beyond the boundaries of everyday laymen, is commonplace. Many a faith holds that there are individuals whose authority to perform rites, rituals, and ceremonies comes directly from God, or via one who has received it from the divine. Indeed, in many traditions ordinances preformed without this authority are considered invalid. Consequently, this aspect of ritual is an important one, both in how it authorizes a rite or ordinance, but also in what those who authoritatively preform those rites represent.

In many traditions—particularly in denominations of Christianity—there are rites or rituals of ordination that must be followed in order for an ordination to be valid. One scholar noted that ordination prayers of the Christian church have "undergone considerable revision" during the years between the fourth and twentieth centuries.[2]

The New Testament seems quite clear that the laying on of hands was a ritual commonly utilized to convey or confer priesthood authority.[3] In addition, by the early third century, Christians had developed written extra-canonical ceremonies describing the process for ritually conferring authority.[4] Of the practice of laying on of hands to confer priesthood, one expert in the ordination rites of the ancient church wrote: "The imposition of the hand is almost universally attested as the principal ritual gesture of ordination . . . The [majority of] ancient sources all agree that the imposition of hands was originally performed during the time that prayer was being offered for the ordained."[5] In other words, anciently hands were laid upon the head of the one being ordained and, while the hands were thus placed, a prayer of ordination was uttered. One LDS source noted that the laying on of hands can symbolize "transmission of power from on high (D&C 36:2)."[6] Thus, the ordained has received some of God's authority or power to act in His name here upon the earth. Elsewhere we are told that, symbolically, ordination implies "attachment to the deity."[7] The ordained does not simply operate under God's authority, but actually in concert with God. If worthy, there is a oneness that is to exist between the priesthood holder and God, who speaks to and through him during the act of laying on of the hands.

> Both the Jacobite[8] and Maronite[9] rites display a unique feature in relation to the imposition of the hand: the [person performing the ordination] first extends his hands over the consecrated [or blessed] bread and wine three times before proceeding to lay his right hand on the ordained . . . This ceremony seems to have been introduced in order to express the idea that it was not the [person preforming the ordination] but Christ who ordained his ministers, and it was his spiritual power that was bestowed upon them.[10]

These Middle East branches of the Christian church seek to symbolically depict whose authority they are operating under by extending their hands over the sacramental symbols, representative of Christ, prior to performing the laying on of hands. The triple action (i.e., thrice extending the hands over the symbols of the sacrament) suggests that the priesthood holder is acting under the direction of all three members of the Godhead—the power of each being operative in the blessing in some unique way.

The prayer utilized when this rite of ordination is performed in these two aforementioned branches of Christianity says, in part, the following: "God, who adorn[s] your universal Church by these high-priests through the imposition of hands . . . ; adorn this your servant also, who you have made worthy to receive the high order of bishops from you . . . . Not now by the imposition of my weak hand but by the descent of the Holy Spirit, . . . by your grace and the mercies and kindness of your only-begotten Son and of your good and most-holy Spirit."[11]

Similarly, the late fourth/early fifth century Church Father, John Chrysostom, taught: "For this is ordination: the man's hand is imposed, but God does all and it is his hand which touches the ordained's head when he is rightly ordained."[12] Again and again commentators on the ritual of laying on of hands for priesthood authority note that the man who ordains or blesses simply symbolizes God or Christ—but it is the Father or Son who is truly operative in the ordinance. Hence, a Latter-day Saint giving a blessing may state, "By the authority of the Melchizedek Priesthood . . ." (which indicates what priesthood he is operating under), but he may also add, "In the name of Jesus Christ . . ." (suggesting that the words to be spoken are not his own, but rather are Christ's words and Christ's will). One recent text on symbols in the Restored gospel noted:

> The priesthood holder acts in Christ's stead, doing the things the Lord would do if he were here. In that process, the priesthood holder is an agent and representative of the Savior himself. This truth is underscored in a principle the Lord expressed to Edward Partridge: "I will lay my hand upon you by the hand of my servant Sidney Rigdon . . ." (D&C 36:2). The Lord did not actually place his hands upon Edward Partridge's head. Instead, he commissioned Sidney Rigdon . . . In the process, though, it was truly as though the Lord himself were laying his hands upon Brother Partridge's head . . . . Priesthood holders are . . . types or shadows of the great High Priest.[13]

Hands, of course, are ancient symbols of one's actions or works.[14] They function as representations of power.[15] The individual laying hands upon another represents Christ. Consequently, his hands are Christ's hands—or, in other words, he is doing Christ's work and conveying Christ's power. Hence, one source on biblical and Semitic symbols records: "By stretching out the hand towards a person . . . one symbolized the transference of power from one party to another."[16]

The location of the hands of the person performing the blessing or ordination is also symbolically significant. In antiquity, as is the case today, the head was the location of blessing. As a symbol, anciently the head represented three main ideas: the entirety of the person,[17] the life of the person,[18] and the source of governance or rulership.[19] The former of these ideas seems to be the focus of the symbolism during the giving of a blessing, or in the conferral of priesthood. Thus, blessings are traditionally pronounced upon the head as a symbol that the entirety of the person is being blessed.[20]

One LDS source insightfully notes: "The head represents the entirety of a person. It rules the body and gives it all it needs: food, oxygen, information, and so forth. As the head is the ruling part of the body, Christ is the head or ruling part of each of us. He gives us all we need, both temporally and spiritually. To have hands laid on our head signifies that . . . we yield ourselves to Christ, who is our head and the head of the priesthood."[21]

When multiple individuals are involved in the giving of a blessing, or in the act of conferring priesthood authority, it is common for those participating in the rite to stand in a circle around the individual being blessed. Of this emblematic act, one commentator wrote: "The symbol of the circle as a reflection of the eternal is a powerful symbol . . . The prayer circles of blessings and ordinations are symbolic of the eternal powers of heaven. In our families and in the temple we gather in prayer circles as we petition the Eternal Father."[22] Thus, to gather around one being blessed represents both the eternal nature of what is being done, but also the idea that those participating are calling upon God for assistance in blessing the encircled soul.

Related to our discussion of the symbolic meaning behind the manner in which men are ordained, is a curious practice among the early Christians. In Romans 16:1 the Apostle Paul writes: "I commend unto you Phebe our sister, which is a servant of the church which is at Cenchrea." In our King James translation Phebe is referred to as a "servant." However, the Greek word translated as such is *diakonos*, which means quite literally "servant," but would traditionally be translated as "deacon." Thus, Paul refers to "Sister Phebe" as a "deacon" in the Church at Cenchrea.[23] One text highlights the fact that by the early second century you begin to see references to women serving in the church as "deacons"[24]—though, as we shall see, this was not the same office held by young Aaronic Priesthood holders of today's Church.

It is unclear exactly when this office of *deaconess* developed. We know of written sources that make reference to it from the early second century onward, and it appears that the position of *deaconess* continues to exist in Western Christianity until around the sixth century, and in Eastern Christianity until about the eleventh century.[25] Some have actually suggested that it may have begun in the first century church.[26] While not all branches of Eastern Orthodoxy had this female office, at the very least the Armenian, East Syrian, and Georgian Orthodox traditions did.[27] The office was generally present in the early Roman Catholic movement.

So what exactly was the role of these *deaconesses* within the early Christian church? Their primary responsibilities were three in number. First of all, they would visit other sisters in their homes, where they would teach them the gospel. Second, they were responsible for performing an "anointing of the bodies of female" candidates who had presented themselves to the Church for initiation.[28] As one source notes: "women . . . ought to be anointed by a deaconess with the oil of anointing; . . . It is not fitting that women should be seen [naked] by men."[29] Another text notes: "Women deacons were prominently engaged in liturgical ministry to women . . . Singularly important was their preparation of women catechumens and their role in . . . [the] anointing of women."[30] Yet another source states: "St. Epiphanius strictly limited the functions of deaconesses to working with other women, performing those services, either liturgical or charitable, that modesty and decency forbade men. Moreover, their activities were limited to what a priest directed them to carry out, assisting at the baptism [or, more accurately, in the initiatory rites] of women where nudity was required, for example."[31]

Thus, these deaconesses were responsible for washing and anointing other sisters, as part of an early Christian initiation ritual. Finally, the women holding this position in the church had the assignment of seating the women in the liturgical assembly.[32]

One sixth century canon from a Jacobite Christian community speaks of priestly clothing worn by the *deaconesses*. This aforementioned text states of *deaconesses* that, like men who were serving in a liturgical capacity, women engaged in similar rituals were to wear "an *orarion* on the shoulder" also.[33] The "orarion" or "stole" was a "band of vestment cloth" that, for certain orders of the priesthood, was worn over the left shoulder, across the breast and back of the torso, and attached at the hip on the right side of the body.[34] It extended from the shoulder to mid-calf in the front and back of the wearer. The location or placement of the garment symbolized the rank held by the wearer.[35] Thus, *deaconesses*, like men ordained to the priesthood, would wear "robes of the priesthood" when they served their sisters during certain sacred rites or ceremonies.

It seems worth pointing out that Hippolytus (circa AD 170–236), in his *Apostolic Tradition*, was quite clear that women were *not* "ordained" to the priesthood, but rather "appointed" or set apart to their calling to minister as *deaconesses*.[36] They *did* receive the laying on of hands prior to their service, but this was *not* perceived as an ordination. Similarly, James (or Jacob) of Edessa (circa AD 640–708), in his *Canonical Resolutions*, specifically states that a *deaconess* is "instituted" in her office. She is not "ordained" in the way a deacon is "ordained." He highlights that, whereas a deacon has power "to serve at the altar" or sacrament table, and has power to "take the Hosts [or blessed bread] off the altar," a *deaconess'* work is focused on the sisters, "anointing" the adult women, and visiting them when they are ill. But James is emphatic that their setting apart is *not* akin to that of a deacon (who holds the priesthood), nor is their calling akin to his in its focus.[37]

In the *Apostolic Constitutions*[38] we find the following blessing text for women being set apart (by the laying on of hands) as a *deaconess*:

> O Eternal God, the Father of our Lord Jesus Christ, the Creator of man and of woman, who didst replenish with the Spirit Miriam, and Deborah, and Anna, and Huldah; who didst not disdain that Thy only begotten Son should be born of a woman . . . — do Thou now also look down upon this Thy servant, who is to be ordained[39] to the office of a deaconess, and grant her Thy Holy Spirit, and "cleanse her from all filthiness of flesh and spirit," that she may worthily discharge the work which is committed to her to Thy glory . . . Amen.[40]

Two Georgian prayers, dating from around the tenth century, reflect the content of the one found in the *Apostolic Constitutions*, just cited. The first reads as follows:

> O Lord, God of hosts, who before all the women commanded Miriam, sister to Moses, to invoke his name; who gave the gift of prophecy to Deborah; . . . deign now to promote to that same dignity your female servant here present so that she may anoint with oil . . . Give her also the gift of instructing and convincing the young in the fulfilling of their duties. Give her the grace to express everything in your name so that, serving you in a worthy manner and without fault, she may be emboldened to intercede at the house fixed by your Christ.

The second of these tenth-century setting apart blessings reads: "You who gave the grace of your Holy Spirit not only to men but also to women—establish now officially your female servant here present in this service, O all-powerful God. Give her the grace of your spirit that she may walk in pleasing fashion and without reproach in the works of justice and thereby be given the pardon of your Christ."[41] Each of these blessings implies that *deaconesses* were seen by the early Church as individuals whom God could inspire and work through to bless the faithful Saints who fell under their stewardship.

Beyond the benefit gained from knowing such an office existed, one must question what the symbolic implications are of women serving as *deaconesses*. A number of symbolic teachings are potentially present in the office of *deaconess* among the early Christians. For example, as men were anciently initiated as priests and kings, the women seem obvious symbols for priestesses and queens. As Truman Madsen once noted: "Women and men are equal partners: a king only with a queen, a priest only with a priestess, a patriarch only with a matriarch."[42] The early Christians, much like their pagan counterparts, seemed to have a sense that women symbolized the divine—but *not* the masculine side of God.[43] Rather, women typified the feminine in heaven; the mother goddess, or Mother in Heaven. One text notes: "The idea of God as mother has a rich and long tradition in Christian spirituality."[44] This same source reminds us: "There is a feminine face of God in the Hebrew Scriptures—images and metaphors for God and God's activities that are drawn from the world of women's experience."[45] Note how often the Judeo-Christian scriptures speak of this feminine aspect of the divine—which *deaconesses* appear to symbolize.

- "The Hebrew word for one of the most important attributes of God is *rahum*, generally translated 'compassion.' However, the literal meaning is 'womb love.' . . . This same Hebrew term is the basis for the word *rahamim*, generally translated as 'mercies.'"[46] Consequently, God's love is painted in feminine terms—using the image of a woman's womb as the metaphor.
- In Isaiah 49:15 we read: "Can a woman forget her sucking child, that she should not have compassion on the son of her womb? yea, they may forget, yet will I not forget thee." Here God is depicted as a nursing mother—a metaphor entirely foreign to men.
- In Deuteronomy 32:11–12 we find this: "As an eagle stirreth up her nest, fluttereth over her young, spreadeth abroad her wings, taketh them, beareth them on her wings: So the LORD alone did lead [Jacob] . . ." Again, God is seen in terms that are feminine, rather than masculine. God is depicted as a mother eagle teaching, protecting, and supporting her children.
- In Hosea 13:8 God promises: "I will meet [your enemies] as a bear that is bereaved of her whelps [or cubs], and will rend the caul of their heart . . ." God describes divine love as being like what a

mother bear feels for her young cubs—including a willingness to do anything to protect her children.

- Curiously, in Matthew 23:37 Jesus states: "O Jerusalem, Jerusalem, . . . how often would I have gathered thy children together, even as a hen gathereth her chickens under her wings, and ye would not!" Thus, even Christ uses feminine language to describe the type of love that God and Christ have for those who profess a belief in them.

- As the reader will likely be aware, one ancient scriptural expression of "the feminine face of God" is found in the pre–New Testament figure of Sophia/Wisdom—an undefined divine being who is found frequently in the Jewish and Christian theology of an earlier era.[47] In the Apocrypha's Wisdom of Solomon (10:18–19), for example, we read: "She [Sophia] brought them over the Red Sea, and led them through the deep waters; but she drowned their enemies, and cast them up from the depth of the sea." Similarly, in Proverbs 8:22–31 we find Sophia at God's side prior to the creation of the universe, and before the waters and mountains of this earth existed. She is depicted as a coworker with God, and we learn that He delights in her, just as she delights in the newly created cosmos and its inhabitants.[48]

Of this phenomenon of scripture using female images to depict God and His attributes, one commentator noted: "If the idea of God can be expressed with the metaphor of mother, then women are in the image of God."[49] Certainly we know that among Jewish worshipers at Elephantine, there was commonly understood to be a "mother goddess at Yahweh's side."[50] Indeed, one text suggests: "Although the early Israelites engaged in the worship of female deities, at some point goddess worship was removed from the religious tradition."[51] Another author penned this: "In the lands that brought forth Judaism, Christianity, and Islam, God was once worshiped in the form of woman."[52] Consequently, the actions, activities, and responsibilities of early Christian *deaconesses* seem to clearly categorize them as symbols for the divine—namely for this mother goddess figure once so common in ancient worship. Beyond a liturgical context, note how often the roles and characteristics of God (in scripture) seem to parallel the roles and work of mothers, as well as fathers. For example, God is the creator; and women are the mortal creators of human life. Thus, in the capacity of creator, God is the life-giver to all—as are women. God is nurturing and compassionate; attributes we associate more with women then we do with men. God is the one who feeds us (spiritually and physically); women traditionally are associated with the role of feeder. God is seen as sacrificer—He gives His Son, and His Son gives His life on our behalf; women sacrifice themselves to carry and deliver a child, and then, in many cases, sacrifice career and personal goals to nurture their offspring. Many parallels exist that force a comparison between *deaconesses* and the mother goddess figure of antiquity.[53]

On another symbolic note, Eve's role in ritual—as a symbol of the bride of Christ, or the Church—seems to represent the foolishness of man (male and female). It shows the weakness of the bride of Christ, so readily influenced by the enticements of the adversary. (For a fuller discussion of this symbol, see chapter 4, specifically the section on Narrative in Ritual) However, the *deaconess* seems to be placed in juxtaposition to Eve in ritual settings. Whereas Eve symbolizes men and women—fallen and foolish; the *deaconess* appears to be only a representation of women, and everything she symbolizes is positive. She draws (for her symbolism) the positive attributes of faithful women to teach us about the exalted attributes of the Feminine in heaven.

One Roman Catholic text offered a number of interrelated explanations as to what women serving as *deaconesses* symbolize.[54] They are said to be symbols of "the universal call to holiness." In other words, both sexes—men and women—are called to be holy and consecrated to God and His work. Thus, the office of *deaconess* offered women an opportunity to consecrate their lives to God in a way akin to how men do through service in priesthood callings. Jesus gave Himself for the Church. His was a life of total devotion and complete sacrifice. The role of priesthood holder symbolically mirrors that life of devotion and sacrifice, and calls men to be as Christ (e.g., "what manner of men ought ye to be? Verily I say unto you, even as I am."—3 Nephi 27:27). The position of *deaconess* in the early Church gave women an opportunity to also live lives of devotion and sacrifice—to serve as symbols of the divine, just as men did.

Anciently, the *deaconess* "saw the worship of God and the service of man as one single worship of God, one single service of the Church. Her inspiration in this was Christ, who fulfilled the Old Testament type of the servant both in his life of loving labor and in his sacrificial death for others."[55] As King Benjamin informed us: "When ye are in the service of your fellow beings ye are only in the service of your God" (Mosiah 2:17). The Lord Himself stated: "Inasmuch as ye have done it unto one of the least of these my brethren, ye have done it unto me." (Matthew 25:40). Thus, to be a *deaconess* was a call to be a servant, and to live the life of Christ, ever serving one's brother or sister as He would serve them. The *deaconess* represents one who is "constantly living for others." Indeed, our Catholic text informs us, the *deaconess's* role during the rituals was to quietly sit by until someone needed her service. Her role or position of responsibility was not for personal gain or aggrandizement. She played no part but servant. Consequently, she is as Christ, who patiently waits upon us as servant, in that all that He does on our behalf is evidence of His desire to serve and to save.[56] On a related note, sisters functioning as *deaconesses* symbolize the principle that the gifts of the Spirit can be as operative in righteous women as in righteous men within the Church.

In a slightly different vein, the priestly "garb" of the *deaconess*—which often reminds us of her "renouncement of the world"[57]—is also a symbol that God has authorized her to serve in His stead, in some appointed capacity, wherein she performs sacred rites, rituals, and ceremonies which He has revealed and authorized her to perform. The role places women in a teaching responsibility—authorized to speak and apply God's words—and, symbolically, reminds us that God speaks to any (male or female) who qualifies to be receptive to His spirit. Finally, our Catholic text informs us that a *deaconess* represents "the handmaid of the Lord"[58]—meaning one who has turned her will over to God's. Serving in that office anciently was a symbol of the dedication and commitment of the women set apart to so serve.

Ordained men and set apart women (or *deaconesses*) both symbolize the divine. The way in which each represents God is clearly different. Men often symbolize God and His actions in the world as Father, Son or Savior. *Deaconesses*, on the other hand, appear to represent both the scripturally declared feminine attributes of the divine and likely also what the ancient Jews and potentially early Christians could have seen as a mother goddess figure. They are distinct symbols for the servant side of God.

Notes

1. The "Priesthood of all Believers" is the principle, often associated with Luther, that any baptized believer of Christ holds the "priesthood," in that God does not distinguish between the "secular and the spiritual work." Thus, according to this teaching, an ordained priest has no more authority before God than does a lay member who believes and is baptized. See C. Scott Dixon, "Martin Luther," in Bowden (2005), 718. One scholar wrote:

> It was only comparatively late in the first millennium in the West that there was a steady development towards a celibate Roman Catholic priesthood, whose main task was to offer the mass. Along with this came an increasingly wide divide between clergy and laity, which the sixteenth-century Reformers rejected in their attempt to return to the early church. Against it they set the priesthood of all believers, a doctrine drawn from the phrase in 1 Peter 2.9, "you are a chosen race, a royal priesthood," read as removing the possibility of any hierarchy among Christians. (John Bowden, "Ministry and Ministers," in Bowden [2005], 757)

See also McBrien (1995), 1051, S.v. "Priesthood of all Believers."

2. See Bradshaw (1990), 46.

3. See, for example, Acts 6:5–6, where Stephen and six other men are ordained to the priesthood by the laying on of hands. In Acts 13:1–3 individuals are ordained by the laying on of hands. In 1 Timothy 4:14 we read of the laying on of hands for Timothy's ordination. In addition, in 2 Timothy 1:6 Paul makes reference to when he ordained Timothy by the laying on of hands. As an example from the Hebrew Bible, in Deuteronomy 34:9 we are told that Joshua was ordained by the laying on of Moses's hands. Commentators on these passages frequently highlight that this laying on of hands is the ritual transferal or conferral of priesthood authority. See,

for example, I. Howard Marshall, *Tyndale New Testament Commentaries: Acts* (Grand Rapids: Eerdmans, 1998), 127; Richard N. Longenecker, "The Acts of the Apostles," in Gaebelein (1976–92), 9:331, 497–98; Joseph A. Fitzmyer, *The Anchor Bible: The Acts of the Apostles* (New York: Doubleday, 1998), 351; Luke Timothy Johnson, *Sacra Pagina: The Acts of the Apostles* (Collegeville, MN: The Liturgical Press, 1992), 107, 221, 345; E. F. Scott, *The Moffatt New Testament Commentary: The Pastoral Epistles* (London: Hodder and Stoughton, 1957), 52–53, 91; Donald Guthrie, *Tyndale New Testament Commentaries: The Pastoral Epistles*, revised edition (Grand Rapids: Eerdmans, 1998), 109, 139; Ralph Earle, "2 Timothy," in Gaebelein (1976–92), 11:395; Ian Cairns, *International Theological Commentary: Deuteronomy—Word and Presence* (Grand Rapids: Eerdmans, 1992), 306; Earl S. Kalland, "Deuteronomy," in Gaebelein (1976–92), 3:234.

4.   See Martos, in Bowden (2005), 1070.

5.   Bradshaw (1990), 22, 33.

6.   Parry and Parry (2009), 12.

7.   Van Gennep (1960), 12.

8.   Syrian-rite Christians are traditionally called "Jacobite" Christians. The Oxford *Encyclopedia of Christianity* states that of Christian denominations extant today, the Jacobite branch "can lay some claim to be the oldest expression of Christianity." John Fenwick, "Orthodox Christianity," in Bowden (2005), 861. Fenwick adds: "The Syrian communities did not generally accept the Chalcedonian Definition [of Christ's nature] and for a century or so suffered some persecution from the Byzantine authorities." (Fenwick, in Bowden [2005], 861.) Chalcedon declared that Jesus was one person with two natures—human and divine. He was united in His personhood, but had a duality of natures that existed without division or separation.

> In 543 CE a monk named Jacob Baradeus was secretly consecrated by Patriarch Theodosios of Alexandria, a leading figure in the opposition to Chalcedon. For the rest of his life Jacob travelled [sic] extensively in the Middle East, from Egypt to Iran, consecrating bishops, ordaining priests and deacons, and helping the communities regroup as a single identifiable unit—the Syrian Orthodox Church. Jacob's reversal of this low point in the church's fortunes has led to the church often being called "Jacobite." (Fenwick, in Bowden [2005], 861)

9.   The Maronite Christian church has its origins in the late fourth century, and its stronghold in Lebanon, where it is the largest Christian

denomination in that country, or in any modern Middle Eastern country. While it technically existed as a separate denomination from Roman Catholicism until AD 1182, Maronites often deny that they ever "lacked communion with the Holy See." Today they are seen as a tradition within *The* tradition. See Ronald G. Roberson, "Maronite Catholic Church," in McBrien (1995), 818–19; John Fenwick, "Christianity in the Middle East," in Bowden (2005), 747.

10.   Bradshaw (1990), 45, 183.

11.   Ibid., 197–98.

12.   John Chrysostom, "Homily on Acts 14:3," in "Homilies on the Acts of the Apostles," cited in Bradshaw (1990), 77.

13.   Parry and Parry (2009), 8–9. See also Jae R. Ballif, "Melchizedek Priesthood," in Ludlow (1992), 2:883.

14.   Julien (1996), 191; Todeschi (1995), 128. Hands can also invoke images of strength, providence, authority, or blessings. J. F. McConkie (1985), 261; Cirlot (1962), 137.

15.   Farbridge (1923), 274–75; Conner (1992), 137. In all probability, the hand is a symbol of power, not simply because we rely heavily upon its manifest strength, but also because the Hebrew root for hand can mean "power" and "strength." Francis S. Brown, S. R. Driver, and Charles A. Briggs, eds. *A Hebrew and English Lexicon of the Old Testament* (Peabody, MA: Hendrickson Publishers, 1999), 388, 1094; Tresidder (2000), 22; J. F. McConkie (1985), 261. One text notes: "While the touch of the human hand conveys differing intentions and evokes a gamut of feelings, the gentle, firm gesture that is the laying on of hands intends the sense of imparted power." Ryken, Wilhoit, and Longman (1998), 362. Joseph Fielding McConkie suggested that, because of this concept of hands possessing and transferring power, it is traditionally held that the laying on of hands "symbolizes the placing of God's hand or power upon the one so blessed (See D&C 36:1–2)." McConkie (1985), 261–62. Elsewhere we read: "The hand of God is divine power; transmission of spirit; protection; justice." Cooper (1995), 78.

16.   Farbridge (1923), 274–75.

17.   When Jacob blessed his sons, he stated that "the blessings of thy father . . . shall be on the head of Joseph (Genesis 49:26). Solomon stated that "blessings are upon the head of the just" (Proverbs 10:6). Numerous times in the Doctrine and Covenants we read of blessings being placed or poured out upon the head of one individual or another (see D&C 39:8, 52:37, 107:83, 124:21, 57, 133:34). Each of these pronouncements is designed to emphasize the head as a symbol for the entire person.

Similarly, as evidence of an all-encompassing grief or mourning, ancients would shave their heads (Job 1:20), cover their heads (2 Samuel 15:30), or place dirt or ashes on their heads (2 Samuel 13:19, 15:32).

18. Since the head was sometimes a representation of the seat of one's life, the severed head was frequently employed in scripture as a representation of the "decisive defeat of the enemy." see Ryken, Wilhoit, and Longman (1998), 367. See also Unger (1966), 461. Thus, we are told that Christ will "crush" Satan's head (see Hebrew of Genesis 3:15), symbolizing His eventual "utter defeat" over the adversary of all mankind. David forewarned Goliath that he would cut off his head (1 Samuel 17:46). The Philistines took Saul's head and hung it in the temple of their god, Dagon (1 Chronicles 10:9–10). At the request of Herodias, Herod Antipas had John the Baptist beheaded (Mark 6:24–28). Reluctantly, but at the command of the Lord, Nephi smote off the head of Laban who had been seeking to thwart God's will (1 Nephi 4:17–18). And Coriantumr concluded his battle with Shiz by cutting off his head (Ether 15:30).

19. As the head rules the body, time and again Christ is spoken of in scripture as the "head of the Church" (Ephesians 4:15, 5:23; Matthew 21:42; Mark 12:10; Luke 20:17; Acts 4:11; 1 Peter 2:7; 1 Corinthians 11:3; Colossians 1:18, 2:10; Jacob 4:17; Mosiah 5:8) that gives it all that it needs. Ryken, Wilhoit, and Longman (1998), 367. See also Walter L. Wilson, *A Dictionary of Bible Types* (Peabody, MA: Hendrickson Publishers, 1999), 214. This same concept of governance is behind the metaphor that describes the leaders of armies and nations as the "head" (Alma 47:8, 49:10, 60:24). Additionally, if one learns to govern one's head which, in turn, will govern one's body, salvation is said to be sure.

20. Ryken, Wilhoit, and Longman (1998), 367. See also Wilson (1999), 214.

21. Parry and Parry (2009), 12.

22. Green (2004), 81.

23. Frederick J. Cwiekowski, "Deacon, Woman," in McBrien (1995), 397.

24. Ibid., 397.

25. See Cwiekowski, in McBrien (1995), 397. One source noted that it appears that "deaconesses" took over the work previously performed by the widows of the early Church. Consequently, the term "deaconess" may be of late origin, but their work appears to be something present in the early Church. See Mary Lawrence McKenna, *Women of the Church: Role and Renewal* (New York: P. J. Kenedy & Sons, 1967), 53. This same source suggests that the transition between "widows" and "deaconesses" may have taken place as late as the third century (See McKenna [1967], 68, 79), though

comments made by Pliny the Younger early in the second century imply that McKenna is too late on her dating of the development of this female office.
26. For example, one book suggests: "The last thirty years of American scholarship have produced an amazing range of evidence for women's roles as deacons . . . in Christian churches from the first through the thirteenth century." Torjesen (1993), 2, 19–20. This same source suggests that the position or office of *deaconess* (under a different title) may have existed in pre–New Testament Judaism, and continued within that faith at least until the sixth century CE. See Torjesen (1993), 2, 19.
27. See Bradshaw (1990), 89.
28. Ibid., 84, 86–87.
29. R. Hugh Connolly, *Didascalia Apostolorum* (Oxford: Clarendon Press, 1929), 146, cited in Mitchell (1978), 30.
30. Cwiekowski, in McBrien (1995), 397. A "catechumen" is one who has been converted and is being instructed prior to and in anticipation of his or her baptism.
31. See Martimort (1986), 114. See also 113.
32. See Bradshaw (1990), 86.
33. See Martimort (1986), 139–40.
34. See McBrien (1995), 935, S.v., "Orarion."
35. Ibid., 1225, S.v., "Stole."
36. Hippolytus wrote: "When a widow is appointed, she shall not be ordained but she shall be appointed by the name. . . . The widow [or deaconess] shall be appointed by the word alone, and so . . . hands shall not be laid upon her [to ordain her] because she does not offer the oblation nor has she a sacred [priesthood] ministry. Ordination is for the clergy on account of their ministry, but the widow is appointed for prayer . . ." Hippolytus, "Apostolic Tradition," Part 1, 11:1–5, in Burton Scott Easton, trans., *The Apostolic Tradition of Hippolytus* (Ann Arbor, MI: Archon Books, 1962), 40. See also Bradshaw (1990), 83–84; McKenna (1967), 78. One modern text states: "There is no ordination of women to the priesthood. It is known that a female diaconate existed in some Oriental Orthodox traditions. There exist ancient texts and prayers for consecrating deaconesses . . ." However, these are setting apart blessings rather than priesthood ordinations. Christine Chaillot, "The Ancient Oriental Churches," in Geoffrey Wainwright and Karen B. Westerfield Tucker, eds., *The Oxford History of Christian Worship* (New York: Oxford University Press, 2006), 135.
37. See Martimort (1986), 142–43. Martimort points out that "both the discipline and the liturgy of the churches insisted upon a very clear

distinction between deacons and deaconesses" when it came to having conferred priesthood authority. Martimort (1986), 247.

38. This document, also known as the "Constitution of the Holy Apostles," has been dated (as a compilation) as early as AD 250 and as late as AD 394. Because it is a compilation of several earlier works, it does not all date from the same period, nor are its contents all originally from the same pen. The mid-third to late–fourth century date represents when it was complied, rather than the composition date of the original documents from which the "Apostolic Constitutions" were drawn. Thus, this is a third or fourth-century composition which drew upon works likely dating from the early to mid–second century. One text notes: "The work is divided into eight books, and is primarily a collection of and expansion on previous works such as the *Didache* (c. 140) and the *Apostolic Traditions*. Book 8 ends with eighty-five canons from various sources and is elsewhere known as the *Apostolic Canons*." Arthur A. Just, Jr., *Ancient Christian Commentary on Scripture—Luke* (Downers Grove, IL: InterVarsity Press, 2003), 400. See also James Donaldson, "Introductory Notice to Constitutions of the Holy Apostles," in Roberts and Donaldson (1994), 7:388; Edgar J. Goodspeed, *A History of Early Christian Literature* (Chicago: The University of Chicago Press, 1966), 12.

39. While the translator of this text renders the verb "ordained," as noted, Hippolytus and James of Edessa both emphatically taught that the women were "set apart" rather than "ordained."

40. "Constitution of the Holy Apostles," book 8, section 3, chapters 19–20, in Roberts and Donaldson (1994), 7:492.

41. Both prayers are found in Martimort (1986), 181.

42. Madsen (2008), 51. See also a very curious comment regarding women as priestesses in Smith (1998), 3:178.

43. One Roman Catholic source suggests that, in the image of priestess or *deaconess*, there is no tension being depicted (i.e., God has a masculine and feminine side). Rather, the office simply implies that in heaven both the masculine and feminine exist—the "goddess" being a representation "of divine power and sovereignty embodied in female form." See Elizabeth A. Johnson, *She Who Is: The Mystery of God in Feminist Theological Discourse* (New York: Crossroads, 1994), 55–56. See also James J. Preston, "Goddess Worship: An Overview," in Eliade (1987), 6:43.

44. Torjesen (1993), 265.

45. Ibid., 259, 260–62.

46. Ibid., 259.

47. See Torjesen (1993), 260–61. Of "wisdom's" mysterious identity, one

source notes that she "seems to be a communication of God." This same source states "that wisdom is the form in which . . . Jahweh makes himself present and in which he wishes to be sought by man." See Roland E. Murphy, "Wisdom in the OT," in David Noel Freedman, ed., *The Anchor Bible Dictionary*, 6 vols. (New York: Doubleday, 1992), 6:927.

48. See Torjesen (1993), 261.

49. Ibid., 264.

50. See Johnson (1994), 92. See also E. O. James, *Myth and Ritual in the Ancient Near East* (New York: Barnes & Noble, 1958), 63, 125–28.

51. Preston in Eliade (1987), 6:39.

52. Merlin Stone, "Goddess Worship: Goddess Worship in the Ancient Near East," in Eliade (1987), 6:48. See also Merlin Stone, *When God was a Woman* (New York: Harcourt Brace Jovanovich, 1976), 22–24. It should be noted that scholars generally agree that the presence of goddess worship in ancient Israel was likely due to a corruption of the faith (i.e., the influence of Israel's pagan neighbors). See, for example, Stone (1976), 57.

53. Thus one commentator on the symbolic meaning of the office of *deaconess* highlighted the power of feminine symbols in any liturgical setting.

> The powers to produce life inherent in female sexuality provided the most potent symbols for the divine in the societies of Old Europe . . . The Christian ritual of baptism, for instance, draws its meaning from women's work of giving birth. In some of the earliest baptismal rites, converts entered the waters naked, like the baby in the womb. After being immersed they came forth from the water as people who had been born again. The first food these "newborn" converts received was in fact made of milk and honey—an imitation of breast milk—signifying their entrance into the Christian community as babes. (Torjesen [1993], 254, 258)

54. See McKenna (1967), 167–83.

55. Ibid., 171.

56. Ibid., 180.

57. See Cooper (1995), 184; William F. Orr and James Arthur Walther, *The Anchor Bible: 1 Corinthians* (New York: Doubleday, 1976), 261; Morris N. Kertzer and Lawrence A. Hoffman, *What is a Jew?* (New York: Collier Books, 1993), 91; Nicholas de Lange, *Judaism* (Oxford: Oxford University Press, 1987), 32–33.

58. McKenna (1967), 183.

Four

Narrative in Ritual

Narrative, or the telling of stories, has long been part of ritual. From antiquity down to the present, certain stories have been told and retold as a means of teaching people about their own history and their personal relationship with God.[1] In certain ritual settings, prominent biblical narratives have been woven into sacred ceremonies in an effort to give those rites symbolic value or in an attempt to make otherwise meaningless ceremonies personally relevant.[2]

Chief among those narratives employed in ancient and modern liturgies are the Creation and the Fall. One text on symbolism notes that "the stories with which the Bible begins"—namely the Creation and the Fall—are "symbols of truths learned in history." The Bible presents events of the past and applies them to mankind in general. Thus the Creation is my story and my creation; the Fall is my story and my fall.[3] One who participates in a rite in which the story of the Creation or the Fall is told must ask himself or herself: What is this narrative telling me about my own creation or my own fall? How does this story highlight the good and/or evil I have done in my own life, or in the world? and What divine or sacred knowledge does this narrative seek to reveal to me?[4]

THE CREATION

We know of a number of liturgical contexts in which the Creation drama was acted out as a teaching device for initiates or parishioners. For example, in the book of 2 Enoch[5] we read of how Enoch was "stripped of his earthly garments and [then] anointed with holy oil" after which he was "brought by the archangel Michael [or Adam] before God's face" where he was "instructed" regarding "the story of creation."[6] The stages of Enoch's preparation prior to being instructed give this episode a clearly ritual context.

Curiously, in England in the late Middle Ages there existed a set of biblically based "mystery plays" that were presented annually[7] to the people of York (and the surrounding region), beginning in the fourteenth century and running continuously through the late sixteenth century. These were religious plays designed to increase the spirituality of those who observed them. One commentator noted that their "spiritual purpose was the glorification of God, and [their] didactic intention to instruct the unlettered in the historical basis of their faith."[8] Another expert on these liturgical dramas noted that the plays were "sacramental theater . . . . In them theater and sacrament" became "profound investigations of each other's opportunities and limits."[9] These plays, taking their cues from biblical narratives, focused on key events in the plan of salvation, including the Creation and the Fall.[10] One text notes: "The mediaeval audiences of the plays felt themselves to be deeply implicated in this presentation of sacred history. The essential episodes were the Creation of the world and of man, man's deception by the Devil, resulting in the Fall and the expulsion from Paradise."[11] This same text adds:

> One of the principal effects of the cycle [of plays] . . . was to place the audience in a position of God-like omniscience [with] regards [to] the continuing history and nature of their spiritual predicament on earth. Out of this arose a need for them to examine their consciences and to decide where their allegiance lay in the conflict between good and evil for possession of the souls of the human race. . . . The Creation and Fall were . . . to show the

predicament of fallen man and his need for redemption, and to prefigure the coming of the Redeemer and his earthly existence.[12]

As noted, one of the York Mystery Plays depicted the Creation and drew heavily upon the first two chapters of the book of Genesis.[13] One text noted that "the presence of music was essential to the depiction of heaven in the *Creation*" play.[14]

Another liturgical setting in which the story of the Creation has been employed as a teaching device is the Roman Catholic Easter Vigil (i.e., the Mass celebrated on the eve of Easter). On that holy occasion the story of the Creation is recounted as part of the Mass, and then the homily is traditionally drawn from that same scriptural theme.[15] Thus, the story of the Creation is central to the teaching at that liturgical gathering.

As can be seen, the story of the Creation has its place in ritual or liturgy. It is an excellent teaching device, and has many potential symbolic meanings. When found in a liturgical context, the focus of the symbolism and interpretation is not generally on the minute details of the story, but rather on the general overarching message to be found in the story and its application. What follows are but a few of the many metaphorical approaches to the Creation that have been proffered over the centuries.[16]

Perhaps the most common symbol associated with the Creation is that of God's efforts to "re-create" you and I in His image and pattern, or after His likeness. Thus, at the Roman Catholic Easter Vigil the story is read and interpreted as a symbol of re-creation, resurrection, renewal, and salvation. Indeed, the placement of a discussion of the story of the Creation in a service held just before the dawn of Easter morn is not coincidental. For, just as Easter celebrates the resurrection of Christ, and the promise of a resurrection for all; so also, the story of the Creation celebrates God's power to change each fallen individual—to bring all back to life, and specifically back to a life of faithfulness and obedience (something each of us falls short of). Similarly, just as the Creation story talks of God separating the light from the darkness, we see how God can do the same in our own lives. And just as the Creation story speaks of God giving life to all of His creations, we see how God can give life to those who accept Him and embrace His ways. Like the Creation story, which teaches us that God made men and women after His own image, we understand that each of us are not only children of God, but have the potential (as all children do) to become as our Father is. Each of these symbolic messages are tied up in the reality that God must re-create or resurrect us into something greater than we, of ourselves, can become.[17] One commentator wrote that the repetition of depicting or discussing the story of the Creation over and over again in a liturgical setting "reflects the belief that the act of creation is not simply what happened once in history but something eternally accomplished by God's creative word. In fact, one could argue that [the Creation story] really recounts what God intended in creation, not what really resulted, and that . . . [the] creation happens among us through Christ."[18] In other words, in a liturgical setting it is appropriate to begin with the Creation story because the story is about our creation more than it is about the earth's creation. "The account of the creation of this earth becomes a part of each individual's personal story about his or her place in the universe and kingdom of God."[19] Just as the Fall of Adam and Eve is really the story of our personal fall, so also the Creation account is actually a metaphorical retelling of our creation and our placement in the divine plan. The popular LDS author, James Ferrell, wrote:

> For most of my life, I thought the Creation story was just about the formation of an earth. I wasn't so sure that it mattered much today.
>
> But then I noticed something amazing: The creation story was about me.
>
> I'm quite serious. The Creation is not merely the story of a heavenly body. It is also, metaphorically, the story of the creation of heavenly beings—me, you, all of us. So when we study the creative progression of the earth, we're actually also learning about our own mortal and eternal progression. When we see that, the Creation matters. Today.[20]

Ferrell's point is that the story of the Creation is a story of God re-creating you and me from fallen humans to new creations in Christ (see 2 Corinthians 5:17).[21] He continues:

> Let's consider the Creation in broad strokes to see how completely the earth was transformed by the creative process, and how that change mirrors the conversion that is offered to man.
>
> In the beginning, before it had taken up orbit around a source of light, the earth was empty, desolate, and dark. This seems a pretty good description of man's state so long as he insists on living for himself, on his own terms, refusing to hearken to the light of Christ. But the Spirit moved upon this darkness, and the earth moved into proximity with the light. Under the influence of the light, a 'firmament' or atmosphere of life-sustaining air was formed above and around the earth. In application to ourselves, we might consider this to be a representation of the nourishing influence of the Spirit in our lives. Under the influence of this light and within the protective canopy of this air or spirit, the earth began to come to life. Isn't this exactly what happens to us when we are nourished by the Spirit and bathed by the light? We, too, come to life, as it were, and begin to bring forth good fruit.
>
> Interestingly, it is at this point in the process, after the Lord has sown his seeds and nourished his creation by his own light and spirit, that he then guides that creation into the orbit of those that he has set up to govern—the "lights in the firmament of the heaven," the "greater light to rule the day, and the lesser light to rule the night." This too, I think, is analogous to what happens with us, as the light of Christ and the whisperings of the Spirit both enliven us and direct us to the Lord's representatives on earth. These representatives, who have been called to govern in this sphere, then shed forth the Lord's light on the issues of our day, helping us to discern the light from the darkness . . .
>
> As we obey the counsel of these governing ones and follow in the light they reveal . . . we, like the earth, bring forth more abundantly. In fact, under the combined influence of the light of Christ, the Spirit, and the direction of those called to govern over the earth, the earth itself becomes a sustaining source of life, nourishing and strengthening everything in its presence—fish, fowls, insects, animals. As the earth grows more abundant and more beautiful, finally, the life that appears on the earth begins to be in the image of God.

Isn't this how we grow as well? As we stay in the orbit, as it were, of the light of Christ, the Spirit, and the Lord's representatives on earth, and as we observe and follow that light, do we not bring forth more abundantly? Do we not sustain and nourish all that is around us? Do we not ultimately receive the image of God in our countenances?

At this point in the Creation story, the parallelism between man and the heavenly body known as the earth becomes one . . .

As with the earth, the transformation from dark, desolate solitude to glorious abundance in the presence of God is in and through the power of Christ. He is the creator of heaven and earth.[22]

Ferrell goes on to point out that over and over again the various Creation accounts state of the earth that it was obedient to God's commands. "The key to each stage of progression [during the creation] was obedience." He adds: "This is as true of man's progression as it was for the earth's."[23] God was able to take desolate, useless earth and give it life, beauty, purpose, and productivity because it was willing to be obedient to His commands. Such can be the case with us, if we are willing to allow Him to change us; to mold and shape us; to stretch and use us.

As attested to by commentator after commentator: the story of the Creation in liturgy is particularly valuable for what it can teach us about ourselves: our origin, our divine nature, and what God has done *for* us and wishes to do *to* us. For those of us who are willing, it reminds us that God is constantly trying to make us into something usable, better, and new—just as He did to the unorganized matter from which He composed this earth.

A second common symbol often pointed to in the story of the Creation is that of Jesus as Creator. There is little question but that the story of the Creation is a Christocentric event. As John 1:3 reminds us: "All things were made by him; and without him was not anything made that was made."[24] Though much could be said to prove this point, note just a few of the very Christocentric elements of the story. The main activity on day one of the Creation was the dividing of the light from darkness. This is not a reference to a distinction between day and night or a creation of the sun and the moon.[25] According to the Genesis account, that happened on day four of the Creation. Indeed, as Basil the Great[26] wrote: "The condition in the world before the creation of light was not night but darkness."[27] In other words, God had yet to create day and night on the first day; but light and dark most certainly *did* exist! So what was the division of light from darkness that took place at the very beginning of the Creation? It appears to be a dividing of the divine light (D&C 88:6–11) from the demonic dark (1 Nephi 12:17).[28] It appears to be a reference to the separation that took place between those who followed Lucifer and those who followed God and Christ.[29] That introductory miracle during the Creation highlights Jesus' presence from the very beginning, as do other components of the Creation that seem to be mentioned almost in passing. Thus, just as light reminds us of Christ because it banishes the dark and because of its necessity for the sustaining of life, so also water (prominently present during the Creation) can serve as a strong symbol for Christ's life-giving work in the creative process—and in our day-to-day lives.[30] One source notes:

> Water is one of the most essential elements on earth for the growth and continuing life of plants and animals and humans. Without water, all fish and sea creatures die within minutes. Most animals and all humans die within days without water. Water can take a lifeless, arid desert and turn it into a fertile, teeming land. Water is necessary for cleansing that which has become dirty or befouled. The movement of water is a major source of electrical power on earth.
>
> Water is an impressive symbol of the atonement. The atonement is essential for our growth and continuing life. It can take a spiritually lifeless, arid soul and help it become fertile and vital. It is necessary to cleanse souls that have become dirty or befouled. It is a major source of the spiritual power on earth.[31]

Thus, the significant presence of water during the story of the Creation has been taken by some as a divine reminder of Jesus' role in the creation of all things, and of His atoning role on behalf of all things. Significantly, on day three of the Genesis version of the Creation story, dry land is first manifest. The initial bit of land to come out of the water has traditionally been held to have served as the first post-Fall temple in the new world. One scholar noted: "In the biblical tradition, the first ground to appear after the waters of chaos had receded, where earthly creation first took place . . . became the . . . temple."[32] Hugh Nibley wrote: "It was always believed that . . . the temple . . . was the beginning place of the world, the rock where other things are founded."[33] Isaiah refers to the temple as "the mountain of the Lord" (Isaiah 2:3). Thus, in the initial Creation of the earth, the first rock to come forth out of the waters was sacred, set apart, holy, and different from the rest. It would be the temple; the house of the Lord. That rock was not only the symbol of God's future earthly abode, it too was a representation of Christ Himself.

> The fundamental, foundational (literally) substance of the earth is *rock*. It is the firm base of all else on the planet. The scriptures teach repeatedly that Jesus is the solid rock of the gospel (Deut. 32:4; Ps. 28:1; 62:2; 1 Cor. 10:1–4). As such, Christ and his atonement are the solid foundation upon which we can build. Like a rock, the atonement is steadfast and immovable.
>
> Rock is ground up by other elements into sand and dirt. It is rock on which the earth's soil rests and from which plants and trees grow. Even sea plants and sea creatures require the nutrients that come from the underwater rock as it is gradually pulverized by the forces of nature. Thus the rock, when broken down, contributes to the life of all plants and animals on the entire earth. Likewise, through Christ's atonement we can receive the essential spiritual nourishment we all need.[34]

The first rock that emerged from the waters became the temple because the tip of the mountain was the place upon earth that was closest to God, just as Jesus is the Being that is closest to God. Consequently, you and I are taught through the story of the Creation (and the life of Christ) to become close to the Father as Jesus did, and to do so (as the temples teach us to), by removing ourselves from the world (as mountains and Christ are removed from the world).[35]

At the beginning of the Creation story, we are informed that *all* things are in chaos without God, and that it is God who tames or brings order to the chaos—in the world and in our lives.[36] As one commentator wrote: "The lives of many people are chaotic (cf. Mark 1:32–34). . . . The [Genesis] text claims that even the chaos of our historical life can be claimed by God for his grand purposes."[37] Just as God calmed the chaos of the disorganized waters during the creative process, He can calm the chaos that swirls in our own lives—spiritually, temporally, and in every other way—if we but let Him.[38] Elder Howard W. Hunter of the Twelve, after recounting the miracle of Jesus raising the daughter of Jairus from the dead, said this: "Whatever Jesus lays his hands upon lives. If Jesus lays his hands upon a marriage, it lives. If he is allowed to lay his hands on the family, it lives."[39] One interpretation of the story of the Creation in liturgy is that it teaches us that God seeks to bring order to the chaos in our lives—and He does that by inviting us to come unto Christ and be perfected in Him (Moroni 10:32). He seeks to place His hands upon our heads, upon our lives!

A third common truth seen as symbolically taught in the Creation story is the reality that all things were created "good" by God. Indeed, in the scriptural account again and again God refers to His creations as "good" or "very good" as the King James Version puts it. One commentator interpreted that to mean "wonderful!" or "perfect!"[40] However, all that which was originally created as "good" has been corrupted by you and I. Thus, the placement of the Creation story in juxtaposition to the story of the Fall has been seen by some as evidence that the former teaches us how God made all things perfect and the latter explains how man took those perfect things and made them imperfect through his disobedience. To become like God, the Creation story suggests, is to create good rather than to create evil or to destroy good. The story of the Creation is an invitation for mankind to use its creative powers in such a way that we can say, once we are done with any work, "it is good!" We must not use our creative powers in destructive ways.[41]

Related to this third symbolic message in the story of the Creation is a fourth one—the environmental message. If Christ (as the God of the Old Testament) is the Creator of the earth we must necessarily have reverence for it, for it is His.[42] One of the primary reasons for using the story of the Creation as part of liturgy or ritual is that it serves to give voice to, or expression of, our traditionally unexpressed awe and gratitude for what God has done in the Creation.[43] Representations of the Creation show that we're aware of God's tremendous gift to us through His creating life and a place on which we might live that out.[44] One source states: "To use creation in liturgy is to show reverence for creation through, with, and in which the incarnate God is disclosed and discovered."[45] In other words, the story of the Creation really teaches us about God's character and nature in ways that no other passage of scripture and no other liturgical rite can.[46] In liturgical and scriptural accounts of the Creation we are told that God creates all things, and pronounces all things as "good."[47] Thus the story of the Creation calls us to both respect (and hold as good) all things God has created. But it also calls us to insure that they remain good. "Material things are *sacramenta*, symbols that reveal the goodness and beauty of the Creator. . . . It is only sin that has disfigured the beauty of creation and diverted things from their purpose. . . . Therefore the temporal order cannot [or should not] be despised or neglected."[48]

Fifth, there is an aesthetic message to be found in Creation liturgy.[49] As noted above, the Creation story was an important part of the York Mystery plays. Through the repeated acting out of this biblically based drama, the audience was taught about God as Creator, but also about His role as Artisan.[50] God created all things, but He chose to do so with a brush of beauty. Consequently, we know that beauty is both part of who He is and part of what He expects us to seek out and develop—in our world and in our lives.[51] It is not a passing trait of the divine. It is a central attribute!

As a sixth symbol, some have seen in liturgical depictions of the Creation a message about stewardship and accountability. The

Father creates through a chain of delegation. All who are given assignments are expected to return and report how they fulfilled that which they were assigned to do. As it was in the Creation, so it is in life. What God may assign through several layers of stewards is still to be perceived as directly from God (D&C 1:38), and the call or assignment is no less sacred—and the accountability no less severe for those who shirk their covenant-bound duties.

A seventh symbolic meaning is to be found in the writings of the Church Fathers. Jerome[52] and Ephrem the Syrian[53] each suggested that the comment in Genesis 1:2 that "the Spirit of God moved upon the face of the waters" was a "foreshadowing" of the ordinance of baptism and the fact that such an ordinance could only be valid if the Spirit accompanied it (See Acts 19:1–6).[54] In support of their teaching, D&C 132:7 informs us that ordinances not entered into and sealed by the Holy Spirit of Promise are not valid in the hereafter. Certainly some of the early Christians saw the story of the Creation as teaching that in order for rites, like baptism, to be valid the Holy Spirit must accompany them; meaning it must motivate one to receive the ordinance, and it must certainly be received as a gift after the physical baptism of water has been received.

An eighth symbol potentially present in liturgical discussions of the Creation has to do with employment. One might justifiably take from the story that all godly jobs are acceptable to Him who created all things, and that all worthy forms of employment can be used to build the Kingdom of God upon the earth. The Creation story suggests that aesthetics (including art and architecture) are of God; medicine is of God; zoology and agronomy, along with horticulture, are of God; even astronomy finds a place in the Creation account. If one's work is righteous, God can use the man or woman who performs it. The story of the Creation seems to highlight many potential occupations in which the Father and Son work in their process of fashioning this earth and its inhabitants.

Finally, the creation story is saturated with references to fertility and, consequently, imagery of productivity. The plants are commanded to "yield seeds" (Genesis 1:11) and the trees are commanded to "bear fruit" (Genesis 1:11). The waters are commanded to "bring forth" creatures (Genesis 1:20) and even humans are commanded to "be fruitful, and multiply, and replenish the earth" (Genesis 1:28). All of this suggests a theme of productivity, reproduction, yield, fertility, and so on.[55] Perhaps the story of the Creation is an invitation for mankind to produce in every way that the word implies.

There are likely many other symbols that could be drawn from a general look at the story of the Creation. What has been provided above is but a summary of some of the most commonly developed themes. Though a look at events of each day of creation may uncover an additional layer of symbolism, scholars seem pretty much in agreement that, in a liturgical or ritual setting, examining the Creation's symbolism is best done as a unit rather than in its particulars or minute details. What seems most important to note is that the story of the Creation finds place in liturgical settings, not so much as a means of explaining the science behind how God created mans' abode, but rather the biblical and ritual accounts of the Creation appear to be filled with subtle messages about how God desires to change us, and what He encourages us to seek to change about ourselves.

THE FALL

The belief that the first humans fell from grace through some act of disobedience is a very common theme in many of the world's religions and cultures.[56] Indeed, *The Encyclopedia of Religion* records: "The myth[57] of an earthly paradise, where man is immortal, is an integral part of cosmogony and descriptions of the world's beginning in many cultures. That primordial man enjoys a bliss and freedom that he loses as the result of a fall is a dominant theme of this myth, a theme offering many variations."[58] For example, the Bantu speakers from the region north of the Congo River, the Dogon tribe of West Africa, the people of Cameroon and Burkina Faso each have a similar folklore regarding the fall of primordial man. Stories like theirs are also found among the people of the Ivory Coast, Senegal, Nigeria, sub-Saharan Africa, Ghana, Togo, Kenya and Zaire.[59] Indeed, the story of the fall of man is perhaps the most commonly believed religious tradition of all. It is clearly articulated in Judaism, Christianity, and Islam. But it also appears in Zoroastrianism and Gnosticism, to name only a few faiths focused on the Fall. The story is common in antiquity as well as modernity. Like the story of the Creation, the Fall of man has been told or reenacted as a teaching device for initiates or parishioners in a number of liturgical contexts for millennia. Temple scholar and symbologist, Margaret Barker, suggested that the story of the Fall was commonly enacted in ancient temple rites.[60] Though it is hard to say what role the Fall played in any instruction offered in Solomon's Temple, she notes "the walls of both the inner and outer rooms were decorated 'with carved figures of cherubims and palm trees . . . ' (1 Kings 6:29) . . . . The doors of the inner sanctuary . . . were carved with cherubim, palm trees and flowers . . . The temple interior was a garden representing the . . . Garden of Eden."[61] Thus, in some way that sacred story apparently played a role in rites or rituals of that holy edifice.[62]

Secret societies have existed for millennia, and in many civilizations.[63] And, as one commentator noted, "they all have their initiation" rituals.[64] Participants in Greek mystery rites were considered either *mystai* or *epoptai*, meaning those being initiated were at the temple for the first time (*mystai*) or those attending the rites had returned to watch or engage in the rituals on behalf of the new initiates (*epoptai*).[65] Thus, participation in the rites and rituals of mystery religions[66] was not a one-time encounter. One might participate on a number of levels (e.g., *mystai*, *epoptai*, or officiating priest). The oldest and most important of these mystery rites was that which has come to be known as the "Eleusinian mystery."[67] Though there is much we do not know, central to the Eleusinian version of the mystery religions was the re-enactment of mankind's fall. According to the legend, Persephone, the daughter of the Greek goddess Demeter, is gathering flowers in a garden or meadow when she is accosted by Hades, the god of death and the underworld. The law was that whoever consumed food or drink in the underworld was doomed to stay there for eternity. Persephone is tricked by Hades into eating the forbidden seeds of the pomegranate, and thus damns herself. After her unwary choice to partake, she is asked by one of the divine beings "Child, hast thou eaten of any food in the world below?" She is informed that, if she has partaken of the forbidden fruit, she will experience severe consequences for her choice. She confesses that she has indeed done that which would damn her to the underworld.[68] One commentator on these rites notes that Persephone's fall is symbolic. Metaphorically, she "is the corn which must descend into the earth so that from seeming death new fruit may germinate."[69] In other words, what looks like a tragic fall is really a blessing in disguise; a necessity of sorts. As part of the ritual, the new initiate was required to sacrifice a young pig. The animal would die in the stead of the initiate. Its placement in the earth reminded participants of Persephone's "sinking into the earth"[70]—thereby equating her "fall" with the personal "fall" into sin of the initiate. During the performance of the Eleusinian mystery rites the story of the fall of Persephone was acted out for those being initiated into the secret rites.[71] "The participants hoped to obtain a 'better lot,' a more glorious immortality in the next world."[72] They believed that they would be "transformed to a higher status by initiation" into these rites.[73]

In the Antiochian and Jerusalem Catechisms[74] the story of the Fall was also used as a teaching device when candidates for initiation were preparing to be washed. They would remove their clothing, and then be instructed that, just as they stood naked without shame, they (through this ordinance) would return to Eden, where Adam and Eve were naked but without shame, because they, like the washed initiate, were clean.[75] Consequently, being washed, it is as though the initiate was now Adam or Eve.

As noted above, in the late Middle Ages in England a set of biblically based "mystery plays" were presented to the people annually. These were designed to increase the spirituality of observers while also glorifying God and instructing the observers through "sacramental theater."[76] Among other biblical narratives, these York Mystery plays depicted the Fall.[77] One commentary on the Mystery Plays noted that the story of Adam and Eve's fall "initiates the human drama of the [mystery play] cycle. It sets in motion the chain of events which, though it is answered by Christ's sacrifice in the Passion, continues to implicate the audience in the present, its consequences not being finally exhausted until the Last Judgement."[78] In other words, in York the Fall was depicted liturgically with regularity to remind the observers and participants of truths central to history and to God's plan: namely that the Fall of mankind is our fall. The story implicates you and me. And while Jesus' Atonement is the answer to the woes we have brought upon ourselves, nevertheless, the message of the Fall is sure—We have done this! We are Adam and Eve! This is our story!

During Lent season leading up to Easter, the story of the Fall finds place in the liturgy of the Roman Catholic Church today. The readings in the lectionary for Mass[79] for the first Sunday of Lent (Genesis 2:7–9 and 3:1–7)[80] speak of the Fall of man, and how that compares to Christ's faithfulness.[81] The priest conducting the service develops the theme as he sees fit, but traditionally the message is one of fall and needed redemption.[82] The congregation is seen as "fallen Adams" who are living in "exile" from God—who, like Adam of old, through their disobedience have been driven from paradise and can only return via their personal choice to turn to Christ.[83] Thus, the Catholic liturgy that kicks off the season of Lent—or the season leading up to Easter and the celebration and commemoration of Christ's redemption of fallen man—begins with a discussion of the Fall of man, and how, through Christ (the "new Adam") all may be saved.[84]

In looking at the story of the Fall in a liturgical or ritual context, it is important to remember that most often it is presented in that setting more for its symbolic teaching, and less for its detailed doctrinal messages. In other words, like with the story of the Creation, to get bogged down in the endless details of the story (during a ritual) is to miss the overall message the rite is seeking to convey. Thus the participant in the ceremony is traditionally encouraged to look at the broad picture, or the overarching symbolic message of the Fall. And what is that message?

It is generally understood that Adam and Eve were typological symbols for the human race. They serve as representations of each of us, and our own personal fall from grace.[85] Of course, this concept is recognized by Latter-day Saints and non-Latter-day Saints alike. Indeed, non-LDS scholars and theologians commonly acknowledge that the story of the Fall—whether scripturally or ritually based—is *primarily* designed to teach us about ourselves. Entire books have been written on the subject that the story of the Fall is really a story about mankind's fall—and to read it otherwise is to miss the point of the story. As one scholar noted:

> Adam . . . is the Representative of the human race . . . . This story must be taken seriously but not literally . . . . It is a [scriptural story] that accurately reveals the existential situation in which man finds himself in the world . . . . While it is anchored in history, its significance is not limited to a particular history . . . . The language or terminology employed is, for the most part, symbolic . . . . To affirm that there are [figurative and symbolic] elements in Scripture is not to detract from its divine inspiration nor from its historical basis but to attest that the Holy Spirit has made use of various kinds of language and imagery to convey divine truth . . . . The tale . . . concerns not only a first fall and first man but a universal fall and universal man. Adam is not so much a private person as the head of the human race. He is a generic as well as first man. He is Everyman and therefore Representative Man. He is the representative of both our original parents and of all humankind.[86]

Similarly, another scholar noted that in marriage and life the man is symbolically living out the role of Adam, and the woman that of Eve.[87] Our first parents are symbols for the whole of "Israel" or "the children of Zion."[88] When a man and woman marry, they adopt the roles of Adam and Eve and hope that their home can become a new Eden or, better put, a temple.[89] One scholarly commentary on the Genesis account states: "The fall [is] a prototype of all sins . . . . The snake, the woman, and the man are not depicted as individuals involved in a personal crisis; rather, they are representatives. We are left with the impression that this is not their story so much as it is our story, the story of humankind."[90] Likewise, one popular Christian author wrote:

> The whole story of the Fall is a parable of every sinner's experience . . . It is generally accepted that the details [of the Fall] are to be interpreted symbolically rather than literally . . . They are in marvelous agreement with the real facts of human nature and experience. Adam is the representative of the human race . . . When [a man] reads this narrative, his conscience says to him, like a prophet of God: "Thou art the man; the story is told of thee!"[91]

Adam and Eve are our pattern. Their story is ours. Symbolically speaking, you and I are to consider ourselves as if we were Adam and Eve.[92] We are to see the story of the Fall as the story of our fall.[93] Consequently, when that sacred story is utilized in a liturgical or ritual setting, it is traditionally seeking to teach us less about the historical figures, Adam and Eve, and more about how you and I—who in the story of the Creation were made perfect—came to be in this fallen state, cut off from the God who loves us. The story of the Fall in liturgy serves as a message about *our* need for obedience, the consequences of *our* sins, and *our* desperate need for a Savior to redeem us from *our* fallen condition. To misunderstand this is to misunderstand the reason why the Fall is employed in ritual, anciently as well as today.

Certainly many parallels may be drawn between Adam and Eve's Fall and our own; and consequently many lessons exist for us in the story of the Fall. For example:

- Adam and Even began their earthly journey in Eden, and, consequently they were in a state of innocence—worthy of the Father's presence. Likewise, you and I began our mortal sojourn as innocents, and worthy of the Father's presence.[94]
- It has become somewhat of a colloquialism to point out that Eve was "not made out of [Adam's] head to rule over him, nor out of his feet to be trampled on by him, but out of his side to be equal with him, under his arm to be protected, and near his heart to be

beloved."[95] Thus, we are taught through their relationship about what God wants for our relationships.

- God created for Adam and Eve a place of paradise. During the Millennium the earth will return to a paradisiacal state. The abundance in Eden is a symbol of what God ultimately wishes for each of His children. While temporal abundance is not always possible in this life, spiritual abundance (including "fruits" or "gifts" of the Spirit) is, and temporal and spiritual abundance for all in the eternities is the promised blessing to those who strive to be faithful. Thus one commentator noted that "the Garden of Eden became a byword for prosperity and fruitfulness (see Isaiah 51:3; Ezekiel 36:35; Joel 2:3)."[96]

- Adam is depicted as being basically "up to nothing" when Satan comes to tempt him. So it is in our own lives. When we are idle, Satan has the most access to us.

- Adam and Eve are accosted by the adversary, who seeks to destroy them through tempting them to disobey God. So it is in our own lives. The devil daily desires to deceive us into being our own god—living our own law—all with an ultimate goal of making us "miserable like unto himself" (2 Nephi 2:27).[97]

- At the center of the garden, God placed the tree of life—a symbol for Christ[98]—and encouraged Adam and Eve to freely partake of the fruits of that tree (Genesis 2:9). If, in our own lives, Christ is central and we choose to freely partake of the fruits He offers, our lives (like the lives of Adam and Eve) can take on a somewhat paradisiacal nature.

- God's first command to Adam and Eve was to multiply and replenish the earth—which was really a command to be selfless (Genesis 1:28). Curiously, that is the first command LDS husbands and wives are given when they are sealed in the holy temple.[99]

- Adam and Eve were not only commanded to abstain from eating the "forbidden fruit," they were also prohibited from even touching it (Genesis 3:3). We find in this command the old adage, "don't play with fire." If we do not flirt with temptation, we reduce the likelihood that we will be tempted beyond that which we can withstand (1 Corinthians 10:13).

A list of potential lessons from the Fall could continue for pages. The aforementioned examples are but a few of the commonly noted lessons seen by exegetes in the textual accounts of the Fall, some of which may also be drawn from liturgical versions of the story. However, one of the most important symbolic lessons of the Fall has to do with the symbolism of the Groom and His bride. Scripture frequently highlights Christ's covenant relationship with His Church by employing the symbols of bride and bridegroom for the Church and Messiah respectively.[100] In that symbolic context, Adam stands as a representation of God the Father; His Son (and our Savior), Jesus; and their Prophets. Eve, on the other hand, serves as a typological symbol of the Church, the bride of Christ, or Covenant Israel.[101] Thus, when the story of the Fall is employed in liturgy, this metaphorical interpretation is often intended. As would be expected, many lessons can be learned from this imagery.

Just as Adam was the first human to be created, Christ is the Firstborn of the Father (D&C 93:21). Adam was created in the image of God,[102] as was Jesus, who is said to be in the express image of the Father (Hebrews 1:3). Michael became the "first Adam" and Jesus is the "last Adam" (1 Corinthians 15:45).

God made Adam a "help meet" (Genesis 2:18: Moses 3:18). We must remember, this is Christ's work. It is His Church. But it was not in the design and will of the Father that He do it alone. As Eve was Adam's help and support, Christ's bride—the Church— serves as His help and support. The Church's members aided Him in the Creation, in the writing of scripture, in the preaching of His message, in the administration of ordinances, and so on. Their hands are His hands. Their work is His work. Adam and Eve were commanded to be one, and in a like manner, Christ and His Church are to be one.

Eve was said to have been made from Adam's side or rib (Genesis 2:21–24; Moses 3:21–24). The Church is called "Christian" because it comes out of the Man, Christ. And the covenant relationship between the bride and the Bridegroom is the most important of all eternal relationships. Adam and Eve were to become one; husbands and wives are all commanded to become one; and Christ and His Church are to be one. One typologist wrote: "[Eve is] a type of the church as Adam is a type of Christ. As Eve was made out of a part of Adam, so the church is a part of the Lord Jesus. The church is called His bride as Eve was Adam's bride."[103]

> It is significant that the man calls the woman "bone of my bone and flesh of my flesh," a statement he could not have made about the animals. In Hebrew, these phrases indicate a closeness, a blood relationship between the two parties, and in this case a unified companionship between the man and the woman. But the phrases are also used in other places in the Old Testament to describe two parties who are not necessarily blood relatives but who have made a covenant with each other, such as when the northern tribes of Israel made a covenant with David, their new king, and confirmed: "Behold, we are thy bone and thy flesh." David makes a similar covenant with the elders of Judah: "Ye are my brethren, ye are my bones and my flesh." Some of the participants may have been related, but the phrase refers to a mutual covenant the two parties have made with each other.[104]

There is a covenant relationship that exists between Christ and His Church. This is foreshadowed by Adam's relationship with Eve. The fact that the man was made first, and that the woman was made from the man, has been seen as a statement about the covenant people's dependence upon Christ—who was the Firstborn of Father's spirit offspring.[105] The rib metaphor suggests that human existence is intended to be a partnership of man and woman[106]—or Christ and His Bride.[107]

In the scriptural accounts of the Fall, Eve is not present when the Father gives the commandment for them to avoid eating of the "forbidden" fruit. Adam receives God's word, and then conveys it to Eve. She then is expected to exercise faith in the divinity of the command and be obedient to it. Similarly, God gives to Christ and His prophets commandments, which they in turn convey to us. We do not receive these directly from the Father, but rather through mediators He has chosen. We are then expected to exhibit faith in the divinity of these revealed dictates, and be obedient to them. Hence, Ambrose noted that Satan "aimed to circumvent Adam by means of the woman. He did not accost the man who had in his presence received the heavenly command. He accosted her who had learned of it from her husband and who had not received from God the command which was to be observed."[108] So it is with us—Christ's Church; Satan tempts us to get at God and Christ. We are susceptible to his enticings, but they are not. The story of the Fall informs us that Adam (representing Christ) fell, not because he was tricked, but because Eve (symbolic of the members of the Church) gave into the serpent's enticings (i.e., the devil's temptations), and thus Adam (Christ) needed to come to mortality to fix what Eve (God's other children—male and female) had done. Adam's act clearly mirrors Christ's choice to redeem us (His bride or Church) from sin and spiritual death.[109]

Commentators have suggested that the "deep sleep" which came upon Adam foreshadowed Christ's sacrifice on our behalf. Augustine put it this way: "Adam's sleep was a mystical fore-shadowing of Christ's death, and when his dead body hanging from the cross was pierced by the lance [in] his side."[110] In addition, just as through that sleep Eve was "formed or builded," so also through Christ's death, the Church was built up or given strength.[111] "Since Eve had been created from the side of the sleeping Adam, . . . from the side of Christ hanging on the cross the church . . . must be created. In fact the church is 'the woman'."[112] Christ's bride, the covenant people, certainly existed before His Atonement. However, it was the death of Christ that gave their work efficacy and turned a localized religion of ancient Israel into the worldwide faith of Christianity. This "deep sleep" coming upon Christ (represented by Adam) may highlight the fact that Christ came here, took upon Himself a mortal body, and subjected Himself to the veil of forgetting, the trials, and the tests of mortality. However, through His exact obedience and perfect faithfulness, that veil of forgetting—that "deep sleep"—was rent, and His communion with the Father was made possible. In this Christ sets for us the perfect example.

In Eden, Adam and Eve were given two specific commandments. The first was that they "multiply" and "replenish" (Genesis 1:28). The second command was that they not eat of the fruit of the tree of knowledge of good and evil (Genesis 2:16–17). All too frequently these two dictates have been labeled as "contradictory commandments." From a doctrinal perspective, efforts have been made to explain why they are not contradictory.[113] However, knowing that this metaphor is about you and I, then there is no contradiction in these two commandments. Whereas Adam and Eve *had to* partake of the "forbidden fruit" in order to multiply, you and I, on the other hand, needn't do so. On the contrary, we are commanded to multiply and replenish the earth, all the while being expected to *avoid* partaking of that which has been forbidden. And you and I *are* capable of keeping both of these commandments at the same time.[114]

In Genesis 3:16 the Lord God declares to Eve, who has just transgressed God's law, "thy desire shall be to thy husband, and he shall rule over thee." Metaphorically speaking, Eve was deceived but Adam was not. Thus, the transgression of Eve established (at the beginning of her mortal probation) her need to be saved by her husband—who could see through the adversary's sophistry. Thus, the "husband" that the woman (or Church) should desire is Christ; and He shall rule over His bride (the Church).[115] This position is rightfully His because He is perfect and cannot be deceived by the devil.

As Eve's act in Eden introduced this telestial, mortal probation, she would be sent forth to be tried and tested. However, she would not be expected to brave the "lone and dreary world" alone. God would send with her as a help, Adam—he being much stronger than she, that he might serve as a protector and provider. So also God has not sent us (the Church) to walk the danger-strewn path of mortality alone. He has sent us a companion in Christ. His strengths far exceed ours. He will serve as our protector and provider throughout this daunting existence, so long as we keep His spirit with us. Adam was Eve's husband; she, his bride. Christ is our Groom; we (the Church), His bride.

When the story of the Fall appears in a liturgical setting, we find distinct hints of Christ's covenant relationship with His Church. The tale's figurative description of Eve's choice to hearken to the devil, and Adam's resistance to any form of disobedience, strongly mirror the weakness of the mortals who comprise the Lord's Church, and the strength of the Messiah, who seeks to redeem us. We often find the Creation and Fall being recounted or enacted in ritual or liturgical settings because these two narratives are really parallel stories. The former speaks of God and all that He has created as entirely "good." Thus, God, who is holy, cannot be the author of evil. The latter, on the other hand, explains how evil entered the world, and highlights the fact that God is not the cause of wickedness. Thus, the liturgical juxtaposing of the Creation and the Fall reminds us that "God is the cause of everything that is good and man is the cause of everything that is vain."[116] We who have introduced evil through our choice to fall must now turn to Christ that we might be made "new creature[s]" through Him (2 Corinthians 5:17), banishing evil forever from our lives.

Notes

1.   One expert on the ancients and their exegesis (or methods of scriptural interpretation) wrote:

> The early Christian interpretation of the prophecies of Isaiah and other Old Testament figures are another well-known instance of making ancient works relevant. . . . The same fundamental assumption was held to be true about *all* of the Hebrew Bible . . . Everything was held to apply to present-day readers and to contain within it an imperative for adoption and application to the readers' own lives. Paul's observation about the biblical narrative of the Israelites' wanderings in the desert,

>> Now these things [that happened to the Israelites in the desert] happened to them as a warning, **but they were written down for our instruction**, upon whom the end of the ages has come—1 Cor. 10:11

> is merely one formulation of an assumption that had long characterized ancient biblical interpretation. For Paul, as for all ancient interpreters, the Bible is not *essentially* a record of things that happened or were spoken in the past. That they happened is of course true; but if they were written down in the Bible, it was not so as to record what has occurred in some distant past, but "for our instruction," so that, by reading the sacred text whose material comes to us from the past,

we might learn some vital lesson for our own lives. (Kugel [1998], 16–17; emphasis in original)

2.   Indeed, one scholar of world religions pointed out that narrative in ritual "point to truths of a kind that cannot be told in other ways." He added that narratives sometimes "provide us with explanations of ritual." See John Bowker, *World Religions: The Great Faiths Explored & Explained* (New York: DK Publishing, 2006), 8.

3.   See Ricoeur (1967), 242, n. 4.

4.   One source suggested: "As the initiate re-enacts the sacred drama, he is endowed with the knowledge and power possessed by the gods. The initiate becomes one who knows." Lundquist, in Lundquist and Ricks (1990), 1:439.

5.   The book of 2 Enoch is a pseudepigraphical text that dates roughly to around the late first century of the Common Era. It has been described as "an amplification of Genesis 5:21–32" and is basically the equivalent of Jewish Midrash on those verses. [See F. I. Andersen, "2 (Slavonic Apocalypse of) Enoch—A New Translation and Introduction," in Charlesworth (1983, 1985), 1:91.] The work is likely a composite of various earlier manuscripts, or has been created out of material taken from a large and older work. Though the oldest version of the text only exists in Slavonic, it is believed to be reliant on a Greek version of an Enoch text. [See Andersen, in Charlesworth (1983, 1985), 1:94.]

6.   See Alexander, "Introduction" in Charlesworth (1983, 1985), 1:248.

7.   These plays were presented on the "Feast of Corpus Christi," which could fall on any day between May 23 and June 24. This feast was an annual commemoration of the Roman Catholic belief that the consecrated or blessed Eucharistic bread contained "the Real Presence of the Body of Christ." It was a celebration of the redemptive effects of the sacrament of the Lord's Supper. The Feast of Corpus Christi was Roman Catholicism's "midsummer festival" during the Middle Ages. See Richard Beadle and Pamela M. King, eds., *York Mystery Plays: A Selection in Modern Spelling* (Oxford: Clarendon Press, 1984), x; McBrien (1995), 369. One commentator noted: "The York plays were performed off and on from 1376 to 1569." Sarah Beckwith, *Signifying God: Social Relation and Symbolic Act in the York Corpus Christi Plays* (Chicago: The University of Chicago Press, 2001), 4.

8.   Beadle and King (1984), ix. The term "didactic" means literally "designed or intended to teach."

9.   Beckwith (2001), xv.

10. See Timothy Thibodeau, "Western Christendom," in Wainwright and Tucker (2006), 247; Pamela M. King, "Mystery Plays," in Bowden (2005), 816–17.

11. Beadle and King (1984), xi.

12. Ibid.

13. Ibid, 1.

14. Ibid., xxvii. The Protestant Reformation had much to do with the cessation of the York Mystery plays. [See Beckwith (2001), 4, 121–57.] A number of those caught up in the reformation movement thought it blasphemy for mortals to depict the divine—even if the purpose was to teach the gospel to the illiterate. One text informs us: "In a profound shift in the mnemonic landscape of the sacred, England's Blasphemy Laws rendered performance of religious materials both practically impossible and conceptually unthinkable." Beckwith (2001), 3. See also John McManners, ed., *The Oxford Illustrated History of Christianity* (New York: Oxford University Press, 1990), 253.

15. See, for example, National Conference of Catholic Bishops, *Lectionary for Mass* (New Jersey: Catholic Book Publishing Corporation, 1998), 323–27; see also pp. 328–55.

16. Not surprisingly, most religions and cultures have a story of the Creation. In the various non-Christian tribal religions of Africa (e.g., the Yoruba, the Dogon, the Nuer, the Dinka, the BaMbuti, and the Khoisan) the belief that God (whatever He may be called) created all things, or oversaw the creation of all things, is commonplace. See Willard G. Oxtoby and Alan F. Segal, eds., *A Concise Introduction to World Religions* (New York: Oxford University Press, 2007), 19.

Similarly, the Native American tribes of North America (e.g., the Tewa of the Pueblo, the Zuni, the Hopi, the Iroquois, and so forth) all have strong Creation myths, which are central to both their theology and their liturgical acts. See Oxtoby and Segal (2007), 35–36.

The Dogon people of West Africa, for example, have a number of rituals that stem from their story of the Creation. This same text notes:

> The Dogon . . . possess an extraordinary complex body of cre-
> ation myths. According to oral traditions . . . the supreme being,
> Amma, created the world because he was lonely. Accounts differ as
> to how he did so, but according to one he transformed himself into a
> womb, within which he created four spirit beings called Nummo. . . .
> Then Amma and the Nummo created and placed on the Earth eight
> beings [four male and four female] who were to become the ancestors

of humans. . . . Dogon communities are organized around four major ritual societies, each of which was organized by one of the four ancestral fathers [created by Amma and the Nummo]. The oldest of these, Amma Seru, is associated with the supreme being, and the oldest member of each extended family performs rituals in his honor. Oxtoby and Segal (2007), 26–27.

The shrines of the Dogon are painted with murals depicting creative events, and they have rituals associated with events of the creation, such as the "descent of the Celestial Granary" and the giving of life to God's earthly representative. (See Oxtoby and Segal [2007], 27.) In African indigenous religions, ritual is a very important and central part of their faith. Our text notes: "The rituals associated with life transitions—events such as puberty, marriage, birth, and death—are often referred to as rites of passage. Many of these rituals have a three-stage structure. In the first stage the initiates are separated from their familiar world." (Oxtoby and Segal [2007], 21.) Rituals of separation are common in certain cultures. Like the aforementioned African tribes, the Papuans of New Guinea and the Melanesians of Malekula also have rites or rituals of separation from the familiar as a means of initiation. (See Ellwood [1992], 35–36.) Curiously, this is exactly what the Creation story teaches us. The Creation is a separation from our "familiar world"—our former world in the presence of God. It is a transition to a new, unfamiliar existence that, though created by God, nevertheless, places us in a situation that, at times, can feel rather desperate and precarious.

17. See James A. Wallace, Robert P. Waznak, and Guerric DeBona, *Lift Up Your Hearts—Homilies for the "A" Cycle* (New York: Paulist Press, 2004), 102–106. This same text notes: "The resurrection of Christ is not just about the glorious event of the past but about seemingly impossible transformations that occur in the present because of Christ's power and the Holy Spirit." See Wallace, Waznak, and DeBona (2004), 94.

18. Kevin W. Irwin, "The Sacramentality of Creation and the Role of Creation in Liturgy and Sacraments," in Kevin W. Irwin and Edmund D. Pellegrino, eds., *Preserving the Creation: Environmental Theology and Ethics* (Washington DC: Georgetown University Press, 1992), 79.

19. Andrew C. Skinner, *Temple Worship: 20 Truths that will Bless your Life* (Salt Lake City: Deseret Book, 2007), 196.

20. James L. Ferrell, *The Hidden Christ: Beneath the Surface of the Old Testament* (Salt Lake City: Deseret Book, 2009), 9.

21. See Ryken, Wilhoit, and Longman (1998), 181–82.

In Pauline language, the passage from the "old man" to the "new man" [2 Corinthians 5:17] . . . expresses the incorporation of the individual in the reality signified by the "types" of the first and the second Adam; the inner mutation—"putting on the new man"—is the shadow cast on the place of experience by a transformation which cannot be wholly experienced subjectively, nor observed from outside, but can only be signified symbolically as a participation in the "types" of the first and second Adam. It is in this sense that St. Paul says that the individual is "'transformed" [μεταμορφοῦσθαι—metamorphosed] into the same image [εἰκών] (2 Cor. 3:18), "conformed" [σύμμορφος] to the same image [εἰκών]' of the Son (Rom. 8:29), and that he "bears the image of the heavenly" after having "borne the image of the earthly" (1 Cor. 15:49)." (Ricoeur [1967], 274–75)

22. Ferrell (2009), 13–15.
23. Ibid., 16.
24. See Irwin, in Irwin and Pellegrino (1992), 80–81. "The doctrine of creation . . . underlines and validates the truth that history, from beginning to end, is under the sovereign purpose of God as revealed in Jesus Christ." Bernhard W. Anderson, "Creation in the Bible," in Philip N. Joranson, ed., *Cry of the Environment* (Santa Fe, NM: Bear and Company, 1984), as cited in Irwin, in Irwin and Pellegrino (1992), 100, n. 33.
25. See Kugel (1998), 47.
26. Basil the Great (AD 330–79) was a bishop of the church in Caesarea and one of the Cappadocian fathers who sought to clarify the meaning of the Trinity as originally defined at the Council of Nicaea (in AD 325). See Frederick W. Norris, "Basil of Caesarea," in Ferguson (1990), 139–41; Andrew Louth, ed., *Ancient Christian Commentary on Scripture: Genesis 1–11* (Downers Grove, IL: InterVarsity Press, 2001), 186.
27. See Basil the Great, "Hexaemeraon," 2.8, in Louth (2001), 7.
28. Though on day one the light and dark were divided, it was on day four of the Genesis account that a solar system was organized to provide us with days and nights, times and seasons, and so forth. Origen of Alexandria (flourished AD 200–54) wrote:

As those lights of heaven that we see have been set "for signs and seasons and days and years," that they might give light from the firmament of heaven to those who are on the earth, so also Christ, illuminating his church, gives signs by his precepts, that one might know how, when the sign has been received, to escape the "wrath to come," lest "that day overtake him like a thief," but that rather he can reach "the acceptable year of the Lord." Christ, therefore, is the "true light which enlightens every man coming into this world." (Origen, "Homilies on Genesis," 1.6, in Louth [2001], 19)

So we must follow Christ and trust in His word, and thereby we obtain the promise that we will not be caught unprepared at His second coming! Origen also wrote:

> Just as the sun and the moon are said to be the great lights in the firmament of heaven, so also are Christ and the church in us. But since God also placed stars in the firmament, let us see what are also stars in us, that is, in the heaven of our heart. Moses is a star in us, which shines and enlightens us by his acts. And so are Abraham, Isaac, Jacob, Isaiah, Jeremiah, Ezekiel, Daniel, and all to whom the Holy Scriptures testify that they pleased God. For . . . each of the saints, according to his own greatness, sheds his light upon us. (Origen, "Homilies on Genesis," 1.7, in Louth [2001], 19)

Thus, like our obligation to follow Christ, so also we must follow the Prophets who are the lights (as are their words) given to us to illuminate our paths in this dark and dangerous world.

29. At least one Jewish source suggests that the dividing of the light from the dark is a separation of God's life from the devil's influence. (See Louis Ginzberg, *The Legends of the Jews*, 7 vols. [Philadelphia: The Jewish Publication Society of America, 1967–69], 1:8–9, 12–13.) Bishop Ambrose of Milan (AD 333–97), instrumental in the conversion of Augustine of Hippo, also suggested that the light was a symbol of God/Christ and the darkness the devil. (See Ambrose, "Hexaemeron" 1.9, 4:1, in Louth [2001], 7, 17.) John Chrysostom (AD 347–407) took a similar position (See John Chrysostom, "Homilies on Genesis" 6.14, in Louth [2001], 16.) On a tangential note, Parry and Parry wrote:

> Light is one of the most important elements of life on earth. It enables photosynthesis, which allows plants to develop the nutrients we all need—and which also produces oxygen for us to breathe. Natural light helps the human body produce vitamin D, without which humans would die. Light is energy and a source of power. It reaches across the universe faster than anything else we know. And light is necessary to enable us to see—it reveals those things that are around us. It makes it possible for people to perform their daily labors. Jesus Christ is literally the light of the world (John 8:12; 12:46; Mosiah 16:9; 3 Ne. 18:2; D&C 10:57–58). As such, he possesses all the

qualities of light listed above, both physically and spiritually. As inhabitants of the earth, we receive the blessings of physical light as a pure gift. All humankind also receives the blessings of spiritual light, or the Light of Christ. . . . As our Light, then, Jesus Christ is the very source of our life. He energizes and empowers us to "live, and move, and have our being" (Acts 17:28). By his light we can see and know truth. Without it we are in darkness. . . . Surely it is no coincidence that when God created the earth, on the very first day he said, "Let there be light" (Gen. 1:3). (Parry and Parry [2009], 161–62)

30. Water is not solely a positive symbol. Sometimes it is associated with sanctifying and cleansing (e.g., John 7:37–39) and other times with chaos, disorder, or death (e.g., Romans 10:7; Luke 8:33). See Alonzo L. Gaskill, *The Lost Language of Symbolism* (Salt Lake City: Deseret Book, 2003), 265, 360 n. 75, 400–401 n. 42.

31. Parry and Parry (2009), 154. This same work continues: "When we come unto Christ through ordinance and obedience, we receive the Holy Ghost, who will help to quench all our spiritual thirst. The Spirit can act as an agent of our spiritual cleansing. He can change us from dry, arid souls, those who are spiritually dead, to those who are teeming with spiritual life. We thus have a source of power within us that never ends. All these things are made possible through the atonement of Christ . . . ." (Ibid., 155)

32. John M. Lundquist, "What Is Reality?" in Lundquist and Ricks (1990), 1:429–30. See also Ginzberg (1967–69), 1:12, 5:16, n. 39.

33. Nibley (1992), 284.

34. Parry and Parry (2009), 152–53.

35. One source records: "The primordial mound" or mountain that arose when God parted the waters and the land "represented order and definition amidst the unruly chaotic waters." Donald W. Parry, "Garden of Eden: Prototype Sanctuary," in Parry (1994), 137.

36. See Ryken, Wilhoit, and Longman (1998), 179–80.

37. Walter Brueggermann, *Genesis: A Bible Commentary for Teaching and Preaching* (Atlanta: John Knox Press, 1973), 29.

38. In Mosaic symbolism water was often a symbol for chaos. Lucifer has been referred to as the "chief" of "the waters" and as "the Angel of the Sea." (See Ginzberg [1967–69], 1:18.) Thus, in the Creation story water is frequently used as a symbol of the adversary—shifting, unstable, chaotic. The fact that the earth was covered with water (at the beginning of the Creation account) is traditionally interpreted as a symbol for its chaotic and disorganized state—and potentially for his influence prior to

God's intervention through the Creation. (See, for example, Clifford and Murphy, "Genesis," in Brown, Fitzmyer, and Murphy [1990], 10–11, 541, 545.)

39. Howard W. Hunter, "Reading the Scriptures," in *Ensign*, November 1979, 65.

40. See Ryken, Wilhoit, and Longman (1998), 180. Curiously, this "stands in marked contrast to later Greek and other philosophical and theological perspectives, which view the material realm as intrinsically evil and morally suspect." (Ryken, Wilhoit, and Longman [1998], 180.) God sees good in the material creation, uses the material creation, is the source of the material creation, and only expresses concern in the material creation when it is misused.

41. "Everything exists because God existed first. Therefore grace is prior to creation. The world has only a relative independence, and is—in its goodness—God's self-expression. Nothing in creation is essentially unclean. Sin is a secondary concept, and redemption means restoration. Some idea of a continuous creation is necessary. Nature must be seen as a single coherent event." Irwin, in Irwin and Pellegrino (1992), 100, n. 26.

42. See Irwin, in Irwin Pellegrino (1992), 89.

43. Ibid., 74.

44. "The fact that all things find their origin in the creative work of God means that everything, in some way, bears witness to the creation and is revelatory of the Creator. According to the Bible every rock and tree and creature can be said to testify of God, declare his glory and show forth his handiwork (Ps 8:1; 19:1; 104; 148). We might accurately speak of the creation as [a] divine messenger (cf. Ps 104:3–4)." (Ryken, Wilhoit, and Longman [1998], 181.) As Alma testified to Korihor: "All things denote there is a God; yea, even the earth, and all things that are upon the face of it, yea, and its motion, yea, and also all the planets which move in their regular form do witness that there is a Supreme Creator" (Alma 30:44).

45. Irwin, in Irwin Pellegrino (1992), 73.

46. One commentator suggested that "creation can serve the mediating function of coming to know God." Irwin, in Irwin Pellegrino (1992), 101, n. 41.

47. See Irwin, in Irwin Pellegrino (1992), 90.

48. Ibid., 90.

49. The late Pope John Paul II stated:

> The aesthetic value of creation cannot be overlooked. Our very contact with nature has a deep restorative power; contemplation of

its magnificence imparts peace and serenity. The Bible speaks again and again of the goodness and beauty of creation, which is called to glorify God (cf. Genesis 1:4ff.; Psalm 8:2; 104:1ff . . .). More difficult perhaps, but no less profound, is the contemplation of the works of human ingenuity . . . that ought to motivate people to care for their surroundings. (John Paul II, "Peace with God the Creator, Peace with All Creation: Message of His Holiness Pope John Paul II for the celebration of the World Day of Peace, 1 January, 1990," in *Origins* vol. 19, no. 28, p. 467)

50. See Beckwith (2001), 42–44.

51. One Catholic commentator suggested that the Creation story, when used as part of ritual or liturgy, teaches us about "God's nature and goodness." It also teaches us "the value of aesthetics." In a liturgical presentation of the Creation story, we learn that "that which is aesthetically pleasing reflects the glory of God." See Irwin, in Irwin and Pellegrino (1992), 88. This same source notes that "various arts collaborate with the celebration of the liturgy." Those include "architecture, painting, sculpture, music, choreography" and the like. "Everything that participants [in a ritual] see: lights and colors, the harmony of the space; everything they hear . . . ; voice, song, [music]; . . . everything they touch: offering the sign of peace, . . . contact with the various objects in worship; and every movement they are engaged in: . . . everything about the liturgy presumes a creation focus." See Irwin, in Irwin and Pellegrino (1992), 88.

52. Jerome (circa AD 347–420) was a skilled biblical exegete (or commentator) best known for his translation of the Latin Vulgate, which became the accepted biblical text in the West for centuries. Though ordained a priest, he is not known to have formally functioned in that capacity. He attended the Second Council of Constantinople (AD 381), and is known to have vigorously defended the doctrine of Mary's perpetual virginity. Jerome supported a lifestyle of extreme asceticism (or self-sacrifice), and even lived for a time as a hermit in the desert of Syria. See Michael P. McHugh, "Jerome," in Ferguson (1990), 484–86; Louth (2001), 188.

53. Ephrem the Syrian (flourished AD 363–73), a fourth-century exegete, teacher, and deacon in the Church, was also a noted writer of commentaries and hymns. He has been classed among Christian literary masters such as Dante, and was known as the "Harp of the Spirit." See Just (2003), 402; Kathleen McVey, "Ephraem the Syrian," in Ferguson (1990), 304–305; Louth (2001), 187.

54. See Jerome, "Homilies 10," and Ephrem the Syrian, "Commentary

on Genesis I," cited in Louth (2001), 6. Regarding the connection patristic sources made between the waters of the Creation and the waters of baptism, note the following about the Roman Catholic Easter Vigil. It is the time of conversion, and the Creation is seen as a perfect story to teach the participant about how God, through Christ, creates all things "good," and is about to re-create the convert from a fallen state to a status of "good" via the atonement of Christ. (See National Conference of Catholic Bishops, *The Sacramentary* [New York: Catholic Book Publishing Company, 1985], 188.) Thus as part of the liturgy of the Easter Vigil, the waters of Creation and the waters of baptism are equated, one with another, and are referred to as "the waters of rebirth" (ibid., 193). Indeed, the blessing upon the baptismal waters—given in the form of a hymn—states:

> Father, . . . in baptism we use your gift of water, which you have made a rich symbol of the grace you give us . . . At the very dawn of creation your Spirit breathed on the waters, making them the well-spring of all holiness . . . Father, look now with love upon your church . . . By the power of the Holy Spirit give to the water of this font the grace of your Son. You created man in your own likeness: cleanse him from sin in a new birth of innocence by water and the Spirit. We ask you, Father, . . . to send the Holy Spirit upon the waters of this font. May all who are buried with Christ in the death of baptism rise also with him to newness of life. We ask this through Christ our Lord." (ibid, 198–200)

The Roman Missal states that "those who are to be baptized renounce the devil individually" (ibid., 203). Baptism is a means of so doing. During this same aforementioned liturgy we find these words: "This water . . . we shall use to recall our baptism. May he renew us and keep us faithful to the Spirit we have all received." Then this prayer is added: "Be with us as we recall the wonder of our creation and the greater wonder of our redemption. Bless this water: it makes the seed to grow, it refreshes us and makes us clean . . . . By water . . . you made our sinful nature new in the bath that gives rebirth. Let this water remind us of our baptism" (ibid.). As life comes from the waters of the Creation, at baptism you are given eternal life by being made a new creation through the waters of that rite, and through Christ's Atonement, which makes those waters efficacious.

55. See Ryken, Wilhoit, and Longman (1998), 180.

56. See Julien Ries, "The Fall," in Eliade (1987), 5:256–67.

57. The term "myth," as used in reference to religious or scriptural stories, is not a derogatory term. Nor does it mean in theology what it means in

popular culture today (i.e., a fiction or made-up story). Indeed, of "myth" in religious writings, one text states that it "is not merely a tale told, but a reality lived. It is not the nature of fiction such as we read today in a novel but it is a living reality, believed to have once happened in primeval times, and continuing ever since to influence the world and human destinies." See James (1958), 17. One LDS author penned this: "The use of the word 'myth' . . . should not unsettle Latter-day Saints as it often does. In this context, 'myth' refers to sacred stories that explain the interventions of the divine into human affairs—the interventions that reveal covenant laws, temple rites, and the purpose of human existence." Lundquist, in Lundquist and Ricks (1990), 1:442.

58.   This same text continues:

> The Jorai cosmogony of the autochthonous peoples of Indochina gives an idyllic description of original man. Living with the god Oi Adei, man enjoyed a deathless existence in a paradise where he could fly like a bird and talk with plants and animals, where bundles of wicker grew on trees and shovels turned over the earth by themselves. Man had only to feed his tools; but he got drunk and did not do so, and the tools revolted. In the Sre cosmogony of Indochina, man had no need to work in the earthly paradise, since the god Ong Ndu had made him immortal; but when the primordial couple refused the god's command to dive into a well, they were punished for their disobedience by suffering, old age, and death. (Julien Ries, "The Fall," in Eliade [1987], 5:256–57)

59.   Ibid., 5:267.

60.   See Barker (2008), 81.

61.   Barker (2008), 26–27. Likewise, Richard D. Draper and Donald W. Parry pointed out:

> The Garden of Eden account (Genesis 2–3) is composed of several powerful symbols that look forward to or anticipate later temple systems. . . . For instance, the text of Genesis 2–3 explicitly identifies items directly connected to Israelite sanctuaries (including the Mosaic Tabernacle and Solomon's Temple), such as the tree of life, cherubim, sacred waters, sacred vestments, Eden's eastward orientation, and divine revelation. The Eden story also contains words and phrases used in later biblical texts that refer to the temple. (Richard D. Draper and Donald W. Parry, "Seven Promises to Those Who Overcome: Aspects of Genesis 2–3 in the Seven Letters," in Parry and Ricks [1999], 121)

62. The plants carved into the walls and doors of Solomon's Temple (1 Kings 6:29–35) certainly created the appearance of Eden for the priests who served therein. But so did a number of other elements. Real animals were constantly in use as sacrifices by ancient Israel, just as animals were constantly present in Eden, and used by Adam as sacrifices once he left the Garden (Moses 5:6.). In each of Israel's temples, cherubim are found on the veil and atop the ark (Exodus 25:18–22, 26:1, 31, 36:8, 35, 37:7–9; Numbers 7:89; 1 Samuel 4:4; 2 Samuel 6:2; 1 Kings 6:23–35, 8:6–7; 2 Kings 19:15; 1 Chronicles 13:6; 2 Chronicles 3:7–14, 5:7–8; Psalms 80:1, 99:1; Isaiah 37:16; Ezekiel 41:18–25), reminding us of the cherubim with flaming swords that served to guard or veil Eden from fallen man (Genesis 3:24; Moses 4:31; Alma 12:21, 42:2–3.). The entrance to Jerusalem's temple was oriented toward the east, recalling the situation of Eden's gate. Even the duty of the Levites to guard the sanctuary (Numbers 1:53) reminds us of the commission God gave to Adam to till, serve, protect, or guard the garden (Genesis 2:15; Moses 3:15; Abraham 5:11). Eden was said to have been filled with gold and onyx (Genesis 2:12; Ezekiel 28:13; Moses 3:12), and Israel's temple employed gold and onyx stones abundantly (Exodus 25:7, 28:9–20, 35:9, 27, 38:24, 39:6, 13; Numbers 7:86; 1 Chronicles 29:2). Adam's garden had its tree of life, and Israel had its branched and flowering lampstand, representative of Eden's tree (Exodus 25:31–40).

63. See Kurt Rudolph, "Mystery Religions," in Eliade (1987), 10:230–39.

64. Walter Burkert, *Greek Religion* (Cambridge, MA: Harvard University Press, 1985), 277.

65. Burkert (1985), 283. See also Burkert (1985), 287; Rudolph, in Eliade (1987), 10:231.

66. The ancient Greek "mystery" rites offer us curious insights into secret religious instruction. "The mysteries were so called because they were rites which were kept secret from all except the initiates. . . . The candidates underwent (1) a preparatory purification, such as a . . . washing . . . , (2) instruction in mystic knowledge, usually given behind closed doors . . . , (3) a solemn beholding of sacred objects" or symbols (Rudolph, in Eliade [1987], 10:231). The "sacred symbols" were shown to, or demonstrated for, the initiates by the temple's "hierophant"—a Greek word meaning "he who shows the sacred things" (See Fritz Graf, "Eleusinian Mysteries, in Eliade [1987], 5:83.)—"followed by (4) the enactment of a divine story, generally in the form of a pageant or play, in which the . . . divinities were impersonated, and (5) a crowning or wreathing of each of the candidates

as a full-fledged initiate" (John B. Noss, *Man's Religions*, fifth edition [New York: Macmillan, 1974], 60). See also Burkert (1985), 286. As part of the "cult of Isis," initiates were cleansed by the sprinkling of water, and then clothed in a linen garment. Next they were given a symbolic "journey through the lower world and the upper world." Finally, there was the "vesting of the initiate as the sun god . . . , or in other words [the initiate] experienced a deification." (See Rudolph, in Eliade [1987], 10:235–36.) As the rites began, nearly all light was extinguished. "Darkness shrouded the crowd thronged in the hall of mysteries as the priests proceeded to officiate by torchlight" (Burkert [1985], 288). At certain points during the rites the *epoptai* would veil themselves while the ritual was enacted (ibid., 287). This same source suggests there may be a connection between how ancient Greek mystery religions practiced their rites, and how modern Greek Orthodox usher in Easter—lights initially extinguished, the candle light spread throughout the sanctuary, and then, eventually, all lights illuminated again. (See ibid., 289; and see Graf, in Eliade [1987], 5:84.) For a description of the Greek Orthodox Easter Sunday rite, see George L. Papadeas, *Greek Orthodox Holy Week and Easter Services* (New York: no publisher listed, 1975), 448. One text notes that: "Much of Greek religion had to do with purification and holiness. The *temenos* or sanctuary was 'cut off,' set apart. The temples we admire were not places for public worship in the modern sense." Rather, they were sacred sites where only the initiated or the initiates had a right to enter. (Geoffrey Parrinder, *World Religions From Ancient History to the Present* [New York: Facts on File Publications, 1983], 150. See also Burkert [1985], 286.)

67. These mysteries were associated with the temple of Demeter Eleusinia on the hillside just outside of Eleusis, which was some fourteen miles northwest of the city of Athens. Some hold that these rites began as early as 1600 BCE, and later spread from Greece to Rome. See Graf, in Eliade (1987), 5:83.

68. The story informs us that Persephone was raped by Zeus who had taken "the form of a snake" (Burkert [1985], 297). One text notes that, at the beginning of the ceremonies, the officiator "handled a serpent" because of its symbolic connections to Demeter and Kore (or Persephone). See Rudolph, in Eliade (1987), 10:233. The parallels with the fall of Adam and Eve seem obvious.

69. Burkert (1985), 160.

70. See ibid., 286. See also Graf, in Eliade (1987), 5:84.

71. See Rudolph, in Eliade (1987), 10:233–34; Graf, in Eliade (1987), 5:83. According to one work on this subject, "mysteries are accompanied

by tales—some of which may be secret, *hieroi logoi*—mostly telling of suffering gods." Burkert (1985), 277.

72. See Noss (1974), 61. See also Burkert (1985), 159–60, and Graf, in Eliade (1987), 5:83. Sophocles said of these rites: "Thrice blessed are those mortals who have seen these rites . . . : for them alone there is life, for the others all is misery." Parrinder (1983), 289.

73. Burkert (1985), 276. One commentator on the rites stated that "the eschatological hopes"—meaning a hope for the end of the wicked world and the salvation of the faithful—"offered by the rites attracted philosophers and emperors alike." Graf, in Eliade (1987), 5:83. Related to the Eleusinian mysteries were the Orphic or Dionysian mysteries. These dated from around the sixth century BCE, (See Burkert [1985], 296.) and spread throughout the Mediterranean world, including southern Italy, Crete, and Cyprus. As part of these rites, covenants were made by the initiates to live "rules of purity," to wear certain "white garments" associated with their initiation, to avoid immorality, to live a somewhat ascetic lifestyle, and to seek to rid one's life of those things which would send the initiate, like Persephone, to the underworld. These mysteries had power to influence the reward of the initiate in the next life: "By being worthy he might hope to enjoy a better lot in the next world and at the same time increase his sense of spiritual security in this" (Noss [1974], 61). As one commentator noted, the mystery rites consisted of "things said," "things shown," and "things performed" (Christopher Partridge, ed., *Introduction to World Religions* [Minneapolis: Fortress Press, 2005], 82). Through engaging in these rites, the initiate believed he or she would have the possibility of beholding "a glorious vision of the god" and "a unification with the gods or . . . a deification of the human" in the next life. (See ibid. See also Burkert [1985], 277, 337; Rudolph, in Eliade [1987], 10:231.) One texts notes that it was "the yearning of the initiate . . . to hear the words: 'Happy and blessed one, you have become divine instead of mortal'" (Parrinder [1983], 155). So important were these rites, that in the belief of the ancient Greeks, "outside the mysteries there was little hope beyond the grave" (ibid.). As one text noted, "if the chance of initiation has been let slip in this life, it is impossible to make up for the omission after death" (Burkert [1985], 277).

74. Our English word "catechism" comes from a Greek word, and means literally to "echo" or "repeat." A catechism is a manual of instruction often used by those preparing initiates for conversion and baptism through memorization and recitation. In modern times the best-known U.S. example of such a book would be the Roman Catholic *Baltimore Catechism*. (See McBrien [1995], 236.) The Antioch catechism would have been in use

by at least the late fourth or early fifth century, and the Jerusalem version by no later than the mid-fourth century.

75. See Martimort (1986), 131.

76. Beadle and King (1984), ix; Beckwith (2001), xv. See also Beckwith (2001), 44–46.

77. As a means of instructing the illiterate of the thirteenth and fourteenth centuries, the great European Gothic cathedrals of that era were filled with stained glass windows, carvings in wood, and stone embellishments. In the fourteenth and fifteenth centuries, these were supplemented by the aforementioned "mystery plays"—ritual re-enactments of biblical stories, such as the Creation and the Fall. See Parrinder (1983), 435.

78. Beadle and King (1984), 8.

79. The "Lectionary for Mass" is the book that contains the scriptural readings to be used on any given day of the liturgical calendar in the Roman Catholic Church. Currently the lectionary is divided up into a three-year rotating cycle.

80. In the Liturgy for the "1st Sunday in Lent—Year A" the three readings used during the liturgy consist of Genesis 2:7–9, 3:1–7 (which deals with the Fall of Adam and Eve), but also include Romans 5:12–19 (which deals with Christ, as the "new Adam," redeeming man from the Fall), and Matthew 4:1–11 (which deals with the temptations of Christ which are common to all man). Regarding Matthew 4, note that Satan first tempts Jesus to satisfy the cravings of the flesh, ordering Him to turn stones into bread (Matthew 4:3). Next the devil entices Jesus to misuse His power for prideful unrighteous reasons (Matthew 4:6). Finally, Jesus is encouraged by the adversary to seek the meaningless things of this world (Matthew 4:8–9). The Romans and Matthew passages have obvious ties to the Fall. The congregation is invited to contemplate which example they have chosen to follow. Do they fall, with Adam and Eve, or do they resist Satan's temptations, as did Christ (Matthew 4:1–11). The two stories are our own. The story of the Fall depicts our personal fall, and the story of Christ's resisting the devil's temptations is a cue for each of us to do the same. (See Wallace, Waznak, and DeBona [2004], 55–60.)

81. See West (1997), 94. One text states: "On Ash Wednesday, the starting-point for the lenten journey, we view our salvation in Christ from the sober standpoint of our sinful mortality" (ibid., 91).

82. "In our reading today, the essential goodness of creation stands in stark contrast to human disobedience." (See "Liturgical Calendar and Bible Study for First Sunday in Lent—A," [Picayune, MS: St. Charles Borromeo Catholic Church, n.d.], 1, a copy of which is in the possession of

this author.) Elsewhere we read: "The Book of Genesis, the first book of the Bible, teaches that all that God has made is good. It is very good. Not until one of God's creatures decided not to serve was there chaos. The rebellion of man brought chaos. We must restore order to this chaotic world. We must realize that the world is good. It is man that must be brought to acknowledge God and His goodness and that of His creatures" (James D. Walker, *Commentator's Lectionary* [Milwaukee: The Bruce Publishing Company, 1965], 82).

83. "In choosing these readings, the Lectionary for Mass is suggesting a typological relationship between Exile and our separation from God, a parallel between expulsion and sin reminiscent of God driving the disobedient Adam and Eve from the garden. In all of the . . . readings selected for the Easter vigil, there is a strong sense of anticipation that God's promises are about to be fulfilled, that the return to God . . . is imminent" (West [1997], 100–101). In other words, the ritual teaching for that Sunday is entirely about our fall, and Christ's power to redeem us from it.

84. In one version of the children's liturgy for the first Sunday of Lent we find a recitation of the story of Satan's temptation of Adam and Eve, and their subsequent fall, followed by this statement:

> Today's story is all about temptation. . . . Like Adam and Eve, we are all tempted sometimes to do something wrong. . . . God wants us to choose to do what is right, but this is not always easy. During Lent we make promises [or covenants with God] . . . to do . . . good. Whatever we do, we try to keep in touch with God, to be less selfish and more generous. . . . The emphasis should be on doing things for Jesus, rather than simply on giving things up. (See Katie Thompson's *The Complete Children's Liturgy Book: Liturgies of the Word for Years A, B, C* [Mystic, CT: Twenty-Third Publications, 1995], 26)

In Dr. Moira Laidlaw's "liturgies online" the "lectionary generated liturgy" for the first Sunday of Lent suggests that the story of the Fall of man should be acted out. See: http://www.liturgiesonline.com.au/liturgies/main/index.php?ch_table=link4&year=A&SID=

85. For example, President Gordon B. Hinckley, in speaking of the holy temple and the story taught therein, stated that "we have sketched before us the odyssey of man's eternal journey from premortal existence through this life to the life beyond" (Gordon B. Hinckley, *Teachings of Gordon B. Hinckley* [Salt Lake City: Deseret Book, 1997], 636). Likewise, Elder Bruce C. Hafen expressed the following: "The experience of Adam and

Eve is an ideal prototype for our own mortal experience. Their story is our story. The complete cycle of their fall from innocence and their ultimate return to God typifies a general human pattern" (Bruce C. Hafen, *The Broken Heart* [Salt Lake City: Deseret Book, 1989], 37). BYU's Hugh Nibley wrote this: "The Mormon endowment . . . is frankly a model, a presentation in figurative terms . . . . It does not attempt to be a picture of reality, but only a model . . . setting forth the pattern of man's life on earth with its fundamental whys and wherefores" (Nibley [2005], xxix). Echoing the sentiments of the aforementioned brethren, another Latter-day Saint scholar has written: "What, then, . . . of the Eden story? . . . A rehearsal of the key events of Eden brings the realization that we too are privileged to leave the lone and dreary world and enter the sacred sanctuaries of the Lord, where we participate in essentially the same experiences known to our first parents before the Fall. The temple is to us as Eden was to Adam and Eve . . . . The story of Eden, in fact, [is] a light that reveals the path all must travel to return to the divine presence" (Joseph Fielding McConkie, "The Mystery of Eden," in Joseph Fielding McConkie and Robert L. Millet, eds., *The Man Adam* [Salt Lake City: Bookcraft, 1990], 23, 29–30). Similarly, in an LDS publication dedicated to an examination of the life of Father Adam, one author informed his readers: "In the mind of first-century Jews and Christians, what Adam was, we are; what Adam could become, we can become" (Stephen E. Robinson, "The Book of Adam in Judaism and Early Christianity," in McConkie and Millet [1990], 128). Indeed, it is generally held within Mormonism that Adam and Eve "are symbolic representations of all men and women" (Jolene Edmunds Rockwood, "The Redemption of Eve," in Maureen Ursenbach Beecher and Lavina Fielding Anderson, eds., *Sisters In Spirit* [Chicago: University of Illinois Press, 1992], 18). Even when in sacred precincts, Latter-day Saints are instructed that, when contemplating the Fall, they should substitute themselves for the persons of Adam and Eve. Clearly their story is our story. The message of the Fall is about us. See also Hansen (2009), 25–26, 34–35; Green (2004), 16.

86. Donald G. Bloesch, *Essentials of Evangelical Theology*, 2 vols. (Peabody, MA: Prince Press, 2001), 1:104–106. See also Elaine Pagels, *Adam, Eve, and the Serpent* (New York: Vintage Books, 1989), xxi, 74; Ricoeur (1967), 236.

87. See Jacob Neusner, *The Enchantments of Judaism* (Atlanta: Scholars Press, 1991), 53–65.

88. Ibid., 62. See also Jacob Neusner, *Genesis Rabbah: The Judaic Commentary to the Book of Genesis* (Atlanta: Scholars Press, 1985), 174,

208–209, 211, 213, 224, 230. "The story of the 'fall' is a paradigm of human conduct in the face of temptation" (Bruce Vawter, *On Genesis: A New Reading* [New York: Doubleday, 1977], 81, 90).

89. Neusner (1991), 62. One LDS author suggested: "We in essence enter Eden when we enter the temple, for there, as in Eden, we are in a place wherein God can dwell, wherein we can make covenants, receive ordinances, and learn all that is necessary to find our way back to our heavenly home" (Beverly Campbell, *Eve and the Choice Made in Eden* [Salt Lake City: Bookcraft, 2003], 57).

90. John H. Sailhamer, *The Pentateuch as Narrative* (Grand Rapids: Zondervan, 1992), 105–106, emphasis added. See also John H. Sailhamer, "Genesis," in Gaebelein (1976–92), 2:54–55.

91. J. R. Dummelow, ed., *The One Volume Bible Commentary* (New York: Macmillan Publishing, 1936), 6, 9.

92. Curiously, Muslims have specific movements they perform during prayer. For certain Muslims these prayer "forms" or movements are "connected with the name Adam, the model of humanity." For example, standing up forms the Arabic letter *alif* (ا). Bending forms the Arabic letter *dāl* (د). When prostrate, the person praying takes the shape of the Arabic letter *mīm* (م). These three letters combined form the Arabic name Adam. Thus, the person praying takes upon himself the role of Adam (آدم). See Schimmel (1986), 153.

93. As one reads scripture, it is hard to escape the fact that a recurring Adamic theme is present. The story of Adam and Eve and their Fall appears as the backdrop for numerous scriptural stories. It is not just our personal fall that appears to be depicted. But Adam clearly stands as an archetype for *all* human beings. His story can be seen in their story—and, more importantly, they are to see themselves in him. For example, Noah steps forth from the ark as the beginning of a race of humans, and immediately after God's judgments have been poured out upon the earth. Such was also the case with Adam. As with the first man, Noah was commanded by God to "Be fruitful, and multiply, and replenish the earth" (Genesis 9:1). Even Noah's relationship with the animals seems to draw upon the Adamic motif. And knowing that the great prophet of the deluge was familiar with Adam's story, surely Noah would have recognized these parallels. Likewise, Abraham's life was also filled with Adamic motifs. He and his seed are promised that they will be fruitful and multiply (Genesis 12:2–3; 17:2, 6, 8; 22:16–18; 26:3–4; 28:3; 35:11–12; 47:27; 48:3–4). In so doing, Abraham's offspring generates Israel, just as Adam and Eve give birth to the human race. Covenant Israel is no different. Her story is just as

saturated with this same Adamic symbolism—from her constant struggle with obedience to God's commands (which reminds us of the story of Adam and Eve's disobedience), to the architecture of her temples (which mirrors the Garden of Eden, as we have already pointed out).

94.   Indeed, Latter-day Saints teach that "all children who die before they arrive at the years of accountability are saved in the celestial kingdom of heaven" (D&C 137:10).

95.   Leslie F. Church, ed., *The NIV Matthew Henry Commentary in One Volume* (Grand Rapids: Zondervan, 1992), Old Testament page 7. See also Jeffery R. Holland and Patricia T. Holland, *On Earth As It Is In Heaven* (Salt Lake City: Desert Book, 1989), 107; Ginzberg (1967–69), 5:90, n. 47.

96.   Parry, in Parry (1994), 146.

97.   One text suggests that the serpent's role in Eden is a multi-faceted symbol. The serpent can represent the influence of the devil—an obvious symbol in the storyline. Thus, he symbolizes the outward influence upon each of us which seeks to tempt us and to drag us downward. Consequently, in Eden the "serpent" is already present when Adam and Eve arrive—representing the reality that there is a negative influence which exists in this Telestial world, independent of any of us. But the symbol of the serpent also highlights "a part of ourselves which we do not recognize; [the serpent] would be the seduction of ourselves by ourselves . . ." (Ricoeur [1967], 256). Thus, James says: "Let no man say when he is tempted, I am tempted of God: for God cannot be tempted with evil, neither tempteth he any man: But every man is tempted, when he is drawn away of his own lust, and enticed" (James 1:13–14). Though the devil has his day in all of our lives, we also are guilty, at times, of placing ourselves in tempting situations, or of allowing our natural man to reign, thereby bringing upon ourselves enticements and temptations. And like Eve, we are prone to shift the blame for such weakness to someone else (e.g., "the serpent beguiled me, and I did eat"—Genesis 3:13).

98.   One text notes:

> Trees are symbols of stability and strength. . . . They provide shade for those who are hot and weary. . . . They give necessary oxygen to both man and animals on the earth. Many trees are a source of delicious food . . . . The bark and leaves of certain trees have been found to have valuable medicinal qualities. Symbolically, Jesus Christ is represented by a tree . . . . The fruit also directly represents the atonement . . . . As a tree, Christ has all the symbols mentioned above. He stands firm when other plants wither. He is a place

of refuge. He provides life to all—in fact, he is *the* Life, our eternal life (John 11:25; 14:6). The fruit of his tree is nourishing above all other fruit. That fruit brings the greatest joy on earth and in eternity. He heals us through the "balm in Gilead" (Jer. 8:22), a salve that was prepared from a tree. All this points to the atonement of our Savior performed through his infinite love. (Parry and Parry [2009], 156)

99. I am convinced that one of the major reasons for this command is because of its ability to teach selflessness. We live in a day and age when modern society sees the command to "multiply" as antiquated and irrelevant. Indeed, in a twist of irony those who curtail their families for selfish reasons—careers and money being chief among them—claim that those who are obedient to this command are *really* the selfish ones. Cries of "overpopulation" and "the depletion of resources" are heard, even though numerous countries (such as Austria, Germany, Greece, and Italy) actually have a zero or negative population growth. Contrary to the reasoning of man, the Lord has said: "I, the Lord, have decreed to provide for my saints, that the poor shall be exalted, in that the rich are made low. For the earth is full, and there is enough and to spare; yea, I prepared all things, and have given unto the children of men to be agents unto themselves. Therefore, if any man shall take of the abundance which I have made, and impart not his portion, according to the law of my gospel, unto the poor and the needy, he shall, with the wicked, lift up his eyes in hell, being in torment" (D&C 104:16–18). Selfishness often keeps us from being obedient to God's commands. And yet through that selfishness we actually rob ourselves of the very blessings the commandants were designed to provide. One commentator noted: "The greatest opportunity of all, to learn eternal values and achieve heavenly potentials, resides in the responsibility and the privilege to create bodies for others of God's spirit children" (Rasmussen [1993], 7–8). We grow and become more like God when we are obedient to His command to each of us to create tabernacles for our brothers and sisters who are awaiting their chance at mortality. The First Presidency of the Church wrote:

> The Lord has told us that it is the duty of every husband and wife to obey the command given to Adam to multiply and replenish the earth, so that the legions of choice spirits waiting for their tabernacles of flesh may come here and move forward under God's great design to become perfect souls, for without these fleshly tabernacles they cannot progress to their God-planned destiny. Thus, every husband and wife should become a father and a mother in Israel to

children born under the holy, eternal covenant. (Heber J. Grant, J. Reuben Clark, Jr., and David O. McKay, in James R. Clark, comp., *Messages of the First Presidency of The Church of Jesus Christ of Latter-day Saints,* 6 vols. [Salt Lake City: Bookcraft, 1965–75], 6:177)

See also Milton R. Hunter, *Pearl of Great Price Commentary* (Salt Lake City: Stevens and Wallis, 1951), 147–48; Brigham Young, *Journal of Discourses* 4:56.

100. See, for example, Isaiah 54:1–6; Jeremiah 31:32; Ezekiel 16:8; Hosea 2; Romans 7:1–6; 2 Corinthians 11:2; Ephesians 5:21–33; Revelation 19:7 and 21:2, 9. See also Gaskill (2003), 79, 191–97, 321.

101. As the bride, Eve's covenanting through Adam represents the Church making covenants with the Father through Christ, her mediator. Parry and Parry wrote: "Because our sins separate us from God, we cannot act in our own names and have our acts be recognized by God. We must have a mediator, a savior, whose power of redemption will validate our righteous acts. We need One who is not separated from God to stand between us and God. Hence, all of our righteous acts, all of our testimonies and teachings— and all ordinances—must be done in the name of Jesus Christ, that perfect Redeemer" (Parry and Parry [2009], 9). Adam, as a representation of the Lord, has the ability to covenant directly with the Father because Adam/Christ (unlike His bride/the Church) is not disobedient.

102. Elder McConkie spoke of Adam as being "a similitude of Christ." See McConkie (1978), 449. Elder McConkie's comment comes in the context of the Apostle Paul's declaration that Christ is the "second Adam."

103. Wilson (1999), 139.

104. Rockwood, in Beecher and Anderson (1992), 17–18.

105. See, for example, Louth (2001), 67, 71; Quodvultdeus, "Book of Promises and Predictions of God" 1:3, in Louth (2001), 71; Augustine, "City of God" 22:17, in Louth (2001), 70; Jerome, "Homilies" 66, in Louth (2001), 70; Ambrose, "Letters to Laymen" 85, in Louth (2001), 71.

106. See Sailhamer, in Gaebelein (1976–92), 2:47.

107. "As Eve was bone of the bones of her husband and flesh of his flesh, we also are members of Christ's body, bones of his bones and flesh of his flesh" (Ambrose, "Letters to Laymen" 85, in Louth [2001], 71). Late in the fourth century Ambrose noted that Eve was not made in the same way Adam was. She was created from a rib, whereas Adam came from the dust. (See Ambrose, "Paradise" 10:48, in Louth [2001], 68.) Similarly, Christ's mortal birth (represented by Adam's creation) was different than that of each of us (typified by Eve's creation). Whereas we have come entirely from

another mortal (symbolized by the rib), Christ's origin is clearly different (as highlighted by the dust utilized in the creation of Adam). It is this difference in His origin and makeup that enables Him to atone, and us to exercise faith in Him.

108. Ambrose, "Paradise" 12, in Louth (2001), 76. See also Ginzberg (1967–69), 3:85; Campbell (2003), 61.

109. The book of Hebrews informs us that Christ "was in all points tempted like as we are, yet without sin" (Hebrews 4:15). In some liturgical accounts of the Fall, Adam is approached by the devil before Eve is. However, the man rejects Satan's enticements. Therefore, Lucifer moves on to Eve—and she succumbs. So it is with Christ and His Church. He was tempted or tried in all things, but did not fall. We (His bride), on the other hand, too often do give in to the allures of the adversary. Thus, just as Adam is figuratively depicted as leaving Eden to reverse the effects of what Eve had done, so also Christ left His Father's abode in the heavens in order to rectify the wrongs we have committed. "While Eve is described as 'enticed' . . . , Adam acts decisively out of obedience to God . . . (1 Timothy 2:14)" (Judd King, *A Handbook to the Pearl of Great Price* [Unpublished manuscript: 1995], S.v. Moses 4:18–19).

110. Augustine, "City of God" 22:17, in Louth (2001), 70.

111. See Ada R. Habershon, *Study of the Types* (Grand Rapids: Kregel Publications, 1974), 43–44. "We have heard about the first Adam [and how he was injured in his side in order to produce Eve]; let us come now to the second Adam and see how the church is made from his side. The side of the Lord Savior as he hung on the cross is pierced with a lance" (Jerome, "Homilies" 66, in Louth [2001], 70). "The taking of Eve from Adam's side also bears a resemblance to the relationship between the church and the Son of God, who permitted himself to become weak that others of his body (the Church) might have strength" (Roger R. Keller, "Adam: As Understood by Four Men Who Shaped Western Christianity," in McConkie and Millet [1990], 177). See John Calvin, *A Commentary on Genesis*, 2 vols., John King, ed., (Edinburgh: The Banner of Truth Trust, 1964), 1:97.

112. Quodvultdeus, "Book of Promises and Predictions of God" 1:3, in Louth (2001), 71.

113. On several occasions, President Joseph Fielding Smith taught: "The Lord said to Adam, here is the tree of knowledge of good and evil. If you want to stay here then you cannot eat of that fruit. If you want to stay here then I forbid you to eat it. But you may act for yourself and you may eat of it if you want to. And if you eat it you will die" (Joseph Fielding Smith,

"Fall—Atonement—Resurrection—Sacrament," in *Charge To Religious Educators*, second edition [Salt Lake City: The Church of Jesus Christ of Latter-day Saints, 1982], 124). See also Joseph Fielding Smith, *Answers to Gospel Questions*, 5 vols. (Salt Lake City: Deseret Book, 1993), 4:81; Joseph Fielding Smith, from a typescript, approved by President Smith, of an address given at the LDS Institute of Religion, Salt Lake City, Utah, 14 January 1961, quoted in Robert J. Matthews, *A Bible! A Bible!* (Salt Lake City: Bookcraft, 1990), 185–86, in which President Smith stated: "Mortality was created through the eating of the forbidden fruit, if you want to call it forbidden, but I think the Lord has made it clear that it was not forbidden. He merely said to Adam, if you want to stay here [in the garden] this is the situation. If so, don't eat it." One LDS scholar similarly taught:

> What, therefore, did God really say to them in the garden? I suggest that He might have said something like the following: "If you want to stay in the Garden of Eden with no cares and no possibility of growth, you should not eat from the tree of knowledge of good and evil. However, if you desire to grow and receive all that I have in store for you, you will have to leave the garden. If you eat of the tree, you will be cast out of the garden into the earth and into mortality, and you will die both temporally and spiritually, but you will open the door for yourselves and for all humanity to receive eternal life like I have. The choice is yours." In other words, God gave them information. (Roger R. Keller, "Teaching the Fall and the Atonement: A Comparative Method," in *The Religious Educator: Perspectives on the Restored Gospel*, vol. 5, no. 2 (2004), 104)

According to President Smith (and others), God was quite clear with Adam and Eve that they had a choice—and that choice was *not* which of the two contradictory commandments will you keep. On the contrary, the two choices given them were as follows. If they wanted to stay in Eden, then the fruit of knowledge of good and evil was forbidden. However, if they wanted to leave, they would have to partake of that fruit. The first couple would have been quite clear on what their options were, and what the repercussions of either choice would be.

114. President N. Eldon Tanner noted: "God has pointed out to us, as to Adam, that if we are to enjoy life to the full, there are things we must do and things we must not do. In other words, we are given everything for our benefit and blessing but we must remember that there are a few 'forbidden fruits' that will deprive us of full enjoyment and bring sorrow and regret

to us if we partake" (N. Eldon Tanner, "Where Art Thou?," in *Ensign*, December 1971, 32).

115. In Isaiah 4:1 we read: "And in that day seven women shall take hold of one man, saying, We will eat our own bread, and wear our own apparel: only let us be called by thy name, to take away our reproach." Victorinus, a fourth-century father of the church, interpreted Isaiah's words basically as follows: "In the coming day the Bride of Christ, His Church, will lay hold upon Him, saying we will eat of our own bread and wear our own clothes (i.e., "We know that it is by grace that we are saved, *after all WE can do*" — 2 Nephi 25:23), but let us be called after thy name—'Christians'—that we might have our shame or sins removed" (See Victorinus, "Commentary on the Apocalypse of the Blessed John," in Roberts and Donaldson [1994], 7:345–46). It is Christ that rules over the woman, not a mortal husband. A man may be called to preside in righteousness in the home, but he and his wife are equal partners before the Lord. It is Christ that is their head.

116. Ricoeur (1967), 240, 243.

Five

Clothing Rituals

The important place of clothing in ritual is evident to anyone who has ever attended a Roman Catholic Mass, the Divine Liturgy of the Eastern Orthodox tradition, or an LDS Temple Endowment. Clothes have a transforming effect upon those who don them, and upon those who view the ceremonial garments. Almost without exception, ritual clothing is symbolic, and is intended to be a teaching device for the wearers and for those who observe the ritual being performed.

CHANGING CLOTHES

Before beginning a rite or ordinance, it is common today—as it was in antiquity—for the participants to remove their street clothes and dress themselves in sacred or symbolic clothing.[1] Hugh Nibley noted that, throughout the ancient world—when temples still had their place as the central component of religious life— "the candidate begins on his arrival" at the temple or holy place "by removing his dusty clothes" and then he gets "dressed in white robes and slippers."[2] Elsewhere we read that "common ground or dirt must not fall from the shoe onto sacred ground, because common ground represents the flesh, morality, and humanness."[3]

Not bringing the world's filth into God's abode was considered imperative. However, the symbolism behind the physical act was more important than the act itself. This changing of apparel so common prior to participation in religious ritual suggests a transition—not just physically, but mentally or spiritually. One avoids bringing physical filth into God's house, and one must avoid bringing spiritual filth into one's own life. "White garments" we are informed, "were a symbol of inner purity" in the early church.[4] One expert in ritual apparel noted that in ancient times "all vestments were originally plain and white."[5] The color served as a sort of symbol of the sacred; something generally associated with priesthood rites and rituals. One Catholic text notes that "white is a symbol of the Creator, light, joy, purity, innocence, glory, and perfection."[6] It is certainly the most commonly employed of the scriptural and liturgical colors. Even in the secular world, white carries stronger connotations than any other color—black being a distant second. As we have suggested, the color white is associated with the concepts of purity, righteousness, holiness and innocence, victory, light, and revelation.[7] Beyond these standard ideas, white is also occasionally equated with happiness, virginity, the presence of the Holy Ghost, and spiritual dedication or mastery.[8] One commentator on the color suggested that, "as white is a reflection of all the beautiful colors of the spectrum, so too our lives must reflect all the multifaceted beauty of the Savior's gospel light."[9]

Elsewhere we read: "Inevitably, white, the absolute colour [sic] of light, became a symbol of purity, truth, innocence and the sacred or divine . . . . White is the positive side of the black-white antithesis in all symbol systems. It is also the colour [sic] of initiation, the novice, neophyte or candidate (the Latin word for which means 'shining white') and of rites of passage, including baptism, confirmation, marriage."[10]

The changing of one's clothes, and the donning of white apparel (or liturgical clothing) meant that the individual engaging in the ceremony or ordinance was aware that he or she was about to enter into a covenant to be new or different than he or she had previously been.[11] It was a public statement about an inner transition—a transition of heart, mind and desires. In the fourth century Cyril wrote: "As soon, then, as ye entered, ye put off your tunic; and this was an image of *putting off the old man with his deeds.*"[12] One commentator wrote the following regarding the act of changing from street clothes to ritual clothing: "We symbolically leave the world behind by changing our worldly garments. *We change into clothing of white, symbolic of the Atonement cleansing, as if we were washed white in the blood of the Lamb.*"[13] The white garments of the initiate have ever been "a sign of innocence and purity."[14] Applying this practice of ritually changing clothes to the Latter-day Saints, Hugh Nibley noted: "When we enter the temple, we leave one world and step into another. Conversely, when we leave the temple, we leave one world . . . and return to the other. If the Latter-day Saints are going to continue building temples, they must make up their minds as to which world they are going to live in."[15] The transition from street clothes to sacred clothes symbolized among the ancients that they *had* decided which world they wished to live in!

Because the clothing donned tends to vary, the symbolic meaning also varies. As suggested above, the simple white clothing of the early Christian initiates was primarily a symbol of purity, victory, atonement, fidelity, and any related concept. Other pieces of ritual apparel likely have additional meaning. However, the general concept of clothing an initiate—regardless of the garb—consistently suggests separation or consecration. It implies a rejection of the world and its ways. As one text noted, in the ritual investiture of the initiate "there is a leveling process—they may be . . . dressed in such a way as to erase individuality . . . . Neophytes are often isolated from the everyday world."[16] Elsewhere we are told that in sacred ceremonies "everyone wears white clothing, which symbolizes . . . an equality in the sight of God that creates unity and oneness in his children."[17] Thus, one invested with a ritual article of clothing is now set apart—apart from the world, from the profane, from one's secular associations, and so forth.[18] But one is also made "level" or "equal" to those with whom he or she worships. Of this principle, Andrew C. Skinner wrote:

God is not whimsical, requiring some things from one person but a little more or a little less from another. That is precisely one powerful message of the temple. No one is better than another. As President James E. Faust said: "Fundamental to temple worship is the principle that God is no respecter of persons." Within the hallowed walls of the temples, there is no preference of position, wealth, status, race, or education . . .

Sometimes we hear it said that life isn't fair. True enough, I suppose. But we never have to worry about that being true in the temple. All is fair, and all are equal . . . So important is this status of equality before the Lord that in the temple all are dressed alike. That is, every sister wears white clothing, the same as every other sister; every brother wears white clothing, the same as every other brother.

. . . The beggar and the banker, the learned and the unlearned, the prince and the pauper sit side by side in the temple and are of equal importance if they live righteously before the Lord God.

From his own experience, Elder Russell M. Nelson of the Quorum of the Twelve Apostles provides a masterful lesson about equality in the temple: "In the temple . . . age, nationality, language—even position in the Church—are of secondary significance. I have attended many endowment sessions when the President of the Church participated. Every man in the room was accorded the same high regard that was extended to the President. All sit side by side and are considered equal in the eyes of the Lord. Through a democracy of dress, temple attendance reminds us that 'God is no respecter of persons.'"

It is significant that the holiest spot on earth, the place where heaven and earth intersect, strongly reaffirms our equal status before God the Father and his Son Jesus Christ. All are alike unto God. Temple clothing is a symbol not only of purity but also of equality.[19]

The changing of clothing prior to engaging in ritual was an important symbol among the ancients and is an important symbol among modern practitioners of religious rites. The physical change represents a spiritual transition, and a rejection of the world. The color white (where present) reminds the practitioner of the need to be clean, and the means by which that may be accomplished. The uniformity of clothing among initiates teaches that all are alike unto God.

VESTING AND VESTMENTS

The vesting of those who would serve in the temple with "sacred vestments" was a standard feature of ancient Israel's practice.[20] One source notes:

> When high priests and priests served in the temple, they wore sacred clothing, which was an integral part of the temple setting . . . . Sacred vestments served a number of purposes: 1. Putting on sacred vestments is related to putting on Christ and his holiness . . . . When we put on Jesus Christ we accept him and his atonement, and we become like him. 2. Sacred vestments carry with them symbolisms that point to the blessings of the atonement . . . . 3. Sacred vestments represent the person who wears them. The expression "keep your garments spotless" (Alma 7:25) means to keep yourself spotless, and the person who is "clothed with purity" and who wears "the robe of righteousness" (2 Ne. 9:14) is the one who is pure and righteous. . . . When mortal worshipers wear sacred vestments, they are imitating celestial beings, including God, angels, and redeemed souls, who all wear sacred clothing. . . . 5. Sacred vestments anticipate the resurrection, when we will be clothed with an immortal body.[21]

As in ancient Israel, in Mesopotamia those who participated in temple rites had to wear special linen priestly garments.[22] The "priestly clothing" worn during temple service to God "was intended to represent the garb of God and of the angels . . . . Dressing in special clothing in the temple denotes a change in role, from that of mortal to immortal, from ordinary human to priest or priestess, king or queen."[23] Implied in this statement is the idea that the priest or priestess is somehow functioning as a symbol for the divine. Priestly services, and the accompanying liturgical garments, suggest a divine investiture of authority in the individual functioning in the capacity of priest or priestess. One text notes: "Because the priestly clothing [of biblical times] was considered to be divine in origin, it gave the wearer authority to act as a representative of God among men."[24] The common practice of donning "priestly clothing" has long been a sign of consecration and preparation for "spiritual duties" (Exodus 29:1–9, 40:12–15; Leviticus 6:11, 16:1–4).[25] The belief that the priestly garments were sacred or holy is evidenced by the fact that when they wore out, they were not to be discarded, but rather had to be burned in the temple during the Feast of Tabernacles.[26]

In a rather curious account of a vision had by Levi, the third son of Jacob and Leah, we learn that he saw in vision seven men dressed in white clothing who initiated him for priestly service. The account tells that, as part of that initiation, these men or angels whom he viewed in his vision "washed [Levi] with pure water," and "anointed [him] with holy oil." He also indicates that these ministers "put on [him] something made of linen" and spoke to him of "a new name." The beings "dressed in white" commanded Levi to "arise [and] put on the vestments of the priesthood." Among the articles of clothing he was commanded to don were "the robe of truth," a cap or miter for his head, a "girdle" or sash, and "the apron for prophetic power."[27] Levi's clothing mirrors items worn by the high priest of Hebrew Bible times.[28] And the ritually clothed high priest mirrored Christ—the "great high priest" (Hebrews 4:14). One text on the symbolic clothing of those functioning in ancient temples states:

> As the High Priest was a type of the Great High Priest, Jesus, so the garments of the High Priest were typical of the character of Jesus Christ. Likewise, as the sons of the High Priests were priests and as we who are the sons of God are called to be priests, even so the dress of the priests typifies the character of believers. The chief lesson to be learned from these robes is, therefore, the character which is essentially Christ's, and then the character of believers in their relationship to Him.[29]

In other words, the high priest's temple vestments were each a symbol of Jesus' "character," divine attributes, or some aspect of His ministry.[30] "Aaron [as the high priest] was clothed upon with these garments, thus fitting him for the office to which he was called, and covering him with a dignity he did not otherwise possess, for the robes were part of his consecration. What a contrast to the Lord Jesus Christ. Character, not clothes, fitted Him."[31] The priests of the temple were fallen human beings, as all mankind are. The clothes of the temple and tabernacle mirrored the righteous attributes of Christ. The imperfect human high priest needed them to qualify him for the work, as he did not naturally possess Christ's attributes to the degree necessary to save himself. Christ, on the other hand, having the divine attributes, needed no ceremonial robes to qualify Him for His divinely appointed assignment. He was what all priests were called to be—holy! The ritual clothing utilized in ancient temples was a reminder to those who viewed the priest, whom he represented. For the priest himself, the clothing was a symbol of what he was being called to become and what the scope and focus of his service were to reflect. Every item of priestly clothing has some symbolic meaning or merit. To assume they were aesthetic only is to miss the teaching intended.[32]

Aprons and Ephods

In the twenty-eighth chapter of the book of Exodus, we are told of the clothing to be worn by a temple priest when he officiated before the Lord. In verse four we read: "And these are the garments which they shall make [for the priest to wear]; a breastplate, and an ephod, and a robe, and a broidered coat, a mitre, and a girdle: and they shall make holy garments for Aaron thy brother, and his sons, that he may minister unto me in the priest's office." Although there is not absolute agreement in the scholarly community, there is ample support for the belief that the priestly ephod was an apron.[33]

As with the ancient temple priests of Hebrew Bible times, the wearing of an apron during religious rituals also takes place today in certain Judeo-Christian traditions. For example, in Roman Catholicism bishops and popes are wont, during certain liturgical rites, to wear "a small, silk [or linen] apron" known as a "gremial" or "gremiale" (which means literally "lap").[34] One commentator pointed out that "The wearing of the . . . apron . . . by Roman Catholic clergy is a vestige of ancient priestly dress used in the temple."[35] The original symbolic meaning of the apron in Roman Catholicism appears to have been lost. Thus today it is primarily for practical purposes. In a slightly different vein, in certain rites celebrated by U.S. Jews in the nineteenth and early twentieth centuries, we find the use of ceremonial clothing.[36] Significantly, an "apron" was donned during these rituals, and was said to be "an ancient garment symbolizing purity and [was authorized to be] worn only by the 'elect of the Lord'."[37] These Jewish initiates also "wore a white robe 'from shoulders to feet'."[38]

We know that anciently aprons often served as symbols for "priesthood"[39] and "work."[40] Consequently, when the high priest who served in the tabernacle or temple prepared for his service therein, he donned the apron (Exodus 28).[41] He was engaged in the "work" of the Lord; a work that required that he be in possession of "priesthood" power.

In Genesis 3:7 we learn that Adam and Eve "sewed fig leaves together, and made themselves aprons."[42] Of the relationship between Adam and Eve's aprons and those worn by the priest of the ancient temple, one source informs us:

> Adam and Eve, while in the garden, possessed two items of clothing that apparently held ritual meaning: the apron (Genesis 3:7) and the garment of skins (see Genesis 3:21) . . . . No doubt [the apron] held some sort of ceremonial significance for the first couple . . . . It is quite likely that these vestments, belonging to Adam and Eve and obtained while in the garden, served as archetypes for later sacral vestments belonging to the Israelite temple system.[43]

While the Adamic apron may have been the prototype for the high priest's temple apron, Adam and Eve's article seemed to have symbolism beyond simply priesthood and work (though it likely represented that also). We know that anciently both aprons and figs symbolized fertility and reproduction.[44] One scholarly source noted, "In ancient Semitic custom, young children ran about with a loose shirt or cloak. As they reached sexual maturity, they began to wear an 'apron' or loincloth . . . wearing [an apron] represented adulthood."[45] Of course, the symbols of fertility and reproduction are important because it wasn't until the fall that Adam and Eve were able to "multiply and replenish" the earth as they had been commanded (Moses 5:11). Thus, appropriately, upon placing themselves in a position to "be fruitful and multiply," Adam and Eve donned the very symbols of their newly received power.[46]

In what might appear to be a different interpretation of the same symbol, Elder James E. Talmage associated figs with the covenant people.[47] Thus when Adam and Eve, in accordance with God's will, provoked the Fall, they became the first of God's covenant people, and for that reason donned fig leaves.[48] In reality this explanation is completely in line with aprons as symbols of work, priesthood, and procreation.[49] The conscious choice to obey God and become one of His covenant people is also a conscious choice to enlist in His work of building His kingdom upon the earth. Part of that "work" is the rearing of a righteous posterity, as He commanded all from Adam and Eve onward. Thus the aprons properly stand for a call to work and serve in a priesthood capacity as God's covenant people.

HEAD COVERINGS

The head is a fairly common symbol in scripture, and is regularly the focus in religious rites or rituals. Heads are anointed, blessed, bowed, cursed, covered, and crowned. In each case a ceremonial act is performed on a head that has implications for the entirety of the person receiving the rite. As it relates to liturgical head coverings, that which men don and that which women wear is traditionally different, both in appearance and in symbolic intent.

In the scriptures, men are constantly said to be wearing hats or "miters," particularly in association with temple service (Exodus 28:4, 37, 39; 29:6; 39:28, 31; Leviticus 8:9, 16:4; Zechariah 3:3–5). Hats, caps, crowns, and the like can represent "authority," "victory," "wisdom," and "power."[50] Anciently, the covered head was also a symbol of nobility and freedom.[51] The Mosaic high priest wore simultaneously a miter and crown (Leviticus 8:9) because his life typified Christ, the eternal King, who possessed both power and authority. The caps or bonnets worn by the priests that worked in the Mosaic tabernacle (Exodus 39:28) were apparently different from the turbanlike hat worn by the high priest. The headdress of the temple priests was made of white linen. Some Jewish sources suggest they too may have been turbanlike,[52] while others hold that the priests' caps were flat on top.[53] These caps worn by the Mosaic priests, during their priestly service in the temple, symbolized "holiness and righteousness"—two attributes which are "an important factor for those who hold the responsibility of leadership, and particularly those who lead in religious affairs. This was decidedly true of the Lord Jesus Christ, our Great High Priest."[54] This same call to be "holy" and "righteous" is extended to all who lead or serve in the kingdom.

One commentary on the clothing of the priests who served in the Old Testament temple or tabernacle notes: "The word 'bonnet' is derived from a word which means 'to elevate' or 'lift up.' How suggestive! . . . Has not Christ our Great High Priest lifted us to heavenly places and made us kings and priests unto Him? Not one of us was of ourselves worthy of such honor. He humbled Himself that we might be exalted. Let us therefore walk worthy of the vocation to which we have been called."[55]

Thus, when the temple priests donned their priestly "bonnets" or "caps" the act implied that they were entering into a covenant to walk up to the promises made and the calling received.

In Exodus 28:36 we learn that the high priest wore a metal plate on the front of his cap, which bore the inscription "Holiness to the Lord." Though only the high priest was commanded to wear such an inscription, certainly what it represented was expected of all of God's priests. Without personal worthiness—holiness—all that the temple priests did was a mere form and a mockery of holiness! The high priest represented the people before God. Thus God's call to him to be holy before the Lord was a call to all priests in Israel to be holy before the Lord—to consecrate their hearts and minds to Jehovah. That declaration of "holiness to the Lord" was to influence their labors, their utterances, their thoughts and desires, and the paths they pursued—not just in the temple, but in their daily walk.[56] Thus, symbolically speaking, all who donned the cap of the priest were really donning a commitment to live in "holiness *before* the Lord" because they had dedicated their lives *to* the Lord.[57] The placement of the plate on the forehead reminds us of the fact that: "It is the head that controls the whole of the body."[58]

Curiously, when the book of Exodus speaks of priests "putting" on caps or bonnets, the meaning of the Hebrew is to "tie" or "bind" them on. One commentary on the clothing of the Mosaic tabernacle's officiants states: "The word 'put' in Exod. xxix.9, where we read: 'And put the bonnets on them,' is the word 'bind' in the original" Hebrew.[59] Confirming this claim, *The New Oxford Annotated Bible* translates Exodus 29:9 as follows: "Then you shall bring [Aaron's] sons . . . and tie headdresses on them."[60] *Young's Literal Translation* reads: "And his sons thou dost bring near, and hast . . . bound on them bonnets."[61] Another translator renders the salient portion of this passage: "You must also have [Aaron's] sons come up, and then . . . fasten caps on them."[62] The *Good News Bible* gives the command: "Tie caps on their heads."[63] Finally, the *Moffatt Translation* renders the verse: "Bring his sons and robe them, . . . tying on their caps."[64] In each of these translations it appears that the cap worn by the Aaronic priests who functioned in Moses' tabernacle was in some way tied or bound to their head, body, or the robe that they wore.[65] While we cannot be dogmatic about exactly how these caps were "tied" to the priests, the idea of binding or connecting the cap to the other priestly clothing seems likely. Symbolically speaking, the implications of this act are highlighted by a statement from the book of Proverbs. There we read: "For as he thinketh . . . , so is he" (Proverbs 23:7). We know that anciently, among other things, the head served as a symbol for ruling or leading.[66] We use phrases like "he is the head of his family" or "he is the head of the company." These colloquialisms imply literal leadership (i.e., the person is the head or ruler of some organization or body). However, the head as a symbol for ruling can also imply the truism that one's head governs one's body. As President Spencer W. Kimball pointed out: "The statement, 'As a man thinketh, so is he,' could equally well be rendered 'As a man thinketh, so does he.' If one thinks it long enough he is likely to do it."[67] Thus, what one thinks rules, governs, or determines what one does. The body follows the mind, as it were. Tying the cap to the body (or clothing of the body) suggests that what one thinks will determine how one lives and what one does. If one learns to control the mind one learns to control the entire person. The converse is also true. If one does not control his mind, he will have no control over his body. Indeed, the body (with all of its passions and desires) will rule the man, rather than the man ruling it.[68]

Hugh Nibley wrote that the "white robe and linen cap of the Hebrew priesthood" as "described in Exodus [28:4, 39:1–31] and Leviticus [8:7–9] and the third book of Josephus's *Antiquities*" [7:1–7] seem to parallel "some Egyptian vestments" and also the robes and hats worn at college commencement ceremonies.[69] One Roman Catholic scholar made a similar connection between the cap worn during university commencement exercises and that worn by Christian clerks as part of their ecclesiastical dress.[70] Apparently the university usurped that which had initially been reserved for the priesthood. Nibley referred to the tassel or ribbon attached to the commencement hat as the "the emergent Flame of Full Enlightenment."[71] Another source spoke of these same ribbons or tassels as "the resplendent Light [of] God"[72]—a representation of revelation and the influence of the Holy Spirit on the wearer. During graduation exercises the tassel is transferred from one side of the head to another. This act is seen as both a symbol of graduation (from one degree or order to a higher degree or order), and also as a symbol of the opposites that necessarily exist in all things (see 2 Nephi 2:11, 15).[73] One LDS source suggested: "The wearing of the cossack [sic] (robe), the apron, the stole, and the mitre by Roman Catholic clergy is a vestige of ancient priestly dress used in the temple."[74] If that is the case, then the "lappets," "infula," or "fanons" (i.e., ribbons) that hang from the back of the mitre of the Catholic Bishop (and some abbots) during liturgical rites seem curious. Could these be connected to the ribbons or tassels of the academic cap, which themselves stemmed from the Jewish priestly cap? One can only conjecture, but the consistent design element is curious. Regardless, the symbolism of the priestly cap is important. It reminded the priest who donned it of who he represented and what authority he operated under. It symbolized the fact that his thoughts would control his actions. It highlighted his need to think and act as God would—for he stood as a symbol of his God when he officiated in the priesthood. It reminded him of the need to be Spirit-directed, and the need to be a recipient of revelation in his priestly calling. And it foreshadowed not only the opposites that exist in life but also the dual authority that was extant in the earthly Church.

In many ancient cultures, priestesses were depicted as wearing veils.[75] So it was in early Christianity. Indeed, one scholar suggested that "the practice of women covering their heads in the Catholic and Eastern churches (traditionally with a veil)" stems directly from the Apostle Paul's dictate that a "woman's head should be covered during prayer" (see 1 Corinthians 11:4–7, 13–15).[76] The symbolic meaning of veils is typically contingent upon their cultural and liturgical employment. For example, in many cultures, veils symbolize chastity personified. They indicate that one is modest and filled with virtue.[77] They suggest a "renunciation of the world."[78] Thus, in an apparent display of modesty, we read that Rebekah "lifted up her eyes, and when she saw Isaac . . . she took a veil and covered herself" (JST Genesis 24:69–70).[79]

An additional symbolic meaning of the veiled face can be that of submission to righteously held and exercised authority.[80] As we have noted earlier in this text, the veiling of the face makes one a symbol of the bride of Christ and, consequently, should not be seen as a representation of the oppression of women by men who exercise "unrighteous dominion" (D&C 121:36–37, 39, 41–44). Highlighting the bride/bridegroom relationship, the apostle Paul counseled: "Wives, submit[81] yourselves unto your own husbands, as unto the Lord. For the husband is the head of the wife, even as Christ is the head of the church: and he is the saviour of the body. Therefore as the church is subject unto Christ, so let the wives be to their own husbands in every thing. Husbands, love your wives, even as Christ also loved the church, and gave himself for it" (Ephesians 5:22–25). One scholar pointed out that anciently

> the relation between a god and his people was represented as one of marriage . . . . Thus, in the Old Testament Jahveh is frequently imagined as the husband of Israel . . . . Hosea, for example, thinks of Israel as an unfaithful wife who is still beloved by her husband and is forgiven and restored. Paul takes up the Old Testament idea and conceives of the relation between the Church and Christ as one of marriage . . . . The book of Revelation culminates in the glowing description of the Church as the Bride of Christ, and . . . the submission of a wife to her husband is in some way to represent the obedience which the Church owes to Christ.[82]

Note Paul's emphasis in Ephesians 5. He indicates that a wife's "subjection" to or "cooperation with" her husband is a symbol for the bride (Church) subjecting herself (male and female) to the Bridegroom, who is Christ. The bride of Christ, His Church, is to live in subjection to its Bridegroom and Savior. The donning of a veil symbolizes the Church's willingness to do so. Anciently, the veil carried very strong connotations of blindness, unbelief, a lack of faith, obscured vision or sight, the concealment of certain aspects of truth or deity, and so on. To be veiled implied that one stood in a "pre-enlightened state," and was in ignorance of certain bits of "hidden or esoteric knowledge."[83] The veiled face is not a statement about the spiritual ignorance of women. On the contrary, it is a statement about the spiritual blindness of all mankind, including those in the Church—covenant Israel. Thus, one commentator wrote, "Paul reinterprets and spiritualizes this veil to represent the Jewish inability to understand the Scriptures correctly."[84] Similarly, Isaiah scholar Edward Young noted that God depicts the bride of Christ as veiled because she is spiritually blind

and ignorant outside her relationship with the Lord.[85] One dictionary of biblical imagery states: "As an image of concealment, the veil
also has the negative meaning of a mind that is cut off from the
truth. Paul pictured the unbelieving mind as having a veil over it
(2 Corinthians 3:12–16) and the gospel as being veiled to people
who disbelieve it (2 Corinthians 4:3)."[86] Thus, in antiquity when
the woman clothed herself in a veil, in part, that act symbolized her
acknowledgment that the Church (or covenant Israel) did not see
clearly, and therefore needed its God (and His earthly representatives) to guide the members of the Church safely home. Submission
of the will to the bridegroom was the only way that this safe return
could be accomplished—and the veil was a frank acknowledgment
of that fact. Thus, contrary to modern attitudes, the veiled face can
be a strongly positive image in scripture.[87]

There is one other symbolic connotation behind the scriptural
and liturgical employment of facial veils that seems important
here. Again from the Apostle Paul we read that a woman (during
prayer) "ought . . . to have power on her head because of the angels"
(1 Corinthians 11:10). The *RSV* translates the verse, "The woman
should have a veil on her head."[88] The Greek, however, would be
more accurately rendered "the woman should have Authority on
her head."[89] The meaning of this passage is somewhat unclear,
and scholars are far from united on what Paul intended his readers to understand. Some commentators and translators have suggested that the verse is implying that women should always be in
subjection to a man.[90] However, the Greek does not support this
reading. One commentator on the passage noted, "Far from being
a symbol of the woman's subjection to man, therefore, her head-
covering is what Paul calls it—authority: in prayer and prophecy
she, like the man, is [acting] under the authority of God."[91] In
the writings of Ambrosiaster, we are informed "the veil signifies
power."[92] One commentator suggested that the phrase "because
of the angels" meant that the angels would not recognize the
"authority" of the Corinthian women when they participated in
the ordinance of prayer if they did not choose to come attired as
God had commanded them.[93]

Though the veil has many potential meanings, the ancient use of veils among Christians meant at least this: she who donned the veil was committed to living a virtuous life—faithful to covenants. The veiled woman symbolized the bride of Christ (male and female), and the need of that bride to be closely associated with the Bridegroom if salvation was to be achieved. And finally, the veiled woman implied divine authority acknowledged by angels and God.

ROBES OR STOLES

There are numerous references in the scriptures to people wearing robes, particularly in relation to their serving in the temple or tabernacle. One source states, "In priestly tradition, special outerwear depicted power."[94] The British typologist, J. C. Cooper, indicated that robes are standard symbols for "the power of heaven" or priesthood, and the wearer is to be viewed as the "earthly representative" of God.[95] One expert in biblical clothing wrote, "some traditions," both in the Old and New Testaments, "portray the outer garment of special persons as conveying power."[96]

The early Christians had an article of liturgical clothing—a robe of sorts—which they would wear during sacred rites. It was often referred to as an "orarium" or "orarion," though today it is more commonly known as a "stole"—a term that comes from a classical Greek word meaning "a long flowing robe." There are written accounts of priesthood holders wearing the stole or orarion during sacred ceremonies at least as early as the Council of Laodicea (AD 363).[97] The item is still worn today (in a somewhat modified manner) in Roman Catholicism, Eastern Orthodoxy, and in certain protestant denominations. One text suggested that the wearing of the robe or stole "by Roman Catholic clergy is a vestige of ancient priestly dress used in the temple."[98]

This sacred vestment originally consisted of a plain white long piece of fabric—usually linen[99]—which was worn over the left shoulder (if one was a lower order of the priesthood), but would be moved to a different position if one was ordained to a higher order of the priesthood.[100] After the fourth century deacons (during sacred rituals) would wear it over their left shoulder, with it tied (on their right side) at the hip via a string or cord.[101] It extended from the shoulder to mid-calf in the front and back of the wearer. The location or placement of the garment symbolized the rank held by the wearer.[102]

The robe, stole, or orarion was not limited to men. One sixth century canon from a Jacobite Christian community states of deaconesses that, like men who are serving in a liturgical capacity, women engaged in similar rituals were to wear "an *orarion* on the shoulder" also.[103] This established the divine authorization of all who participated in the rites—male or female.[104]

We find numerous interpretations of the symbolism supposedly inherent in the orarion or robe. For example, one text notes that whereas the sacred undergarment worn by officiants in priesthood rites was designed to "cover" the nakedness of the wearer, the robe was "worn as the symbol of office and authority."[105] Thus, one text on the history of religious vestments notes that when the "stole" or "orarium" was worn by the pope it stood as a symbol of his "universal jurisdiction" or priestly authority.[106] Elsewhere we are informed that "the robe carries with it dignity, and also that which belongs to royalty."[107] This same source states: "Royalty is the underlying truth of the garment" referred to as "the robe." It symbolizes "that royalty which belonged to the Christ of God, the Great High Priest."[108] Consequently, it symbolizes the royalty of the office that those who serve in His stead have been called to. They are not just priests, but also kings! The orarion was often seen as a representation of the divine nature of the wearer—or of his or her call to be deified by God. As an example, one text dealing with the fourth-century Synod of Laodicea makes the following points about the stole or orarium. "St. John Chrysostom . . . [says] that this piece of dress was worn over the left shoulder, and that as it swung back and forth [when the wearer moved] it called to mind the wings of angels."[109] Similarly, one Eastern Orthodox text states:

Byzantine vestments . . . hold a kind of functional mystical significance in that their symbolism is directed toward "transforming" the celebrant as he assumes them for liturgical celebration. In accordance with [his] preparation for the liturgy, the clergymen take on the garments of the divine. The priest is girded in purity and his outer appearance tells the congregation of the "new man" as he appears in the liturgy. The deacon, moving his orarion [stole] in the manner of the movement of the angels' wings, prepares the congregation for the heavenly experience. And, indeed, the bishop [or robed priesthood holder] becomes the icon [or visible symbol] of Christ as the congregation is lifted into the divine presence. . . . The vestments themselves become mystically the wings of angels, the robe of Christ, and the glorious garments of the Saints.[110]

In other words, as the robed priesthood holder moves about in the sanctuary or temple, his orarion or priestly robes wave or flap as the wings of angels. Symbolically, those viewing the rites performed are to be reminded that the robes and the rituals are to make those who participate like God and one with God.[111]

Related to the idea that the robe, stole, or orarion suggests the divinity or potential deification of the wearer, one Catholic text suggests: "The *stole* . . . represents immortality, the yoke of obedience, and the reign of Christ."[112] Those who wear it are committing to take upon themselves a spirit of obedience to Christ in the hope of gaining the immortality that Christ offers to all those who love and serve Him. One author penned this about the priestly robes of antiquity and their connection to immortality: "The classic robe of the initiate throughout the East has always been and still is the pure white wrap thrown over the shoulder, which also represents an embrace . . ."[113] The embrace itself is a symbol of God's love and acceptance.

In the fourth century "Ephrem the Syrian . . . used the veil [of the temple] and the robe [of its priest] to describe the incarnation" of Jesus.[114] In other words, both were symbols of Christ. Consequently, to take upon oneself the orarion or robe was to symbolically take upon oneself Christ (or His attributes). The "white robe reaching to the ground"—worn by Roman Catholic priests, and sometimes called an "alb"—"signifies purity of life and also recalls the white garment in which Christ was robed by the mocking Herod."[115] Consequently, the robe is a call to purity, but also to sacrifice and submission.

One commentator explained why a priestly robe, stole, or orarion would be commanded by God to be worn during sacred services. "When [robes] are used [in ritual or ceremonies] the attention of the worshipers is more easily focused on the religious messages conveyed by the words spoken . . . , and the feelings which are associated with the . . . service of divine worship are naturally sustained by their use."[116] In other words, the priestly garments worn by the ancients and some moderns in their most holy rites are designed to help participants focus on the message behind the rituals. They are teaching tools that, when understood, add to the meaning of the covenants or oaths taken in association with those articles of clothing.

Sashes and Cinctures

In the Hebrew Bible the Mosaic priests were to wear a sash or girdle around their waist (Exodus 29:9; Leviticus 8:7) when working in the tabernacle.[117] This sash or belt was worn on top of the priestly robe, tied, with the ends hanging down.[118] Modern priests, such as those in the Eastern Orthodox tradition, also wear a sash or "cincture" as part of their priestly vestments.

Multiple symbols have been associated with this ancient liturgical garment. For example, in certain periods and regions the wearing of a sash symbolized chastity or virginity.[119] One commentator suggested that the priestly sash was "symbolic of continence, self-restraint, chastity, and patient suffering."[120] Thus, just as the priest physically bound himself with the sash, he morally and spiritually bound himself to the Lord—promising to keep the covenants he had entered into.[121] Since priests in the Mosaic dispensation donned the girdle in anticipation of performing their sacred work, some have suggested that the sash or cincture may also represent the principle of work (e.g., "Therefore, gird up thy loins for the work"—D&C 112:7). One text on the clothing of ancient temple priests states: "The girdle . . . is nearly always a symbol of service, the girded loins denoting readiness for action. This must always be the attitude of the priest and it is certainly true of Christ."[122] One who believes himself worthy to participate in sacred ceremonies must first qualify himself by being a servant in the kingdom. One's willingness to lay down his or her life in building the kingdom in large measure qualifies him or her to participate in such holy rites. Finally, as an additional insight into the possible symbolic meaning of the priestly sash or cincture,[123] one text states: "[It] is symbolic of the scourge ordered by Pilate (John 19:1)."[124] In other words, he who binds himself with the sash is willingly taking upon himself the role of Christ, including the obligation to suffer and sacrifice for the kingdom, and for God's children. The imagery is a powerful metaphor for the Christian's covenant responsibility to live Christ's life—to give (as much as possible) as He gave. It reminds the wearer that being a faithful Christian will not be easy. Rather, it will require sacrifice and, at times, a degree of pain or suffering.

Although never explicitly mentioned in scripture, the tying of bows is implied (Exodus 29:9; Leviticus 8:7). If a sash was worn around the waist of the priest, it was most likely tied in a knot or bow. One LDS commentator noted that the temple is "the knot that ties earth and heaven together."[125] Consequently, the ancient priest who tied a bow knot on his liturgical clothing was reminded (through that act) that via the covenant process, he binds or ties himself to God which, of course, is exactly what covenants do. President John Taylor is said to have taught that making a bow knot represents "the marriage covenant between man and wife."[126] Similarly, one British typologist indicated that bows on clothing were a symbol of the combination of the "masculine and feminine."[127] In some Eastern cultures, the tying of a bow knot was a marriage custom that symbolized the binding of the two people; hence came the old cliche, "tying the knot."[128] Of course, in religious rites (other than marriage), the bride is the Church and the groom is Christ. Thus, the tying of bow knots suggests the participant's covenant relationship with Christ.

FOOTWEAR

Shoes have basically three symbolic connotations in scripture and ancient temple worship: enslavement and poverty (Isaiah 20:2–4; Micah 1:8; 2 Samuel 15:30), entrance into a hallowed place (Exodus 3:5; Joshua 5:15), and covenant-making (Ruth 4:1–8). It is the last of these three categories that seems of most interest to us here.

In the fourth chapter of the book of Ruth, we find the highlighting of a rather curious ritual associated with the buying or trading of property or land. The salient portion reads: "(Now in earlier times in Israel, for the redemption and transfer of property to become final, one party took off his sandal and gave it to the other. This was the method of legalizing transactions in Israel.) So the kinsman-redeemer said to Boaz, 'Buy it yourself.' And he removed his sandal" (*NIV* Ruth 4:7–8).[129] This "ceremony of the shoe," as it has been called, [130] is alluded to in the Hebrew Bible and the records of ancient Mesopotamia.[131] Indeed, it appears from a number of sources (scriptural and otherwise) that the transfer of property in ancient times was traditionally accompanied by a rite or ritual consisting primarily of the removal of shoes. The Hebrews referred to this ritual by the name of "Halitzah" (meaning "to draw off").[132]

One text notes: "When someone sells his property . . . he loses permanently or temporarily his legal right to it . . . and he 'lifts up his hand or foot from it, and places that of the new owner in it.' Thus it is logical to conclude that this expression which had at first only a legal meaning developed into a symbolical meaning. Then the biblical tradition took a further step. The 'lifting up of the foot' became more concrete and real with the 'pulling off of the shoe.' "[133]

This act before witnesses was a legal attestation[134] that the party divesting itself of a particular piece of property was doing so willingly—and had formally and officially relinquished all future claims on that particular piece of property.[135] The removal of the sandal, slipper, or shoe at the end of the rite signified that the transaction was completed and the ritual was legally binding.[136]

One commentary described the meaning of the rite as follows: "A person's garments are, so to speak, part of himself, and . . . if a person removes his garments in order to show his willingness to deprive himself of everything in life, he ought also to remove his shoes."[137] This same author continues:

> Amongst the Hebrews business transactions took place publically [sic.] in the market-place so that the presence of the whole community, or at least ten of the elders, served to confirm them. (Gen. xxiii.) . . . As an aid to the memory, therefore, there arose the custom of drawing off the shoes in transferring a possession or domain. (Ruth iv, 7.) The idea was that the person who gave up a possession should show by removing his shoe that he was thus divesting himself of something before the witnesses. This could then be regarded as a public declaration that he was withdrawing from the property and handing it over to another person.[138]

Because the shoe was a natural symbol of possession, the removal of the same implied divestment.[139] As noted, this act (although symbolic) had binding, legal implications clearly understood by all who were called upon to witness the rite[140]—and in a time when the ability to write was greatly limited, it allowed even the illiterate to participate in legal transactions. Because of biblical evidence, and extra-canonical support, scholars believe that this rite was at one time very widespread in the ancient Near East.[141]

Thus, from the "ceremony of the shoe" we learn that anciently one who wished to enter into a covenant—specifically giving up one's "first estate" for a "second estate" or "better estate"—would do so by removing his shoes and putting them on again.[142] This established both the covenantally binding nature of the act, but also implied that the one performing the rite was doing so of his own free will and choice.

Undergarments

As has already been suggested, the priests and high priest who served in the Mosaic Tabernacle wore various articles of ritual clothing. Among those were a type of symbolic undergarment.

Thus, in Exodus 28:39 we read: "And thou shalt embroider the coat of fine linen." The Hebrew of this verse may also be rendered: "And thou shalt weave a shirt-like undergarment of fine white cloth."[143] Thus, this article of priestly clothing appears to be a cotton undershirt of sorts, to be worn by the temple (or tabernacle) high priest. The simpleness of the garment, seemingly plain in appearance, was reminiscent of Christ's seeming plainness, as predicted by the prophet, Isaiah (e.g., "he hath no form nor comeliness; and when we shall see him, there is no beauty that we should desire him"—Isaiah 53:2).[144] However, the "fineness" of the weave is indicative of the greatness of the God whom Israel rejected. The whiteness of the shirt was a symbol of the purity and holiness of Christ's life and character. Of this garment, one commentator noted:

> Profit will be gained by considering the Hebrew word here translated "coat". It is "Kethoneth". The root meaning of this word is twofold—"To cover" or "to hide". It is exactly the same word as is used in Gen. iii.21, and there translated "coats". In the literal translation the verse reads: "And Jehovah God doth make to the man, and to his wife coats (Kethoneths) of skin and doth clothe them." (Note that in the original the word is "skin".[145] It is singular and not plural as in our Authorized Version. This suggests that one sacrifice was sufficient for them both.) When Adam [partook of the "forbidden fruit"] he tried first *to cover* his nakedness with leaves, and then he sought *to hide* behind the trees of the garden. Both were of no avail . . . . Then it was [God that] made for them a Kethoneth to cover their sin and to hide their shame. This we know was only accomplished through the death of another, and also through the shedding of blood. Thus in this first garment of the High Priest is secreted some of the wonder of the holiness and righteousness of the Christ.[146]

From this we learn that this white undershirt represented the atonement of Christ, and His willingness to "cover" our sins, thereby "hiding" our shame.[147] Consequently, when the high priest donned the garment, he was donning Christ's attribute of perfection or cleanliness. Christ was clean because of His perfect obedience. The priest who dresses in the garment is clean because, in so dressing, he symbolically received of the cleansing power of Christ's Atonement, and thereby received His attributes of perfection, cleanliness, righteousness, and so forth.[148] Again, we read:

> Notice that the coat was put on the moment the priest was washed . . . As the sons of God [temple priests] have been clothed in His righteousness because they have been washed in His Blood. Having received this imputed righteousness we are able to say with the prophet Isaiah: "I will greatly rejoice in the Lord, my soul shall be joyful in my God: for He hath clothed me with the garments of salvation, He hath covered me with the robe of righteousness . . ." (Isa. lxi.10).[149]

This same source states that "attached to this embroidered coat" or woven undershirt "was the girdle. . . . This linen girdle was not the curious girdle of [Exodus 28:8]. It was attached to the undergarment and so was not seen . . ."[150] It was a waistband or belt, per se. Today it might be equivalent to the waistband on a pair of underpants, serving to hold them up, but remaining hidden from view. Though "it was not seen . . . it was there girding the loins. Perhaps we are not always conscious that the Lord is ministering on our behalf especially when we see no outward evidence, but we can encourage our hearts with the fact that He is always working on our behalf."[151]

Of course the books of Exodus (28:42) and Leviticus (6:10) both tell us that the priests were to wear, in conjunction with their undershirt, "linen breeches" that extended "from the loins even unto the thighs" (Exodus 28:42).[152] Of the combination of this white cotton/linen shirt and pant set, one commentator wrote: "The subject of holiness . . . is seen typified in each of the garments made of the fine twined linen, giving us an appreciation of the term 'Holy Garments'. The coat [or undershirt] that clad his person would signify an holiness of the heart that beat beneath it . . . . whilst these linen breeches [or underpants] that covered his nakedness declare an holiness of the flesh" or "desires and passions."[153]

Numerous symbols have been seen in the liturgical garments worn by those of the priestly class. Some have been suggested above. However, others come to mind. For example, because articles of priestly clothing were received as part of a call to service—particularly service in the temple or tabernacle—they are commonly understood to represent the fact that the wearer has entered into covenants with God.[154] One text on rites of passage noted that exchanging things or receiving gifts binds the receiver to the giver. This same text notes that receiving ritual garments would be included in such acts of binding. The receipt (or exchanging) of such items is equivalent to "pronouncing an oath" or entering into a covenant.[155] Because of their association with covenants, the sacred priestly garments can also remind the wearer of the constant need for repentance, and the need to be faithful to covenants through living a virtuous life.[156] The wearing of priestly garments can remind the initiate that God has called him to do the work of the divine.[157]

Beyond their symbolic reference to covenants, the garments of the high priest have also been said to symbolize "the angelic state" the wearer should be in "when he entered the holy of holies, the presence of the Lord. This changing of garments was an important piece of temple symbolism."[158] Anciently, the high priest had the image of God upon him, as represented by his clothing.[159] "The white linen garment was the dress of the angels, given to favored human beings upon their ascent to heaven"[160]—the ascent being something acted out in ancient temple rites. Because the ancient undergarment was a representation of the wearer's worthiness to enter God's presence, it also insured his modesty and purity—and functioned, in a sense, as armor against the temptations of the world.[161] Related to the symbolism of protection is that of atonement.[162] As the garments covered the flesh of the initiate, this article of clothing associated with the flesh of Christ represented God's intention to "cover" the sins and shortcomings of the faithful wearer.[163] Just as the garment covered the wearer's nakedness, Christ's Atonement covers mankind's sins.[164]

Because the priestly garments of old were connected with

atonement, they are also symbols for exaltation. One author, drawing on the imagery of the book of Revelation, wrote: "Clothing initiates in the temple garment is a ceremonial . . . *pre*-enactment . . . of God's giving 'white raiment' to the faithful, and thus it serves as [a] symbol of the promise of exaltation."[165] Hence, if a priest anciently received the garments of the holy priesthood, it foreshadowed or typified God's intention to exalt him, if he lived true and faithful to the covenants he had entered into.[166]

CONCLUSION

Ritual clothing, anciently as well as today, symbolically represents station, attributes, authority, covenant relationship, and so forth. To change clothes is to change identity, status, and nature. Among most religious peoples—but particularly the ancient Hebrews—there was something very sacred about the receiving of, and the symbolism behind, articles of ritual attire. One who changed into such clothing was making a covenant to be different. The very act of disrobing from one's street clothes and robing in priestly apparel, suggested transition and empowerment. One commentator suggested that much of the raiment of those associated with temple worship was representative of the "divine nature." Hence, as one was "clothed" during temple rites, one was symbolically putting on "robes of righteousness." The "more completely clothed" the initiate was—meaning the more priestly articles donned—the more "priesthood power" was ceremonially being received until the initiate was in possession of "a fullness of priesthood" or priesthood power—as found in the divinely given rites and rituals.[167]

Notes

1. Cyril, Bishop of Jerusalem [circa AD 315–87], indicated that, prior to engaging in the "mysteries" or sacred rites of the Church, Christians living in the fourth century would change out of their street clothes. This prepared them to partake of the holy, as they had symbolically set aside the worldly. See Cyril of Jerusalem, "Catechetical Lectures," Lecture 20:2, in

Schaff and Wace (2004), 7:147.
2. See Nibley (2008), 497.
3. Donald W. Parry, "Sinai as Sanctuary and Mountain of God," in Lundquist and Ricks (1990), 1:487.
4. Madsen (2008), 135.
5. Janet Mayo, *A History of Ecclesiastical Dress* (London: B. T. Batsford, 1984), 145.
6. Rest (1987), 46.
7. Conner (1992), 61; Bayley (1993), 2:38; Farbridge (1923), 277–78; Smith (1998), 289; Myers (1987), 227; Unger (1966), 212–14; McConkie and Parry (1990), 33; McConkie (1985), 105, 256–57; Parry and Parry (1998), 59, 278.
8. Todeschi (1995), 73; Henry (1925), 80–81; Fontana (1994), 67; Rest (1987), 46.
9. Wilcox (1995), 24.
10. Jack Tresidder, *Symbols and Their Meanings* (London: Duncan Baird Publishers, 2000), 156. It should be noted that on very rare occasions white functions as a negative sign. In the secular world it is a sign of aging, and gray hair. In certain parts of the world it provokes images of winter, coldness, and the accompanying death of plant life. More than a dozen times in the book of Leviticus, white is noted as the color of leprosy. (See Ryken, Wilhoit, and Longman [1998], 944.)
11. To participate in ancient temple rites, the priest "divested himself of the multicolored garb of the material world and put on the glorious robe of the angels" (Barker [2008], 116).
12. Cyril of Jerusalem, "Catechetical Lectures," Lecture 20:2, in Schaff and Wace (2004), 7:147; emphasis in the original.
13. Green (2004), 59; emphasis in original.
14. Mayo (1984), 135.
15. Nibley (2008), 409.
16. Fiona Bowie, "Ritual and Performance," in Partridge (2005), 33.
17. Wilcox (1995), 24.
18. Drawing a parallel with LDS practice, Elder Dean L. Larsen of the Seventy wrote:

> When member patrons come to the temple, they change from their street clothes to white temple clothing. All who serve in the temple, both the patrons and the officiators, wear white clothing in the temple. The white dress is symbolic of purity and spiritual cleanliness. Changing from street clothes to white temple clothing

when entering the temple adds to the effect of leaving the influences and cares of the world outside. It enhances an atmosphere of reverence and worship and a sensitivity to being in the house of the Lord. (Dean L. Larsen, *Setting the Record Straight: Mormon Temples* [Orem, UT: Millennial Press, 2007], 77)

19. Skinner (2007), 32–34.

20. See Parry, in Parry (1994), 145. One Catholic commentator pointed out: "It is certain, from early documents, that both the celebrant and the laity who were present [at sacred rites], were expected to wear special, and not everyday, garments in assisting at so august a rite" (Henry [1925], 72–73).

21. Parry and Parry (2009), 26–29.

22. See Wilson, in Parry and Ricks (1999), 313.

23. John A. Tvedtnes, "Priestly Clothing in Bible Times," in Parry (1994), 665–66. "Priestly clothing, by its symbolic nature and pure whiteness, replaces the everyday garb which reminds us that we are in the world, thus bringing the wearer closer to heaven" (ibid., 677).

24. Ibid., 694.

25. Ryken, Wilhoit, and Longman (1998), 319.

26. Tvedtnes, in Parry (1994), 665.

27. See "The Testaments of the Twelve Patriarchs—Testament of Levi," 8:1–19, in Charlesworth (1983, 1985), 1:790–91.

28. "The priests [of the Old Testament] were clothed in 'holy garments' of white linen, including a cap, robe, sash, and trousers (see Exodus 28–29)" (Cowan, in Parry and Ricks [1999], 106).

29. Charles W. Slemming, *These Are The Garments: A Study of the Garments of the High Priest of Israel* (London: Marshall, Morgan Scott, 1945), 22.

30. See Slemming (1945), 23; Barker (2008), 125.

31. Slemming (1945), 23.

32. As it relates to LDS temple clothing, Hugh Nibley pointed out: "There is nothing theatrical about the garments of the Holy Priesthood, nor is there anything secret about them, since they may be viewed by anyone at funerals. It has been my experience that [those engaged in temple work] are inclined to dismiss . . . as meaningless embellishments those parts of the clothing which they do not understand. My conviction is that every detail of the garments is indispensable" (Hugh Nibley, "Endowment History," 18, unpublished paper dated February 2, 1990, a copy of which is in the possession of this author).

33. For example, *The Anchor Bible Dictionary* states of the ephod: "It apparently was an apronlike garment, suspended from the waist level downward . . ." (Carol Meyers, "Ephod," in Freedman [1992], 2:550). Another Bible Dictionary states: "The ephod described in Ex 28:6–14; 39:207 is a garment something like an apron" (McKenzie [1965], 241). Elsewhere we read that it was "an apron worn over a longer robe" (Myers [1987], 342). One commentary on the book of Exodus notes that scholarly sources sometimes interpret the ephod to be "an apron" worn at the waist. (See Walter C. Kaiser, Jr., "Exodus," in Gaebelein [1976–92], 2:468.) Another commentary also refers to it as an "apronlike" garment (George Arthur Buttrick, ed., *The Interpreter's Bible*, 12 vols. [New York: Abingdon Press, 1951–57], 1:1039). The *New Oxford Annotated Bible* states: "The *ephod* is a garment similar to an apron" (Michael D. Coogan, ed., *The New Oxford Annotated Bible—New Revised Standard Version*, third edition [New York: Oxford University Press, 2001], 122 [Hebrew Bible section]). Indeed, some English translations render the Hebrew word, "ephod," as "apron." (See, for example, James Moffatt, trans., *A New Translation of The Bible* [New York: Harper & Brothers Publishers, 1950], 92 [Hebrew Bible section]; *The Complete Bible—and American Translation*, J. M. Powis Smith and Edgar J. Goodspeed, translators [Chicago: The University of Chicago Press, 1949], 76 [Hebrew Bible section].)

34. See McBrien (1995), 593; F. L. Cross and E. A. Livingstone, eds., *The Oxford Dictionary of the Christian Church*, second edition (New York: Oxford University Press, 1990), 601–02, S.v., "Gremial"; Mayo (1984), 155; Wainwright and Tucker (2006), 844. In early Roman Catholic practice the gremial was worn by the presiding officer (e.g., popes, bishops, and eventually priests) in various liturgical settings wherein oil was used, such as during confirmations, ordinations, and the dedication of altars. Eventually it became common for the bishop to wear this apron during the mass, specifically when he was seated.

35. Tvedtnes, in Parry (1994), 694.

36. See Soyer (1999): 164.

37. Ibid., 168.

38. Ibid., 170.

39. Conner (1992), 141; Unger (1966), 317.

40. Julien (1996), 14.

41. It may be that the original symbolic meaning of the gremial (in Roman Catholicism) was also "work," though, as suggested, that meaning has now been lost.

42. The Hebrew here translated "apron" is a word more often rendered "girdle," and only sometimes "apron."

43. Parry, in Parry (1994), 145.

44. Julian (1996), 23–24; Cooper (1995), 14; McConkie & Parry (1990), 49; Bayley (1990, 1993), 2:248; Carol Meyers, "Apron," in Freedman (1992), 1:319.

45. Meyers, in Freedman (1992), 1:319.

46. As noted later in the chapter, President Joseph Fielding Smith taught: "The Lord said to Adam, here is the tree of knowledge of good and evil. If you want to stay here then you cannot eat of that fruit. If you want to stay here then I forbid you to eat it. But you may act for yourself and you may eat of it if you want to. And if you eat it you will die" (Smith, in *Charge To . . .* [1982], 124. See also Smith [1993], 4:81). The choices God gave to Adam and Eve were quite simple. Option number one consisted of God giving them the right to stay in Eden forever. They would never really have to work, as everything would be provided for them. They wouldn't really grow because they wouldn't be tried, tested, or placed in difficult circumstances. According to this option, Adam and Eve would be allowed to focus on the things which they wanted, and the things which they wanted to do. Of course the major drawbacks to this choice included: (1) they would never become as God is because of their lack of growth, and (2) none of their potential offspring, namely you and I, would ever have a chance at becoming like God either, as Adam and Eve's choice would prevent us from being born. Option number two, as President Smith reads the account, consisted of Adam and Eve sacrificing their opportunity for guaranteed ease and pleasure so that others could be born and have a chance at godhood also. This option promised hard work, requisite sacrifice, and trials and tests that would stretch the first of the human family to the core. They would likely have to give up some worldly goals and aspirations in order to make it back to God. According to this option, they were assured that, no matter how good a life they lived, in the end they would still die. However, in this elective, the very things that would make the mortal experience so hard would be the very things that would make it possible for Adam, Eve, and all of their posterity to return to God, having become like Him. The two choices Adam and Eve were given in Eden are the very same two choices every couple are given when they kneel at an altar in the temple and enter into the new and everlasting covenant of marriage. Their first option, if it can even be called such, is to be self-serving and put off their family until they've done all that they want to do, and have obtained all that they want to obtain. The second option is to sacrifice what they

want and what the world tells them that they should and must have, in order that others can have a chance at mortality and exaltation. Adam and Eve's choice was really to have a family or not to have a family. Hence, Adam says, "I will partake that man may be!" Thus, If nothing else can be seen in the fig leaf aprons, this much is certain—Adam and Eve had made the right choice. They were going to be "fruitful and multiply." They had decided to put God's will before their own—and at great cost and sacrifice on their part. Such is the commitment God asks of us.

47.   See James E. Talmage, *Jesus the Christ* (Salt Lake City: The Church of Jesus Christ of Latter-day Saints, 1981), 443; Cooper (1995), 66.

48.   Curiously, Jewish legend held that the forbidden fruit was the fig. (See Ginzberg [1967–69], 1:75, 96–97; 5:97–98, 122; *Books of Adam and Eve* 20:5, in Charlesworth [1983–85], 2:281.) Thus, when Satan told Adam and Eve to cover their nakedness with fig leaves, he was really seeking to trick them into guaranteeing that their transgression would be discovered. Finally, one LDS source states that, "By sewing fig leaves together and making aprons for themselves, Adam and Eve covered their nakedness (Moses 4:13). In so covering themselves with leaves, they became trees, as it were." Trees that are green represent "righteous men" and women (McConkie and Parry [1990], 15, 103–104).

49.   Curiously, BYU religion professor Rodney Turner wrote: "Priesthood is not only a divine power of attorney by which men on earth act, lead and rule in God's behalf, it is also the means by which all things are organized and controlled. If the sick are healed, if the dead are raised, if mountains are moved, if the winds are stilled or life is begotten, it is by virtue of this power. To the extent that anyone organizes or controls matter, he or she is drawing upon the *principle* of priesthood" (Rodney Turner, *Woman and the Priesthood* [Salt Lake City: Deseret Book, 1972], 287–88). Consequently, Turner would reason, procreation is a priesthood act—wherein God's power is utilized to create human life.

50.   J. F. McConkie (1985), 257; Conner (1992), 137; Cooper (1995), 80, 106; Tresidder (2000), 134–35.

51.   Cooper (1995), 29, 80.

52.   See, for example, Nachmanides, *Commentary on the Torah*, 5 vols. (New York: Shilo Publishing House, 1973), 2:486.

53.   See Nahum M. Sarna, ed., *The JPS Torah Commentary: Exodus* (Philadelphia: Fortress Press, 1991), 185.

54.   Slemming (1945), 118.

55.   Ibid., 119.

56.   One commentator on the clothing wrote: "The mitre [or cap] that

adorned [the temple priest's] head would speak of holiness of thought and control" of the mind (Slemming [1945], 127).

57. See ibid., 124–25.

58. Ibid., 118.

59. Ibid.

60. Coogan (2001), 124.

61. Robert Young, *Young's Literal Translation of the Bible*, revised edition (Grand Rapids: Guardian Press, 1976), 57.

62. Smith and Goodspeed (1949), 77.

63. *Good News Bible* (New York: American Bible Society, 1978), 97.

64. Moffatt (1950), 94.

65. See also Parry and Parry (2009), 133.

66. See Ryken, Wilhoit, and Longman (1998), 368.

67. Spencer W. Kimball, *The Miracle of Forgiveness* (Salt Lake City: Bookcraft, 1989), 106.

68. Related to this rite of tying a cap to the body (as described in the book of Exodus) is a practice in Jewish Mysticism known as "putting on the name." Briefly stated, the initiate is clothed in a "sleeveless garment, modeled after the high priest's ephod, covering shoulders and chest down to the navel and falling along the sides to the loins, and [is also adorned with] a hat connected with [or to] the garment. On this magic garment the secret names of God are inscribed." According to one commentator, through the ritual associated with this clothing, the initiate is endowed with "adept irresistible strength" (Scholem, in Rothenberg and Rothenberg [1983], 304).

69. Hugh Nibley, "Leaders to Managers: The Fatal Shift," Commencement Address delivered at Brigham Young University, August 19, 1983, in *Brother Brigham Challenges the Saints* (Provo, UT: Foundation for Ancient Research and Mormon Studies, 1994), 493.

70. See Mayo (1984), 137, 155.

71. See Nibley (1994), 493.

72. See Bayley (1990–93), 2:64.

73. See also Hugh Nibley, who wrote: "The well-known shifting of garments from left to right in initiation ceremonies (e.g., of the tassel on the mortarboard at graduations) is a reminder, according to St. Hippolytus of Rome, that 'nature consists of opposites, good and bad, even as right and left—light and darkness, night and day, life and death'" (Nibley [2005], 443). This does not imply one side is bad and another good. Hippolytus is simply highlighting the fact that all things have their opposites. Just as men and women are opposite but complementary, so also are many of the opposites that exist in this life.

74. Tvedtnes, in Parry (1994), 694.

75. See, for example, Asia Shepsut, *Journey of the Priestess* (San Francisco: Harper Collins, 1993), 105, 107–109, 190.

76. John A. Tvedtnes, "Temple Prayer in Ancient Times," in Parry and Ricks (1999), 89.

77. See, Hall (1979), 318; Ryken, Wilhoit, and Longman (1998), 911; McConkie (1985), 274; Torjesen (1993), 41–42.

78. Cooper (1995), 184. So, for example, some Islamic and Jewish women veil themselves to keep men from being distracted. (See Orr and Walther [1976], 261; Ira G. Zepp, Jr., *A Muslim Primer* [Wesminster, MD: Wakefield Editions, 1992], 176–77; Glassé [1989], 413; Kertzer and Hoffman [1993], 91; De Lange [1987], 32–33.) Women in modern Eastern cultures are traditionally veiled. In secular Western wedding ceremonies women also commonly wear a veil.

79. A friend recently pointed out: "You cover your head and pray, creating your own little temple inside. You set yourself apart from the world to draw closer to God" (Lori Denning, personal correspondence, July 14, 2010).

80. Cooper (1995), 184; McConkie (1985), 274; Torjesen (1993), 166. Note that the emphasis is on righteously held and exercised authority. What woman should be offended by being an equal partner (1 Corinthians 11:11) with a male (holding a different but not more important role) who honors his priesthood (D&C 121:36) and bears accountability before God for what happens in his home and family (D&C 68:25, 84:33–41)? If he is doing these things, what fear would a woman have in following him, except if her desires and goals were contrary to the will of the Lord?

81. Actually, the Greek word translated "submit" does not mean to "give in" or "blindly obey." One scholar noted that the verb never implies "servile submissiveness" or the "elimination or breaking of the human will." Rather, it is a "voluntary" sustaining of the spouse (Barth [1974], 609). Another wrote, "'cooperate' is a loose translation, but that is the working concept that Paul asks of all Saints—cooperation with Church and civil leaders, and cooperation of wives with the family leadership of their husbands" (Richard Lloyd Anderson, *Understanding Paul* [Salt Lake City: Deseret Book, 1983], 353).

82. E. F. Scott, *The Moffatt New Testament Commentary: The Epistles of Paul to the Colossians, to Philemon, and to the Ephesians* (London: Hodder and Stoughton, 1952), 236–37. See also W. Robertson Nicoll, *Expositor's Greek Testament*, 5 vols. (Grand Rapids: Eerdmans, 1983), 3:366. Regarding the ancient Christian use of veils, one source points out: "The virgins were part of the ecclesiastical order, part of the clergy, and sat in

special seats reserved for them with the presbyters, widows, and bishops. Their number and their commitment to a life of chastity was one of the church's most esteemed emblems. These virgins signified their unmarried state by not wearing veils" (Torjesen [1993], 166). If virgins were an office, and not wearing a veil symbolized being unmarried, then donning a veil represents getting married or entering into a covenant relationship with a bridegroom (namely Christ), as anciently it was the cultural practice for married women to wear veils so as to show "propriety, specifically sexual modesty, since it preserved the sight of [their] hair for only [their] husband and family" (ibid., 41).

83.   Wilson (1999), 444; Conner (1992), 177; Cirlot (1971), 359; Todeschi (1995), 274; Cooper (1995), 184.

84.   Myers (1987), 1036.

85.   See Edward J. Young, *The Book of Isaiah*, 3 vols. (Grand Rapids: Eerdmans, 1997), 2:194–95.

86.   Ryken, Wilhoit, and Longman (1998), 911.

87.   Ibid.

88.   See also *JST* 1 Corinthians 11:10.

89.   The *NIV, NRSV, The Jerusalem Bible*, and *New World Translation* also render the Greek word translated "power" in the *KJV* and "veil" in the *RSV* as "authority."

90.   For example, the Moffatt translation of this verse reads, "in view of the angels, woman has to wear a symbol of subjection on her head." (See also Dummelow [1936], 910.)

91.   Leon Morris, *Tyndale New Testament Commentaries: 1 Corinthians*, revised edition (Grand Rapids: Eerdmans, 1998), 152. Perhaps this has something to do with Kevin Todeschi's claim that a woman veiled stands as a symbol of "intuitive abilities" (Todeschi [1995], 275).

92.   See Gerald Bray, ed., *Ancient Christian Commentary on Scripture: New Testament Volume 8, 1–2 Corinthians* (Downers Grove, IL: InterVarsity Press, 1999), 108. "Ambrosiaster" was the name given by Erasmus to the author of a work once thought to have been composed by the fourth-century Ambrose of Milan.

93.   See Brown (1999), 157–58.

94.   Douglas R. Edwards, "Dress and Ornamentation," in Freedman (1992), 2:233. See also Geoffrey W. Bromiley, ed., *The International Standard Bible Encyclopedia*, revised edition, 4 vols. (Grand Rapids: Eerdmans, 1979–88), 4:204; Rest (1987), 51.

95.   Cooper (1995), 140.

96.   Edwards, in Freedman (1992), 2:233, 236. One source suggests of

the robe of the Old Testament high priest that it represents priesthood. (See Nibley [2005], 489–90.)

97. One "Council of Braga forbade priests to say mass without having a stole . . . upon their breast" ("Excursus on the Vestments of the Early Church," in Schaff and Wace [2004], 14:142). There were no less than nine Church councils at Braga (modern-day Portugal), in addition to various synods.

98. Tvedtnes, in Parry (1994), 694.

99. "The high priest wears a white robe . . . The linen robe symbolizes the heavenly . . ." Linen was often worn instead of wool because its source was not subject to death, as a lamb would be—and the priest, dressed in linen, was a symbol of the divine, who cannot die. See Barker (2008), 114, 116.

100. "The Council of Toledo, in 633, . . . specifies that the deacon should wear his [stole or robe] over his left shoulder, and . . . it should be white, without any mixture of colours [sic] or any gold embroidery" ("Excursus on the Vestments of the Early Church," in Schaff and Wace [2004], 14:142).

101. See McBrien (1995), 935, S.v., "Orarion."

102. See ibid., 1225, S.v., "Stole." Thus, a deacon wore the article over the left shoulder, but a bishop wears it "over both shoulders" symbolizing his higher order in the priesthood, and representative of both the left and right shoulder being covered by the garment. (See also ibid., 1308, S.v., "Vestments.")

103. See Martimort (1986), 139–40.

104. Curiously, outside of Christianity certain garments are given to those ordained or endowed into the highest ranks of spirituality in various traditions. For example, the ritual that initiates Hindu boys (of the three upper castes) is called *upanayana* (which means "coming close to a teacher" to get knowledge) or *brahma upadesa* ("receipt of the sacred teaching concerning the Supreme Being"). As part of his initiation, he is ceremonially washed. Then he is given a "sacred thread," which he wears over his shoulder (across the chest). This cord or thread is a symbol of the garment the initiate is to wear when he performs sacrifices or functions in a ritual capacity. It has also been said to symbolize the "spiritual umbilical cord" of "rebirth" associated with the young man's initiation. In other words, the cord is a sacred reminder to he who wears it that he has made covenants that, if kept, constitute a rebirth and a new beginning—*tabula rasa*—and also an authorization to function in a priestly capacity. After endowing the boy with the sacred garment, he is taken outside to view the sun, which he is informed is "the source of light, knowledge, and immortality." He is also shown how to "twine his fingers in a particular way" as a means

of "warding off" harmful rays—itself a potentially powerful symbol. (See Oxtoby and Segal [2007], 305.) In the Confucian ceremony, known as a "clapping" rite, a young man is initiated into adulthood. As part of that initiation—which typically takes place somewhere between the ages of fifteen and twenty—the initiate receives a ceremonial hat, a robe, and a name. All of these represent the receipt of a new identity—in this case, the transition from childhood to that of adulthood, and an identity that is now one of responsibility specifically to one's deceased ancestors. By engaging in this rite, the initiate is committing to perform the rituals and ceremonies necessary to ensure the spiritual well-being of his kindred dead. To shirk one's responsibilities after engaging in this covenant-making ritual is to bring accountability and, potentially, disaster upon the head of an uncommited initiate. (See ibid., 463.) While these articles are not identical to each other, or to the orarion of Christianity, the meanings seem similar (i.e., authorization, priestly status, covenant relationship, and so on).

105. Slemming (1945), 30. This same source says that the "robe was an emblem of kingly grace" (ibid., 35). It also informs us: "The robes dignify a man for the office he holds . . . . Every servant of the Lord who ministers in holy things should himself respect his office and should be respected because of his office" (ibid., 31).

106. See Herbert Norris, *Church Vestments: Their Origin & Development* (London: J. M. Dent & Sons, 1949), 88–89. See also Mayo (1984), 134.

107. Slemming (1945), 30.

108. Ibid., 31.

109. See "Excursus on the Vestments of the Early Church," in Schaff and Wace (2004), 14:142.

110. Archimandrite Chrysostomos, *Orthodox Liturgical Dress: An Historical Treatment* (Brookline, MA, 1981), 71. One text on modern Greek Orthodox liturgical garb also states of the *orarion* (or "deacon's stole") that it "symbolizes the wings of angels" (Evagoras Constantinides, *Orthodoxy 101: A Bird's Eye View* [Northridge, CA: Narthex Press, 2006], 52).

111. One LDS commentator suggested: "The robes of righteousness . . . represent the acquisition of a divine or holy nature" (Green [2004], 61). This same source states: "These priesthood robes symbolize the purity (see 2 Nephi 9:14) and righteousness (see Revelation 19:8) of the divine nature of a Saint who emulates the divine nature of Christ" (ibid., 63). Margaret Barker penned this: "The linen robe is 'the bright array of glory' and the one who wears it 'is now replenished with insatiable contemplation face

to face'" (Barker [2008], 125). John Tvedtnes suggests: "The white robe, along with the anointing, symbolized the Holy Ghost's protection against Satan" (Tvedtnes, in Parry [1994], 672).

112. Rest (1987), 53.

113. Nibley (2005), 443. See also Mayo (1984), 137, 155.

114. Barker (2008), 126.

115. Henry (1925), 69. See also Rest (1987), 52. Another commentator also emphasized the symbolism of purity represented by the robes—along with a suggestion of equality before "God the Father and his Son Jesus Christ"—specifically because all who participate in holy ordinances wear the same basic robes (Charles [1997], 70).

116. Rest (1987), 51.

117. Edwards, in Freedman (1992), 2:234.

118. J. Philip Hyatt, "Dress," in Hastings (1963), 223; Edwards, in Freedman (1992), 2:234.

119. See Edwards, in Freedman (1992), 2:237; Tresidder (2000), 134; Henry (1925), 69–70.

120. Rest (1987), 53. See also Henry (1925), 69–70.

121. One source indicates that bows were "once a sacred symbol, and signified the concealment or secrecy surrounding sacred mysteries" (Julien [1996], 226). On the surface, this insight might seem unrelated. However, on a deeper level it may well be in harmony with our discussion of bows on pages 156–57, as fidelity to covenants implies concealment of certain secret or sacred truths one has received.

122. Slemming (1945), 28.

123. See Mayo (1984), 154.

124. Rest (1925), 53.

125. Nibley (2008), 313. On a related note, the ancient symbol of the ankh had strong ties to "the mysteries" or rites of initiation among the Egyptians. Indeed, one encyclopedia on symbolism noted that the *ankh* is a symbol of "the key of knowledge of the mysteries and hidden wisdom" (Cooper [1995], 13, S.v., "Ankh"). Nibley has suggested that, in ancient Egyptian practice, upon the birth of a child it would be presented with the *ankh* sign, or the symbol of life. (See Theodore H. Gaster, "Amulets and Talismans," in Eliade [1987], 1:244; Leonard H. Lesko, "Egyptian Religion: An Overview," in Eliade [1987], 5:50; Cooper [1995], 13, S.v., "Ankh"; Julien Ries, "Cross," in Eliade [1987], 4:155–56, 162; Gaster, in Eliade [1987], 1:244.) This was placed over, or (like a navel or earring) was attached to, the navel of the baby, specifically because both the *ankh* and the umbilicus represented life. The symbol was worn as an amulet, of sorts,

throughout the life of the individual. Consequently, Nibley conjectures that "the mysterious *ankh*" represented "a knotted cord" or "the navel-string" we commonly call the umbilical cord. He writes: "It is interesting that *ankh* also means 'oath,' the idea being . . . that one swears by one's life, so that if the oath is broken, so likewise 'the cord of life,' i.e., the umbilical cord, is broken" (Nibley [2005], 454). Like Nibley, one typologist noted that the *ankh* represents the idea of a covenant or oath, and, consequently, the symbol of the *ankh* is tied to the principles of "power" and "authority"—as it is through the making and keeping of oaths or covenants that one obtains power and authority, and it is through the breaking of the same that one loses such. (See Cooper [1995], 13, S.v., "Ankh.")

126. See, the "Record Book" of Shadrach B. Roundy, Church Archives, Salt Lake City, Utah, cited in David John Buerger, *The Mysteries of Godliness* (San Francisco: Smith Research Associates, 1994), 145. See also Odgen Kraut, *The Priesthood Garment* (Salt Lake City: Pioneer Press, 1971), 18.

127. Cooper (1995), 24. Like bow knots, Cooper indicates that knots in general are symbols of "continuity, connection, a covenant [or] a link" (ibid., 92). See also Cirlot (1962), 191; Todeschi (1995), 155; Fontana (1994), 75; Hall (1979), 184.

128. Tresidder (2000), 36, 152; Todeschi (1995), 155.

129. Some academics have assumed that the rite being performed in this passage is an example of the ancient law of "levirate" marriage, wherein the surviving brother of a deceased man is expected to unite in an intimate relationship with the childless widow of his brother in order to raise up seed unto the name of his prematurely deceased sibling (See Deuteronomy 25:5–6). Near the end of Deuteronomy 25 we learn what, according to the Law, a woman should do if her surviving brother-in-law (or *levir*) refuses to marry her. "Then shall his brother's wife come unto him in the presence of the elders, and loose his shoe from off his foot, and spit in his face, and shall answer and say, So shall it be done unto that man that will not build up his brother's house. And his name shall be called in Israel, The house of him that hath his shoe loosed" (Deuteronomy 25:9–10). Admittedly, on a superficial level there appear to be significant correlations between these two passages (Ruth 4 and Deuteronomy 25). In the end, however, there are a number of reasons why Ruth chapter four is likely not intended to be a representation of a traditional levirate marriage ritual. First of all, unlike the widowed woman in Exodus 25, Ruth does not spit in the face of the man who refuses to marry her—which many sources indicate is a requisite part of the ceremony of levirate marriage. Second, in the story of Ruth and Boaz it is *not* the woman who removes the man's shoe. Rather, it

is the male who is depicted as removing his own shoe. Third, in the Book of Ruth the unnamed kinsman-redeemer (*gō'ēl*) is *not* Ruth's husband's brother—as required by Jewish law. Fourth, the root words for the levirate obligation (*yābām*) and for the kinsman-redeemer (*gā'al*) are totally unrelated. Fifth, Obed—the son born to Boaz and Ruth—is spoken of as the son of Boaz rather than as the son of Ruth's deceased husband, Mahlon (see Ruth 4:18–22; see also LXX Ruth 4:13). This would be contrary to levirate marriage—which is primarily for the purpose of raising seed up to a deceased brother. And finally, whereas levirate marriage did not require—nor allow—a marriage contract to be initiated (as the couple were considered already married), in the Book of Ruth a formal marriage is expected, and in the end, performed.

130. E. A. Speiser, "Of Shoes and Shekels," in *Bulletin of the American Schools of Oriental Research*, 77 (1940), 18. See also John Hamlin, *International Theological Commentary: Ruth—Surely There Is A Future* (Grand Rapids: Eerdmans, 1996), 57; Buttrick (1953), 2:849.

131. Recently recovered records from Nuzi, an ancient Mesopotamian city, attest to a ceremony of property transfer or land ownership wherein the person selling (or transferring property) must remove his shoes as evidence that the transfer had indeed taken place. See Hamlin (1996), 58.

132. David Bridger, ed., *The New Jewish Encyclopedia* (New York: Behrman House, 1962), S.v. "Halitzah" 185.

133. Ernest R. Lacheman, "Note on Ruth 4:7–8," in *Journal of Biblical Literature*, vol. 56, no. 1 (Mar., 1937), 53, 56. Thomas and Dorothy Thompson ("Some Legal Problems in the Book of Ruth," in *Vetus Testamentum* 18 [1968], 92) make a similar claim.

134. Farbridge (1923), 274; Ryken, Wilhoit, and Longman (1998), 787; Speiser (1940), 15; Charles F. Pfeiffer and Everrett F. Harrison, eds., *The Wycliffe Bible Commentary* (Chicago: Moody Press, 1975), 271; Eakin (1971), 238; G. A. Cooke, *The Book of Ruth* (Cambridge, England: Cambridge University Press, 1913), cited in Cundall and Morris (1968), 306; Francis I. Andersen and David Noel Freedman, *The Anchor Bible: Amos* (New York: Doubleday, 1989), 312–13; G. M. Tucker, "Shorter Communications: Witnesses and 'Dates' in Israelite Contracts," in *The Catholic Biblical Quarterly* 28 (1966): 42.

135. As one commentator put it, "The meaning of this custom was that the adopter would never go again and put his foot in his former property" (Lacheman [1937], 53). Elsewhere we read that by removing the shoe he was "intimating in this that, whatever right he had to walk or go on the land, he conveyed and transferred it . . . *This was the method of legalizing*

transactions in Israel" (Church [1992], O.T. 293. See also David R. Mace, *Hebrew Marriage: A Sociological Study* [New York: Philosophical Library, 1953], 97–98; Tucker [1966], 44).

136. Arthur E. Cundall and Leon Morris, *Tyndale Old Testament Commentaries: Judges and Ruth* (Downers Grove, IL: InterVarsity Press, 1968), 307.

137. Farbridge (1923), 223–24.

138. Ibid., 9.

139. Mace (1953), 98.

140. One commentator on the rite noted: "To confirm whatever was agreed upon, one man drew off . . . his sandal . . . . It is a curious custom, but at least its unusualness would mean that it attracted attention, and this probably was its object . . . . People would know of the agreement reached" (Cundall and Morris [1968], 306). Elsewhere we read: "A man renouncing property rites removed a sandal . . . , a gesture that everyone understood and considered binding if witnessed by the elders" (Readers Digest, *Great People of the Bible and How they Lived* [Pleasantville, New York: Readers Digest, 1974], 133, cited in Church Educational System, *Old Testament: Genesis–2 Samuel [Religion 301] Student Manual*, second edition revised [Salt Lake City: The Church of Jesus Christ of Latter-day Saints, 1981], 263.)

141. See, for example, T. and D. Thompson (1968), 90.

142. Anciently the foot (and, consequently, footwear) symbolized power or possession (e.g., Psalm 8:6, Psalm 36:11, Joshua 10:24), and also territorial claims (e.g., Deuteronomy 1:36, 11:24, Joshua 1:3, 14:9). See Hamlin (1996), 58.

143. The optional rendering given above is based on the following: "And thou shalt **embroider** [Hebrew: *shabats*, meaning to "weave" or "plait"] the **coat** [Hebrew: *kthoneth* or *kuttoneth*, meaning an "undergarment" or "shirtlike garment" sometimes rendered "tunic"] of fine **linen** [Hebrew: *shesh* or *shshiy*, meaning something "bleached white" or of white "linen"]." Admittedly, scholars have translated the passage variously, and thus that which we have offered is but one rendering—but it appears to be a valid rendering of the Hebrew. (See Kenneth Barker, ed., *The NIV Study Bible* [Grand Rapids: Zondervan, 1995], 128, S.v., Exodus 28:39 and footnote 28:39; *Good News Bible* [New York: American Bible Society, 1978], 96, S.v., Exodus 28:39.)

144. The idea that the garment symbolized Christ seems significant. Anciently, the garments of the high priest and the veil of the temple were parallel in their appearance and symbolism. One commentator noted: "Texts which describe [the high priest's] vestments show that these were

made in exactly the same way as the temple curtain" or veil (Barker [2008], 111). Another wrote: "The priest in his robes of 'glory and beauty' was adorned in harmony with his surroundings—the tabernacle; . . . This again reminds us of the great fact that God loves harmony, and that *all* His work is harmonious" (Slemming [1945], 24). Blake Ostler wrote: "It should be noted that the ancient garment bore the same tokens as the veil of the temple at Jerusalem . . . Many ancient texts confuse the garment with the veil of the temple, such as Ambrose of Milano's *Tractate of the Mysteries* or the *Hebrew Book of Enoch* where the 'garment' and 'veil' are used interchangeably" (Blake Ostler, "Clothed Upon: A Unique Aspect of Christian Antiquity," in *BYU Studies* vol. 22, Winter 1982, no. 1, p. 35). Nibley noted: "There is a persistent tendency to compare the veil of the temple and the ritual garment, if not actually to identify them . . . According to the important 'Second Coptic Gnostic Work' the holy garment of the initiate and the veil of the temple have the same significance; they are both symbols of obedience, both representing that virtue which separates the initiate from the wicked world even as it separates existence from nonexistence, the pure from the impure, the elect from all that contaminates and injures—and the two actually follow the same design" (Nibley [2005], 439, 450). As noted elsewhere in this text, the book of Hebrews states that the veil of the temple was a symbol for the flesh of Christ (Hebrews 10:19–21). Nibley pointed out that the garment and the veil of the temple bore "the same markings" and had "the same cosmic significance" (Nibley, *Mormonism* . . . [1987], 75). "Inseparable from the veil were the vestments of the high priest . . . . Veil and vestments were complementary imagery. . . . The veil and the priestly vestments provided the first Christians with ready imagery to convey what they meant by the incarnation" (Nibley, *Mormonism* . . . [1987], 75). In other words, the veil was a symbol for the flesh of Christ—God incarnate. Margaret Barker wrote: "The veil of the temple was used by Christians from the beginning to describe the incarnation. Further, they used not only the veil but also the robe of the high priest, which symbolized the second divine being [i.e., Jesus] being robed in the material world of the veil. The first Christians knew the intimate connection between the two. . . . The veil torn in two at the moment of Jesus' death [was] a graphic illustration of the identity of flesh and veil (Matt. 27:51; Mark 15:38; Luke 23:45)" (Barker [2008], 124). Similarly, LDS scholars, Don and Jay Parry penned this: "Entering the veil of the tabernacle or the temple . . . teaches us of Jesus' atonement. The veil that separated humankind from God's presence . . . symbolizes Jesus Christ's flesh (Heb. 9:3; 10:19–20). The temple veil stood between humans and their entrance into the temple's holiest place; in the same way, the Savior stands between the celestial kingdom and us. 'No man cometh unto the Father, but by me,' Jesus declared (John 14:6)" (Parry and Parry [2009], 33, 128). The fourth-century commentator and hymn writer "Ephrem the Syrian . . . used the veil and the robe to describe the incarnation" (Barker [2008], 126). Since the veil is the garment, and the veil and garment are the flesh of Christ, then Barker's statement that "the veil of the temple is the robe of the angel" or the divine seems significant (ibid., 124). The ancient priest, when clothed in the sacred priestly garment was symbolically being clothed in the flesh of Jesus, representing his call to act on behalf of the divine and to develop the attributes of the divine.

145. The two Hebrew words for "light" and "skin" differ in only the initial letters, and are pronounced alike in modern Hebrew. This explains why some traditions have the garments of Adam and Eve made of light, others have them made of skin. (See Tvedtnes, in Parry [1994], 651.)

146. Slemming (1945), 27. Slemming draws a connection between the garments of the temple high priest and the garments given to Adam and Eve in the Garden of Eden. In Genesis 3:21 we learn that God personally clothed Adam and Eve in their garments, which He had apparently made from the skin of some animal (likely a lamb) which He had slain on their behalf. Of the fact that the Father clothed them Himself, one text notes: "Such personal attention by Deity to the matter of the coats of skins underscores the liturgical import of the garments" (Parry, in Parry [1994], 142). One LDS source notes: "The vestments given to Adam symbolize . . . the possibility of restoring to him the glory of God that he had originally enjoyed" (Stephen D. Ricks, "The Garment of Adam," in Parry [1994], 721). Symbolically speaking, the garments can represent the glory Adam and Eve lost through their fall, and the glory God offers to all who overcome the world. Nibley wrote: "The garment represents the preexistent glory of the candidate. When he leaves on his earthly mission, it is laid up for him in heaven to await his return. It thus serves as security and lends urgency and weight to the need for following righteous ways on earth. For if one fails here, one loses not only one's glorious future in the eternities to come, but also the whole accumulation of past deeds and accomplishments in the long ages of preexistence" (Nibley [2005], 489). Nibley also wrote: "The white undergarment is the proper preexistent glory of the wearer, while the . . . garment of the high priest [or outer garment] . . . is [or represents] the priesthood later added to it [i.e., the undergarment]" (Nibley [2005], 489–90). Another source states: "The resurrection . . . is conceived [of] as the putting on of a new garment" (Carl Clemen, *Primitive Christianity and*

Its Non-Jewish Sources [Edingburg: Clark, 1912], 173–74, cited in Nibley, *Mormonism* . . . [1987], 38, n. 78). John speaks of those who inherit God's kingdom as being clothed in "white raiment" (Revelation 3:5). "The color of the garment is important. The Greek *leukos* denotes brilliance, a state of heavenly splendor . . . . The brilliant, white garment covers those who enter the sacred space of God" (Draper and Parry, in Parry and Ricks [1999], 135–36). The garment appears to mirror the glory of resurrected beings. That which was lost through the Fall shall be returned to all the faithful. The garments of Adam and Eve and the garments of the temple high priest each can symbolize the reality that mankind dwells in a world in which we do not belong, and in which we find ourselves constantly threatened by the powers of darkness. Thus, the story of the Fall informs us that Adam received the garment to protect him as he went forth into the world, not only against it, but against himself, i.e., from the temptations and enticements in which he would find himself. (See Nibley [2008], 350.) The doctrine of the Atonement is clearly at the root of the garments— whether they be those of the priest or those of our first parents. We read:

> "Unto Adam also and to his wife did the Lord God make coats [garments] of skins, and clothed them" (Genesis 3:21). . . . There are two chief connections between the garments of skins and Christ's atoning sacrifice. First, ancient tradition suggests that the skin gar- ments were made of sheep's wool. Wool reminds us of Jesus Christ and his atonement, for the scriptures refer to sacrificial lambs that typify Jesus' death. Christ also is called . . . the "Lamb of God, which taketh away the sin of the world" (John 1:29), and the "lamb without blemish" (1 Peter 1:19). . . . Second, the English word *atone- ment* (at-one-ment) originated from the Hebrew word *kaphar*, which means "to cover." When the Lord covered Adam and Eve with gar- ments of skin, he was, as it were, covering or protecting them by the power of his atonement. Though leaving the presence of God, they were not leaving his protection. (Draper and Parry, in Parry and Ricks [1999], 134–35)

"The Hebrew root *kpr* not only means 'to atone' but it also denotes 'to cover.' This denotation can pertain to covering temple worshipers of ancient Israel with sacred vestments" (Parry and Parry [2009], 29; see also Green [2004], 61). God, in clothing Adam and Eve, shows His concern for their spiritual well-being, and acts as the ultimate parent, teaching them of the Atonement that would "cover" their sins. Additionally, in a liturgical setting, the individual who "clothes" the initiate (in the image and pattern of Adam and Eve being clothed) is a representation of the Father.

147. "The white coat [was] the emblem of righteousness" (Slemming [1945], 31).

148. As Paul noted, Jesus, "who knew no sin," took upon Himself our sins "that we might be made the righteousness of God in him" (2 Corinthians 5:21).

149. Slemming (1945), 28. John Tvedtnes noted that Jewish scholars,

> [Theodor] Reik and [Karl] Abraham . . . saw the prayer shawl, or *tallith,* worn by Jews during certain prayers, as a representation of the sacrificial ram. Though often made of silk, the prayer shawl is ideally made of sheep's wool, and some worshipers prefer the wool of lambs raised in the Holy Land. The rectangular shawl has tassels (*zizzith*) attached to each corner, each tassel consisting of four white and four blue threads and bound together by knots formed by the longest thread. Reik suggests that "the tallith, made from the wool of a ritually clean animal, might be the substitute for the fleece of a ram, originally roughly cured and worn by the Hebraic tribes. The zizzith would then allude to the animal's four legs, and the knotting of the many threads would represent the joints," to which I would add that the blue threads may have originally represented the veins running through the legs. Reik concludes that wearing the *tallith,* a garment sacred to the Jews, was originally intended to identify the wearer with the God of Israel. To the Christian—and to Latter-day Saints in particular—this would suggest that the wearer "put on Christ" (Galatians 3:27; compare Romans 13:14), thus representing "the Lamb of God, which taketh away the sin of the world" (John 1:29). When, therefore, the priests wore the prayer shawl and raised their arms to bless the people, they unknowingly symbolized the Messiah to come. (Tvedtnes, in Parry and Ricks [1999], 86–87)

150. Slemming (1945), 28.

151. Ibid.

152. It is widely accepted that priests who served in the temples of the Judeo-Christian tradition wore special undergarments known as linen breeches. (See Edwards, in Freedman [1992], 2:234; Hyatt [1963], 223.) One text refers to these as "femoralia," "breeches," or "drawers." "*The Oxford English Dictionary* describes femorals as 'clothing for the thighs—breeches'. See Leviticus 6:10: 'The priest shall be revested with the tunike [sic] and the linnen [sic] femoralles'. (Douay Bible 1609)" (Mayo [1984], 153).

153. Slemming (1945), 127.

154. See Dean L. Larsen's comments in *Setting the Record Straight: Mormon Temples* (Orem, UT: Millennial Press, 2007), 77.

155. See Van Gennep (1960), 29–30.

156. See Carlos C. Asay's comments in "The Temple Garment: 'An Outward Expression of an Inward Commitment,'" in *Ensign*, August 1997, 21. The ancient priestly undergarments are typically understood to have been rather simple and plain; at least such was likely the case in Hebrew Bible times. However, a version of these same garments may have existed in New Testament times—and, yet, may not have been so plain. The apostle Paul said: "I bear in my body the marks of the Lord Jesus" (Galatians 6:17). Elder McConkie referred to these "marks" as "the holy symbols typifying faith in Christ and his gospel, which are borne by all the faithful" (McConkie [1987–88], 2:487). On a related note, but predating the New Testament, Nibley suggested of the ancient Egyptians: "Holy insignia were worn . . . on ritual garments or marked on the body itself" (Nibley [2005], 335). In this same text Nibley wrote: "Adam and Eve had ' . . . the names of the Father, Son and Holy Ghost . . . written on their bodies in seven places'" (ibid., 335–36). One source suggested that ritual markings on priestly liturgical clothing served to remind the wearer of the importance of keeping "covenants exactly and honorably," and of the need of God's people "to control [their] thoughts and actions" at all times, in anticipation and preparation of "the Lord's second coming" (Charles [1997], 60). Consequently, symbolic adornments of ancient liturgical garb (when it *did* exist) reminded the wearer of covenants entered into. However, any symbolism beyond that given generally was not described in writing by any of the ancients.

157. See Charles (1997), 60. Seemingly unrelated to the practice of the priests of the Mosaic temple cult is the following curious insight: "I like to think of the garment as the Lord's way of letting us take part of the temple with us when we leave. It is true that we carry from the Lord's house inspired teachings and sacred covenants written in our minds and hearts. However, the one tangible remembrance we carry with us back into the world is the garment. And though we cannot always be in the temple, a part of it can always be with us to bless our lives." Asay (1997), 22.

158. See Barker (2008), 97.

159. See ibid., 112–13.

160. Ibid., 113.

161. See Evelyn T. Marshall, "Garments," in Ludlow (1992), 2:534; Larsen (2007), 77–78; Asay (1997), 19–21.

162. See Green (2004), 61–62.

163. See Charles (1997), 59.

164. One LDS author penned this: Being "covered with the 'garment of salvation'" represents "the cleansing and covering power of the Atonement." Green (2004), 61.

165. Charles (1997), 58.

166. A related point is worth mentioning. The notion that the garments given to Adam and Eve (upon their fall) symbolized the glory possessed by God, the Messiah, and all exalted beings is a common one. Sources suggest that prior to their fall, Adam and Eve wore "garments of light" akin to the glory and light that radiated from the Father (Ginzberg [1967–69], 5:97, n. 69; See also Tvedtnes, in Parry [1994], 651–52; 1 Enoch 62:13, 16, in Charlesworth [1983, 1985], 1:44). When they partook of the "fruit of the tree of knowledge of good and evil" God stripped them of those garments of light and made coats of skins for them as a replacement. (See Ginzberg [1967–69], 1:79; 5:103–104; See also Tvedtnes, in Parry [1994], 651–52.) They "received their garments [of skin] from God after the fall . . . and [Adam's] descendants wore them as priestly garments at the time of the offering of the sacrifices. Furthermore they . . . [are said to have had] supernatural qualities" (Ginzberg [1967–69], 5:103, n. 93). Consequently, the priestly garments can symbolize exaltation because they represent what God has, what man once had, and what God seeks to offer the faithful.

167. See Green (2004), 225.

Six

Covenant-making Rituals

The making of covenants, vows, or promises to God has ever been part of revealed religion. In the Judeo-Christian-Islamic tradition, various promises or oaths are required of those who seek to faithfully live their religion and establish their acceptability before their God. The manner in which these pledges are entered into or enacted varies from one religion to another—and even from one denomination to another. However, the central idea of covenant-making is commonplace in these traditions.

More often than not, covenant-making rituals are laden with symbolism. Whether those symbols are to be found in the language of the oath, in the manner in which the pledge is entered into, or in the defined consequences for breaking the covenant, varies from one religion to another. But what can be said dogmatically is this: for most traditions symbolism is the language of covenant making. This fact requires the participant in the vow to seek understanding of his or her promise (thereby discouraging passive participation in oath making). But it also enables the covenant-maker to gain from the oath (through prayerful contemplation) a fuller understanding of the meaning of the vow as he or she progresses spiritually in the ensuing years. Thus, the covenant has the ability to be non-stagnate because of the symbolism's potential to continually teach anew.

To list every symbol related to or utilized in covenant or oath-making would be an impossibility. Suffice it to say, "signs of recognition," "tokens," "passwords," and "penalties" are common symbolic components in covenant-making rituals. Indeed, the commonality of these symbolic forms among various ancients and moderns alike is surprising. For example, the Essenes,[1] several sects which have broken off of Islam (such as the Ansayrii or Nusairis,[2] and the Druses[3]), the Lamaist sect of *Mahāyāna* Buddhism,[4] and even certain Christian churches (such as the Oriental Orthodox denominations[5]), have and do employ covenant-making elements such as "signs," "tokens," "key words," and "penal oaths" as part of their liturgical rituals.[6] The meaning of such oath-making rituals is sometimes defined, and at other times left for the participant to discover. But each is clearly laden with symbolic meaning and, consequently, with a divine offering to the inquisitive participant who seeks understanding.

Penalties as Part of Oath-making

In the first chapter of the book of Ruth we find a rather curious ritual depicted. The biblical author mentions the rite, but does not elaborate, perhaps because the meaning behind the ceremony was (at that time) common knowledge. The frequently cited passage reads: "And Ruth said, [Naomi,] entreat me not to leave thee, or to return from following after thee: for whither thou goest, I will go; and where thou lodgest, I will lodge: thy people shall be my people, and thy God my God: Where thou diest [Naomi], will I die, and there will I be buried: *the LORD do so to me, and more also, if ought but death part thee and me*" (Ruth 1:16–17 emphasis added). Ruth's promise to Naomi is simply this: I am entering into a covenant that I will stay with you until the end. Where you live and die, I will live and die. And if I break this covenant or promise, may God do the following to me. At that point Ruth apparently made some gesture symbolizing the taking of her life. It is not clear from the English text what sign she made, though she clearly made some penal sign representative of what God would do to her if she was unfaithful to her covenant or oath. Hence her statement to Naomi, "the LORD do so to me, and more also, if . . ." One scholarly source notes:

> This solemn oath formulary appears only here and in eleven passages in Samuel and Kings. The first part of it was presumably accompanied by a symbolic gesture, something like our index finger [being drawn] across the throat.[7] Deep behind this lay, in all probability, a ritual act involving the slaughter of animals, to whom the one swearing the oath equated himself. The best indications that this is so are the portrayals of elaborate covenant ratifications, containing solemn oaths, in Gen 15:7–17 and Jer 34:18–20. The slaughtered and spilt animals represent what the oath-taker invites God to do to him if he fails to keep the oath.[8]

Elsewhere we read: "The formula [Ruth] uses . . . suggests but does not define the punishment that should follow the breaking of the oath. So [it] was perhaps accompanied by some expressive gesture (touching the throat?). Otherwise [the verse] is incomprehensible."[9] Ruth appears here to be "cutting a covenant" with Naomi—meaning, as was anciently the custom, when one wished to enter into a covenant one attached a penalty to that covenant, often by making a penal sign when swearing the oath or through slaying an animal as part of the oath. In either case, part of the covenant was a promise that if the maker of the covenant did not live up to his or her promise, he or she was to be slain in the way the aforementioned animal was slain, or in the way the penal sign suggested. Ruth's oath or covenant to Naomi was sworn or made with such a penalty in mind.[10] John Milton wrote: "An Oath is that whereby we call God to witness the truth of what we say, with a curse upon ourselves, either implied or expressed, should it prove false."[11]

Though the utilization of penalties as part of oath making is particularly commonplace in ancient Semitic covenant rituals, the practice is found elsewhere in antiquity, and also has its parallels in modernity. For example, in one Roman Catholic oath ritual we find this statement made by the initiate: "If then—which may God forbid!—anyone is tempted to reveal our secrets, let him think well before he acts. Such a one would surely incur the curse of God."[12] Similarly, in rites celebrated by U.S. Jews in the nineteenth and early twentieth centuries we find the use of pronounced penalties for "those who violated the covenant" entered into.[13] Even in Islam, certain Muslim mystics, like the Bektashi order of Sufism, take oaths that have penalties attached. They are to keep confidential the secret or esoteric teachings of their order "on pain of death."[14] Those who break the vow of secrecy are subject to several "punishments."[15] Of the act of "cutting a covenant" as an initiation ritual, one scholar wrote: "The mutilated individual is removed from the common mass of humanity by [this] rite of separation (this is the idea behind cutting . . . , etc.) which automatically incorporates him into a defined group; . . . the incorporation is permanent."[16] In other words, making covenants with penal signs attached sets the participant apart from the world, and incorporates him or her into a new group, family, or circle—the initiated or endowed.

In each case the penalty is symbolic but certainly highlights the sacral nature of oaths or covenants. The symbolic implications of such oaths varies from people to people and religion to religion. From a Christian perspective the penal sign is likely not to be taken literally as evidence that one will be physically sacrificed for breaking his or her covenant. Rather, the death implied by the penal signs among Christians who use such oath-making gestures would be spiritual. One who breaks his or her oath, therefore, should expect to lose his or her salvation. A multiplicity of signs implies a multiplicity of penalties, though usually with the same ultimate consequence—a loss of salvation or, in LDS terms, exaltation. Thus, if God is traditionally seen by most Christians as omnipotent,[17] omniscient,[18] and omnipresent,[19] the person who breaks his or her covenant should expect to lose the blessing of heaven, including the divine promise that the faithful would become as God is.[20] The reverse is also true: the individual who keeps his or her covenants should expect to become as the Father is and to receive all that the Father has; including the traits of omnipotence, omniscience, and (in God's way) omnipresence.

SIGNS OR RITUAL GESTURES

The making of "ritual gestures" or "signs" during the covenant-making process is common to most ancient and many modern religions. "All our own well-known manual gestures are not simple conventionalities, the outcome of accident, but . . . each has some distinct meaning."[21] Indeed, the importance of the gestures, and the need for them to be performed in an exact specified manner, is evidenced by the fact that they are "carefully prescribed" in the rubrics or manuals of the Catholic Church.[22] One recent LDS text noted:

> Religious rituals (or ties) are sacred actions or "ceremonial movements." Some scholars refer to these rites of transition as "gestures of approach" because they are religious gestures (or acts or movements) that worshipers make as they approach God during sacred worship. The ancient temple, especially, included sacred gestures that enabled and empowered worshipers to move from the outer gate inward to the most holy place of all, the holy of holies. The gestures of approach are vital to a temple society because they symbolically cleanse and prepare worshipers for entry into and movement through sacred space as they transition from the profane world into the sacred temple.[23]

Again, these "gestures of approach" vary from religion to religion. One of the most common is the raising of the arm to the square. What this "gesture" or "sign" represents depends upon the religion and the rite being enacted. For Christians, other than symbolizing one's willingness to sustain another, or the representation of one's entrance into a covenant, the raised right hand is often understood to be "a sign of power and command."[24] The right arm raised was known as the "right hand of power." When raised, it symbolized receiving the "gift" God was offering (and that which God offers us through rituals or ordinances is a portion of His power).[25] One LDS source suggested that the "sign" or "gesture" of raising the arm to the square was a Christocentric symbol. "The square in the carpenter's toolbox (remember who the Carpenter is) represents exactness in all we do. Christ, as the only person who was perfectly exact in his mortal life, could himself be symbolized as a square. When we participate in covenants involving the symbol of the square, we are reaching up to God in a way that reminds us of Christ, in whose name the covenants are made."[26]

Of course, the raised arm to the square is not the only "gesture of approach" found in ancient or modern liturgical rites. For example, the Hebrew word traditionally translated "ordain" in the *King James Version* of the Bible means quite literally to "fill the hand," and seems to have some ritual significance.[27] The very fact that "filling" one's empty or cupped hand became synonymous with "ordaining" a man implied that the ordained is given something—namely, power or authority. Thus, the ceremonial act of "filling one's hand" is a ritualistic way of saying that one is "receiving" power or authority. The "filling of the hand" may also symbolize the receipt of blessings, as ancient temple priests (when consecrated) had their hands filled with portions of the temple offerings—thus they were being endowed with God's gifts (each token of His sacrifice on their behalf).[28]

Though the making of "gestures of approach" or ritual "signs" may seem to be exclusively the practice of ancient peoples,[29] various faiths in modernity utilize "signs" in the covenant-making process. Roman Catholicism is a prime example. They have certain ceremonies or rites in which "signs" are utilized by initiates.[30] One Roman Catholic text notes that in making a covenant, the initiates are instructed: "Raise your right hands and repeat after me."[31] This same source states that it is important to "teach your members the mode and use of the secret signs."[32] In the nineteenth and early twentieth centuries, Jews who immigrated to the United States came up with a set of ritual "signs" which initiates would employ as part of a fraternal order created to ease the transition into a new culture and nation.[33] Each of these "signs" had symbolic meanings associated with the faith to which they were attached. For Christians these may have been Christocentric, or even penal connotations—though, once again, the penal signs tended to have a Christocentric meaning among Christians because of their association with Godly powers promised to the faithful.

Tokens and Passwords

The early Christians had what some have referred to as "tokens of recognition."[34] These were handclasps utilized for a number of reasons, and which carried a number of symbolic meanings. One text on rites of passage noted that exchanging things or receiving gifts binds the receiver to the giver. This same text notes that clasping hands, embracing, or receiving ritual garments would be included in such acts of binding. The receipt (or exchanging) of such items is equivalent to "pronouncing an oath" or entering into a covenant.[35] Handclasps as "tokens of recognition," covenant, and reconciliation were common in ancient cultures and religions, including that of the early Christians.[36] Indeed, one historian wrote: "We cannot but admit that a very important function is accorded to the hand, in various parts of religious ritual, by all Christians, Hebrews, and by many others."[37] In his article on "The Sacred Handclasp in the Classical and Early Christian World," LDS scholar Stephen D. Ricks spoke of "a solemn and ceremonial handclasp" known by the Greeks as *dexiosis*, and in Latin as *dextrarum iunctio*, which means "giving" or "joining of [the] right hands." Ricks noted the commonality of these "gestures" or "tokens" in antiquity when taking an oath of allegiance, or when receiving "the mysteries." Indeed, he points out that initiates into the mysteries were typically called *syndexioi*, meaning "joined by the right hand."[38]

Nibley suggested that such handclasps or "tokens of recognition" were "used extensively in regulating ancient social and religious gatherings; they are all means of identification, whose main purpose is security"[39]—security in the sense that they carried the potential of revealing one's friends and exposing one's enemies.[40] Anciently tokens were "proof of identity."[41] By them you knew whom you dealt with, and whether he be friend or foe.[42] One commentator pointed out: "The giving of the hand," for example, "showed that a relationship was established between two persons (2 Kings 10:15; Jeremiah 50:15; Ezekiel 17:18)."[43] To clasp another's hand was a sign of a "pledge" or an expression of "solidarity."[44] He who had such "tokens" also carried authority—divine authority—and, thus, could be trusted.

One dictionary of symbols suggests that, "In esoteric doctrine, the position of the hand in relation to the body, and the arrangement of the fingers, convey certain precise symbolic notions."[45] Consequently, the meaning of a given "token of recognition" is contingent upon its context, religious affiliation, and manner of conveyance. Generally speaking, ancient Christian tokens commonly symbolized "the eschatological union" or man's return to his God. Thus, one source states: "the handclasp . . . expresses salvation, the saving and the saved."[46] In the illuminated Bible of S. Paolo fuóri le Mura, which dates from the ninth century, we find an illustration of God's hand clasping that of a mortal in an apparent depiction of an ascension motif. God's hand is coming from behind a cloud (i.e., a veil?), and he grasps the other hand in a rather curious and unusual way as he is apparently drawing the human into his presence.[47] One commentator wrote: "The ritual handclasp in the mysteries and early Christianity was linked with concepts of equality, friendship, agreement, liminality, entrance, marriage, sexuality, salvation, starting the path of initiation, ending the path of initiation, resurrection, forgiveness, reconciliation, communion of man with man, of human with god, of god with god, and apotheosis."[48] In the giving or receipt of a "token of recognition" the two separate hands, each representative of the giver, would "intertwine" fingers with the other "to make a new unity, complex yet simple."[49] The man estranged from his God gave or received a "token of recognition," and in so doing became "one" with his God once again.[50]

The ancient practice of employing "tokens of recognition" in the covenant-making process is attested to in scripture. For example, in the book of Genesis we find the following: "And Abraham said unto his eldest servant of his house, that ruled over all that he had, Put, I pray thee, thy hand under my *thigh*: . . . And the servant put his hand under the *thigh* of Abraham his master, and sware to him concerning that matter" (*KJV* Genesis 24:2, 9; emphasis added). Curiously, the *JST* of this same passage is slightly different, and reads as follows:

> And Abraham said unto his eldest servant of his house, that ruled over all that he had; Put forth I pray thee thy hand under my *hand*, and I will make thee swear before the Lord, the God of heaven, and the God of the earth, that thou shalt not take a wife unto my son, of the daughters of the Canaanites among whom I dwell; but thou shalt go unto my country, and to my kindred and take a wife unto my son Isaac. . . . And the servant put his hand under the *hand* of Abraham his master, and sware to him concerning that matter (*JST* Genesis 24:2, 8, emphasis added).

In the passage under consideration, Abraham makes a request of Eliezer (whose name means "God is my help"). Abraham doesn't just send Eliezer out to find a wife for Isaac; he requires an oath or covenant from him. This highlights how important this is to Abraham. This is no mild request.

Scholars of the Hebrew universally agree that Eliezer is placing his hand under (or on) Abraham's reproductive area.[51] There isn't anything sexual or inappropriate implied here. It is highly symbolic, but easily misunderstood in the permissive society in which we live. One source recorded: "The person binding himself put his hand under the thigh of the person to whom he was to be bound; i.e., he put his hand on the part that bore the mark of circumcision, the sign of God's covenant, which is tantamount to our . . . laying the hand upon the New Testament" when swearing an oath.[52] Another text notes that anciently the reproductive organs represented "the life-giving power of deity"—something inheritors of the Judeo-Christian tradition sought to obtain.[53] The Hebrew word translated "loins" in the Old Testament is also often translated "thigh." Both imply reproduction, offspring, or procreative powers. Thus, we read: "And all the souls that came with Jacob into Egypt, which came out of his loins [or thigh] besides Jacob's sons' wives, all the souls were threescore and six" (Genesis 46:26). Also, "And all the souls that came out of the loins [or thigh] of Jacob were seventy souls" (Exodus 1:5). So Abraham's oath with Eliezer had to do with offspring or posterity. Abraham was trying to insure that the Abrahamic Covenant was received and entered into by Isaac. Several commentaries offer interpretations, such as the following: "The rite . . . place[s] the one who swears under the penalty of sterility if the task is not carried out."[54] And "Since sons are said to issue from their father's thigh, an oath that involved touching this vital part might entail the threat of sterility for the offender or the extinction of his offspring."[55] One of the primary promises of the Abrahamic Covenant was "innumerable posterity" (Genesis 22:17). Abraham appears to be saying to Eliezer, if you do not keep this oath, you will *not* inherit exaltation—the only heavenly reward that includes the power of procreation.[56] One non-LDS biblical scholar wrote: "The symbolism [behind Abraham's act] may receive its biblical meaning as a peculiarly appropriate conclusion to the story of Abraham and Sarah, which begins in their childlessness (11:30) and God's promise [to make them a great nation through whom all nations of the earth would be blessed] (12:1–3). Does the symbolic act combine notions reflected in the Latin word *testis*, which means both 'testator' and 'testicle'?"[57]

Of course, the *JST* changes "thigh" to "hand." Of this change, one source notes: "The gesture seems to have been a token of the covenant being made between the two men, perhaps similar to our shaking hands."[58] The point of the passage is to say that, one who does not keep his covenants shall not inherit the blessings of the Abrahamic covenant, including all of the blessings of Abraham, Isaac, and Jacob. Included in those blessings are godhood and eternal increase (or "innumerable posterity"). The *JST* version of the verse represents this idea through the receipt of a token and sign symbolic of omnipresence, or eternal increase. If one breaks his or her covenants—including the covenant of marriage—that person will *not* become as God is, nor will he or she have eternal increase, as gods do. So that which may seem disgusting or sexual in modern western culture, is really about the promises of godhood that all who enter into revealed covenants have offered to them.

The giving of one's hand, or offering a "token," as part of a covenant-making ritual, is not exclusive to the ancient patriarch. Other scriptural examples might be pointed to in the Hebrew

Bible[59] and the Greek New Testament.[60] Similarly, in the texts of the intertestamental period, we commonly see reference to the utilization of "tokens of recognition." For example, Enoch takes Noah by the hand.[61] He also speaks of the angel Metatron[62] (or Michael) who presented him before God's throne: "He grasped me with his hand," Enoch reports, "and said to me, 'Come in peace into the presence of the high and exalted King . . .' Then I entered . . . and [he] presented me before the throne of glory."[63] In one text Enoch informs the reader of a vision he had of several heavenly beings: "There came forth from heaven (a being) in the form of a snow-white person . . . and three others with him. Those ones which had come out last [i.e., the three] seized me by my hand . . ."[64] Three heavenly beings "wearing snow-white clothes" appeared to Enoch and clasped his hand before giving him an ascension experience.[65] Enoch also reported: "The angel Michael, one of the archangels, seizing me by my right hand . . . , led me [through] all the secrets of mercy, and he showed me all the secrets of righteousness."[66] Like Enoch, intertestamental literature suggests that the ancient patriarch, Abraham, also received "tokens of recognition" from divine beings. Indeed, Abraham reports several experiences with an angel who "took [him] by the right hand."[67]

Various sects associated with Christianity in one way or another (in the early years of the Common Era) seemed to employ "tokens of recognition" as part of their rites, rituals, or covenant-making acts. One text reports that Gnostic-Christians had "their own secret distinguishing signs. . . . According to Epiphanius (circa AD 315–403) the (Barbeliote[68]) Gnostics, by way of greeting, made a tickling stroke on the palm of the hand."[69] Elsewhere we read: "The Manicheans[70] . . . had secret forms of recognition, three in number, described by St. Augustine as the word, the grip, and the breast."[71] Certain modern Christian, Jewish, and Islamic denominations are found to employ "tokens of recognition." For example, one scholar pointed out: "In all the Oriental Orthodox Churches . . . the priest greets the deacon at the altar, and then the deacon comes down among the faithful to transmit [the] sign of peace, from row to row or all around the Church. The gesture

itself is performed in different ways. Among the Syrians, the faithful touch hands . . . . Among the Copts it is similar."[72] In Roman
Catholic practice you see, in certain ceremonies or rites, the utilization of "grips" or "tokens."[73] One Catholic text states: "The grip
is given by shaking hands in the ordinary way, and giving two distinct pressures with all the fingers. This is answered by one sharp
pressure."[74] Accompanying the grip is a question to be answered
by the individual being examined.[75] One text dealing with nineteenth and early twentieth century Jewish immigrants and their
rites speaks of handclasps, "grips," or "hand signals."[76] "Some
Orthodox religious congregations . . . adopted customs from the
world of the lodge, including . . . [the use of] hand . . . signals."[77]
Curiously, in certain Sufi initiation rites one sees several essential
elements that make up the ritual of initiation. First of all there is
the receipt of "secret instruction." Then there is the taking of the
"compact" or "covenant"—which often includes a "handclasp"
and the investing with sacred clothing.[78] The Bektashi order of
dervishes—a branch of Sufism—have "signs they use" and "special phrases" as "part of the symbolic side of their secret" typically
referred to as "the symbolic secret."[79] One of the Bektashi signs
consists of closing the last two fingers on the right hand, and then
placing them over the heart. The remaining three fingers are left
open with the thumb extended. Another symbolic token used by
this same group consists of touching the fingers and thumb of the
left hand while resting them just under the chin. An additional
sign or token consists of touching the lips with the thumb, and
then immediately lowering the hand to just below the heart, and
slightly to the left while barely and briefly bowing the head. A
fourth token consists of shaking hands while pressing the ends of
the thumbs together. Symbolically speaking some see this token
as representing unity and the idea that the hearts of the two participants are "attached to one another."[80] In Sufism the symbolic
meaning of letters is "extremely important." Each letter is said to
have, for the Muslim Mystics, a "secret meaning hidden" within.[81]
The Arabic letter *alif,* which is the first letter of the alphabet, symbolizes (for some Sufis) "the whole wisdom" of Sufism, Islam, and

the Qur'an. More specifically, the *alif* for many mystics symbolizes God, the source of all wisdom and truth.[82] Indeed, that character of the Arabic alphabet has been called "the divine letter."[83] It symbolizes the unity of God, and also God's uniqueness.[84] But it also represents "the spiritually free, the true mystics who have reached union with God."[85]

What is to be made of these rather common practices found in ancient and modern rites? The symbolism is dependent upon the faith in which the token or gesture is found.[86] In some traditions the symbolism behind the "token of recognition" is not given to the initiate, but the participant is apparently to discover it for himself. In others, "tokens" and their meanings are disclosed to those participating in the rite. Certain general meanings regarding the symbolism are known. For example, in many religious traditions the right hand is the "hand of power" and is associated with "rectitude," whereas the left hand often has negative connotations, such as "deviousness."[87] Thus, tokens are more often than not received by clasping right hands, but seldom (if ever) by gripping left hands.

Not surprisingly, in Islam at least some of the "tokens of recognition" employed are symbols of Allah.[88] Consequently, one would expect that those utilized by various Christian denominations (ancient and modern) would most likely be Christocentric.[89] In what one text refers to as "Jesus' round dance,"[90] we see the Savior kneeling and praying while encircled by His Twelve Apostles, who say "Amen" or "so be it" after each clause in Jesus' prayer. In so doing, they make the prayer their own, as though they had uttered the words themselves. Significantly, one commentator on a Gnostic account of this ritual states that the redeemer "must be wounded" and then his followers must "repeat the acts and sufferings of [their] god in [or during] the mystery action" or ritual. In so doing they are promised "deification."[91] In the ritual (which will be discussed more fully in the chapter on prayer rituals), this same source states, "the believer must incur the same sufferings as his [or her] god, and therefore he [or she] must mourn with him."[92] In other words, during the "round dance" or prayer circle, symbolic signs were made or tokens were exchanged, each of which represented some aspect of suffering that the participant's God had endured. These symbols, according to our early Christian source, were Christocentric—focused specifically on the Atonement.[93]

Finally, frequently accompanying the signs and tokens[94] mentioned in this chapter are certain "secret" words or phrases. They are found in specific Catholic rites,[95] in some rare rites associated with Judaism,[96] and even in certain branches of Islam.[97] These "secret" words or "passwords" symbolized fidelity to covenants, if they were kept secret. They represented to the recipient an endowment or gift, as they were considered symbols of God's holy words. Thus to receive them implied both that God had endowed you, but also that God had entrusted you. Consequently, they were also symbols of divine friendship and acceptance. In some cases they functioned as keywords or passwords—and thus enabled the one in possession of them to know friend from foe; demons from the divine.

Notes

1.   The Essenes were a Jewish sect that flourished from about the middle of the second century BC until about AD 70. Of them, one text states: "The Essenes were founded in the late second century BCE by a man known as the Teacher of Righteousness and were isolationists, rejecting in particular the right of the Hasmoneans and their successors to hold the high priesthood and claiming as invalid much of the ritual of temple worship, while recognizing the importance of the temple itself. Essene ideas are characterized as more apocalyptic and messianic than other trends within Judaism, and were influential on the Diaspora. The Qumran sect, which produced the Dead Sea Scrolls, is thought to have been Essene" (Hugh Bowden, "Origins and Background," in Bowden [2005], 846). See also John J. Collins, "Essenes," in Freedman (1992), 2:619.

2.   The Ansayrii or Nusairis (aka 'Alawī) are a prominent (though minority) religion in Syria that is often seen as a sect of Shiah Islam, though the faith clearly has borrowed (in doctrine and liturgy) from Christianity, Gnosticism, ancient Babylonian belief, probably Zoroastrianism, and Islam. Though it is uncertain, it is believed that the sect dates from somewhere around the mid–tenth century CE. They are certainly heterodox (i.e., non-orthodox), by Islamic standards, and would be considered mystics in every sense. (See Glassé [1989], 30–31.)

3.   The Druses or Druzes are a sect who have historical ties to eleventh-century Islam, but are hardly Muslim today. They are seen as "unitarians" who have been influenced by Gnosticism, Islam, and the Occult. Though they retain a few Muslim doctrines, they also have a number of teachings that would be foreign to Islam, like an acceptance of reincarnation. They practice extreme asceticism and offer several degrees of secret initiation. (See Glassé [1989], 103–104.)

4.   Lamaism is a branch of *Mahāyāna* Buddhism common in Tibet and Mongolia, as well as in parts of Nepal and northern India. Though Buddhism was introduced into Tibet in the mid–seventh century, this branch of Buddhism likely has its origins in the mid–eighth century.

5.   The Oriental Orthodox Churches, such as the Armenian, Coptic, Ethiopian, and Syriac Orthodox Churches, have their origin in the split that resulted from the Christological doctrines pronounced at the Council of Chalcedon (AD 451). Those that accepted the Council's Christology (or doctrine of Christ) are known as Eastern Orthodox (e.g., Greek, Russian, or Romanian Orthodox), and those who rejected it are known as Oriental Orthodox. The latter of these two branches of orthodoxy are sometimes known as "non-Chalcedonian churches"—distinguishing them from the Eastern Orthodox who were generally comfortable with the dualistic Christological definitions of Chalcedon. (See Betty Jane Bailey and J. Martin Bailey, *Who Are The Christians in the Middle East?* [Grand Rapids: Eerdmans, 2003], 48–49, 66–67.)

6.   See Bernard H. Springett, *Secret Sects of Syria and Lebanon* (London: George Allen and Unwin, 1922), 92, 122, 140–141, 173, 176–177, 241, 250.

7.   One commentator notes: "The thumb extended as a manual gesture is not confined to Christian ritual." This same source points out that the ritual extending of the thumb was, anciently, part of Jewish cleansing rites, Islamic rites of circumcision, Buddhist begging practices, and even certain practices of Danish royalty. (See Frederick Thomas Elworthy, *Horns of Honour* [London: John Murray, 1900], 153–54.) In some cases the extended thumb stood as a symbol (such as a knife) in the hand of the initiate acting out the penalty.

8.   Edward F. Campbell, Jr., *The Anchor Bible: Ruth* (New York: Doubleday, 1975), 74. Hugh Nibley wrote: "Anciently the principle of proxy was carried out . . . . A clear case comes from Leviticus 8:12–15 . . . . Aaron kills the bullock, puts the blood on the altar . . . to make atonement for [the people]. The rites with the Levites are the same. Thus the sacrifices are carried out in the temple without the shedding of human blood, but

if human blood can be spared, why not all blood? Because this was the similitude of the shedding of blood for the atonement of sin. Properly, of course, the sinner's own blood must be shed, unless a *gō'ēl*, a representative substitute advocate or redeemer, could be found to take one's place. *The willingness of the candidate to sacrifice his own life . . . is symbolized by the blood on the right thumb and right earlobe, where the blood would be if the throat had been cut*" (Nibley [1992], 57–58, emphasis added).

9. Cundall and Morris (1968), 261. Curiously, in Moses 5:29 Satan insists Cain swear an oath to him "by [Cain's] throat." See also Alma 46:21 where the people swear a covenant that if they should break their oath they should be rent as their garment has been rent.

10. Typically when the King James Version of the Bible speaks of "making a covenant" the Hebrew is "to cut a covenant." (See Brown, Driver, and Briggs [1993], 503.) For interesting studies on the subject of "Cutting a Covenant," see H. Eilberg-Schwartz, *The Savage in Judaism* (Bloomington, IN: University of Indiana Press, 1990), 100; Theodor H. Gaster, *Myth, Legend, and Custom in the Old Testament.* (New York: Harper and Row, 1969), 140–56, 362–63; Ginzberg (1967–69), 1:234–37; Keil and Delitzsch, *Commentary on the Old Testament: The Pentateuch.* (Grand Rapids: Eerdmans, 1986), 209–19; Meredith G. Kline, "Oath and Ordeal Signs," in *Westminster Theological Journal.* Vol. 26 (1967): 115–39; Martin Noth, *The Laws In The Pentateuch and Other Studies* (Philadelphia: Fortress Press, 1967), 108–17; Gordon Wenham, *Word Biblical Commentary: Genesis 1–15.* (Waco, TX: Word Books, 1987), 322–35; Claus Westermann, *Genesis 12–36: A Commentary.* (Minneapolis: Augsburg Publishing House, 1981), 212–31.

11. See John Milton, *A Treatise on Christian Doctrine* (Cambridge: Cambridge University Press, 1825), 579. Elsewhere we read: "The ritual performance of a curse was anciently an imitation of sacrifice . . . . All of this, of course, was 'a similitude of the sacrifice of the Only Begotten' (Moses 5:7), which atoned for the sins of all, and thus redeems or saves from death. . . . We are told that a covenant must be made by the shedding of one's own blood unless a substitute can be found to *redeem* one (see Numbers 8:13–15). In ancient times, all the sacrifices were symbolic. . . . One penalty is particularly interesting because of a very early Christian writing known as the *Discourse on Abbatôn*, which goes back to apostolic times in Jerusalem. . . . It tells how . . . Satan refused to recognize [Adam], saying, ' . . . bring a sharp sickle and cut him at breast level from shoulder to shoulder, on this side and on that, right through his body . . . ' " (Nibley [2008], 361–62).

12. Knight (1920), 92.
13. See Soyer (1999): 169.
14. Springett (1922), 79, 92.
15. See ibid., 79.
16. Van Gennep (1960), 72.
17. Sometimes symbolized by the throat and its power to command.
18. Sometimes symbolized by the heart, the seat of knowledge in the minds of the ancients.
19. Sometimes symbolized by the loins, the location of the procreative powers through which we become omnipresent via our offspring.
20. Related, but not identical, is the following offered by Hugh Nibley. "The Egyptian . . . embalming rites included ritual blows [or wounds] inflicted on the corpse in imitation of the sacrificial death of Osiris" (Nibley [2005], 382). Nibley suggested that the act of embalming in ancient Egypt was a ritual designed to imitate the treatment the deceased God has previously experienced. Consequently, the embalmed person, through this ritual, was being initiated in the image of his God. "To enjoy the blessing of Osiris—eternal life—one must do the works and suffer the vicissitudes of Osiris" (Nibley [2005], 133.) Thus, the act of embalming was really a ritual re-enactment of how God Himself had been slain. Consequently, in death man becomes "the peer of the gods" (W. Brede Kristenesen, *Het leven uit de dood: Studeien over Egyptische en oud-Griekse godsdienst*, second edition [Haarlem: Bohn, 1949], 40–41, cited in Nibley [2005], 133). The ancient Egyptians had a popularly told legend about Osiris, the god of the dead—and founder of religion, temples, and rituals—and how he was dismembered by his rival brother, Set—"the personification in the battle against good" (Richard Carlyon, *A Guide to the Gods* [New York: Quill, 1982], 287–89, 294–95; Donald A. Mackenzie, *Egyptian Myths and Legends* [New York: Gramercy Books, 1994], 17, 21). Consequently, ever concerned about their own dismembering by the evil one, the Egyptians were wont to petition their gods to protect them from such penalties. One text notes: "When the soul sets forth [on the journey to the other side] . . . evil spirits and fierce demons compass him about . . . But his most formidable enemy is the fierce god Set, the murderer of Osiris, the terror of the good gods and of men . . . . Fain would that wrathful demon devour the pilgrim on his way" (Mackenzie [1994], 97). Thus, exercising faith in the assistance of Osiris, the petitioner would announce (in a sort of faith-based plea) things such as "my bowels shall not perish" or "my head shall not be separated from my neck; my tongue shall not be carried away" (E. A.

Wallis Budge, *Egyptian Religion: Ideas of the Afterlife in Ancient Egypt* [New York: Gramercy Books, 1959], 100).

21. Elworthy (1900), 148.

22. See Elworthy (1900), 153; Frederick Thomas Elworthy, *The Evil Eye* (London: John Murray, 1895), 269, n. 417.

23. Parry and Parry (2009), 22.

24. Julien (1996), 189. "The power of the human hand . . . is an article of very ancient belief, and remains almost unaltered to this day." Elworthy (1900), 159.

25. See Elworthy (1900), 160.

26. Parry and Parry (2009), 14.

27. See Kaiser, in Gaebelein (1976–92), 2:471, n. 9; R. Alan Cole, *Exodus: An Introduction and Commentary* (Downers Grove, IL: InterVarsity Press, 1973), 203; Richard J. Clifford, "Exodus," in Brown, Fitzmyer, and Murphy (1990), 57; Parry and Parry (2009), 30; Victor P. Hamilton, *Handbook on the Pentateuch* (Grand Rapids: Baker Book House, 1982), 266.

28. See Clifford, in Brown, Fitzmyer, and Murphy (1990), 57; Joseph H. Hertz, *Pentateuch and Haftorahs*, second edition (London: Soncino Press, 1962), 344; Parry and Parry (2009), 29–30. In slaying an animal, as part of ancient temple sacrifices, "the hand is held in such a manner as to hold the blood, as it holds the oil in the anointing" (Nibley [2008], 396).

29. For example, of the ancient Essenes, we read: "When addressing their chiefs they stood with their right hand extended below their chin and the left dropped to their side" (Springett [1922], 92).

30. See Knight (1920), x.

31. Ibid., 86.

32. Ibid., 29.

33. See Soyer (1999): 168.

34. See, for example, Todd M. Compton, "The Handclasp and Embrace as Tokens of Recognition," in Lundquist and Ricks (1990), 1:611–42.

35. See Van Gennep (1960), 29–30.

36. See Compton, in Lundquist and Ricks (1990), 1:611–42. Even in apocryphal stories of antiquity, the symbolic act of conveying tokens in the covenant-making process is found. For example, one ancient text suggests that the devil tried to deceive Adam, and in so doing sought the exchange of a sacred token: "Satan, the hater of all good, took the form of an angel, . . . and greeted Adam and Eve with fair words that were full of guile. Then Satan . . . said, 'Rejoice, O Adam, and be glad. Lo, God has sent [me] to thee to tell thee something.' . . . But Adam said, 'I know you not.' . . . And Satan said unto him 'Swear, and promise me that thou wilt

receive [the message God has sent me to bear].' Then Adam said, 'I know not how to swear and promise.' And Satan said to him, 'Hold out thy hand, and put it inside my hand.' Then Adam held out his hand, and put it into Satan's hand; when Satan said unto him, 'Say, now . . . I will not break my promise, nor renounce my word.' And Adam swore thus" ("The First Book of Adam and Eve," or "The Conflict of Adam and Eve with Satan," 70:1, 2, 5, 8, 12–16, in Rutherford H. Platt, Jr., ed., *The Forgotten Books of Eden* [Cleveland, Ohio: The World Publishing Company, 1927], 49–50). While initially the handclasp was primarily associated with the making of contracts, it spread as a form of salutation throughout Europe primarily because of the influence of Christianity, or perhaps via Manicheanism, a heretical break-off group associated with third-century Christianity. (See Compton, in Lundquist and Ricks [1990], 1:622.)

37.   Elworthy (1900), 155.

38.   See Stephen D. Ricks, *"Dexiosis and Dextrarum Iunctio*: The Sacred Handclasp in the Classical and Early Christian World," in *The FARMS Review* 18/1 (2006): 431–32. Nibley wrote: "A token, according to the Oxford English Dictionary, is 'something given as the symbol and evidence of a right or privilege, upon the presentation of which the right or privilege may be exercised.' To be more specific, a sign (*signum*) was both a pointing (related to *zeigen*, teach, didactic, etc.) and a touching (touch, take, tactile, *dactyl*). In particular, it was the *dexter*, the right hand or taking hand, and as such is universal in the *dexiosis* of the mysteries" (Nibley [2008], 362). One source states: "There are a number of words in Greek and Latin that mean 'token' in recognition drama – e.g., *anagnōsmata* ('things for making known again'), *spargana* (the swaddling wrappings of the lost child, often figured), *sēmeia* ('signs, marks, signals'). But one of the most interesting token-words is the basis for our word 'symbol': *symbolon* (singular; plural: *symbola*), found as a name for tokens both in recognition and mystery. This word means 'things thrown together' (i.e., something thrown together after it has been once broken apart, from *ballo*, 'thrown,' and sun-, 'with or together'). . . . The halves 'thrown together,' unified, are the symbol of two separate identities merging into one. . . . The handclasp and the embrace perfectly express [the] concept of two separate halves coming together to create a unity" (Compton, in Lundquist and Ricks [1990], 1:612–14).

39.   Nibley (2008), 362–63. "The hand, the emblem and instrument of power, naturally became in itself one of the earliest of protective amulets." Elworthy (1895), 241. "The earliest examples we have of the hand as an amulet . . . are found . . . from early Etruscan tombs . . . They are described

as belonging 'to the first age of iron,' a period of extreme antiquity." The earliest examples were almost universally intended to represent an open hand with its fingers extended. "But as skill improved, we find attempts more or less successful to represent the hand in definite positions or gestures." Elworthy (1895), 241–42.

40. Certain "manual gestures" made with the hands were believed, among the Italians, to have the power to "ward off" the influence of the devil or evil. See Elworthy (1900), 146. See also Elworthy (1895), 234.

41. Compton, in Lundquist and Ricks (1990), 1:614.

42. On a related note, Joseph Smith stated: "I preached in the grove on the keys of the Kingdom, Charity &c The keys are certain signs and words by which false spirits and personages may be detected from true, which cannot be revealed to the Elders till the Temple is completed —The rich can only get them in the Temple—the poor may get them on the Mountain top as did Moses. The rich cannot be saved without Charity, giving to feed the poor when and how God requires as well as building. There are signs in heaven, earth, and hell, the Elders must know them all to be endowed with power, to finish their work and prevent imposition. The devil knows many signs but does not know the sign of the Son of Man, or Jesus. *No one can truly say he knows God until he has handled something, and this can only be in the Holiest of Holies*" (Andrew F. Ehat and Lyndon W. Cook, eds., *The Words of Joseph Smith* [Provo, UT: Religious Studies Center, 1980], 119–20, emphasis added).

43. Farbridge (1923), 275. See also J. F. McConkie (1985), 262; Todeschi (1995), 128.

44. Cooper (1995), 78; Cirlot (1971), 137; Bayley (1990–93), 2:331. For the ancient Greeks, "tokens of recognition" commonly represented principles like "love, brotherhood, and reconciliation" (Compton, in Lundquist and Ricks [1990], 1:116, 617). Bayley noted: "An extended hand [was anciently] the symbol of Fidelity and Faith" (Bayley [1990, 1993], 2:330). He also pointed out: "When clasped . . , the Hand was obviously an expression of concord and . . . love" (Bayley [1990, 1993], 2:331).

45. Cirlot (1962), 137.

46. See Compton, in Lundquist and Ricks (1990), 1:115–16, 617.

47. See Louisa Twining, *Symbols and Emblems of Early and Mediaeval Christian Art*, new edition (London: John Murray, 1885), 4. See also illustration 12.

48. Compton, in Lundquist and Ricks (1990), 1:622–23. See also 1:617. Apotheosis is the elevation of a human (after he or she has died) to a divine status. In ancient mystery religions, the handclasp tokens were symbols of

"love, initiation, arrival, salvation, union with the god, and apotheosis" (ibid., 1:614).

49. Compton, in Lundquist and Ricks (1990), 1:614.

50. The notion of the hand being contorted to symbolize God, Christ, Atonement, or union with the divine is more widely dispersed among the various Christian denominations than one might think. Thus we find the related practice in Christian circles of the thumb sometimes seen as a symbol of God the Father; the middle finger representing the Son; and the index finger being perceived as standing for the Holy Spirit. (See Bayley [1990, 1993], 2:334; Heath [1909], 118.) Similarly, when the thumb and first two fingers are extended upwards (as is common in Roman Catholicism), the two fingers of the hand that remain downward (pressed against the palm of the hand) are seen as symbols of Christ's mortal and divine natures. [See Bayley (1990, 1993), 2:334–35; Heath (1909), 118–19.] So the fingers of the hand are commonly symbols for the divine, or the members of the Godhead, or of a given member of the Godhead. Various "manual gestures" can (and often do) represent specific gods (Elworthy [1900], 148). One such "gesture" "in ancient times" was seen as a "sacred sign" (ibid., 204)—so much so that one ordained priest who wrote a text on "manual gestures" avoided entirely any reference to this token out of respect for its sacral nature (ibid., 203). Other manual gestures can symbolize the omnipotent God being called upon for protection. (See ibid., 175.) The *dextera Dei* (or hand of God) symbolizes that God is "pouring down" or giving out blessings to those who receive His hand or token. (See ibid., 157–58.) "The source of the power to be conveyed is from above, *i.e.*, from the supreme deity, . . . the unseen Almighty of the Christian, whose hand only is exhibited. The open hand, coming down from above, is . . . 'indicative of the Divine favour' . . ." (ibid., 158).

51. For examples see Hertz (no date given), 1:147; Buttrick (1951–57), 1:652; Clifford and Murphy, "Genesis," in Brown, Fitzmyer, and Murphy (1990), 27; Speiser (1962), 178; J. Gerald Janzen, *International Theological Commentary: Genesis 12–50—Abraham and All the Families of the Earth* (Grand Rapids: Eerdmans, 1993), 86; Kidner (1967), 147.

52. Adam Clarke, *Clarke's Commentary*, 6 vols. (New York: Methodist Book Concern, no date given), 1:147.

53. Buttrick (1951–57), 1:652.

54. Clifford and Murphy, in Brown, Fitzmyer, and Murphy (1990), 27.

55. Speiser (1962), 178.

56. President Joseph Fielding Smith taught: "Those who receive the

exaltation in the celestial kingdom will have the 'continuation of the seeds forever.' They will live in the family relationship. In the terrestrial and in the telestial kingdoms there will be no marriage. Those who enter there will remain 'separately and singly' forever. Some of the functions in the celestial body will not appear in the terrestrial body, neither in the telestial body, and the power of procreation will be removed" (Smith [1998], 2:287). Elder Henry B. Eyring stated: "There is only one place where there will be families—the highest degree of the celestial kingdom. That is where we will want to be" (Henry B. Eyring, *To Draw Closer to God: A Collection of Discourses* [Salt Lake City: Deseret Book, 1997], 162).

57. Janzen (1993), 86.

58. Church Educational System, *Old Testament: Genesis – 2 Samuel (Religion 301) Student Manual* (1981), 84. Scholars trace the common practice in Western culture of greeting people through the extending of one's hand back to the ancient ritual of requesting a "token of recognition" from individuals encountered. See, for example, Todd M. Compton, "The Whole Token: Mystery Symbolism in Classical Recognition Drama," *Epoche* 13 (1985): 1–81; Compton, in Lundquist and Ricks (1990), 1:611–42; Nibley, in Parry (1994), 557–59; Farbridge (1923), 274–75; Brown (1999), 48, n. 37; 135; 154, n. 109; 156, n. 130–32; 236, n. 19.

59. For example, in Ezekiel 17:18 we read: "Seeing he despised the oath by breaking the covenant, when, lo, he had given his hand, and hath done all these things, he shall not escape." Of this one commentator wrote:

> The giving of a hand may function as an oath-sign by solemnly depicting the covenant commitment. The gesture of giving one's hand in a handshake . . . appears with plausible covenant-making implication in 2 Kgs. 10:15; Jer. 50:15; Ezek. 17:18; Lam. 5:6; Ezra 10:19; 1 Chron. 29:24; and 2 Chron. 30:8. . . . There are a number of references to handshakes in extra-biblical texts and in ancient Near Eastern iconography which support the biblical evidence for the use of this gesture as a pact or covenant-making rite. The biblical text perhaps the clearest in its association between the gesture of giving the hand and covenant making, is Ezek. 17:18: "Because he despised the oath and broke the covenant . . . , because he gave his hand and yet did all these things . . . , he shall not escape . . ." . . . "There are two covenant-making acts in Ez 17, 11–21: an oath . . . sworn in the name of God (2 Chr 36,13) and the rite of *nātan yād* (v. 18) which was not merely a gesture of assent to the covenant terms, but a sign which effected the covenant relationship." (Gordon Paul Hugenberger, *Marriage as a Covenant: A Study of Biblical Law and*

Ethics Governing Marriage Developed from the Perspective of Malachi
[Leiden: E. J. Brill, 1994], 211–12)

One Jewish scholar associates the scriptural practice of giving of one's hand (e.g., Ezekiel 17:18) as "a gesture of promise and compact" (Moshe Greenberg, *The Anchor Bible: Ezekiel 1–20* [New York: Doubleday, 1983], 315. See also Carl F. Keil, *Biblical Commentary on the Prophecies of Ezekiel*, 2 vols. [Grand Rapids: Eerdmans, 1950], 1:242–43).

60.   One LDS text states: "The New Testament teaches that during his forty-day postresurrection ministry, Jesus spent time specifically with the apostles, 'to whom also he showed himself alive after his passion by many infallible proofs . . . and speaking of the things pertaining to the kingdom of God' (Acts 1:3). The phrase 'infallible proofs' is the King James translation of the Greek word *tekmeriois* and means, literally, 'sure signs or tokens.' The book of Acts is really saying that Jesus taught the apostles about his resurrection and about the kingdom of God through many sure signs and tokens. It is the same in the Lord's temples today" (Skinner [2007], 112–13. See also Ogden and Skinner [1998], 30; Nicoll [1983], 2:52). Fitzmyer ([1998], 202) seems to agree with Skinner's rendering, though in a weaker sense, implying that Jesus proved Himself resurrected using "signs."

61.   See 1 Enoch 65:9, in Charlesworth (1983, 1985), 1:45.

62.   Metatron is the name of an angel primarily associated with Judaism, but also known in Islam and some branches of Christianity. His name, though absent from the Hebrew Bible and Greek New Testament, does appear in the Jewish Talmud and in several Medieval texts popular with Jewish mystics. We also find reference to him numerous times in the Old Testament Pseudepigrapha. In Rabbinic tradition he is the highest of the angels.

63.   3 Enoch 1:5–6, in Charlesworth (1983, 1985), 1:256.

64.   1 Enoch 87:2–3, in Charlesworth (1983, 1985), 1:63.

65.   1 Enoch 90:31, in Charlesworth (1983, 1985), 1:71.

66.   1 Enoch 71:3–4, in Charlesworth (1983, 1985), 1:49.

67.   See The Apocalypse of Abraham 10:4, 11:1, in Charlesworth (1983, 1985), 1:693–94.

68.   These were a group of second-century Gnostic-Christians who believed that "the Father of all" people (whom they referred to as "*Barbēlo*") had a "female aspect" or "mother goddess." See Rudolph (1987), 80.

69.   Rudolph (1987), 214.

70.   Manichaeism was a "sub-Christian" movement that began in the third century with its founder, Mani [AD 216–76]. Though the religion at

one point had strong ties to Christianity, it was clearly influenced by the doctrines and practices of Zoroastrianism, Buddhism, Gnosticism, and the Elkesaites' Jewish Christian baptismal sect. Mani claimed to be an "apostle through the will of Jesus Christ" who began to receive divine revelations when he was twelve years of age. St. Augustine was once a practicing Manichaean, though later he wrote against the teachings of the sect; and many Christian bishops persecuted the Manichaeans for being heterodox in their beliefs. (See Robin Lane Fox, *Pagans and Christians* [New York: Alfred A. Knopf, 1987], 561–71; Ferguson [1990], 562–63; J. Rebecca Lyman, "Heresy," in Bowden [2005], 520; Blake Leyerle, "Manichaeism," in McBrien [1995], 810–11.)

71. Springett (1922), 56. (See also Augustine, "On The Morals of the Manichaeans," Chapter X, Verse 19, in Schaff and Wace [2004], 4:74–75.) "The Manicheans were divided into classes or grades. The first grade were known as Disciples, and were more or less probationers. The second grade were known as Auditors, who were permitted to hear the writings of Manes read, and interpreted in a mystical form. The third grade were the Perfect, or Elect, who were the priestly order of the sect. From these last were chosen the Magistri, or Council, who were twelve in number . . , with a thirteenth as President. In common with other sects professing Gnostic tenets they had secret forms of recognition, three in number, described by St. Augustine as the word, the grip, and the breast" (Springett, (1922), 56).

72. Chaillot, in Wainwright and Tucker (2006), 135.

73. See Knight (1920), x. These are isolated in Catholicism to the Knights of Columbus.

74. Knight (1920), 90–91.

75. See ibid., 91.

76. See Soyer (1999), 165, 168, 170.

77. Ibid., 173.

78. See Trimingham (1998), 171, 182, 186. See also Springett (1922), 78–80. In one sect of Sunni Muslims each of the fingers were "taken to personify one of the holy family" (meaning Mohammed's family). The thumb was a symbol of Mohammed; the index finger represented Abubakr (the first of the caliphs); the middle finger stood for Umar (the second of the caliphs or "successors to Mohammed" in the Sunni denomination of Islam); the ring finger was a symbol for Uthmám (the third caliph); and the pinky (or little finger) was an image of Ali (the fourth of the caliphs). Similarly, among some Shiite Muslims the thumb represented Mohammed, while the first finger represented his daughter (Fatima), the second her husband (Ali), the third and fourth symbolized Hasan and

Husain (the sons of Fatima and Ali). (See Elworthy [1900], 173.)
79. See Birge (1937), 159–60. See also Springett (1922), 79.
80. See Birge (1937), 160. It is generally held that the Bektashi have borrowed much of their beliefs and practices from Christianity. (See Trix, in Esposito [1995], 1:213; Glassé [1989], 71; Lapidus [1989], 309, 327; Trimingham [1998], 2, 68–69, 81–82, 136, 194; Schimmel [1986], 340; Birge [1937], 210, 215–16.)
81. See Schimell (1975), 411.
82. See ibid., 18, 377, 417.
83. See ibid., 417.
84. See ibid.
85. See ibid., 418.
86. The same hand gesture can have variant meanings. For example, one Neapolitan sign made with the hands means ignorance or stupidity. However, the same gesture or token among Christians has been understood to be a symbol of adoration or supplication toward God. (See Elworthy [1900], 147.) Elworthy states that the "manual gesture" sometimes referred to as the "horned hand"—which consists of "the index and little finger extended, [and] the middle and ring finger clasped by the thumb"—"has very many different meanings" (Elworthy [1895], 260). The *mano cornuta* (i.e., a hand gesture where the index and little fingers are extended while, at the same time the middle and ring fingers are clasped by the thumb) is seen in much of the Mediterranean as a crude gesture (often with sexual connotations), but, as one sixth-century mural from San Vitale (in Ravenna, Italy) shows, it can also be a symbol for the *dexera Dei* or "hand of God." (See Elworthy [1895], 262, 265, figures 113 and 266.) Elworthy pointed out: "When we see the same thing in the early Christian art of the sixth century at Ravenna, and in the present day pagan art of India, we are compelled to admit that . . . there is something in special positions of the hands, which both pagan and Christian alike recognize" (ibid., 266–67). The same author notes that a given hand gesture or token common in Hinduism is identical to "that of a Roman [Catholic] priest when he blesses his flock" (Elworthy [1900], 151), and one gesture representative of contempt among the Italians symbolizes "devout worship" in Java (or Batavia). (See ibid., 177.) He also suggested that the symbolic gestures and mudras of Hinduism and Buddhism are "linked" to the sacerdotal or priestly gestures of Christendom. (See ibid., 208.) In support of Elworthy's claim, Tibetan Buddhist scholar, Robert Beer, noted: "The Sanskrit term *mudra* derives from the verb *mud*, meaning 'to please (the gods)', and the word generally refers to a seal, mark, or sign." (See Robert Beer, *The Handbook of Tibetan*

Buddhist Symbols [Chicago: Serindia Publications, 2003], 221.) Beer goes on to present a series of mudras which seem liturgically significant— particularly for Latter-day Saints. (See, for example, Beer [2003], 223–24, 227–28.)

87. See, for example, Cooper (1995), 78; Cirlot (1971), 137; Fontana (1994), 128; Tresidder (2000), 22; Janzen (1993), 185. More often than not, distinctions are made between the meaning of the left hand and that of the right hand. However, at times "we find both hands used symbolically with seeming indifference" (Elworthy [1900], 166).

88. See Schimell (1975), 18, 377, 417.

89. In support of this is Skinner's claim that the "most significant symbols" in temple liturgy would naturally "point to Christ in one way or another." (See Skinner [2007], 47, 53, 176.) One way of holding the hand is said to symbolize Christ's name—consequently, symbolizing the Messiah Himself. (See Heath [1909], 118.) Regarding the hand as a symbol for God, YHWY or Jehovah within Christianity, one text informs us: "There are many varieties in the form and position of the Hand" that suggest its symbolic place and value in Christian art. "This symbol . . . was the only one expressive of the Divine Presence during the first eleven centuries of Christian Art" (Twining [1885], 2–3). Elsewhere we read: "In Europe during the first eight centuries of Christianity, and even until the twelfth, God the Father was invariably represented by a Hand" (Bayley [1990–93], 2:333–34. See also Heath [1909], 117). "The use of the hand as a sign of the divine presence and power is thus fixed at least as early as the sojourn of Israel in Egypt, and some time before the birth of Moses; it has continued to be so used throughout the ages down to the present day— alike by pagans, [Muslims], and Christians" (Elworthy [1895], 243). One very common Catholic manual gesture or token symbolizes the Trinity. (See Elworthy [1900], 152, n. 156; Heath [1909], 118.)

90. Nibley wrote:

> Lucian, a clever Syrian who wrote in Greek and spoke for the whole Near East, reports that "You cannot have a single ancient *teleten* (high religious celebration, a mystery) without an *orchesis* or pantomime dance." Plato says dancing is mandatory at every public offering . . . . The Old Testament is rich in dancing situations. Israel came out of Egypt dancing, and the victory dances that followed were by choruses of maidens (see Exodus 15:20; 1 Samuel 18:6). We read of a company of prophets carrying instruments (see Psalm 149:3); they danced as they prophesied. There was a daily procession,

with song and dance around the altar in the temple; David and Solomon both participated in it. . . . I have shown elsewhere that the round dance of the creation drama takes the form of the prayer circle in the temple. (Nibley [2008], 463–64)

91.   Max Pulver, "Jesus' Round Dance and Crucifixion According to the Acts of Saint John," in Joseph Campbell, ed., *The Mysteries: Papers From the Eranos Yearbooks* (New York: Princeton University Press, 1980), 185–86.
92.   Ibid., 186.
93.   One text notes: "The sacrificial ordinances connected with Sinai were probably an archetype to those of the later temples" (Parry, in Lundquist and Ricks [1990], 1:493). The sacrifices that were the center of the Old Testament temple rites are traditionally understood to be typological symbols of the Messiah's future sacrifice for sin. (See Larsen [2007], 32). They were tokens of what Jesus would do for those who lived before Him and those who came after. Though they were general symbols, ultimately they represented the four wounds of the cross (i.e., the nail through His heels, the spear between the ribs in His side, the nails in His hands, and those in His wrists). (See Michael Glen Reed, *The Development of the LDS Church's Attitude Toward the Cross* [Sacramento, CA: California State University, Sacramento, Master's Thesis, 2009], 49, and see n. 113; Albert G. Mackey, *An Encyclopedia of Freemasonry and its Kindred Sciences* [Philadelphia: Moss and Company, 1879], 570, S.v. "Pentalpha.") Though the sacrifices of the Hebrew Bible were general symbols foreshadowing every aspect of Christ's suffering and atoning work, the four aforementioned symbols were paramount. In his typical veiled language, Nibley wrote: "*Every follower of Abraham must receive certain signs and tokens relating to sacrifice*; Abraham and Isaac were both tested as offerings on the altar, and both arose unharmed *in similitude of the Only Begotten and the resurrection*" (Hugh Nibley, "Abraham's Temple Drama," in Parry and Ricks [1999], 7, emphasis added). Sacrifices are always in similitude of Christ's ultimate sacrifice on our behalf. In Moses 5 we read: "And after many days an angel of the Lord appeared unto Adam, saying: Why dost thou offer sacrifices unto the Lord? And Adam said unto him: I know not, save the Lord commanded me. And then the angel spake, saying: This thing is a similitude of the sacrifice of the Only Begotten of the Father, which is full of grace and truth. Wherefore, thou shalt do all that thou doest in the name of the Son, and thou shalt repent and call upon God in the name of the Son forevermore" (Moses 5:6–8). President Joseph Fielding Smith wrote: "All the sacrifices of old, from the days of Adam to the atonement

of Jesus Christ . . . were in the similitude of and a reminder of the great sacrifice, and pointed forward to its fulfillment by Jesus upon the cross" (Smith [1993], 1:188). Thus, all symbols of sacrifice are also referential to Christ and His atonement. And the most important of Christocentric symbols always focus our attention on Christ's Atonement. Thus, baptism, the sacrament of the Lord's supper, the utilization of altars, and so forth all point us to Christ's Atonement. Nibley also wrote: "According to Cyril, the candidate was reminded that the whole ordinance [of baptism] is 'in imitation of the sufferings of Christ,' in which 'we suffer without pain by mere imitation his receiving of the nails in his hands *and feet*: the antitype of Christ's sufferings.'" (See Cyril of Jerusalem, "Chatechetical Lectures," Lecture 22:5, "Of Baptism," in Schaff and Wace [2004], 7:148, cited in Nibley [2008], 317, emphasis added.)

94.   Beyond the actual physical grasping of hands as a means of conveying "tokens," it was common in ancient times (e.g., Old Testament, New Testament, Medieval, and so on) for carved hands in the shape of "tokens of recognition" to be utilized, given, or exchanged. "The open hand set up as a trophy or token of triumph was the usual symbol of the Phoenicians" (Elworthy [1900], 163). However, it was also a symbol among the Israelites. Thus, in 1 Samuel 15:12 we read: "And when Samuel rose early to meet Saul in the morning, it was told Samuel, saying, Saul came to Carmel, and, behold, he set him up a *place*, and is gone about, and passed on, and gone down to Gilgal." The word "place" in the King James Version of the passage would be better rendered (from the Hebrew) as "hand." In other words, Saul set up a monument or statue in the shape of a hand in token of his victory over the Amalekites. Additionally, certain deities were often associated with hands in ancient reliefs, statues, carvings, monuments, and the like. When a specific god was associated with a hand, it implied that the blessing or victory came at the hands of the deity. (See Elworthy [1900], 164.) These hand statues or tokens, "in various gestures," were considered by the ancients as "protective amulets" (ibid., 170, 172–73). On many of these tokens, memorials or amulets were carved or engraved symbols "of the attributes of the gods" (ibid, 204–205). They represented "powerful beings in whom their possessors believed" (ibid., 269). Sometimes the symbols or tokens carved on the hand memorials symbolized the blessings or gifts received by the god the statues were dedicated to. Thus one carved set of ears symbolized the blessing of being healed from deafness. (See ibid., 215.) Likewise, symbols of the Atonement might be placed on a hand as a symbol of the spiritual healing Christ had brought into the life of the person creating the "symbolic hand." In these "symbolic hand" statues

multiple symbols would be placed on the hand representing the multiple attributes or gifts of the deity to which the statue was dedicated. (See ibid., 218, 220.) "All ornament or decoration" on these hands "had originally some distinct signification" (ibid., 306). Numerous such hands have been found sporting the initials or name of Jesus (or one of his titles, such as "Word," "Logos," or "Christ"). (See Bayley [1990–93], 2:341.)

95. Of the utilization of passwords in liturgical elements within Catholicism, one Roman Catholic author wrote that it is important to "teach your members the mode and use of the secret . . . words" (Knight [1920], 29). This same text states: "The password . . . must be kept a secret from all outsiders" (ibid., 89. See also p. x).

96. See Soyer (1999): 164–65, 168–71, who speaks of "passwords" being used by nineteenth- and twentieth-century Jewish immigrants to the United States. This same author notes: "Some Orthodox religious congregations . . . adopted customs from the world of the lodge, including . . . [the use of] passwords" (ibid., 173).

97. See Birge (1937), 159–60; Springett (1922), 78–80; Trimingham (1998), 182, 171–86.

Seven

Prayer and
Threshold Rituals

P rayer is a symbolic act that mirrors the participant's union—
or reunion—with the divine. Man, dwelling upon this fallen,
telestial earth, is estranged from God. Supplicating Deity through
prayer represents mankind's desire to be in communion with
Heaven—to return to God's presence and to enjoy His company
throughout eternity.[1]

Anciently the altar was central to liturgical prayer. Its symbolic meanings explain why it was common among the ancients
to gather around an altar when offering prayer to God. In Hebrew
Bible times, for example, covenant Israel utilized altars of prayer
and sacrifice. The altar of incense in the Mosaic Tabernacle
(Exodus 37:25)—which stood just in front of the veil to the Holy
of Holies (Exodus 30:6)—symbolized prayers ascending up to
God (Revelation 8:4).[2] In contemporary Roman Catholicism and
Eastern Orthodoxy altars are utilized as part of the liturgy, and
(among other things) as a location for the offering up of priestly
prayers.[3] They stand as symbols of Christ's presence, God's heavenly throne, and the Savior's atoning sacrifice.[4] Consequently,
prayer at an altar symbolizes prayer to and before God and His
Christ. Such an act intimates one's acknowledgment of his or
her dependence upon the Messiah's saving grace in order to be

authorized to approach God, being in a fallen state. Thus, one text notes: "Anciently, stones were used to build altars on which the Lord's people offered sacrifice and at which they prayed. In other words, the altar was a meditating structure for those who wished to draw closer to God—just as Christ meditates to help us in that quest."[5] Praying before, at, or around a sacred altar is a statement about both the focus of the prayer, and what would be required of the petitioner in order to receive the requested blessings. Indeed, the Hebrew word for "altar" means literally the "place of sacrificing." Thus, the altar becomes a symbol of sacrifice—ultimately Christ's sacrifice, but also a call and covenant to all who approach the altar to be willing to sacrifice everything the worshiper has, if necessary, on behalf of God's work and kingdom.[6]

On a related note, completing the Muslim *hajj* (or "pilgrimage") is, for most practitioners of that faith, a sacrifice; not a sacrifice of blood, but a sacrifice of time, money, and perhaps even one's will. During the *hajj*, the pilgrim making the trip to Mecca "acts as Abraham who 'brought his son Ishmael to sacrifice.' . . . [The pilgrim's sacrifice] could be any one of a number of worldly possessions."[7] One text on the Islamic *hajj* informs us:

> Whoever and whatever, you should have brought it with you to sacrifice here. I cannot tell you which one, but I can give you some clues to help—whatever weakens your faith, whatever stops you from "going", whatever distracts you from accepting responsibilities, whatever causes you to be self-centered, whatever makes you unable to hear the message and confess the truth, whatever . . . causes you to rationalize for the sake of convenience . . . . You are in the position of Ibrahim [or Abraham] whose weakness was in his love for Ishmael (his son). He was teased by Satan. Imagine yourself at the peak of honor, full of pride and there is only ONE THING for which you can give up everything and sacrifice any other love for its love. THAT IS YOUR ISHMAEL! Your Ishmael can be a person, an object, a rank, a position or even a "weakness"![8]

Thus, in Islam approaching the *Ka'bah* symbolizes your willingness to place all upon Allah's altar.[9] You approach it as a symbol of your choice to set aside the world and its attractions. You approach the *Ka'bah*—and thus Allah—to lay upon it (or to give to Him) whatever it is in your life that is keeping you from becoming more like Allah; more as He would have you be. As in Islam, so also in Christianity: approaching the altar is an act of offering, a sacrifice to God; not necessarily of blood, but of one's life, will, desires, possessions—of anything and everything God may ask of you. Again, because the ancients and moderns have seen the altar as a representation of God, as one text informs us, if you should participate in Christian worship or ritual you should "bathe yourself in water when you intend to approach the altar."[10] Muslims would do the same before approaching the *Ka'bah*.

In antiquity it was common for worshipers of the God of Israel to pray standing in a circle, often surrounding one of these afore-mentioned holy altars. For example, in one text, believed to have been penned in the second century, we read of Jesus conducting what some have referred to as a "prayer circle" with His disciples.[11] Likewise, in the early Christian pseudepigraphical text known as *Acts of John*[12] we learn that Jesus "assembled [His disciples] and said, 'Before I am delivered to them [who seek my death], let us sing a hymn to the Father . . . '[13] So he told [the Apostles] to form a circle, holding one another's hands, and he himself stood in the middle and said, 'Answer Amen to me.'" In other words, after Jesus would say a phrase as part of His prayer, He wanted His disciples to say "Amen," implying that they agreed with that part of the prayer, as though they had said it themselves.[14]

Our text continues: "So he [meaning Jesus] began to . . . say, 'Glory be to thee, Father.' And we circled round him and answered him, 'Amen' [after each thing he said] . . . . 'We praise thee, Father: We thank thee . . . In whom darkness dwelleth not.' 'Amen.' ' . . . Say again with me, Glory be to thee, Father, Glory be to thee, Word [or Son of God]. Glory be to thee, Spirit.' 'Amen.' After the Lord had so danced [or prayed] with us, . . . he went out to suffer."[15]

Prayer circles, akin to what we have just offered, apparently were somewhat common among various early Christian sects.

The symbolism is curious. One text notes: "In forming the prayer circle one excludes the outer world." The participants "form closed circles with their backs all turned on the outer world."[16] The altar being their focus, symbolically speaking, the participants are concentrating on the sacrifice of Christ (represented by the altar), while forgetting or rejecting the world (to which they have turned their backs).[17] Nibley noted: "It was from such a circle in heaven that God at the creation of this earth chose those who would be his rulers in it."[18] Thus, he points out, Abraham 3:23 states: "And God . . . stood in the midst [or middle] of them, and he said: These I will make my rulers; for he stood among those that were spirits, and he saw that they were good." Those who turn their back on the world, and make their focus the Atonement (i.e., the altar), find themselves instruments utilized by God in building the kingdom.

Another commentator interpreted the symbolism of standing in a circle as follows: "A circle can represent the protection of priesthood and righteous loved ones—as well as the protection we receive when we submit ourselves to Christ and his plan for us."[19] Thus, the circle offers protection—perhaps, in part, because the participants have rejected the world. Rejection of the world via acceptance of God and His covenants is always protective. The consequence of rejecting Satan's offerings is eventual exaltation. Thus, in his *Theological Dictionary of the New Testament*, Gerhard Kittel writes that the ancient "mystery" rites—dating from approximately 700 BCE to AD 400—symbolically portrayed "the destinies of a god" through "sacred actions before a circle of devotees." Kittel indicates that these "sacred actions" served to give the participant in the rite "part in the fate of the god" being worshiped.[20] In other words, those who anciently were found praying in the "circle" are symbolically acting out the promise of enjoying all God has—specifically exaltation within His heavenly kingdom.

In our ancient example of a "prayer circle" we are told that Jesus commanded the participants to "hold one another's hands" while engaging in the rite.[21] The holding of each others' hands suggests an intimacy that should have or did exist among those who participated in the circle. According to Cyril of Jerusalem,[22] the intimacy of the prayer while surrounding God's altar is a "sign that our souls are mingled together" and that we have banished "all remembrance of wrongs" others in the circle have committed against us. That intimacy, he suggests, "blends souls one with another, and courts entire forgiveness for [and from] them."[23] In other words, Cyril warned participants in this rite or ordinance of prayer that to have ill or unkind feelings toward those with whom you are praying was an offense toward God, and had the ability to harm the influence of the Spirit, which all should seek to have present during the prayer. One modern commentator on the rite suggested: "This mutual support [of interlocking hands] in the circle is necessary where some may be caught away in the Spirit and pass out."[24] In other words, the way in which the rite was performed may have been as much practical as it was symbolic. Of course, in light of the ancient baptismal covenant to support each other in trials, tribulations, and tests (Mosiah 18:9), such an interlocking of hands—as practical as it may be—is clearly symbolic of our covenant responsibility (as Christians) to watch out for the well-being of our brothers and sisters in the gospel, and to support them in their times of need.

It was common in ancient times for those who were petitioning God to do so with their hands raised high above their heads.[25] Indeed, one LDS source notes: "In the setting of the ancient tabernacle and temple, the sacred gesture of lifting up the hands often accompanied the act of prayer."[26] In the book of 1 Kings we read: "And Solomon stood before the altar of the LORD in the presence of all the congregation of Israel, and spread forth his hands toward heaven" (1 Kings 8:22. See also 1 Kings 8:54; 2 Chronicles 6:12). Solomon was not the only biblical figure who prayed to God with "upraised hands" (See, for example, 1 Kings 8:38; 1 Chronicles 6:29; Ezra 9:5; Job 11:13; Psalm 68:31, 143:6; Isaiah 1:15; Lamentations 2:19, 3:41; 1 Timothy 2:8). One pseudepigraphical text suggests over and over again that Adam and Eve often prayed with upraised hands.[27] Methuselah is also said to have prayed with "hands stretched to heaven" while standing at the altar of the temple, clothed in the "designated garments" of the priesthood.[28] There is evidence that this same ritual practice existed among New Testament Christians. For example, in the Gospel of Bartholomew[29] we read: "[V:1] Now the Apostles were . . . with Mary. [V:5] And she . . . said: Let us stand up in prayer. [V:13] Then Mary stood up before them and spread out her hands toward the heaven and began to [pray] thus."[30] The Apostle Paul wrote to Timothy: "I will therefore that men pray every where, lifting up holy hands" (1 Timothy 2:8). Clement of Rome[31] wrote: "Full of holy designs, . . . stretch forth your hands to God Almighty, beseeching Him to be merciful unto you."[32] Similarly, Clement of Alexandria[33] indicated that, in prayer the Saints "converse with God" as they "lift the hands to heaven."[34] On numerous occasions Tertullian[35] spoke of the Christian practice of praying with upraised hands.[36]

As to the symbolism behind this ritual gesture, several suggestions have been made. The most obvious is that suggested by one of the psalms recorded in the *Dead Sea Scrolls*. This text indicates that the reason the ancients prayed with upraised hands was because they were reaching out to God in an effort to gain His aid or assistance.[37] This ritual act is a manifestation of "supplication to God, and of dependence on God (Exodus 17:12; 1 Timothy 2:8)."[38] It evidences one is drawing near to God in order to gain His aid and assistance.[39] Thus, D&C 88:63 states: "Seek me diligently and ye shall find me; ask, and ye shall receive; knock, and it shall be opened unto you . . . , draw near unto me and I will draw near unto you." Prayer with upraised hands symbolizes the petitioner's attempt to metaphorically knock at God's door. The act represents diligently seeking God; an attempt to draw near unto Him. Nibley noted, "the Jews say, there must be a stirring below before there can be a stirring above."[40] Consequently, the ancient practice of raising one's hands toward heaven during prayer was a "stirring"—an effort to gain God's ear.

Praying with upraised hands has also been seen as a symbol of the practitioner's worthiness to approach God. In other words, as the person praying raises his hands high above his head, he testifies to God that He comes before Him clean and worthy of communion. One LDS commentator explained:

> There is symbolism in raising the hands in prayer. The gesture exposes to God both the breast and the palms of the petitioner to show that they are pure (clean). This is reflected in one of the temple hymns found in the Bible, Psalm 24, which Donald W. Parry has suggested may relate to a prayer circle: "Who shall ascend into the hill of the Lord? or who shall stand in his holy place? He that hath clean hands, and a pure heart . . . (Psalm 24:3—4)" The message of the Psalm is clear: In order to enter into the temple (the "hill of the Lord," called "the mountain of the Lord's house" in Isaiah 2:2), one must have clean hands and a pure heart. In other words, both acts (represented by the hands) and thoughts (represented by the heart) must reflect righteousness, along with the lips that utter the prayer. This is probably what the author of Job had in mind when he wrote, "prepare thine heart, and stretch out thine hands toward him" (Job 11:13). Note also Lamentations 3:41, "Let us lift up our heart with our hands unto God in the heavens."[41]

Similarly, Clement of Rome counseled: "Let us draw near to Him with holiness of spirit, lift up pure and undefiled hands unto Him."[42] Consequently, when the ancients raised their hands high to the heavens during their petitions, they were bearing witness to God that they were worthy to do so. Thus, Donald and Jay Parry wrote: "Lifting up the hands is a sacred gesture associated with the atonement—those who are truly righteous may at times lift their hands to heaven and show God that their hands are pure (Ps. 24:4), that is, made pure through the atonement, and they [therefore] expect an answer to their prayers."[43]

Related to this is an interpretation offered by a number of commentators; namely that the extended hands and arms during prayer also symbolize Christ's extended hands and arms during the Crucifixion.[44] Thus, the person praying in this manner is symbolically saying that he is extending himself as a representation of his commitment to give his life for the cause—for the gospel of his God—just as Jesus gave His life for God's work and will.[45] The practitioner of prayer is saying, I will sacrifice because Jesus sacrificed; and, to the degree it is feasible, in the way He gave His life for this work. Consequently, Tertullian spoke of our raised hands during prayer as a symbol of our "preparation for all punishment."[46] In support of this suggestion, Exodus 17 records the famed story of Joshua's fight against the Amalekites (Exodus 17:8–13). As will be recalled, Moses's outstretched or upraised arms gave Israel's army confidence to successfully fight against her enemies. Early Christian sources consistently saw in Moses's actions of raising or stretching out his hands and arms during prayer a symbol for the crucified Christ.[47] In the pseudepigraphical "Odes of Solomon"[48] a similar explanation of the ritual act appears. In Ode 42:1–2 we read: "I extended my hands and approached my Lord, because the stretching out of my hands is *his* sign. And my extension [of my hands and arms] is [a symbol of] the common [or simple] cross, that was lifted up on the way of the Righteous One."[49] Elsewhere in the "Odes" we find this: "I extended my hands and [in so doing] hallowed my Lord; For the expansion of my hands is *his* sign. And my extension is the upright cross. Hallelujah."[50] In both odes we are told that Solomon perceived the act of raising his hands high to heaven as a symbolic gesture representing the Lord's Crucifixion. It is "His sign." It implies that those who make it are committed to being what He is, and living as He lived.

Hence, John Tvedtnes penned this: "Ancient temple prayer was a symbol of Christ. From the wearing of the tallith [or garment] (symbolizing the Lamb of God) to the raised arms with spread fingers (symbolizing the crucified Christ . . .) to the veil that opens when prayers are uttered, everything points to the Savior. It is altogether fitting, therefore, that we are commanded to pray to the Father in the name of Christ (see 2 Nephi 32:9; 3 Nephi 20:31)."[51]

Thus, there is a heavily Christocentric symbol behind the practice of praying with upraised hands. Perhaps such should not be surprising to the reader, as so much of ancient and modern temple work is focused on the primary symbol of the Gospel—Jesus

Christ, and His Crucifixion (1 Corinthians 2:2).

Truman G. Madsen highlighted the following related symbol: "The Hebrew word for 'name' is shem. Ha-Shem is still used sometimes as a 'meta-word,' part of a prayer pattern, used to avoid saying the most sacred name. In Judaism the 'sh' (which in English looks like a 'W') has often had ritual importance because it pictures a position of prayer—arms raised above the head. Thus one symbolizes the name in prayer whether or not he uses it."[52]

The very act of raising one's hands high above one's head forms the first letter of the Hebrew name for God. Thus the practitioner both takes upon himself God's name (through this rite) and also makes clear whom he is petitioning.

As a final symbolic connotation of this ritual behavior, Nibley suggested that "raising both hands high above the head . . . [is] a natural gesture of both supplication and submission."[53] He adds, "it represents submission (the 'hands up' position of one surrendering on the battlefield) while at the same time calling the attention of heaven to an offering one has brought in supplication. . . . The early Christians used the same gesture in anticipation of a visitation from heaven."[54] Associated with this concept of submission in prayer is the following comment by Justin Martyr,[55] who indicated that "everyone knows" that prayer on "bended knees" has the greatest power to appease or "propitiate" God.[56] Like the upraised hand, the bended knee is representative of the submission of one's will to God. Consequently, when one prays with upraised hands, or bended knees, one symbolically offers his submission—and also adoration—to the God he worships.[57]

Related to this practice of praying with upraised hands is another seemingly common prayer behavior—that of repetition during prayer. Apparently the ancients would say certain phrases three times during certain ritual prayers. For example, Noah cried out in tripartite fashion: "Hear me! Hear me! Hear me!" as he began his communion with God.[58] Enoch speaks of a similar pattern of prayer utilized in his day.[59] Isaiah tells of the seraphim or angels who prayed in a tripartite pattern (See Isaiah 6:3). As the number three symbolizes God—or that which is of God—praying in triplicate (or repeating three times certain phrases during prayer) suggests the focus of the prayer, and acknowledges that the source of any answer to that prayer is God.[60]

In the Roman Catholic Mass and the Eastern Orthodox divine liturgy, the clergy and the congregation recite in unison the creed. It has also been the practice in Roman Catholicism that the congregation repeats in unison—as a form of prayer—certain phrases first uttered by the priest, or in response to the words of the priest.[61] For example, as part of the "Penitential Rite," the priest and congregation engage in the following dialogue:

> Priest states: "Lord have mercy."
> Congregation responds in unison: "Lord have mercy."
> Priest states: "Christ have mercy."
> Congregation responds in unison: "Christ have mercy."
> Priest states: "Lord have mercy."
> Congregation responds in unison: "Lord have mercy."

Though, as we have already noted, the triadic formula of the prayer is significant, so is the united recitation of the prayer. One source states that "the purpose of the prayer circle was to achieve total unity of minds and hearts."[62] Another notes that "the participation of the people was manifested especially by the fact that they did not merely listen to the prayers of the priest in silence but ratified them by their acclamations."[63] Elsewhere we read that the unified offering of the prayer "knits the congregation into the closest possible union." This same source adds: "the people are transformed from mute spectators to communicative, human co-offerers" with the person offering the prayer.[64] The fact that the congregation (during the Mass) prays the same words unitedly serves to unify them—and symbolizes the idea that they are one, as commanded by Christ in His great intercessory prayer (John 17:11, 21). Elsewhere Jesus revealed: "Again I say unto you, That if two of you shall agree on earth as touching any thing that they shall ask, it shall be done for them of my Father which is in heaven" (Matthew 18:19). This ritual behavior in prayer represents the doctrinal truism that all those who engage in united or corporate prayer—particularly corporate prayer of the higher form—should be one in their will and desire, one with each other and one with their God. The following text on the ancient practice of corporate prayer suggests a particular symbolism behind praying in unison: "Unisonous prayer was considered particularly valuable for a simple reason: it was more effective than the prayer of single persons. A fragment by Petronius states bluntly: ' . . . Prayers travel more valiantly when united.' It is, therefore, only wise to recite a prayer in unison, if it asks for something extraordinary."[65] Similarly, Athanasius of Alexandria[66] taught that when Christians "stretch forth their hands" and pray, God will more quickly "hear [their] prayer" than if they were to pray alone.[67] One text notes that "joint prayer affords an increased effect: since the earthly prayer mingles with the angels' heavenly praise, it is certainly heard."[68] From the perspective of imagery, praying in unity symbolizes the undivided will of the persons praying and the God to whom they pray. That unity includes their oneness in desire, in basic attributes, and effort. And, as pointed out, their oneness extends not only to themselves and their God, but to the entire Church and the entire host of heaven.

Related to this concept of "oneness" and "unity," Barnabas[69] reminded patrons of prayer to "not go to prayer with an evil conscience."[70] To do so would offend the Spirit of God, and destroy the "oneness" that should exist between those who have chosen to unite their voices in prayer. Tertullian taught that when we, as Christians, approach "God's altar" to pray, we must not do so until we first resolve any "discord or offense we have . . . with our brethren. For what sort of deed is it to approach the peace of God without peace [in our heart]?"[71] Tertullian adds that it is not merely anger that we must jettison prior to approaching the altar of prayer, but also all "perturbation of mind" (or mental distractions).[72] In other words, Tertullian is suggesting that approaching the altar of prayer in a distracted state—focused on things other than the ritual at hand—is as prone to hinder God's spirit as is approaching the altar when one has issues with one's brother. In the Sermon on the Mount, the Lord informed His hearers: "If thou bring thy gift to the altar, and there rememberest that thy brother hath ought against thee; Leave there thy gift before the altar, and go thy way; first be reconciled to thy brother, and then come and offer thy gift" (Matthew 5:23–24). There is the obvious meaning of this passage, as pointed out by Cyril of Alexandria[73]; namely, "whoever bears hard feelings toward his brother is not accepted, since he does not approach the Lord in truth."[74] If one approaches the altar of prayer, having ill feelings toward one of the other participants in the rite, one must withdraw, or he is a hypocrite and stands unaccepted of the Lord. One contemporary commentary on this verse states: "If there are strained relations or friction between us and anyone else, before going to the Temple . . . , we should first be reconciled with that person—talk things over, work them out, resolve differences, forgive, and forget . . . . Then we can approach the Lord and his sacred things with full purpose of heart and, as he says, 'I will receive you' (3 Nephi 12:24)."[75] While clearly the Spirit of the Lord cannot be felt in force if one standing in the circle hinders it through bad feelings, nevertheless, John Chrysostom[76] highlighted the symbolism behind withdrawing from the altar. He asked: "With what motive then doth [the Lord] command [us to withdraw if we have ill feelings]?" Chrysostom then answers: "His will is to point out that He highly values charity [or love], and considers it to be the greatest sacrifice [we can make]: And without it He doth not receive even that other."[77] Chrysostom's point is that, if we offer a "sacrifice" of serving in the church, the temple, or at the altar, but do so without love, God does not accept our offering in any of those settings. Our "sacrifice" of service is negated by the hypocrisy we display in serving without love for our brother or sister whom we meet in the circle. Jerome highlighted a significant point about how Christ describes the problem present at the altar. He wrote: "He did not say, 'If you have anything against your brother' but 'If your brother has anything against you,' so that a greater need for reconciliation is imposed on you [than is imposed upon him]. As long as we are unable to make peace with our brother, I do not know whether we may offer our gifts to God."[78] Jerome points out that one does not withdraw from the altar simply because one has issues with another in the circle. According to Jerome, one should withdraw if someone in the circle has issues with him or her. The implicit suggestion is that none should approach the altar if his or her life is such that others are offended by him or her. It is not enough to feel lovingly toward others at the altar. One must also live in such a way that those at the altar can feel love toward us. Of this Augustine wrote:

> We may interpret the altar spiritually, as being [a symbol] of faith itself . . . , whose emblem [or representation] is the visible altar. For whatever offering [or gift] we present to God, whether [it be our gift of] prophecy, or [our gift of] teaching, or prayer, or . . . a hymn [because we have a gift for music], and whatever other . . . spiritual gift occurs to the mind [that we might choose to offer Jesus], it cannot be acceptable to God, unless it be sustained [or presented to Him] by sincerity of faith . . . .[79]

Thus, Augustine spiritualizes Christ's command to step away from the altar, interpreting it to mean that gifts of sacrifice or talent offered to God—but not in faith—are unpleasing and unacceptable to Him. The worshiper, according to Augustine, must not simply teach the gospel, offer eloquent prayers, sing beautiful music, or serve in the temple, but he or she must do so having faith in God, His plan, His ordinances, His commandments—else all is in vain.

As part of corporate prayer, the Eastern Orthodox and Roman Catholic faiths had, in times past, the tendency to use a *diptych*; a book, folder, or scroll in which was inscribed the names of Christians who were seriously ill and requested a special consideration during the prayer at the altar.[80] Though the names recorded in *diptychs* were often those who were ill, dying, or those who had some special need, it was also common to include the names of church leaders and political authorities within this bundle of names placed upon the altar.[81] Originally the names were read aloud. However, because of time constraints and the typical length of the lists, "the register of names was laid on the altar and merely a reference introduced into the Memento."[82] This Catholic and Eastern Orthodox rite was not an invention of either of those faiths. Indeed, there is evidence that the practice was borrowed from ancient rituals. For example, the Old Testament prophet Zephaniah informs us how "the pious multitude" of his era would "assemble for prayer daily" on behalf of those who were suffering some sort of torment in their lives.[83] We read: "And I also saw multitudes . . . praying before the Lord Almighty, saying, 'We pray to you on account of those who are in all these torments so that you might have mercy on all of them.' "[84] One commentator on the use of the *diptych* wrote: "The practice of laying names on the altar is of unknown origin though it is very old and, it is agreed, may well go back to the days of the apostles."[85] Though we can't date its beginnings, the practice is unquestionably of ancient origins.

Of the symbolism inherent in this practice, one source noted that the *diptych* is the "fullest expression of that altruism by which one saves oneself in saving others."[86] It represents the Christian's covenant-binding responsibility to "mourn with those that mourn; yea, and comfort those that stand in need of comfort" (Mosiah 18:9). The concerns of the individuals whose names are included in the *diptych* become the concerns of those who participate in the prayer. Their worries are our worries; their pains are our pains. Their pleadings to God must become our pleadings. The *diptych* is a symbol for the essence of Christianity—namely a charitable concern for the well-being of all of God's children. As the Apostle Paul stated: If I "have not charity, I am nothing" (1 Corinthians 13:2). The utilization of the *diptych* symbolically reminds us of this truth.

We now turn our attention to what might be called "threshold rituals"—rites or ceremonies that symbolically depict the participant's return to, or entrance into, the presence of God.

One particularly curious example of such a ritual is celebrated every twenty-fifth year in the Roman Catholic Church; the "Holy Year of Jubilee."[87] This is a time of pilgrimage for some, and an opportunity to seek forgiveness for sins by participating in the rituals associated with this holy convocation. A sacred and important part of the "Holy Year of Jubilee" is the performance of a rite known as the knocking at the *Porta Santa*, or knocking at the "Holy Gate." This is a rare ritual, enacted only on Christmas Eve every twenty-fifth year at St. Peter's Basilica in Rome.[88] One commentator on the ritual wrote: "The *Porta Santa*, or 'Holy Gate,' [is] . . . never to be opened except for [the] most special entrance."[89] Indeed, the door (which is used during this ritual) is sealed, or bricked up, after the rite is completed, thereby preventing anyone from passing through it, except during this singular sacred ceremony.[90] On the occasion of the enactment of this ritual, the pope approaches the door with an entourage of pilgrims who have come to participate in this rite of redemption. The pope approaches the location of the door and knocks on the wall three times with a silver[91] or golden[92] hammer. The door is opened from within, and the pope crosses the threshold followed by his entourage of the faithful. Once in the Basilica, the pope makes his way to the high altar, where the Eucharist is housed—symbolic of the presence of the divine.[93] The *Porta Santa* or "Holy Gate" ritual is a highly symbolic rite, which represents the return of the penitent into the presence of God.[94] What is symbolically depicted by the entrance into the sanctuary and the approach of the altar is the redemption of God's people—and their return to Him through His extended grace and mercy.

A seventeenth-century Jubilee Medallion, depicting the pope at the Porta Santa, introducing God's sheep into His presence

Among other things, during the rite the pope prays: "O

God, . . . grant to us Thy servants . . . the pardon of a true indul-
gence and remission of all our sins . . . through Christ our Lord."[95]
Thus, symbolically speaking, when the pope and his entourage
approach the door, they are really approaching the veil that separates God and mankind. The opening of the door from within
represents both our deliverance from the spiritual perils of the
mortal experience[96] and the outpouring of God's mercy for those
who are enabled to cross the threshold and approach the altar.[97]
The reason this rite is performed on Christmas Eve is because it
represents the reality that through the birth of Christ salvation has
come to the world![98] Because the *Porta Santa*, or "Holy Gate," represents the gate of heaven, or the veil between heaven and earth,
those who pass through it are considered "saved."[99] Indeed, during
the ritual some of what the pope says suggests that the act being
depicted is associated with, or in similitude of, the ancient temple
and entrance into the divine presence.[100] The Apostle Paul speaks
of the veil of the temple as the flesh of Christ (Hebrews 10:19–20).
And Jesus, Himself, suggested that he was "the door" (John 10:9).
Thus, the rite has a strong temple theme and a strong Christocentric theme. Curiously, Jerome informs us that one fourth-century
church in Anablatha (near Jerusalem) was discovered to have a veil
hanging in the sanctuary that bore the image of Christ. Epiphanius,[101] upon entering the church, was so unsettled by the discov-
ery that he ripped it down and ordered a plain white veil to be
hung in its place.[102] Thus, apparently some in the congregation at
Anablatha understood the connection between the veil and Jesus.
On a related note, one Catholic scholar suggested that Jesus' declaration, "Enter ye in at the strait gate: for wide is the gate, and
broad is the way, that leadeth to destruction, and many there be
which go in there at: Because strait is the gate, and narrow is the
way, which leadeth unto life, and few there be that find it" (Matthew 7:13–14), might have reference to the *Porta Santa*, or "Holy
Gate" that is central to this Catholic rite.[103]

Curiously, there is an additional Catholic rite—perhaps
related to, or a spin-off of, the *Porta Santa*—that has similar
symbolic underpinnings.[104] It is the "rite of the dedication of a

church." Among other things, the bishop performing the dedication knocks three times (with his pastoral staff) at a closed door. A voice from the other side of the door asks, "Who is this . . . ?" The bishop answers by stating who he represents.[105] After a dialogue (between the two) through the closed door, the individual who had been communicating with the bishop through the door opens it from inside, allowing the bishop entrance into the sanctuary.[106] As with this rite, "question-and-answer successions frequently appear in ritual settings."[107]

One of the most curious portions of the *Porta Santa* and "dedication" rituals is the act of knocking three times with the hammer or pastoral staff. This portion of the ceremony has been interpreted variously.

- The number three is an ancient symbol for God, or the Godhead.[108] Thus, to knock three times implies one is petitioning or approaching deity. It symbolizes who it is that stands behind the closed door or veil. It highlights who we are dependent upon for redemption and return—namely God.
- The knocking three times has been associated with the idea that the opening of the veil or "gate of heaven" would bring joy to (1) those in heaven, (2) those on earth, and (3) those bound in purgatory or spirit prison. Thus, three groups rejoice over God's returning sheep, and hence the pope or bishop knocks three times.[109]
- The knocking three times has been taken to symbolize the fact that there are three things we must have if we wish to enter God's presence and commune with Him for eternity: namely (1) faith, (2) hope, and (3) charity.[110] Consequently, it reminds the worshiper that this is no vain or meaningless ritual. It is a reminder that, when the day comes for you or I to actually approach God's door or veil, our nature or character must necessarily consist of faith, hope, and charity—or the attributes of the divine—if we wish to enter into the presence of the divine.
- Finally, knocking three times has been thought to symbolize our need to call upon God in prayer three times a day; (1) morning, (2) noon, and (3) night. Alma 34:21 reads: "Cry unto him . . . both morning, mid-day, and evening." The Saints have been encouraged to follow that example of petitioning God no less than thrice daily.[111]

The overarching message of the triple knock in this ritual seems to be that we must petition the divine—and do so often, and in a state of purity of heart.

The last important symbol of this rite at the *Porta Santa* is the altar itself. As will be recalled, once the pope and those participating in this ritual enter the portal or "Holy Gate," they head directly toward the high altar[112]—a symbol of the presence of God. Thus, they are admitted into His presence.

In this rite we see depicted man's efforts to regain God's presence. The petitioner is accompanied by His representative as he or she approaches Him at the veil or door. God is petitioned through a triple knock. Those seeking to commune with God are expected to be filled with faith, hope, and charity as they approach Him— indeed, each is to have sought His attributes during his or her mortal journey to the door or veil. In some versions of the rite we have a conversation with the Father through the door or veil.[113] And finally, if He opens the door to us we, through His grace and mercy, regain His presence (as is symbolized by the altar and the Eucharist or emblems of the sacrament, which are found thereon). The entire rite is a symbolic re-enactment of God's grace being poured out upon those who approach Him, making it possible for them to enter His presence.

It is not known for certain where this rite began, how old it is, or how it may have evolved over time. As one Catholic source notes: "It is not easy to ascertain the precise nature of the ceremony in the earlier stages."[114] But, no doubt, this rite was borrowed or adopted from some ancient rite practiced by the early Christian church.

Though our final symbol for this chapter is connected to the preceding one, we will set our formal discussion of the *Porta Santa* aside and now examine the emblematical veil. As seems obvious, the veil is traditionally seen as a symbol of the "boundary between the visible world and the invisible, between time and eternity."[115] There existed an "ancient belief that passing through the veil was passing into heaven."[116] Because the ancient tabernacle's veil was decorated with patterns or symbols that represented the heavens, the veil itself stood as a symbol of the gate to the heavens—it "portrayed a panorama of the heavens."[117] Thus, passing through the veil is a "symbolic pre-*enactment*" of the day when all will seek to "pass the angels who stand as sentinels" and thereby enter God's presence.[118] We read: "The rite of passing between the parts of an object that has been halved"—like a parted curtain or veil—functions as a "rite of passage by means of which a person leaves one world behind him and enters a new one."[119] Veils at times in history other than during the era of the Hebrew Bible have been white—void of cosmic symbolism—and in such cases the veil may have served to symbolize the clouds that shroud the heavens. When one passed through (or beyond) the veil of the temple or sanctuary, one was seen as no longer being bound by time, but rather he or she became the recipient of the visions of eternity.[120]

The veil also carried Christocentric meaning—symbolizing Jesus, the Savior of all. In the book of Hebrews we are informed that the veil of the temple is the "flesh" of Christ (Hebrews 10:20). Consequently, when the ancients sought to commune with God through the veil, they were symbolically speaking to the Father through Jesus—the mediator (as all do each time they pray). And if they passed through the veil into the Father's presence, they were doing so through Jesus—who is the gate or door through which all must enter (John 10:7). Thus the veil (symbolically speaking) says much about the role of Christ in our salvation and in our ability to commune with God and eventually return to God. All is through Christ—All! One commentator noted:

> The veil of the temple was used by Christians from the beginning to describe the incarnation. Further, they used not only the veil but also the robe of the high priest, which symbolized the second divine being [i.e., Jesus] being robed in the material world of the veil. The first Christians knew the intimate connection between the two. [See Hebrews 10:19–21] . . . The veil torn in two at the moment of Jesus' death [was] a graphic illustration of the identity of flesh and veil (Matt. 27:51; Mark 15:38; Luke 23:45).[121]

Similarly, one LDS text reminds us:

233

Entering the veil of the tabernacle or the temple . . . teaches us of Jesus' atonement. The veil that separated humankind from God's presence . . . symbolizes Jesus Christ's flesh (Heb. 9:3; 10:19–20). The temple veil stood between humans and their entrance into the temple's holiest place; in the same way, the Savior stands between the celestial kingdom and us. "No man cometh unto the Father, but by me," Jesus declared (John 14:6).[122]

Margaret Barker wrote: "Inseparable from the veil were the vestments of the high priest . . . . Veil and vestments were complementary imagery. . . . The veil and the priestly vestments provided the first Christians with ready imagery to convey what they meant by the incarnation." In other words, the veil was a symbol for the flesh of Christ—God incarnate.[123] That seems significant in light of the following. Blake Ostler wrote: "It should be noted that the ancient garment bore the same tokens as the veil of the temple at Jerusalem . . . . Many ancient texts confuse the garment with the veil of the temple, such as Ambrose of Milano's Tractate of the Mysteries or the Hebrew Book of Enoch where the 'garment' and 'veil' are used interchangeably."[124] Similarly, Hugh Nibley pointed out that the garment and the veil of the temple bear "the same markings" and have "the same cosmic significance."[125] Thus, to be wrapped in the veil was to be clothed in Christ. To engage in the ritual embrace was to embrace not only the Father, but to be encircled in the arms of the Son. We read: "In the [Egyptian] coronation embrace, 'the god has stretched forth his hands out through [a sort of] sheath (or covering) and clasps the king against his breast.' "[126] Elsewhere we are informed: "The veil of the temple is the robe of the angel" or the divine.[127] Thus, the veil is a very tangible symbol for Christ's presence in the temple, and in the life of the initiate.

We see in ancient sources common reference to a quizzing which was to take place at the Porta Santa, the veil, or the gate of heaven. The deity behind the door or veil would inquire as to the possession of mystic knowledge or secrets that were to be known by the initiate who had approached the door or veil to converse with God. For example, in the Hebrew book of "3rd

Enoch"[128] (or "Apocalypse of Enoch") we read: "A curtain hangs before God's throne separating his immediate presence from the rest of the heavenly world."[129] The text adds: "Ishmael is challenged [or questioned] by the guardian angels at the gate [or veil]. In response to his prayer for help, God sends him the archangel [Michael[130]], who . . . presents him before God's throne. God graciously receives him."[131] One text on Egyptian ritual and religion noted that, in an effort to transition from this life to the next:

> The deceased had to make his way through . . . the doors . . . which were guarded by beings who were prepared, unless properly addressed, to be hostile to the new-comer; he also had need . . . to obtain the help of the gods . . . if he wished to pass safely into the place where he would be [throughout eternity]. The Book of the Dead provided him with all the texts and formulae which he would have to recite to secure this result, but unless the words contained in them were pronounced in a proper manner, and said in a proper tone of voice [i.e., a whisper?], they would have no effect upon the powers of the underworld.[132]

Likewise, one expert on Old Testament pseudepigraphical texts noted: "Ascension of Isaiah[133] 10:24–31 mentions angelic guardians of the gates of the various palaces, to whom passwords have to be given. This recalls the Merkabah notion of the gate-keepers of the seven heavenly palaces, to whom 'seals' have to be shown by the mystic on his way up to heaven."[134] This same author pointed out: "[To] angelic guardians of the gates . . . passwords have to be given. . . . 'seals' have to be shown by the mystic on his way up to heaven."[135] One LDS source suggested: "The gatekeepers are to act as mediators between the deceased and the gods."[136] They assist the initiate when He falls short, just as Christ assists us when we fall short. Elsewhere we are informed: "The process of passing through the veil is symbolic . . . [of] possessing the required knowledge of key words, signs and tokens to be able to pass by the sentinels placed to guard the way to God's presence."[137] The idea of having to pass a divine being or angel who functions as a "gatekeeper" (on one's way back to God's abode) is a theme that is present as far back as "ascension texts" exist.[138] Nibley noted:

All temples are marked by boundaries, stations, levels, doors, stairs, passages, gates, veils, etc.,—they all denote rites of passage going from one condition or state to another, from lower to higher, from dark to light, a complete transition from one world, telestial or terrestrial, to another, ultimately the celestial. At certain crucial passages one must identify oneself by an exchange of names and tokens and show oneself qualified by an exchange of words. This was characteristic of all ancient temples.[139]

The prolific Margaret Barker—whose research has focused heavily on the ancient temple—noted that: "The veil of the temple is . . . a means of revelation as well as of concealment."[140] The quiz at the veil determines which it will be for you. Those who approach God prepared find it "revealing."[141] Those who approach unworthy find it concealing of God's presence, glory, and mysteries. The fact that there were cherubim embroidered on the ancient veil of the temple (2 Chronicles 3:14) symbolically suggested that, as one passed through the veil, they were "passing the angels who stand as sentinels."[142] One text notes, of the initiate's experience at the gate or veil, that "Sometimes secrets are announced by a heavenly voice 'from behind the curtain'."[143] In other words, one comes to the veil, not simply to give, but to receive—just as Barker suggested when she referred to the veil as both a place of revelation and of concealment.

As to what this quiz at the gate, veil, or door consisted of, one text on rites of passage noted that in such rituals in Christianity there was an exchange of sorts that took place. The exchanging of things or the receiving of gifts (or endowments) would bind the receiver to the giver. This same text notes that clasping hands, embracing, or receiving ritual garments would be included in such acts of binding. The receipt (or exchanging) of such items was equivalent to "pronouncing an oath" or entering into a covenant.[144] "The giving of the hand," for example, "showed that a relationship was established between two persons (2 Kings 10:15; Jeremiah 50:15; Ezekiel 17:18)."[145] To clasp another's hand was a sign of a "pledge" or an expression of "solidarity."[146] One dictionary of symbols suggests that, "In esoteric doctrine, the position of the hand in relation to the body, and the arrangement of the fingers, convey certain precise symbolic notions."[147] Thus, it would seem that the ancients, as part of the quiz at the portal, would exchange certain grips, tokens, or handclasps that had an esoteric, symbolic meaning to the initiate. We see this practice in certain ceremonies associated with Roman Catholicism, wherein a grip is employed with an accompanying question to be answered by the individual being examined. Associated with these Catholic "grips" and "questions" were "passwords." Of them, one Roman Catholic source noted: "The password . . . must be kept a secret from all outsiders."[148] The Old Testament pseudepigrapha[149] is filled with references to angels or the divine giving or receiving tokens from figures, such as Enoch. Phrases such as he "seized me by the hand," he "took me by the hand," or he "grasped my hand" appear with frequency in those ancient texts. As a singular example, Enoch reports the following curious encounter: "The angel Michael, one of the archangels, seizing me by my right hand . . . , led me [through] all the secrets of mercy, and he showed me all the secrets of righteousness."[150] Enoch adds that as Michael presented him before God's throne: "He grasped me with his hand . . . and said to me, 'Come in peace into the presence of the high and exalted King . . . .' Then I entered . . . and [he] presented me before the throne of glory."[151] One expert in ancient temple rites wrote:

> Religious rituals (or ties) are sacred actions or "ceremonial movements." Some scholars refer to these rites of transition as "gestures of approach" because they are religious gestures (or acts or movements) that worshipers make as they approach God during sacred worship. The ancient temple, especially, included sacred gestures that enabled and empowered worshipers to move from the outer gate inward to the most holy place of all, the holy of holies. The gestures of approach are vital to a temple society because they symbolically cleanse and prepare worshipers for entry into and movement through sacred space as they transition from the profane world into the sacred temple.[152]

From these aforementioned practices, and dozens like them, we learn that the ancient quiz at the veil included the giving of special handclasps, the answering of certain questions, and the utilization of sacred passwords. These "gestures of approach" were designed to establish the worthiness of the initiate because they symbolized, among other things, that the initiate had qualified himself or herself to approach God. They were symbolic representations of how the individual approaching God had entered into and kept sacred covenants with the divine. They highlighted the fact that the initiate had lived a life worthy of God's presence by "crucifying" his or her "flesh" (Galatians 2:20, 5:24)—setting aside the ways of the world in preference for the ways of God. Consequently, these gestures of approach were often symbols of sacrifice—the sacrifice of the divine and the self-sacrifice of the initiate. These tokens or "gestures of approach" are "proof of identity" in that they establish that the one approaching God is what he or she ought to be in order to enter God's presence.[153] They establish him or her as a "true" Christian; a "true" disciple of Christ. The utilization or exchange of such symbols or tokens represented unity, equality, friendship, agreement, initiation, reconciliation, communion, salvation, and even apotheosis.[154]

If one passed the quiz at the gate, one was embraced and then invited into the presence of the Lord—as depicted in the *Porta Santa* rite shared above. Nibley spoke time and again of this ritual embrace at the veil of the ancient temple. Regarding the symbolism behind this ritual, he wrote: "A spontaneous and natural gesture, embracing is not only a sign of affection but also one of acceptance, recognition, and reception."[155] He added that in Egyptian ritual, someone representing the "Father" or "Creator" embraces the candidate being initiated so as to symbolize the reality that the deceased who is entering into God's presence is "fusing" with, or becoming one with his God. The embrace thus represents God taking the initiate "to his heart."[156] Consequently, the embrace at the veil is a symbol that one has become "one with God"—not metaphysically, but in nature and desires.[157] The embrace implies acceptance, and therefore forgiveness.[158] Thus, we read, the ritual embrace symbolizes "two long separate beings forming a renewed unity, re-creating an identity that had been fragmented and lost."[159]

Todd Compton penned this of the ancient ritual embrace at the veil or gate: "The embrace is the primary emblem of . . . exaltation, and the sign of the child's new status, his re-adoption by his parent."[160] One is saved; one is accepted; one is brought back (through the embrace) into the family of God.[161] This being said, the embrace also connotes revelation, or being brought into the light regarding mystic truths or sacred secrets. Thus, one becomes a new creature—a new creation, as it were. One is born into a new life and a new world through the ritual embrace. Hence Nibley noted, "The birth motif is never far away in the ritual embrace." One might compare "passing through the veil" or door with the birth process—"from one life and one world to another."[162] On a related note, M. Catherine Thomas suggested a birth metaphor (associated with passing through the veil) when she penned the following: "The temple is the narrow channel though which one must pass to re-enter the Lord's presence."[163] Like the fetus that passes through the narrow birth canal in order to be born, the initiate who seeks God's presence must pass through the narrow veil in order to be reborn into His presence. Finally, the ritual embrace has been seen as a story of conferral of divine power from father to son or daughter. "Divine power flows from the old king to his successor . . . ."[164] Those who are embraced at the gate or veil are also, symbolically speaking, ordained to be God's successor in His holy work. It is a commission, a calling of sorts. It is an outward symbol of the fact that God will endow the embraced initiate with all that the He has (D&C 84:38).

One LDS text notes this: "Significantly, it is only after prayer that the veil is uncovered. This is symbolic of the uncovering of the heavenly veil, which also occurs after prayers."[165] Thus the role of prayer is emphasized in a curious way. We approach the veil to commune with God. However in order to successfully do so, we must have frequently communed with God prior to approaching the veil. Our ritual ascent to God's veil—and ideally into God's presence—must be preceded by frequent and sincere prayers, which will give us the power to approach the divine, part the veil, and worthily enter into his presence.[166]

One text reminds us: "The innermost sanctuary of the temple, the most holy place, is a model on earth of the place where God lives."[167] Thus, the action of the ancient high priest in entering the holy of holies symbolically represented the fact that all will eventually seek to enter heaven, and in so doing hope for the conferral of a divine status.[168] That which is beyond the veil represents God's abode—Heaven, the Celestial Kingdom. Those who dwell there experience divinization.[169] Consequently, to pass through the veil is to be as God is. It represents receipt of all that the Father has. It implies complete and total forgiveness through the grace of God and the atoning blood of the Messiah, who is mighty to save (2 Nephi 31:19; Alma 7:14).

Notes

1.   See Constantinides (2006), 58.

2.   See Barker (2008), 122. Curiously, in rites celebrated by nineteenth and early twentieth century U.S. Jews, we find the use of an altar, "on top of which lay a [Hebrew] Bible"—these two being a point of focus during covenant-making ceremonies. (See Soyer [1999], 170.)

3.   See Jeffrey T. Vanderwilt, "Altar," in McBrien (1995), 36–37; Thomas Hopko, *The Orthodox Faith: An Elementary Handbook on the Orthodox Faith—Worship*, 4 vols. (New York: The Department of Religious Education, The Orthodox Church of America, 1983), 2:6.

4.   See Vanderwilt, in McBrien (1995), 37; Hopko (1983), 6; Cooper (1995), 11; Conner (1992), 126. Thus one LDS source noted: "The altar is symbolic of the sacrifice of the Savior who sacrificed all in obedience (see Hebrews 5:8) to His Father to become one with Him" (Green [2004], 136). Elsewhere we read: "A true altar represents a divine presence, heavenly messengers—angels of the Lord—a place for making and receiving covenants and offering up sacrifice . . . . It truly represents the meeting place where Deity accepts man's offerings" (Stephen G. Morgan, *Hidden Treasures of Knowledge: An Abridgement of Ancient Religious Documents which Support the Revealed Word of God* [Salt Lake City: Deseret Book Distributors, 2006], 125).

5.   Parry and Parry (2009), 153.

6.   See Skinner (2007), 184–85. Skinner also noted: "In the Lord's plan, altars have always been the center of sacred action. Around altars in the temples today, the most important and sacred activities occur: the making

of covenants, the offering of prayers, the establishment of eternal marriages and families, and the promises of sacrifice and consecration" (ibid. [2007], 184).

7.   Gaye Strathearn and Brian M. Hauglid, "The Great Mosque and Its Ka)Ba," in Parry and Ricks (1999), 292.

8.   Ali Shariati, *Hajj*, translated by Ali A. Behzadnia and Najla Denny (Houston: Free Islamic Literatures, 1978), 84, cited in Strathearn and Hauglid (1999), 292–93.

9.   The *Ka'bah* is a "large cubic stone structure, covered with a black cloth, which stands in the center of the Grand Mosque of Mecca. In one corner, the *Ka'bah* contains the Black Stone. Neither the stone nor the *Ka'bah* are objects of worship, but they represent a sanctuary consecrated to God . . . , and it is towards the *Ka'bah* that Muslims orient themselves in prayer; thus the *Ka'bah* is a spiritual center, a support for the concentration of consciousness upon the Divine Presence." In this regard, the *Ka'bah* functions a bit like a Christian altar. Our source continues: "The *Ka'bah* was originally founded, tradition says, by Adam, and after his death rebuilt by his son Seth. When the time came, it was rebuilt by Abraham and his son Ishmael . . . . When it was finished, Abraham was commanded by God to go to Mount *Thābir* nearby and call mankind to pilgrimage to 'the ancient house' (*al-bayt al-'atīq*). Afterwards, the *Ka'bah* was rebuilt [several times] by the . . . [various] descendents [sic] of Noah" (Glassé [1989], 214).

10.   "Testament of Isaac" 4:19, in "Testaments of the Three Patriarchs," in Charlesworth (1983, 1985), 1:907.

11.   See "Extract From the Books of the Saviour," #357–58, in G. R. S. Mead, *Pistis Sophia* (London: The Theological Publishing Society, 1896), 358–59. The salient portion of this Gnostic-Christian text reads:

> Then Jesus stood . . . with his disciples, and made invocation with this prayer, saying: "Here me, O father . . ." And while Jesus was reciting this, Thomas, Andrew, James, and Simon, the Canaanite, stood on the west, with their faces turned towards the east; Philip and Bartholomew stood on the south, facing towards the north [thereby representing the four cardinal directions]; the rest of the disciples with all the women disciples stood behind Jesus. But Jesus stood at the altar. And Jesus cried aloud, turning towards the four angles [or directions] of the world, together with his disciples all clad in linen robes.

See also 2 *Jeu* 42–43, 45–50, in Carl Schmidt, ed., *The Books of Jeu and the Untitled Text in the Bruce Codex* (Leiden: E. J. Brill, 1978), 99–102, 104–09, 112–16, & 119.

12. This ancient text was certainly known in the Christian Church by the fourth century. (See Edgar Hennecke and Wilhelm Schneemelcher, eds., *New Testament Apocrypha*, vol. 2 [Philadelphia: The Westminster Press, 1965], 192.) As Clement of Alexandria makes reference to it, it is likely that the *Acts of John* should be dated as early as the second century AD. (See Frederick W. Norris, "Acts of John," in Ferguson [1990], 7.)

13. Nibley noted: "The prayer circle is often called the *chorus* of the apostles, and it is the meaning of *chorus* which can be a choir, but is originally a ring dance." [Nibley, *Mormonism* . . . (1987), 53] It is a hymn, of sorts, unto God, offered in the Spirit of D&C 25:12—"For my soul delighteth in the song of the heart; yea, the song of the righteous is a prayer unto me, and it shall be answered with a blessing upon their heads." Thus, the prayer is as a hymn, which invokes God's choicest blessings upon those who participate.

14. Nibley wrote: "The prayer spoken in the circle differs every time; it is not strictly prescribed. The one leading the prayer expresses himself as the Spirit moves him, and the others either repeat each line after him (which would not be necessary if they all knew it by heart) or add an 'amen' at the end of each phrase, which is the equivalent of reciting the prayer for oneself" (Nibley, *Mormonism* . . . [1987], 56).

15. Acts of John 94–97, in Hennecke and Schneemelcher (1965), 227–28, 232.

16. Nibley, *Mormonism* . . . (1987), 70.

17. Cyril of Jerusalem stated that, while "the Presbyters . . . stand round God's altar . . . the Priest cries aloud, 'Lift up your hearts.'" In the early Christian liturgy of James (the brother of Jesus) the language is "Let us lift up our minds and our hearts." Cyril continues: "In effect therefore the [officiating] Priest bids all in that hour to dismiss all cares of this life, or household anxieties, and to have their heart in [or focused on] heaven with the merciful God" (Cyril of Jerusalem, "Catechetical Lectures," Lecture 23:4, in Schaff and Wace [2004], 7:153–54. Regarding James' alternate wording, see "The Divine Liturgy of James," Section 3:28, in "Early Liturgies," in Roberts and Donaldson [1994], 7:543).

18. Nibley, *Mormonism* . . . (1987), 70.

19. Parry and Parry (2009), 12.

20. See Gerhard Kittel, ed., *Theological Dictionary of the New Testament*, 10 vols. (Grand Rapids: Eerdmans, 1967), 4:803.

21. See Acts of John 94, in Hennecke and Schneemelcher (1965), 227.

22. Cyril (circa AD 315–86) was Bishop of Jerusalem starting around AD 350.

23. Cyril of Jerusalem, "Catechetical Lectures," Lecture 23:3, in Schaff and Wace (2004), 7:153.

24. Nibley, *Mormonism* . . . (1987), 50.

25. Franz Delitzsch wrote: "This [raising of the hands] was the gesture of a man in prayer, who . . . stretched [his hands] towards heaven, or [in] the most holy place in the temple . . . held up the hollow or palm of his hand" (Franz Delitzsch, *Biblical Commentary on the Prophecies of Isaiah*, 2 vols. [Grand Rapids: Eerdmans, 1954], 1:94. See also Madsen, in Lundquist and Ricks [1990], 1:461; Madsen [2008], 142).

26. Parry and Parry (2009), 32.

27. See, for example, Book 1 of "The Book of Adam and Eve" (also known as "The Conflict of Adam and Eve with Satan") 5:3, 26:5, 28:3, 52:2, 58:1, 69:2, 71:6, cited in S. C. Malan, *The Book of Adam and Eve also called The Conflict of Adam and Eve with Satan* (London: Williams and Northgate, 1882), 6, 26, 30, 57, 65, 82, 86. Adam and Eve's righteous children apparently also prayed with upraised hands. (See Book 2 of ibid., 6:10, 17:43 [113, 130].)

28. See 2 Enoch 69:8–14, in Charlesworth (1983, 1985), 1:198, which states of Methuselah that "the elders of the people . . . attired [him] in the designated garments and placed a blazing crown on his head. . . . And [Methuselah] came up to the Lord's altar . . . with all the people in procession behind him. And [he] stood in front of the altar of the Lord, with all the people standing around the place of sacrifice [i.e., the altar]. . . . And [Methuselah] stretched out his hands to heaven and he called out to the Lord." (See also 2 Enoch 70:1, 16, in Charlesworth [1983, 1985], 1:200, 202.)

29. There are no extant versions of "The Gospel of Bartholomew" today. Early sources (e.g., Origen, Jerome, pseudo-Dionysus) acknowledge its existence and quote from the text, but what remains today is fragmentary and likely represents "borrowings" from an earlier document that has not been preserved. It appears certain that the original document (from which other texts have borrowed) existed by the early third century; though it is possible that it dates even earlier than that. (See Jon B. Daniels, "Bartholomew, Gospel [Questions] Of," in Freedman [1992], 1:615–16; Montague Rhodes James, trans., *The Apocryphal New Testament* [Oxford: Clarendon Press, 1960], 166)s.

30. "The Gospel of Bartholomew," 2:1, 5, 13, in James (1960), 170–71.

31. Clement of Rome (circa AD 30–100) was one of the early apostolic fathers—likely a Gentile and a Roman—whose "Epistle to the Corinthians" has been referred to as "one of the most important

documents of subapostolic times." (See Bray [1999], 326.)

32. Clement of Rome, "The First Epistle of Clement to the Corinthians," Chapter 2, in Roberts and Donaldson (1994), 1:5.

33. Clement of Alexandria (circa AD 160–215) was a Christian theologian who sought to draw connections between Christian beliefs and Greek philosophy and culture. He was self-described as "a Christian questioning for understanding about God" (Walter H. Wagner, "Clement of Alexandria," in Ferguson [1990], 214).

34. Clement of Alexandria, "The Stromata," Book 7, Chapter 7, in Roberts and Donaldson (1994), 2:534.

35. Tertullian of Carthage (circa AD 155–225) was an apologist for the Christian Church in North Africa. His christological and theological writings were foundational for later Western Christian thought. (See Weinrich [2005], 424–25.)

36. See, for example, Tertullian, "Apology," Chapter 30, in Roberts and Donaldson (1994), 3:42, wherein he states of Christians, "We lift our eyes [heavenward], with hands outstretched." See also Tertullian, "On Prayer," Chapter 14, in Roberts and Donaldson (1994), 3:685, where he states that the Jews do not raise their hands to the Lord in prayer, but Christians "not only raise, but even expand them . . . in prayer."

37. The aforementioned Psalm states: "O Lord, I cry out to You, hearken unto me. I spread my hands toward Your holy dwelling, give ear and grant my request; do not withhold my boon. Enlighten my soul" (11Q5 Col. 24, in Michael Wise, Martin Abegg, Jr., and Edward Cook, translators, *The Dead Sea Scrolls—A New Translation* [New York: HarperCollins, 1999], 449.) While one may pray in sacred precincts, those precincts are only symbols of a higher reality, namely God's celestial abode. Thus, reaching heavenward is an attempt to draw one's self into the heavenly home, or to draw God down into the earthly sanctuary.

38. Wilson (1999), 209. See also Cooper (1995), 78; Bayley (1990–93), 2:334.

39. One commentator stated that when one prays with upraised hands one is supplicating God and acknowledging his or her ignorance or weakness. (See Elworthy [1900], 148.)

40. Nibley (2008), 324.

41. Tvedtnes, in Parry and Ricks (1999), 84.

42. Clement of Rome, "The First Epistle of Clement to the Corinthians," Chapter 29, in Roberts and Donaldson (1994), 1:12.

43. Parry and Parry (2009), 32. It may be for this reason that one text suggests that "the open hand, when uplifted, was the sign of victory"

(Elworthy [1900], 162). Similarly, "The open hand, whenever depicted, may be taken for the symbol of power and triumph" (ibid., 173). If one is worthy to approach God, one has certainly been victorious over the adversary and the world—one has triumphed!

44. For example, John Tvedtnes wrote: "Ancient temple prayer was symbolic of the crucified Christ" (Tvedtnes, in Parry and Ricks [1999], 89–90).

45. See, for example, Tvedtnes, in Parry and Ricks (1999), 84–85; Nibley, *Mormonism* . . . (1987), 59–60.

46. See Tertullian, "Apology," Chapter 30, in Roberts and Donaldson (1994), 3:42. See also Tertullian, "On Prayer," Chapter 14, in Roberts and Donaldson (1994), 3:685. Minucius Felix wrote: "We assuredly see the sign of the cross . . . when a man adores God with a pure mind, with hands outstretched" (Minicius Felix, "The Octavius of Minucius Felix," Chapter 29, in Roberts and Donaldson [1994], 4:191). Minucius Felix of Rome (circa second or third century) was a Christian apologist who is believed to have been born in North Africa. (See Simonetti [2001], 305.)

47. For example, Cyprian of Carthage (circa AD 200–258) interpreted Moses's outstretched or upraised hands as follows: "In Exodus, when Moses, for the overthrow of Amalek, who bore the type of the devil, raised up his open hands in the sign . . . of the cross, and could not conquer his adversary unless when he had stedfastly [sic] persevered in the sign with hands continually lifted up" (Cyprian, "The Treatises of Cyprian," Treatise 11:8, in Roberts and Donaldson [1994], 5:501). "The Epistle of Barnabas" makes a similar claim. (See "The Epistle of Barnabas" chapter 12, in Roberts and Donaldson [1994], 1:144–45.) Archelaus (flourished circa AD 278), bishop of Carchar, in Mesopotamia, drew a typological parallel between Moses and Christ. He wrote: "Moses . . . stretched forth his hands and fought against Amalek; and . . . the Lord Jesus, when we were assailed and were perishing by the violence of that erring spirit who works now in the just, stretched forth His hands upon the cross, and gave us salvation" (Archelaus, "Disputation With Manes," Chapter 44, in Roberts and Donaldson [1994], 6:220). Augustine also noted the Christological message buried in the typology of Moses' actions. (See Augustine, "On The Trinity," Book 4, Chapter 15, in Schaff [2004], 3:79–80. See also Augustine, "On The Psalms," Psalm 44:8, in Schaff [2004], 8:142.) John Chrysostom wrote the following regarding the symbolic message of Moses's outstretched or upraised hands:

See how the type was "given by Moses," but the "Truth came by

Jesus Christ." (Exodus 17:12) Again, when the Amalekites warred in Mount Sinai, the hands of Moses were supported, being stayed up by Aaron and Hur standing on either side of him (Exodus 17:12) but when Christ came, He of Himself stretched forth His Hands upon the Cross. Hast thou observed how the type "was given," but "the Truth came"? (John Chrysostom, "Homilies on St. John," Homily 14:4, in Schaff [2004], 14:50)

Finally, one of the Cappadocian fathers—Gregory of Nazianzus (circa AD 329–90)—noted: "Moses is to conquer him by stretching out his hands upon the mount, in order that the cross, thus typified and prefigured, may prevail" (Gregory of Nazianzus, "In Defense of His Flight to Pontus," Oration 2:88, in Schaff and Wace [2004], 7:222). Thus, for early Christians the message of Moses's upraised or outstretched hands and arms was Christocentric. They saw this narrative (in Exodus 17) as teaching the importance of faith in the atoning sacrifice of the Lord Jesus Christ. For them, faith centered in that act—and in Christ's mediating role—made it possible to successfully conquer all of our enemies, and overcome all of our trials.

48.   One scholar referred to the "Odes of Solomon" as an ancient "hymnbook," likely dating from around the first century of the common era. Its authorship, original language, and the location of its composition are all unknown. (See James H. Charlesworth, "Odes of Solomon: A New Translation and Introduction," in Charlesworth [1983, 1985], 2:725–34.)

49.   See "Odes of Solomon" 42:1–2, in Charlesworth (1983, 1985), 2:770, emphasis added.

50.   Ibid., 2:259, emphasis added.

51.   Tvedtnes, in Parry and Ricks (1999), 90.

52.   Madsen, in Lundquist and Ricks (1990), 1:460; Madsen (2008), 140.

53.   Nibley, *Mormonism* . . . (1987), 58. Nibley is paraphrasing the non-LDS scholar, Henri Laclercq.

54.   Nibley, *Mormonism* . . . (1987), 59. Here Nibley is drawing on the writings of the German theologian, Friedrich Preisigke.

55.   Justin Martyr (circa AD 100–161) was an early apologist for the Christian church and is one of the most important sources for what Christianity looked like in the second century of the common era. (See Theodore Stylianopoulos, "Justin Martyr," in Ferguson [1990], 514; Weinrich [2005], 420.)

56.   Justin Martyr, "Dialogue with Trypho," Chapter 90, in Roberts and Donaldson (1994), 1:244.

57.   One next notes that prayer with open and elevated hands is a sign of "adoration" and "extreme reverence" for God (Elworthy [1900], 160, 173–74).

58.   See 1 Enoch 65:2–3, in Charlesworth (1983, 1985), 1:45.

59.   See 3 Enoch 40:2, in Charlesworth (1983, 1985), 1:291.

60.   See, for example, Davis (2000), 121, 123; Todeschi (1995), 185; Fontana (1994), 64; Cooper (1995), 114; Bennett, in Hastings (1963), 703; Ifrah (2000), 499; Bullinger (1967), 107–108, 122–23; Smith (1998), 288; Johnston (1990), 39–40; Farbridge (1923), 144; Rest (1987), 17–18, 60–61; Cirlot (1962), 232; Julien (1996), 448.

61.   See, for example, Joseph A. Jungmann, *The Mass of the Roman Rite, Revised and Abridged Edition* (New York: Benzinger Brothers, 1959), 170–71; John H. Miller, *Fundamentals of the Liturgy* (Notre Dame, IN: Fides Publishers, 1959), 248–49. One text notes that a common approach to corporal prayer is "homophonic repetition." The person offering the prayer, sometimes referred to as the "prompter," gives the prayer, phrase by phrase, and then the congregation (or "group" directly participating in the prayer) "repeats each single line in unison." This has been said to likely be the most common mode of corporate prayer in a Christian liturgical setting. (See Matthias Klinghardt, "Prayer Formularies for Public Recitation—Their Use and Function in Ancient Religion," in *Numen*, vol. 46, no. 1 [1999], 20.) This same source notes that an additional approach to corporate prayer, known as "homophonic response," consists of "the prompter alone" reciting

> the entire prayer; the group does not repeat single lines of the formulary, but instead incorporates it by a common response in unison. Most common was the Amen response . . . Since only the homophonic recitation in unison is, literally speaking, a common prayer, the interest concentrates on the question whether a simple response can be considered a valid prayer. The unanimous answer [of scholars] is that the common response resembles a vital and substantial participation in the common prayer and, therefore, must be seen as completely equivalent to the recitation of the prayer by a prompter. (Klinghardt [1999], 20–22)

This implies that, when during the Roman Catholic Mass the congregation says things, such as "amen" after the priest speaks, they are essentially symbolically repeating the entirety of the priest's words as though they had spoken them in unison, line by line.

62.   Nibley, *Mormonism . . .* (1987), 77.

63. Jungmann (1959), 248.

64. Miller (1959), 248.

65. Klinghardt (1999), 22. Gaius Petronius Arbiter (circa AD 27–66) was a Roman attendant and novelist during the reign of Nero.

66. Athanasius (circa AD 295–373) was the bishop of Alexandria Egypt, beginning in AD 328. He was one of the chief opponents of Arius of Alexandria and his unique Christology.

67. See Athanasius, "Apologia Ad Constantium," 16, in Schaff and Wace (2004), 4:244.

68. Klinghardt (1999), 23.

69. Though the "Epistle of Barnabas" is said to have been written by one of the Apostolic Fathers—Barnabas, the missionary companion of the Apostle Paul—scholars today generally hold that it was likely written by someone else and erroneously attributed to Barnabas. The document has been dated as early as AD 70 and as late as AD 135, but the internal evidence is lacking to pinpoint the exact date or location of composition. (See Everett Ferguson, "Barnabas, Epistle of," in Ferguson [1990], 138.)

70. Barnabas, "The Epistle of Barnabas," Chapter 19, in Roberts and Donaldson (1994), 1:149. Barnabas does not specify the need for a clean conscience in a specific form of prayer (e.g., corporate prayer as opposed to personal prayer). He simply states that prayer with an "evil conscience" is a sin that will harm the "light" that should be present when God is being petitioned.

71. Tertullian, "On Prayer," Chapter 11, in Roberts and Donaldson (1994), 3:685.

72. Tertullian, "On Prayer," Chapter 12, in Roberts and Donaldson (1994), 3:685.

73. Cyril (AD 375–444) was the patriarch of the Church in Alexandria, Egypt, and an aggressive fifth-century opponent of the Christological heresy known as Nestorianism, which grew out of the fifth-century Christological controversies, and which held that there was no unity between Christ's human and divine natures. (See Manlio Simonetti, ed., *Ancient Christian Commentary on Scripture—Matthew 1–13* [Downers Grove, IL: InterVarsity Press, 2001], 301; Susan Ashbrook Harvey, "Nestorianism," in Ferguson [1990], 644–47.)

74. Cyril of Alexandria, "Fragment 50," in Simonetti (2001), 104. See also Chromatius, "Tractate on Matthew 21.3.1–3," in Simonetti (2001), 102.

75. D. Kelly Ogden and Andrew C. Skinner, *Verse by Verse: The Four Gospels* (Salt Lake City: Deseret Book, 2006), 193.

76.   Chrysostom (circa AD 344–407) was the Bishop of Constantinople, and became somewhat famous for his eloquence and ardent attacks on laxity among leaders within the Church. He has been called "the greatest preacher in the early church." His name (Chrysostom) means "golden mouth"—an apt description of his gift for words. (See Robert Wilkin, "John Chrysostom," in Ferguson [1990], 495; Simonetti [2001], 303.)

77.   John Chrysostom, "The Gospel of St. Matthew," Homily 16:12, in Philip Schaff, ed., *Nicene and Post-Nicene Fathers—First Series*, 14 vols. (Peabody, MA: Hendrickson Publishers, 2004), 10:112.

78.   Jerome, "Commentary on Matthew," 1.5.23, in Simonetti (2001), 104. Similarly, Elder Bruce R. McConkie wrote: "Not a remembrance that you are angry with your brother, for it is assumed that the true saint will have overcome his own ill feelings, but a remembrance that your brother hath aught against you!" (McConkie [1987–88], 1:223).

79.   Augustine, "Our Lord's Sermon on the Mount," Book 1, Chapter 10, Verse 27, in Schaff (2004), 6:12–13.

80.   The word *diptych* is of Greek origins, and means literally "folded together," as this bundle of names was folded prior to being placed upon the altar.

81.   See McBrien (1995), 1189, S.v. "Diptychs." Prior to Vatican II (1962–65) the Catholic Church offered a prayer at the beginning of the Mass known as the "collect." The name of this prayer stems from the fact that the priest (prior to 1965) would "collect" the prayers or prayer requests of those assembled, and then offer them up to God on behalf of the congregation as he stood before the altar. (See McBrien [1995], 328, S.v. "Collect.")

82.   Marcus Von Wellnitz, "The Catholic Liturgy and the Mormon Temple," in *BYU Studies*, vol. 21, no. 1 (Winter 1981), 32–33. See also Nibley, *Mormonism . . .* (1987), 76. The utilization of *diptychs* has been almost entirely replaced by the requiem or funeral mass.

83.   See O. S. Wintermute, "Introduction" to "Apocalypse of Zephaniah—A New Translation and Introduction," in Charlesworth (1983, 1985), 1:498.

84.   The Apocalypse of Zephaniah 11:1–2, in Charlesworth (1983, 1985), 1:515. See also The Apocalypse of Zephaniah 11:6.

85.   Nibley, *Mormonism . . .* (1987), 76.

86.   Ibid., 75.

87.   Of course, the year of Jubilee in Hebrew Bible times was held every fifty years (Leviticus 25:8–22). However, this rite of Jubilee in Roman Catholicism, though stemming from the ancient Jewish Jubilee, is held more often, as it is deemed proper to offer forgiveness as often as possible.

88.   The pope's appointed representatives or legates are also authorized

to perform this same ritual on that same day at the Basilicas of St. Paul, St. John Lateran, and St. Maria Maggiore. One Catholic commentator on the rite indicated that "the opening of the Holy Gates in four different churches signifies the calling of the faithful from the four quarters of the world" (Herbert Thurston, S.J., *The Holy Year of Jubilee*, 1980 reprint [Saint Louis: Herder, 1900], 227, 244.) The number four symbolizes geographic fullness or totality, and thus suggests that this rite of entrance into God's presence is requisite for all mankind.

89. Thurston (1900), 28.

90. See ibid., 220.

91. See ibid., 29, 115, 218.

92. See ibid., 50, 240.

93. Of course, the rite is much more detailed than I have described above, but the description given highlights the portions of the ritual that will be most curious to the reader and most important for examining the symbolism behind the rite.

94. On a related note, common to certain Jewish rites of the nineteenth and early twentieth centuries was the act of "giving three strong raps of the gavel" (Soyer [1999], 159). This same text notes: "Some Orthodox religious congregations . . . adopted customs from the world of the lodge, including . . . [the use of] gavel signals" (ibid., 173). Similarly, in the Knights of Columbus rites there is a ceremony that is reminiscent of the *Porta Santa* rite. The initiated is to "rap upon the entrance of the Council Chamber. The Inside Guard will open the wicket and [the initiated seeking entrance] will whisper into his ear the last half of the password. He will then admit [the initiated] into the Council Chamber" (Knight [1920], 90).

95. See Thurston (1900), 216, 218.

96. Ibid., 244.

97. See ibid., 30.

98. See ibid., 53, 243–44. According to Catholic explanations of this rite, those who pass through the door with repentant hearts are said to be forgiven of their sins. But the unrepentant who engage in this ritual are making a mockery of God's grace and mercy, and will receive no such forgiveness. (See ibid., 39.) Thus, "How careful then must the faithful be to leave behind them the burden of sin before entering the Holy Gate!" (ibid., 245).

99. See ibid., 53.

100. See ibid., 221–22.

101. Epiphanius (circa AD 315–403) was the Bishop of the Church in

Salamis, in Cyprus. He is best known for his attempts to refute heresy. He was a strong supporter of what might be called "Nicene Orthodoxy," and was one of the chief critics of the ideas of Origen (flourished AD 200–254). (See Weinrich [2005], 417; Frederick W. Norris, "Epiphanius of Salamis," in Ferguson [1990], 307–308.)

102. See Epiphanius, "Letter to John, Bishop of Jerusalem," cited by Jerome in "The Letters of Saint Jerome," Letter LI, in Schaff and Wace (2004), 6:89.

103. See Thurston (1900), 36.

104. The connection between these two rites has been drawn by Catholic commentators. (See ibid., 46.)

105. In the case of this ritual, the knocking bishop apparently symbolizes the Lord seeking entrance into the Church he would then bless via both a verbal blessing pronounced upon entrance (*Pax huic domun*—"Peace be to this house") and also, presumably, through the formal dedication of the building itself. (See ibid., 46–47.)

106. See ibid.

107. David E. Bokovoy, "From the Hand of Jacob: A Ritual Analysis of Genesis 27," in *Studies in the Bible and Antiquity*, vol. 1 (2009): 46. Bokovoy highlights Psalm 24:3–5 as a prime biblical example.

108. See Davis (2000), 121, 123; Todeschi (1995), 185; Fontana (1994), 64; Cooper (1995), 114; Bennett, in Hastings (1963), 703; Ifrah (2000), 499; Bullinger (1967), 107–108, 122–23; Smith (1998), 288; Johnston (1990), 39–40, 55; Farbridge (1923), 144; Rest (1987), 17–18, 60–61; Cirlot (1971), 232; Julien (1996), 448.

109. See Thurston (1900), 244.

110. See ibid. This same source has also suggested that the three knocks, and other symbolic gestures in three (at the door), may symbolize "contrition, confession, and satisfaction" (ibid., 245).

111. Ezra Taft Benson, *Teachings of Ezra Taft Benson* (Salt Lake City: Bookcraft, 1998), 425; W. W. Phelps, "Pray Without Ceasing," Tuesday, June 15, 1841, in *Times and Seasons*, 6 vols. (Commerce and Nauvoo, IL, Nov 1839 through Feb 1846: photo reprint, Independence, MO: Independence Press, 1986), 2:451; Joseph F. Smith, *Gospel Doctrine* (Salt Lake City: Bookcraft, 1998), 221; Spencer W. Kimball, *The Teachings of Spencer W. Kimball* (Salt Lake City: Bookcraft, 1998), 142. See also McConkie (1980–81), 1:368.

112. See Thurston (1900), 29, 111, 218, 223.

113. This portion specifically takes place in the "consecration of a church" ritual.

114. Thurston (1900), 48.
115. Barker (2008), 105. Barker also wrote: "The veil was the boundary between the visible and the invisible creations" (ibid., 111). See also Charles (1997), 93.
116. Barker (2008), 122–23.
117. Ibid., 108–109.
118. See Brigham Young, Discourse delivered April 6, 1853, in Van Wagoner (2009), 2:646. See also Charles (1997), 93.
119. Van Gennep (1960), 19.
120. See Barker (2008), 127.
121. Barker (2008), 124.
122. Parry and Parry (2009), 33. Parry and Parry also wrote: "The temple veil that separated the holy place from the holy of holies symbolizes Jesus Christ's flesh (Heb. 9:3; 10:19–20). In other words, the temple's holiest place (representing the celestial kingdom)" (ibid., 128).
123. Barker (2008), 104. Barker added: "Texts which describe [the high priest's] vestments show that these were made in exactly the same way as the temple curtain" or veil (ibid., 111).
124. Ostler (1982), 35.
125. Nibley, *Mormonism . . .* (1987), 75.
126. Nibley (2005), 447.
127. Barker (2008), 124.
128. Portions of this text date from the first century of the common era. Other parts from the third century. And portions likely date as late as the fifth or sixth century CE. The fact that we learn in the text that "God's right hand cannot operate till the Temple is restored" (3 Enoch 48, footnote 48c, in Charlesworth [1983, 1985], 1:300) establishes that this document was composed after AD 70—as does the following comment: "The right [or covenant] hand of the Omnipresent One . . . has been banished [or become inaccessible] . . . because of the destruction of the Temple" (3 Enoch 48:1, in Charlesworth [1983, 1985], 1:300). One commentator noted: "3 Enoch has arisen through the combination of many separate traditions; it tends to break down into smaller 'self-contained' units which probably existed prior to their incorporation into the present work" (Alexander, "Introduction" in Charlesworth [1983, 1985], 1: 223. See also 1: 226).
129. Alexander, "Introduction" in Charlesworth (1983, 1985), 1:240. See also W. F. Stinespring, "Introduction" to "Testament of Isaac—A New Translation and Introduction," in Charlesworth (1983, 1985), 1:903.
130. The text actually refers to Metatron, rather than Michael, in this verse. However, one text notes that "Metatron and Michael were one and

the same angel: Michael was the angel's common name, Metatron one of his esoteric, magical names" (Alexander, "Introduction" in Charlesworth [1983, 1985], 1:244).
131. Alexander, "Introduction" in Charlesworth (1983, 1985), 1:223.
132. Budge (1959), 170–71. Nibley similarly noted:

> The final and concluding rite of the ancient [Egyptian] initiation was the subject of a study by G. van der Leeuw, who discovered that the non-Christian and early Christian practices were virtually identical. In every case, the final rites . . . consist of . . . an exchange of formulas that are "at the same time" a statement of "creeds, liturgical formulas, and passwords," all befitting an ultimate *rite de passage*. It was an exchange of "symbols," a "Question and Response . . . probably spoken in an undertone both by the priest and the initiand, perhaps . . . at the door of the Holiest." . . . The symbols are exchanged in the concluding rite of the mysteries as a means of identification— . . . the means by which the initiate identified himself "as someone whose life had been united with that of the god." (Nibley [2005], 456–57)

Nibley also wrote: "An important feature of Egyptian architecture of [the] temple . . . is a door, sometimes shown as a curtain . . . , through which a spirit can pass, a means of communication between two worlds; and the literature is full of ceremonial and mythical doors and gates and instructions on how to pass them" (Nibley [2008], 309).
133. The "Ascension of Isaiah" has been referred to as a "Christian expansion of a Jewish pseudepigraphical work." It dates from somewhere between AD 150 and AD 200. While fragments of the document exist in Greek, old Slavonic, and Coptic, the complete text has only survived in Ethiopic. (See Ferguson, "Ascension of Isaiah," in Ferguson [1990], 103–104; J. Flemming and H. Duensing, "The Ascension of Isaiah," in Hennecke and Schneemelcher [1965], 643.)
134. Alexander, "Introduction" in Charlesworth (1983, 1985), 1:248. Related to the temple theme of the book of Isaiah, Truman G. Madsen penned this:

> The highest spiritual aspiration is that there will one day be full harmony of nature in the One who names, the name, and the named. This is the vision of the Temple in Isaiah 56 [which reads]: For thus says the Lord: As for the eunuchs who keep my Sabbaths and choose to do what I will—holding fast to my covenant—to them I will give a handclasp and a name within the walls of my house [the Temple] . . . I will endow them with an everlasting name that shall

not be cut off. (Madsen, in Lundquist and Ricks [1990], 1:474–75; Madsen [2008], 155)

135. Alexander, "Introduction" in Charlesworth (1983, 1985), 1:248.
136. Porter and Ricks, in Lundquist and Ricks (1990), 1:511.
137. Charles (1997), 93.
138. See John Gee, "The Keeper of the Gate," in Parry and Ricks (1999), 237.
139. Nibley (2008), 331.
140. Barker (2008), 126. Barker also wrote: "The veil represented the division between the material and spiritual worlds, between the visible and the invisible, and in this respect it *concealed* the divine. But it also *revealed* the divine in that the veil was the robe of the heavenly high priest when he passed into the visible world" (ibid., 118).
141. Quite literally, the Hebrew and Greek words for "revealing" mean to "uncover," meaning to uncover God—His glory, kingdom, and truth.
142. See Barker (2008), 27.
143. 3 Enoch 45:1, n. 45a, in Charlesworth (1983, 1985), 1:296.
144. See Van Gennep (1960), 29–30.
145. Farbridge (1923), 275. See also J. F. McConkie (1985), 262; Todeschi (1995), 128.
146. Cooper (1995), 137. Harold Bayley wrote that, when clasped, "the hand was obviously an expression of concord" (Bayley [1990–93], 2:331).
147. Cirlot (1962), 137.
148. Regarding these "signs, passwords and grips" in certain Roman Catholic rituals, see Knight (1920), x, 33, 89–91.
149. The pseudepigrapha (literally, "falsely attributed") are a corpus of religious documents with Old Testament themes, written by both Jews and Christians (between 300 BCE and 400 CE). They are referred to as pseudepigraphical primarily because their authorship is assumed to be falsely attributed to some significant figure from the Hebrew Bible, when each text is believed to have been written at a later date by someone other than the person it has been attributed to. One scholar of pseudepigraphical texts described the pseudepigrapha as "ancient writings that are essential reading for an understanding of early Judaism (ca. 250 BCE to 200 CE) and of Christian origins" (James H. Charlesworth, "Pseudepigrapha, OT," in Freedman [1992], 5:537).
150. 1 Enoch 71:3–4, in Charlesworth (1983, 1985), 1:49.
151. 3 Enoch 1:5–6, in Charlesworth (1983, 1985), 1:256.
152. Parry and Parry (2009), 22.

153. Compton, in Lundquist and Ricks (1990), 1:614.

154. See ibid., 1:622–23. See also 1:614, 617.

155. Nibley (2005), 427.

156. See ibid., 429.

157. "The embrace is merely an outward token of the inward meshing of souls" (Compton, in Lundquist and Ricks [1990], 1:625).

158. "The physical symbol of the power of love in the Atonement is the embrace. It is the gesture of reconciliation or at-one-ment between God and man" (Green [2004], 197).

159. Compton, in Lundquist and Ricks (1990), 1:623.

160. Ibid. See also 1:631.

161. It is "the renewed outward token reflecting the renewed inward token of knowledge and love" (Compton, in Lundquist and Ricks [1990], 1:631).

162. See Nibley (2005), 455–56.

163. M. Catherine Thomas, "The Brother of Jared at the Veil," in Parry (1994), 388.

164. See Compton, in Lundquist and Ricks (1990), 1:641, n. 87.

165. Tvedtnes, in Parry and Ricks (1999), 89.

166. Elder Dean L. Larsen wrote: "In temples the curtains to eternity are parted . . ." (Larsen [2007], 3).

167. Lundquist, in Lundquist and Ricks (1990), 1:429.

168. Barker (2008), 74.

169. In other words, they possess the nature, attributes, and divine powers associated with godhood.

Eight

Marriage Rituals

Marriage is a rite, ritual, or sacrament found in nearly every one of the world's religions—ancient and modern.[1] How marriages are solemnized or performed varies from sect to sect, but the central concept of binding of man and woman through a ritual or ceremonial process is commonplace in religious traditions throughout history.

As is well known, during the liturgy of the synagogue in antiquity, men and women were traditionally seated separately,[2] as was the case in the liturgical settings of the early Christians.[3] While this practice may seem unrelated to the rite or ordinance of marriage, there is a symbolic connection. The requirement that men and women be kept separate during the enactment of rituals reminds us of the fact that only in the eternal state of exaltation are men and women, husbands and wives, united forever (D&C 132:7, 15–21). Thus, sitting on separate sides of the room during some sacred ceremony often carries (in the minds of Latter-day Saints) the suggestion that if one does not enter into an eternal union through the rite of authorized marriage, the man and woman will remain single and separate throughout all eternity. It is noteworthy that almost all of the "higher covenants" we make with God are entered into while segregated from those of the opposite sex. However, marriage is an exception. We unit-edly approach God, symbolic of that which God wishes for us; namely, an eternal union. Thus, the separation of men and women that exists in most liturgical settings—particularly those of antiq-uity—is removed in the rite of holy matrimony.

Curiously, in Roman Catholicism the marriage of the bride and groom has traditionally been performed while the couple kneels at an altar, holding hands. The ordained priest preforms the ordinance whilst two witnesses view the holy rite, thereby fulfill-ing the scriptural "law of witnesses" (Deuteronomy 19:15; 2 Cor-inthians 13:1; D&C 6:28).[4] Numerous aspects of this ceremony are undoubtedly symbolic.

First of all, the altar is central to the rite. It is a point of focus in the room in which the marriage is performed; and it is symboli-cally significant.[5] Among other things, altars are symbols of sac-rifice.[6] Indeed, one non-LDS commentator noted that altars are typically raised—sometimes by being placed in an upper room of a temple or on a raised platform of a church. Thus, we must ascend to them, symbolic of Christ's sacrifice and suffering on the cross of Golgotha's hill.[7] Consequently, when kneeling at an altar, in anticipation of one's marriage, one is committing to sacri-fice—particularly to sacrifice his or her will in deference to God's will. The altar at the center of the marriage forewarns the couple of the difficulties that will be present in any marriage. But it also instructs the husband and wife as to how to overcome those—namely, by personal sacrifice, by aligning one's will with God's.[8]

In addition to their connection to sacrifice, altars are also sym-bols of Christ's presence.[9] This becomes significant in the mar-riage ceremony for a couple of reasons. As the husband and wife, kneeling at an altar, make covenants regarding each other (and, by default, their new union), they do so in the presence of Christ, who, in a very real sense, acts as a witness of the covenant before the Father. Additionally, in ideas drawn from certain schools of Jewish thinking, there is a curious numeric symbolism that is present in the marriage of a man and woman. In most ancient societies, letters and numbers were used interchangeably.[10] Each letter of an alphabet had a numerical value. Technically speaking, when the numerical value is substituted for letters in a word the practice is known as gematria.[11] By making this substitution, a word's numerical value could be determined and compared for potential relationships with other words possessing the same numerical value.[12] Anciently some Jews placed a great deal of credence in gematria and its symbolic messages. As an example, the name "Adam" has a numerical total of 45. The name Eve totals 19 in gematria. The numerical difference between the two is 26, which happens to be the number for Yahweh, implying that it is God, and God only, that can make man and woman one.[13] In Judaism the wedding ceremony is performed under a canopy (known as a *chupah*). This symbolizes the new home the bride and groom are about to make with each other,[14] and, for some Jews, it symbolizes the heavens and the idea that God is to watch over and bless the union.[15] Marriage at an altar suggests the need of the man and woman to place Christ at the center of their marriage. In so doing they ensure the success of the union. Removing Him ensures its dismal failure. Thus, one text on Jewish mysticism states: "When a man unites with his wife in holiness, the divine presence is between them."[16] Thus, for a man and woman to kneel at an altar, clasping hands while the rite is being performed—as do Roman Catholic men and women—can suggest their commitment to each other and to God that they will place Christ at the center of their marriage and His attributes at the core of their being.

The handclasp of a husband and wife has already been mentioned more than once in this chapter. Giving your hand to someone shows "that a relationship was established between two persons (2 Kings 10:15; Jeremiah 50:15; Ezekiel 17:18)."[17] Indeed, to clasp another's hand was a sign of a "pledge" or an expression of "solidarity."[18] Roman Catholics are not the only ones who are married while ritually holding each other's hand. Certain Hindus also marry while clasping each other's hands. Indeed, Hindus refer to this portion of the marriage rite as the *pani grahana*, or the "clasping of hands."[19] The words spoken during the hand clasp (in Hinduism) make it clear that the action of taking the hand of one's future spouse symbolizes both the oneness of the bride and groom and also their complementary differences.[20] The rite teaches the man and woman to seek to be united in their goals, hopes, and desires, but to also rejoice in the blessings that exist in the innate differences between a man and a woman. Thus, they should work together to accomplish their righteous desires, but never try to change who the other person is. Handclasps are not the only symbolic gestures in marriage. One commentator noted: "Among the rites of incorporation it is possible to isolate those which have an individual meaning and which unite the two young people to each other: . . . touching each other reciprocally in some way [such as through a handclasp]; . . . sitting on the same seat; . . . entering the new house; and so forth. These are essentially rites of union."[21] Truly there are many symbolic gestures in marriage rites that can be instructive and also symbolic; however, the handclasp is one of the most important, ancient, and sacred of symbols associated with this exalting ordinance. "In the marriage handclasp" we have expressed the symbol of "complete equality" between the partners.[22] "The marriage handclasp . . . represents uniting, love, equality, sexuality, and treaty between husband and wife as marriage begins."[23] As we noted earlier in this text, one scholar pointed out that "the giving of a hand may function as an oath-sign solemnly depicting the covenant commitment."[24] Such a practice was common in antiquity. This same source adds that "'the hand stands for the person'; as such, giving one's hand to another symbolizes the giving of oneself."[25] On a related note, in the Book of Ezekiel we read of the making of an oath or covenant by the giving of one's hand. Of this passage, one commentator wrote: "In [Ezekiel 17] ver. 18 . . . he gave his hand, *i.e.* as a pledge of fidelity. . . . The oath had been sworn by [or in the name of] Jehovah, and the covenant of fidelity . . . had thereby been made *implicite* with Jehovah Himself; so that the breaking of the oath and covenant became a breach of faith towards Jehovah."[26] Thus, in marriage, though I make covenants about my spouse when we are married, to break those covenants is to break an oath to God as much as it is to break a promise to a partner. Indeed, because of the nature of sacred covenants (i.e., God to man and man to God—but not man to man), it is primarily God who is the focus of the covenant, and, consequently it is a breach of faith toward God that is most important. Simply put, the clasping of hands during a marriage rite is designed to remind the participants of their promises and covenants directly to God. One hand-shaped votive, located in a museum in Leyden, depicts a man and wife holding each other's hands over an altar.[27] Of the symbolic hand, one text conjectures: "It must surely be intended as the special household appeal for protection and help, by a newly-wedded pair, to the gods . . . ."[28] But the act of giving one's hand also symbolizes how the man and wife have given themselves to their new spouse, and how each is covenanting to acknowledge that his or her new spouse's differences will be readily and happily accepted as a means by which the couple become complete. The act symbolizes the need not only for unity but for equality in the relationship. This does not mean that the roles of the man and woman will be the same, but it does highlight the commitment to hold each other as equally important in the new marriage, the new family, and in all future decision making.

Related to the ritual "handclasp" in marriage is another act found in both Christianity and Hinduism. One text noted that "binding one [partner] to the other with a single cord" or "tying parts of each other's clothing together" is intended as "rites of union."[29] Indeed, as noted previously (in the chapter on ritual clothing), President John Taylor is said to have taught that making a bow knot represents "the marriage covenant between man and wife."[30] Similarly, one British typologist indicated that bows on clothing were a symbol of the combination of the "masculine and feminine."[31] In some Eastern cultures, the tying of a bow knot was a marriage custom that symbolized the binding of the two people, hence the old cliché, "tying the knot."[32] In certain periods and regions the wearing of a sash tied in a bow around one's waist symbolized chastity or virginity.[33] The wearing of such an item can be "symbolic of continence, self-restraint, chastity, and patient suffering."[34] Each of these aspects is related, in rather obvious ways, to the marriage covenant, and the fidelity that should exist between a husband and wife. In certain marriage rites of the Eastern Orthodox and the Hindus the bride and groom are tied together or bound to each other. For example in the Greek Orthodox marriage rite, the priest places upon the heads of the bride and groom "wedding crowns" (known as *stefana, stepahana,* or *stephania,* from the Greek *stephanos,* meaning a wreath crown). These two crowns are attached together by a singular ribbon. The placement of these upon the heads of the soon-to-be husband and wife may highlight their role as kings and queens or priests and priestesses before God, but the ribbon that connects the two crowns focuses our attention on the fact that, in their marriage, the husband and wife must become one. The fact that the ribbon binding the couple is on their heads suggests that the place to begin their journey into "oneness" is with their thoughts, foci, goals, and desires. The fact that the priest performing the rite three times swaps the two crowns between the heads of the husband and wife symbolizes the need for the husband and wife to have God at the center of their marriage—the number three being a standard symbol for the Godhead or Trinity. Somewhat related to this Orthodox rite is a Hindu practice of "binding" the hands of the bride and groom to each other during the marriage ritual.[35] The hands are clasped and then tied in that grip—the "clasped hands" being a standard symbol for marriage and the unity that should exist between a bride and groom.[36] The binding of the hands highlights the permanence of this relationship; they are bound or sealed to each other.

On a separate note, in one mid–third century Gnostic-Christian text—which has been called "a preparatory manual for a secret initiation ritual"[37]—we read about the importance of the ordinance of marriage.[38]

> Great is the mystery of marriage! For without it the world would not exist. . . . And none shall be able to escape [the devil and his angels] . . . if he does not receive a male power or a female power, the bridegroom and the bride. One receives them from

the mirrored bridal chamber. . . . The woman is united to her husband in the bridal chamber. Indeed those who have united in the bridal chamber will no longer be separated. . . . If anyone becomes a son of the bridal chamber, he will receive the light. If anyone does not receive it while he is here, he will not be able to receive it in the other place.[39]

While Latter-day Saints are fond of pointing out that the "reflecting mirrors that face each other in different rooms of the temple suggest to us eternity,"[40] this aforementioned ancient text seeks to make another point about the "bridal chamber." Philip refers to the place the man and woman are "inseparably" united as "the mirrored bridal chamber." However, his description is not about physical mirrors. Rather, our ancient "preparatory manual" seeks to emphasize that the chamber in which the man and woman are united mirrors the heavenly chamber, the abode of God. It mirrors or symbolizes exaltation or the eternal abode of all those who become deified and dwell with God for eternity. Consequently, while mirrors reflecting endlessly our image as husband and wife can symbolize the eternal nature of the relationship, so also the room in which the marriage is performed is a symbol of God's abode.[41] This is hardly a coincidence, particularly since God desires that marriages be for eternity (D&C 132:7, 15–20), but also because it is through the act of uniting (as Christ's bride or Church) with the Bridegroom (Jesus) that you and I as Christians will eventually find ourselves again in His presence. Thus, the bridal chamber is a symbol of our need to covenantially connect ourselves with Christ. In the context of the Gospel of Philip, the mirroring represents the fact that the bridal chamber mirrors God's abode, and the union between man and God. Symbolically speaking, the marriage performed in the "bridal chamber" should reflect the heavenly in approach and concern and care. One text notes: "Ritual may serve to unite men and gods. The Hebrew root that gives the word for glue or adhesives is also the root of the word signifying attachment to the divine (*dvekut*)."[42] Consequently, marriage becomes the ordinance or experience that tests my commitment to and relationship with God by testing my commitment to and relationship with my spouse.

We must now shift our focus one last time in our attempt to examine the symbols associated with the ordinance of marriage. One text suggests: "The figure of Abraham may be said to be the first [scriptural] answer to the figure of Adam."[43] In other words, while we may traditionally think in terms of the "first Adam" being a typological symbol fulfilled in the "last Adam" (i.e., Jesus the Christ—1 Corinthians 15:44), the Adam/Abraham parallel may be more important for liturgical teaching. For example, in the story of the Fall, Adam and Eve are commanded by God to multiply and replenish the earth, and to heed God's commands that they might enjoy the blessings God has in store for them. However, as the story goes, they reject God's will, and follow, instead, the enticements of Satan. Thus, they lose the promised land and inherit the "lone and dreary world."[44] In the story of Abraham, on the other hand, the patriarch is commanded to heed God's commands that he might enjoy the blessings God has in store for him, and thus, in a spirit of obedience to God, Abraham flees the corrupt world, and seeks a promised land where he can enter into covenants with God and worship Him unmolested by the servants of Satan. The Apostle Paul informs us: "Even as Abraham believed God, and it was accounted to him for righteousness. Know ye therefore that they which are of faith, the same are the children of Abraham" (Galatians 3:6–7). Thus, we each begin our mortal and liturgical journey as the "family of Adam" (Mormon 3:20), but through covenants and obedience, we can become the "children of Abraham." In marriage, Abraham's posterity has pronounced upon them all of the blessings of Abraham, Isaac, and Jacob (see Deuteronomy 1:8), with the command to be "fruitful" and to "multiply" and replenish the earth (Genesis 28:3). This very command takes Abraham back to Eden. It ties him into the Edenic blessings pronounced upon the first couple (Adam and Eve), but fulfilled in the latter couple (Abraham and Sarah). Consequently, liturgically and symbolically speaking, from our creation, throughout our lives, and until we greet the Lord at the heavenly veil, we are to recognize ourselves as symbolized by

Adam and Eve—we are fallen men and women. However, once we return to God we are as Abraham and Sarah—sealed to our spouse and presiding over our posterity for time and all eternity. Thus the story of the Fall represents our entrance into a world filled with sin and weakness. However, our marriage makes us Abrahams and Sarahs, and we are returned to Eden or paradise. We have pronounced upon us all of the blessings of the patriarchs, each of which represent exaltation.

Related to the paradise theme present in marriage rites is this: The two choices Adam and Eve were given in Eden may be the very same two choices all couples are given when they kneel at an altar and make the covenants associated with eternal marriage. Adam and Eve were allowed to stay in Eden and serve their own needs, wants, and desires, or leave Eden and experience a tremendous sacrifice on behalf of others—namely their posterity—which would be greatly blessed by Adam and Eve's seeming loss of Eden. When a couple is married and have pronounced upon them all of the blessings of Abraham, Isaac, and Jacob, their first option—if it can even be called such—is to be self-serving and put off their family until they've done all that they want to do and have obtained all that they want to obtain. The second option is to sacrifice what they want and what the world tells them that they should and must have, in order that others can have a chance at mortality and exaltation. Adam and Eve's choice in Eden was really to have a family or not have a family. Hence, Adam says, "I will partake that man may be!"

The blessings pronounced upon married couples—and the means by which they are pronounced—act as more than just blessings. They are instructions, advice, and counsel. The rites of marriage in various religious traditions (ancient and modern) have much to teach us about promises, covenants, commitment, binding, unity, giving, rejoicing, and God.

Notes
1.   A notable exception would be the "Shakers" or "The United Society of Believers in Christ's Second Coming," who have held to a belief in "the

sinfulness of sexual intercourse" (E. Brooks Holifield, *Theology in America* [New Haven, CT: Yale University Press, 2003], 328, 330. See also Sidney E. Ahlstrom, *A Religious History of the American People* [New Haven, CT: Yale University Press, 1972], 492; McManners [1990], 390).

2.   See I. Sonne, "Synagogue," in *The Interpreter's Dictionary of the Bible*, 4 vols. (New York: Abingdon Press, 1962), 4:486–87; Alfred Edersheim, *The Temple: Its Ministry and Services* (Grand Rapids: Eerdmans, 1963), 48. In Orthodox and Ultra-Orthodox congregations today men and women are seated separately during the Sabbath services.

3.   See William D. Maxwell, *An Outline of Christian Worship: Its Development and Forms* (London: Oxford University Press, 1936), 5; "Constitution of the Holy Apostles," Book 2, Section 7, in Roberts and Donaldson (1994), 7:421; Joseph Rykwert, *Church Building* (New York: Hawthorn Books, 1966), 29.

4.   See Michael G. Lawler, "Marriage," in McBrien (1995), 823.

5.   See Wilcox (1995), 26.

6.   Cooper (1995), 11; Conner (1992), 126.

7.   See Cooper (1995), 11. See also Vanderwilt, in McBrien (1995), 36–37.

8.   The principle symbolized is reminiscent of Elder Neal A. Maxwell's famous comment:

> The submission of one's will is really the only uniquely personal thing we have to place on God's altar. It is a hard doctrine, but it is true. The many other things we give to God, however nice that may be of us, are actually things He has already given us, and He has loaned them to us. But when we begin to submit ourselves by letting our wills be swallowed up in God's will, then we are really giving something to Him. And that hard doctrine lies at the center of discipleship. There is a part of us that is ultimately sovereign, the mind and heart, where we really do decide which way to go and what to do. And when we submit to His will, then we've really given Him the one final thing He asks of us. And the other things are not very, very important. It is the only possession we have that we can give, and there is no lessening of our agency as a result. Instead, what we see is a flowering of our talents and more and more surges of joy. Submission to *Him* is the only form of submission that is completely safe. (Neal A. Maxwell, "Insights From my Life," in *Ensign*, August 2000, 9, emphasis added)

9.   See Henry (1925), 45; Cooper (1995), 11; Ryken, Wilhoit, and Longman (1998), 21.

10. Davis (2000), 126, 140; Draper (1991), 149.

11. The term "gematria" means literally "to reckon by numbers" (Bennett, in Hastings [1963], 703).

12. "Gematria, a Hebraized form of the Greek *geometria*, . . . consisted in indicating a word by means of the number which would be obtained by adding together the numerical values of the consonants of the word" (Bennett, in Hastings [1963], 703).

13. See Joran Friberg, "Numbers and Counting" in Freedman (1992), 4:1145; Ifrah (2000), 254.

14. Kertzer and Hoffman (1993), 252.

15. Parrinder (1983), 403–404. As in Judaism, the Jain wedding ceremony is performed under a canopy (which Jains call a *mandap*). The canopy should only be erected at a happy or joyous time. Otherwise bad luck may come to the bride and groom. (See Robert Pollock, *The Everything World's Religions Book* [Avon, MA: Adams Media Corporation, 2002], 172.)

16. Daniel C. Matt, *The Essential Kabbalah—The Heart of Jewish Mysticism* (San Francisco: Harper San Francisco, 1995), 155.

17. Farbridge (1923), 275. See also J. F. McConkie (1985), 262; Todeschi (1995), 128.

18. Cooper (1995), 137; Bayley (1990–93), 2:331. It should be noted that all covenants are stated in positive terms, meaning, though divorce sometimes happens—and perhaps sometimes even needs to happen—the symbolism behind the covenant of marriage is positive, in that it represents the ideal. Thus one who has suffered a divorce should not take the symbolism present in this rite as offensive. Any who keep their covenants with God should not fear that, because the symbolism is about marriage, their divorce precludes their ability to be exalted, or to be one with the Bridegroom, even Christ.

19. Oxtoby and Segal (2007), 306.

20. The oneness is encapsulated in words, such as these: "Let there be no difference in our hopes and efforts . . . And so we join ourselves (our lives). Let us be of one mind; let us act together and enjoy through all our sense, without any difference." The complementary differences are highlighted by the following words also spoken during the wedding ritual: "I am the sky, you are the earth. I am the seed; you shall bear my seed. I am thought; you are speech. I am the song, you are the lyric" (Oxtoby and Segal [2007], 308).

21. Van Gennep (1960), 132.

22. Compton, in Lundquist and Ricks (1990), 1:617.

23. Ibid., 1:618.

24. Hugenberger (1994), 211.
25. Ibid., 212.
26. Keil (1950), 1:242–43.
27. See Elworthy (1900), 246, 259, figure 149. A "votive" is a religious item, such as a burning candle, that is placed before a picture or statue of Christ as a way of prolonging a prayer.
28. Elworthy (1900), 260.
29. See Van Gennep (1960), 132.
30. See, the "Record Book" of S. B. Roundy, Church Archives, Salt Lake City, Utah.
31. Cooper (1995), 24. Like bow knots, Cooper indicates that knots in general are symbols of "continuity, connection, a covenant [or] a link" (ibid., 92; see also Cirlot (1962), 191; Todeschi (1995), 155; Fontana (1994), 75; Hall (1979), 184).
32. Tresidder (2000), 36, 152; Todeschi (1995), 155.
33. See Edwards, in Freedman (1992), 2:237; Tresidder (2000), 134; Henry (1925), 69–70.
34. Rest (1987), 53. See also Henry (1925), 69–70.
35. See Ellwood (1992), 97.
36. See Rest (1987), 69, 76.
37. See William J. Hamblin, "Aspects of an Early Christian Initiation Ritual," in Lundquist and Ricks (1990), 1:212.
38. See Wesley W. Isenberg, "Introduction" to the "Gospel of Philip," in Robinson (1988), 141.
39. "The Gospel of Philip," 64:31–33, 65:7–11, 70:17–20, 86:4–7, in Robinson (1988), 148–49, 151, 160.
40. See Wilcox (1995), 24.
41. Dr. Gaye Strathearn, whose doctoral dissertation focused on the Valentinian bridal chamber, has recently written a fine article regarding the similarities and dissimilarities between LDS and Valentinian Gnosticism's view of marriage and the bridal chamber. (See Gaye Strathearn, "The Valentinian Bridal Chamber in the Gospel of Philip," in *Studies in the Bible and Antiquity*, vol. 1 [2009], 81–103.) Among other things, Strathearn writes: "It is important to read the *Gospel of Philip*'s references to the bridal chamber within their Valentinian context. . . . The Valentinians seem to have functioned as a school within the Christian church" (ibid., 85, 87). They held that "a sacred marriage was performed" within the bridal chamber "which was believed to be eternally binding" (Gospel of Philip 70:19ff) "and which had to be performed in mortality" (Gospel of Philip 86:1ff; see also Strathearn (2009), 88). According to

Strathearn, "heaven" for the Valentinians consisted "of a number of paired, male-female divine beings that emanated from the high God . . . . The Valentinian bridal chamber ritual is, therefore, . . . to prepare individuals to return to the Pleroma [or heaven] and become a part of that state. . . . Not everyone participated in the bridal chamber, but rather . . . it was reserved for a select few" (Strathearn [2009], 91–92). "The bridal chamber is described" in the Gospel of Philip "as being superior to both baptism and redemption" (Gospel of Philip 69:14–29; Strathearn [2009], 94). When the Gospel of Philip states that through the bridal chamber one "receives light" (Gospel of Philip 86:4–5) it means, according to Strathearn, that the ritual performed therein has a transforming effect on the participant so that "over a period of time" one receives " the light needed to enter the eternal realm" (Strathearn (2009), 97). Dr. Strathearn points out that the phrase "mirrored bridal chamber" means a place that mirrors another place. In the case of the bridal chamber, like the temple of antiquity, it mirrored the heavenly temple (See Exodus 25:9, 40; Hebrews 8:1–5, 9:23; see also Strathearn (2009), 103.) She also argues that the "uniting" that takes place there was, for Valentinian Gnostics, first and foremost about the uniting of one's "divine self" and one's human self. (See ibid.) In other words, though Strathearn acknowledges the divine beings of this Gnostic sect living in pairs in the heavenly realms, this rite helps us to overcome the divide that exists in each of us between our heavenly desires and our fallen earthly desires. In so overcoming, we become prepared to enter the eternal abode—the celestial kingdom in LDS vernacular. In her conclusion she writes:

> The Valentinian bridal chamber shares a number of interest-
> ing parallels with Latter-day Saint teachings about eternal marriage.
> The bridal chamber seems to be the culminating ritual in a series of
> rituals required for individuals to return to the Pleroma [or heavenly
> realms]. This ritual . . . must be performed on earth. It is associated
> with the holy of holies in the temple . . . Although certain passages
> in the *Gospel of Philip* use the language of a man and a woman being
> united in the bridal chamber, . . . the reunification that takes place
> [is the uniting] of an individual with her or her angel [or divine side].
> (Strathearn [2009], 103)

42. Abraham Kaplan, "The Meanings of Ritual: Comparisons," in Truman G. Madsen, ed., *Reflections on Mormonism: Judaeo-Christian Parallels* (Provo, UT: Brigham Young University Religious Studies Center, 1978), 44.

43. Ricoeur (1967), 262.

44. Rudger Clawson, Conference Report, April 1937, 75; James E. Talmage, *The House of the Lord* (Salt Lake City: Deseret Book, 1971), 83; McConkie (1978), 221.

Epilogue

From a Christian perspective, all rites, rituals, and ordinances of the Gospel are Christocentric. Their primary purpose is to draw participants unto Christ, and to place them in a covenant relationship with Him. Beyond their salvific purpose, Christian rituals are also designed to direct the patrons' attention toward Christ through the symbolism they employ. As one text pointed out: "All rituals practiced in early Christianity had a symbolic aspect reminiscent of some act during Jesus Christ's life."[1]

The attentive reader will have already noticed the consistently Christocentric nature of the Christian rites highlighted in this work. However, what follows is a summary of a few of the key examples of Christ's image, as found in the ordinances and rites we have discussed. These symbols not only teach us of Christ, but they also demonstrate what type of being we need to become in order to secure our covenant relationship with Him. We must not simply be passive learners.

In our first chapter, we learned of porters who well symbolize God's presence in the world through His servants—Jesus being the ultimate servant of the Father. Just as the porters were placed to protect the sacred from the profane, Christ (through His earthly representatives) protects that which is sacred to the Father. In this same chapter we also learned that presidencies—particularly the First Presidency of the Church—mirror the Godhead; and that obedience to the Lord's prophet is really obedience to the Lord.

In our second chapter we were reminded that the universally Christian ordinance of baptism points our minds to Christ's death, burial, and resurrection. Indeed, even the oxen—on whose backs rest certain holy fonts (ancient and modern)—symbolize Jesus and His mission to lift, support, and carry those who enter into and keep covenants with Him. In this same chapter, we discovered that to many of the early Christians being washed, anointed, and enthroned was a symbol of Christ's own life, a life that was clean (washed), Spirit-filled (anointed), and had a divine commission (enthroned). We learned that Jesus is the priest and king that the early Christians saw their washing and anointing as representative of. We also learned that this same rite of washing and anointing was a call for those who participated to have the same clean (washed) and inspired (anointed) thoughts and actions that their Savior has. We were taught in this chapter that the receipt of a new name was a call to a new life—a new identity. It was a call to be born again, a call to be as Christ is.

In the third chapter of this work we discussed the idea that the laying on of hands represented the placement of Christ's hands upon the head of the ordained. Indeed, Christ was represented by the one who lays on hands, and the authority conferred is His authority. Those so ordained become His representatives, His messengers. They are authorized, within their individual stewardships, to speak for and in behalf of Him, as so moved upon by the Holy Spirit. We also observed that women, when participating in certain rites, represent the Lord—and specifically aspects of His nature and character that we most rely upon as fallen mortals (e.g., His love, compassion, grace, mercy, servitude, and so forth). The call to represent Christ and the commission to nurture as He nurtured are charges that every Saint—male and female alike— has received from the Father.

In the fourth chapter we discussed two scriptural stories often found in liturgical settings; namely the Creation and the Fall.

We learned that the Creation was an event that typified Christ's efforts to make you and I "new creations" (2 Corinthians 5:17). It well represents our lives of chaos and how, from that chaos, Christ can bring order, life, beauty, and goodness. On the other hand, in the Fall we discovered that—setting aside the actual historical event—the story teaches us about our own propensity to be deceived by the adversary or to disobey God, and in so doing, to bring chaos and spiritual death into our own lives. Yet, the story of the Fall also teaches us that Christ willingly left His paradisiacal place to redeem us—His bride—from our lost and fallen state. Thus, this fourth chapter showed us the cycle that each of us go through: the goodness of Christ's creation, the disappointment of our individual falls, and the glory of our redemption through He who gave all.

In chapter five we discussed clothing worn in rituals. We learned that the removing of secular clothing symbolized our rejection of the world and our desire to approach and become like Christ. Indeed, we were informed that the donning of ritual clothing often symbolizes the receipt of a priestly call to serve others in Christ's image. The procurement of aprons or ephods, we discovered, in many cases represent a call to work; specifically to do the work of the Lord. Additionally, the covering of one's head for men can represent kingship and priestly power—two attributes of Christ. For women, on the other hand, this same act often represented their authority in His presence, and also His bride's dependence upon Him for their spiritual direction and safety. Robes, we learned from several denominations, tend to typify Christ's divine nature and deification, and also His priestly authority. All these He offers to His faithful followers when they humbly and righteously pursue His holy example. Significantly, then, in this chapter we learned that the donning of a sash was a common symbol of fidelity and faithfulness, and also of covenant relationship. What could better describe Christ's relationship with His Father, and, at the same time, the attributes and station we must develop if we are to return to Them. When we discussed footwear, and the removal of the same, we learned of agency and willingness to sacrifice.

Again, we understand these to be indicative of Christ's life. He gave and fought to preserve agency; His every deed was evidence of His willingness to sacrifice, on our behalf, and in accordance with the will of His Father. Finally, in this chapter we discussed the priestly undergarments of the ancient temple priests and the reality that they represent the flesh of Christ. Consequently, those who don them must live as He lived and act as He would act.

In chapter six we discovered that many ancient and modern faiths employ certain signs, tokens, gestures of approach, and the like. Nearly all faiths that have such symbolic gestures as part of their rituals hold them sacred and discuss them only in very limited ways. One thing seemingly common to the various faiths that employ such signs or symbols was their tendency to see such things as Christocentric. Jesus is the sign. Jesus is the token. Jesus is the gesture.

In the seventh chapter of this text, we discussed prayer at an altar. Among other things, we found that Christ is the altar. Thus, as He is focused on in such prayers, He mediates on behalf of those who pray at the altar. In this same chapter we examined the Catholic practice of knocking three times with a small hammer when engaging in certain rites of communion or prayer. We learned that the triple knock symbolized who the petitioner's prayer was addressed to—namely the three members of the Godhead: Father, Son, and Holy Spirit. Latter-day Saints pray to the Father, in the name of His Son, and through His Holy Spirit. This chapter reminded us of what the Book of Hebrews revealed so many centuries ago—namely that Jesus is the veil of the temple. It is through Him that we commune with the Father, and it is through Him that we must pass in order to enter the Father's presence—and, as the previous rites and associated symbols suggest, we cannot pass through Him until He has passed through us.

Finally, in the eighth chapter we discussed the common practice of men and women in various cultures and religions being married while kneeling at an altar. Again, knowing that Jesus is the altar, we were reminded of the importance of placing Him at the center of our marriages.

Though so many more examples could be given and so many more symbols of Jesus could be rehearsed, suffice it to say, truly all things testify of Christ!

If we are to benefit from the symbolism inherit in rites, rituals, and ordinances, we as participants must be more attentive to the symbols that saturate those ceremonies. In so doing we will find more meaning in the covenants we enter into, and we will more fully discover Christ in the rites in which we engage. Consequently, we will also more thoroughly experience in our personal lives His transforming and sanctifying power.

Notes
1.   Becerra (2009), 5.

Bibliography

ANCIENT SOURCES

1 Enoch. In James E. Charlesworth, ed. *The Old Testament Pseudepigrapha.* 2 vols. New York: Doubleday, 1983, 1985. 1:13–89.

2 Enoch. In James H. Charlesworth, ed. *The Old Testament Pseudepigrapha.* 2 vols. New York: Doubleday, 1983, 1985. 1:102–221.

3 Enoch. In James H. Charlesworth, ed. *The Old Testament Pseudepigrapha.* 2 vols. New York: Doubleday, 1983, 1985. 1:255–315.

2 Jeu. In Carl Schmidt, ed. *The Books of Jeu and the Untitled Text in the Bruce Codex.* Leiden: E. J. Brill, 1978. 99–141.

11Q5. In Michael Wise, Martin Abegg, Jr., and Edward Cook, translators. *The Dead Sea Scrolls—A New Translation.* New York: HarperCollins, 1999. 445–49.

Acts of John. In Edgar Hennecke and Wilhelm Schneemelcher, eds. *New Testament Apocrypha.* vol. 2. Philadelphia: The Westminster Press, 1965. 188–259.

Ambrose, "Hexaemeron." In Andrew Louth, ed. *Ancient Christian Commentary on Scripture: Genesis 1–11.* Downers Grove, IL: InterVarsity Press, 2001. 7, 17.

_____, "Letters to Laymen." In Andrew Louth, ed. *Ancient Christian Commentary on Scripture: Genesis 1–11.* Downers Grove, IL: InterVarsity Press, 2001. 71.

_____, "Paradise." In Andrew Louth, ed. *Ancient Christian Commentary on Scripture: Genesis 1–11*. Downers Grove, IL: InterVarsity Press, 2001. 76.

Archelaus, "Disputation With Manes." In Alexander Roberts and James Donaldson, eds. *Ante-Nicene Fathers*. 10 vols. Peabody, MA: Hendrickson Publishers, 1994. 6:179–235.

Athanasius, "Apologia Ad Constantium." In Philip Schaff and Henry Wace, eds. *Nicene and Post-Nicene Fathers—Second Series*. 14 vols. Peabody, MA: Hendrickson Publishers, 2004. 4:236–53.

Augustine, "City of God." In Philip Schaff, ed. *Nicene and Post-Nicene Fathers—First Series*. 14 vols. Peabody, MA: Hendrickson Publishers, 2004. 2:1–511.

_____, "On The Morals of the Manichaeans." In Philip Schaff, ed. *Nicene and Post-Nicene Fathers—First Series*. 14 vols. Peabody, MA: Hendrickson Publishers, 2004. 4:69–89.

_____, "On The Psalms." In Philip Schaff, ed. *Nicene and Post-Nicene Fathers—First Series*. 14 vols. Peabody, MA: Hendrickson Publishers, 2004. 8:1–683.

_____, "On The Trinity." In Philip Schaff, ed. *Nicene and Post-Nicene Fathers—First Series*. 14 vols. Peabody, MA: Hendrickson Publishers, 2004. 3:17–228.

_____, "Our Lord's Sermon on the Mount." In Philip Schaff, ed. *Nicene and Post-Nicene Fathers—First Series*. 14 vols. Peabody, MA: Hendrickson Publishers, 2004. 6:3–63.

Basil the Great, "Hexaemeraon." In Andrew Louth, ed. *Ancient Christian Commentary on Scripture: Genesis 1–11*. Downers Grove, IL: InterVarsity Press, 2001. 7.

_____, "Homilies on the Psalms." In Craig A. Blaising and Carmen S. Hardin, eds. *Ancient Christian Commentary on Scripture: Psalms 1–50*. Downers Grove, IL: InterVarsity Press, 2008. 349.

Chromatius, "Tractate on Matthew 21." In Manlio Simonetti, ed. *Ancient Christian Commentary on Scripture—Matthew 1–13*. Downers Grove, IL: InterVarsity Press, 2001. 102–103.

Clement of Alexandria, "The Stromata." In Alexander Roberts and James Donaldson, eds. *Ante-Nicene Fathers*. 10 vols. Peabody, MA: Hendrickson Publishers, 1994. 2:299–567.

Clement of Rome, "The First Epistle of Clement to the Corinthians." In Alexander Roberts and James Donaldson, eds. *Ante-Nicene Fathers*. 10 vols. Peabody, MA: Hendrickson Publishers, 1994. 1:5–21.

Cyprian of Carthage, "The Treatises of Cyprian." In Alexander Roberts and James Donaldson, eds. *Ante-Nicene Fathers*. 10 vols. Peabody, MA: Hendrickson Publishers, 1994. 5:421–557.

Cyril of Alexandria, "Fragments 50." In Manlio Simonetti, ed. *Ancient Christian Commentary on Scripture—Matthew 1–13*. Downers Grove, IL: InterVarsity Press, 2001. 104.

Cyril of Jerusalem, "Catechetical Lectures." In Philip Schaff and Henry Wace, eds. *Nicene and Post-Nicene Fathers—Second Series*. 14 vols. Peabody, MA: Hendrickson Publishers, 2004. 7:1–157.

Ephrem the Syrian, "Commentary on Genesis." In Mark Sheridan, ed. *Ancient Christian Commentary on Scripture: Genesis 12–50*. Downers Grove, IL: InterVarsity Press, 2002. 63–64.

"Extract From the Books of the Saviour." In G. R. S. Mead. *Pistis Sophia*. London: The Theological Publishing Society, 1896. 358–94.

Gregory of Nazianzus, "In Defense of His Flight to Pontus." In Philip Schaff and Henry Wace, eds. *Nicene and Post-Nicene Fathers—Second Series*. 14 vols. Peabody, MA: Hendrickson Publishers, 2004. 7:203–27.

Hippolytus, "Apostolic Tradition." In Burton Scott Easton, trans. *The Apostolic Tradition of Hippolytus*. Ann Arbor, MI: Archon Books, 1962. 33–61.

Jerome, "Commentary on Matthew." In Manlio Simonetti, ed. *Ancient Christian Commentary on Scripture—Matthew 1–13*. Downers Grove, IL: InterVarsity Press, 2001. 104. (See also Thomas P. Scheck, trans. *St. Jerome: Commentary on Matthew*. Washington, DC: The Catholic University of America Press, 2008. 59–328.)

_____, "Homilies." In Andrew Louth, ed. *Ancient Christian Commentary on Scripture: Genesis 1–11*. Downers Grove, IL: InterVarsity Press, 2001. 6.

_____, "Letters of Saint Jerome." In Philip Schaff and Henry Wace, eds. *Nicene and Post-Nicene Fathers—Second Series*. 14 vols. Peabody, MA: Hendrickson Publishers, 2004. 6:1–295.

John Chrysostom, "Homilies on Genesis." In Andrew Louth, ed. *Ancient Christian Commentary on Scripture: Genesis 1–11*. Downers Grove, IL: InterVarsity Press, 2001. 16. (See also Robert C. Hill, trans. *Saint John Chrysostom: Homilies on Genesis 1–17*. Washington, DC: The Catholic University of America Press, 1986. 20–246.)

_____, "Homilies on St. John." In Philip Schaff, ed. *Nicene and Post-Nicene Fathers—First Series*. 14 vols. Peabody, MA: Hendrickson Publishers, 2004. 14:1–334.

_____. "Homilies on the Acts of the Apostles." In Philip Schaff, ed.

Nicene and Post-Nicene Fathers—First Series. 14 vols. Peabody, MA: Hendrickson Publishers, 2004. 11:1–328.

John of Damascus, "Orthodox Faith." In Philip Schaff and Henry Wace, eds. *Nicene and Post-Nicene Fathers—Second Series*. 14 vols. Peabody, MA: Hendrickson Publishers, 2004. 9:1–101.

John the Deacon, Letter to Senaris. In J. D. C. Fisher. *Christian Initiation: Baptism in the Medieval West*. Chicago: Liturgy Training Publications, 2004. 10. (See also Maxwell E. Johnson. *The Rites of Christian Initiation: Their Evolution and Interpretation*. Revised and expanded edition. Collegeville, MN: Order of Saint Benedict, 2007. 164–67.)

Justin Martyr, "Dialogue with Trypho." In Alexander Roberts and James Donaldson, eds. *Ante-Nicene Fathers*. 10 vols. Peabody, MA: Hendrickson Publishers, 1994. 1:194–270.

Life of Adam and Eve. In James E. Charlesworth, ed. *The Old Testament Pseudepigrapha*. 2 vols. New York: Doubleday, 1983, 1985. 2:249–95.

Minucius Felix, "The Octavius of Minucius Felix." In Alexander Roberts and James Donaldson, eds. *Ante-Nicene Fathers*. 10 vols. Peabody, MA: Hendrickson Publishers, 1994. 4:173–98.

"Odes of Solomon." In James E. Charlesworth, ed. *The Old Testament Pseudepigrapha*. 2 vols. New York: Doubleday, 1983, 1985. 2:735–71.

Origen, "Homilies on Genesis." In Andrew Louth, ed. *Ancient Christian Commentary on Scripture: Genesis 1–11*. Downers Grove, IL: InterVarsity Press, 2001. 19. (See also Ronald E. Heine, trans. *Origen: Homilies on Genesis and Exodus*. Washington, DC: The Catholic University of America Press, 1981. 45–224.)

Quodvultdeus, "Book of Promises and Predictions of God." In Andrew Louth, ed. *Ancient Christian Commentary on Scripture: Genesis 1–11*. Downers Grove, IL: InterVarsity Press, 2001. 71.

Tertullian, "Apology." In Alexander Roberts and James Donaldson, eds. *Ante-Nicene Fathers*. 10 vols. Peabody, MA: Hendrickson Publishers, 1994. 3:1–55.

———, "On Baptism." In Alexander Roberts and James Donaldson, eds. *Ante-Nicene Fathers*. 10 vols. Peabody, MA: Hendrickson Publishers, 1994. 3:669–79.

———, "On Prayer." In Alexander Roberts and James Donaldson, eds. *Ante-Nicene Fathers*. 10 vols. Peabody, MA: Hendrickson Publishers, 1994. 3:681–91.

———, "On The Resurrection of the Flesh." In Alexander Roberts and James Donaldson, eds. *Ante-Nicene Fathers*. 10 vols. Peabody, MA: Hendrickson Publishers, 1994. 3:545–94.

"Testament of Isaac" in "Testaments of the Three Patriarchs." In James E. Charlesworth, ed. *The Old Testament Pseudepigrapha*. 2 vols. New York: Doubleday, 1983, 1985. 1:905–11.

"The Apocalypse of Abraham." In James E. Charlesworth, ed. *The Old Testament Pseudepigrapha*. 2 vols. New York: Doubleday, 1983, 1985. 1:689–705.

"The Apocalypse of Adam." In James E. Charlesworth, ed. *The Old Testament Pseudepigrapha*. 2 vols. New York: Doubleday, 1983, 1985. 1:712–19.

"The Apocalypse of Adam." In James M. Robinson, ed. *The Nag Hammadi Library*, revised edition. San Francisco: Harper and Row, 1988. 279–86.

"The Apocalypse of Daniel." In James H. Charlesworth, ed. *The Old Testament Pseudepigrapha*. 2 vols. New York: Doubleday, 1983, 1985. 1:763–70.

"The Apocalypse of Zephaniah." In James E. Charlesworth, ed. *The Old Testament Pseudepigrapha*. 2 vols. New York: Doubleday, 1983, 1985. 1:508–15.

"The Apostolic Constitutions" or "Constitution of the Holy Apostles." In Alexander Roberts and James Donaldson, eds. *Ante-Nicene Fathers*. 10 vols. Peabody, MA: Hendrickson Publishers, 1994. 7:391–505.

"The Book of Adam and Eve" also known as "The Conflict of Adam and Eve with Satan." In S. C. Malan. *The Book of Adam and Eve also called The Conflict of Adam and Eve with Satan*. London: Williams and Northgate, 1882. 1–207.

"The Divine Liturgy of James." In Alexander Roberts and James Donaldson, eds. *Ante-Nicene Fathers*. 10 vols. Peabody, MA: Hendrickson Publishers, 1994. 7:537–50.

"The First Book of Adam and Eve" or "The Conflict of Adam and Eve with Satan." In Rutherford H. Platt, Jr., ed. *The Forgotten Books of Eden*. Cleveland: The World Publishing Company, 1927. 1–81.

"The General Epistle of Barnabas." In Alexander Roberts and James Donaldson, eds. *Ante-Nicene Fathers*. Peabody, MA: Hendrickson Publishers, 1994. 1:133–49.

"The Gospel of Bartholomew." In Montague Rhodes James, trans. *The Apocryphal New Testament*. Oxford: Clarendon Press, 1960. 166–87.

"The Gospel of Philip." In James M. Robinson, ed. *The Nag Hammadi Library in English*. Revised edition. New York: Harper and Row, 1988. 141–60.

"The Testaments of the Twelve Patriarchs—Testament of Levi." In James

H. Charlesworth, ed. *The Old Testament Pseudepigrapha*. 2 vols. New York: Doubleday, 1983, 1985. 1:788–95.

The Works of Philo: Complete and Unabridged. C. D. Yonge, trans. New updated version. Peabody, MA: Hendrickson Publishers, 1997.

Theophilus of Antioch, "Theophilus to Autolycus." In Alexander Roberts and James Donaldson, eds. *Ante-Nicene Fathers*. 10 vols. Peabody, MA: Hendrickson Publishers, 1994. 2:89–121.

Victorinus, "Commentary on the Apocalypse of the Blessed John." In Alexander Roberts and James Donaldson, eds. *Ante-Nicene Fathers*. 10 vols. Peabody, MA: Hendrickson Publishers, 1994. 7:344–60.

ARTICLES

Alexander, P. "Introduction" to "3 (Hebrew Apocalypse of) Enoch—A New Translation and Introduction." In James H. Charlesworth, ed. *The Old Testament Pseudepigrapha*. 2 vols. New York: Doubleday, 1983, 1985. 1:223–54.

Andersen, Francis I. "2 (Slavonic Apocalypse of) Enoch—A New Translation and Introduction." In James H. Charlesworth, ed. *The Old Testament Pseudepigrapha*. 2 vols. New York: Doubleday, 1983, 1985. 1:91–100.

Anderson, Bernhard W. "Creation in the Bible." In Philip N. Joranson, ed. *Cry of the Environment*. Santa Fe, NM: Bear and Company, 1984. 19–44.

Asay, Carlos C. "The Temple Garment: 'An Outward Expression of an Inward Commitment.'" In *Ensign*, August 1997, 18–23.

Ballif, Jae R. "Melchizedek Priesthood." In Daniel H. Ludlow, ed. *Encyclopedia of Mormonism*. 4 vols. New York: Macmillian Publishing, 1992. 2:882–85.

Banwell, B. O. "Nose." In J. D. Douglass, ed. *The New Bible Dictionary*. Grand Rapids: Eerdmans, 1971. 895.

Bennett, William Henry. "Number" in James Hastings, ed. *Dictionary of the Bible*. Charles Scribner's Sons: New York, 1963. 701–704.

Becerra, Daniel. "Three Motifs of Early Christian Oil Anointing." In *BYU Religious Education 1009 Student Symposium*. Provo, UT: Religious Studies Center, 2009. 3–15.

Bokovoy, David E. "From the Hand of Jacob: A Ritual Analysis of Genesis 27." In *Studies in the Bible and Antiquity*. vol. 1. 2009. 35–50.

Bowden, Hugh. "Origins and Background." In John Bowden, ed.

Encyclopedia of Christianity. New York: Oxford University Press, 2005. 841–53.

Bowden, John. "Ministry and Ministers." In John Bowden, ed. *Encyclopedia of Christianity.* New York: Oxford University Press, 2005. 749–57.

Bowie, Fiona. "Ritual and Performance." In Christopher Partridge, ed. *Introduction to World Religions.* Minneapolis: Fortress Press, 2005. 32–33.

Bridger, David. "Halitzah." *The New Jewish Encyclopedia.* Bridger, David, ed. New York: Behrman House, 1962. 185–86.

Brown, S. Kent. "The Nag Hammadi Library: A Mormon Perspective." In *Apocryphal Writings and the Latter-day Saints.* C. Wilfred Griggs, ed. Provo, UT: Religious Studies Center, Brigham Young University, 1986. 255–85.

Chaillot, Christine. "The Ancient Oriental Churches." In Geoffrey Wainwright and Karen B. Westerfield Tucker, eds. *The Oxford History of Christian Worship.* New York: Oxford University Press, 2006. 131–69.

Charlesworth, James H. "Odes of Solomon: A New Translation and Introduction." In James H. Charlesworth, ed. *The Old Testament Pseudepigrapha.* 2 vols. New York: Doubleday, 1983, 1985. 2:725–34.

_____. "Pseudepigrapha, OT." In David Noel Freedman, ed. *The Anchor Bible Dictionary.* 6 vols. New York: Doubleday, 1992. 5:537–40.

Clawson, Rudger. *Conference Report.* April 1937, 75–78.

Clifford, Richard J. "Exodus." In Raymond E. Brown, Joseph A Fitzmmyer, and Roland E. Murphy, eds. *The New Jerome Biblical Commentary.* New Jersey: Prentice Hall, 1990. 44–60.

_____ and Roland E. Murphy. "Genesis." In Raymond E. Brown, Joseph A. Fitzmmyer, and Roland E. Murphy, eds. *The New Jerome Biblical Commentary.* New Jersey: Prentice Hall, 1990. 8–43.

Collins, John J. "Essenes." In David Noel Freedman, ed. *The Anchor Bible Dictionary.* 6 vols. New York: Doubleday, 1992. 2:619–26.

Compton, Todd M. "The Whole Token: Mystery Symbolism in Classical Recognition Drama." In *Epoche* 13. 1985. 1–81.

_____. "The Handclasp and Embrace as Tokens of Recognition." In John M. Lundquist and Stephen D. Ricks, eds. *By Study and Also By Faith.* 2 vols. Provo, UT: Foundation for Ancient Research and Mormon Studies, 1990. 1:611–42.

Cowan, Richard O. "Sacred Temples Ancient and Modern." In Donald W. Parry and Stephen D. Ricks, eds. *The Temple in Time and Eternity.* Provo, UT: Foundation for Ancient Research and Mormon Studies, 1999. 99–120.

Cross, Frank M. "Gremial." In F. M. Cross and E. A. Livingstone, eds. *The Oxford Dictionary of the Christian Church.* Second edition. New York: Oxford University Press, 1990. 601–602.

———. "Melchites." In F. M. Cross and E. A. Livingstone, eds. *The Oxford Dictionary of the Christian Church.* Second edition. New York: Oxford University Press, 1990. 899.

Cwiekowski, Frederick J. "Deacon, Woman." In Richard P. McBrien, ed. *The Harper Collins Encyclopedia of Catholicism.* San Francisco: Harper San Francisco, 1995. 397.

Daniels, Jon B. "Bartholomew, Gospel (Questions) Of." In David Noel Freedman, ed. *The Anchor Bible Dictionary.* 6 vols. New York: Doubleday, 1992. 1:615–16.

Denny, Frederick Matthewson. "Names and Naming." In Mircea Eliade, ed. *The Encyclopedia of Religion.* 16 vols. New York: Macmillian, 1987. 10:300–307.

Dixon, C. Scott. "Martin Luther." In John Bowden, ed. *Encyclopedia of Christianity.* New York: Oxford University Press, 2005. 716–19.

Draper, Richard D. and Donald W. Parry. "Seven Promises to Those Who Overcome: Aspects of Genesis 2–3 in the Seven Letters." In Donald W. Parry and Stephen D. Ricks, eds. *The Temple in Time and Eternity.* Provo, UT: Foundation for Ancient Research and Mormon Studies, 1999. 121–41.

Earle, Ralph. "2 Timothy." In Frank E. Gaebelein, ed. *The Expositor's Bible Commentary.* 12 vols. Grand Rapids: Zondervan, 1976–92. 11:391–418.

Edwards, Douglas R. "Dress and Ornamentation." In David Noel Freedman, ed. *The Anchor Bible Dictionary.* 6 vols. New York: Doubleday, 1992. 2:232–38.

Ewing, W. "Nose, Nostrils." In James Hastings, ed. *Dictionary of the Bible.* New York: Charles Scribner's Sons, 1963. 701.

"Excursus on the Vestments of the Early Church." In Philip Schaff and Henry Wace, eds. *Nicene and Post-Nicene Fathers—Second Series.* 14 vols. Peabody, MA: Hendrickson Publishers, 2004. 14:142–43.

Fenwick, John. "Middle East, Christianity in The." In John Bowden, ed. *Encyclopedia of Christianity.* New York: Oxford University Press, 2005. 743–49.

———. "Orthodox Christianity." In John Bowden, ed. *Encyclopedia of Christianity.* New York: Oxford University Press, 2005. 854–64.

Ferguson, Everett. "Baptism." In Everett Ferguson, ed. *Encyclopedia of Early Christianity.* New York: Garland Publishing, 1990. 131–34.

_____, "Barnabas, Epistle of." In Everett Ferguson, ed. *Encyclopedia of Early Christianity*. New York: Garland Publishing, 1990. 138.

Filson, Floyd V. "Who Was the Beloved Disciple?," in *Journal of Biblical Literature* 68. June, 1949. 2:83–88.

Flemming, J. and H. Duensing. "The Ascension of Isaiah." In Edgar Hennecke and Wilhelm Schneemelcher, eds. *New Testament Apocrypha*. vol. 2. Philadelphia: The Westminster Press, 1965. 642–63.

Friberg, Joran. "Numbers and Counting." In David Noel Freedman, ed. *The Anchor Bible Dictionary*. 6 vols. New York: Doubleday, 1992. 4:1139–46.

Gaster, Theodore H. "Amulets and Talismans." In Mircea Eliade, ed. *The Encyclopedia of Religion*. 16 vols. New York: Macmillian, 1987. 1:243–46.

Gee, John. "The Keeper of the Gate." In Donald W. Parry and Stephen D. Ricks, eds. *The Temple in Time and Eternity*. Provo, UT: Foundation for Ancient Research and Mormon Studies, 1999. 233–73.

Gifford, Edwin H. "Introduction" to "The Catechetical Lectures of S. Cyril." In Philip Schaff and Henry Wace, eds. *Nicene and Post-Nicene Fathers—Second Series*. 14 vols. Peabody, MA: Hendrickson Publishers, 1994. 7:i-lviii.

Graf, Fritz. "Eleusinian Mysteries." In Mircea Eliade, ed. *The Encyclopedia of Religion*. 16 vols. New York: Macmillian, 1987. 5:83–85.

Habershon, Ada R. *Study of the Types*. Grand Rapids: Kregel Publications, 1974.

Haight, David B. "Come to the House of the Lord." In *Ensign*, May 1992. 15–17.

Hamblin, William J. "Aspects of an Early Christian Initiation Ritual." In John M. Lundquist and Stephen D. Ricks, eds. *By Study and Also by Faith*. 2 vols. Provo, UT: Foundation for Ancient Research and Mormon Studies, 1990. 1:202–21.

Harris, James R. "The Book of Abraham Facsimiles." In Robert L. Millet and Kent P. Jackson, eds. *Studies in Scripture, Vol. 2: The Pearl of Great Price*. Salt Lake City: Randall Book, 1985. 247–86.

Harvey, Susan Ashbrook. "Nestorianism." In Everett Ferguson, ed. *Encyclopedia of Early Christianity*. New York: Garland Publishing, 1990. 644–47.

Hinckley, Gordon B. "Rejoice in this Great Era of Temple Building." In *Ensign*, November 1985. 53–60.

Hunter, Howard W. "Reading the Scriptures." In *Ensign*, November 1979. 64–65.

Hyatt, J. Philip. "Dress," in James Hastings, ed. *Dictionary of the Bible*. New York: Charles Scribner's Sons, 1963. 222–25.

Isaac, E. "1 (Ethiopic Apocalypse of) Enoch—A New Translation and Introduction." In James E. Charlesworth, ed. *The Old Testament Pseudepigrapha*. 2 vols. New York: Doubleday, 1983, 1985. 1:5–12.

Irwin, Kevin W. "The Sacramentality of Creation and the Role of Creation in Liturgy and Sacraments." In Kevin W. Irwin and Edmund D. Pellegrino, eds. *Preserving the Creation: Environmental Theology and Ethics*. Washington, DC: Georgetown University Press, 1992. 67–111.

Isenberg, Wesley W. "Introduction" to the "Gospel of Philip." In James M. Robinson, ed. *The Nag Hammadi Library in English*. Revised edition. New York: Harper and Row, 1988. 139–41.

John Paul II, "Peace with God the Creator, Peace with All Creation: Message of His Holiness Pope John Paul II for the celebration of the World Day of Peace, 1 January, 1990." In *Origins* vol. 19, no. 28, 465–68.

Kaiser, Walter C., Jr. "Exodus." In Frank E. Gaebelein, ed. *The Expositor's Bible Commentary*. 12 vols. Grand Rapids: Zondervan, 1976–92. 2:285–497.

Kalland, Earl S. "Deuteronomy." In Frank E. Gaebelein, ed. *The Expositor's Bible Commentary*. 12 vols. Grand Rapids: Zondervan, 1976–92. 3:1–235.

Kaplan, Abraham. "The Meanings of Ritual: Comparisons." In Truman G. Madsen, ed. *Reflections on Mormonism: Judaeo-Christian Parallels*. Provo, UT: Brigham Young University Religious Studies Center, 1978. 37–56.

Kee, H. C. "Testaments of the Twelve Patriarchs—A New Translation and Introduction." In James H. Charlesworth, ed. *The Old Testament Pseudepigrapha*. 2 vols. New York: Doubleday, 1983, 1985. 1:775–81.

Keller, Roger R. "Adam: As Understood by Four Men Who Shaped Western Christianity." In Joseph Fielding McConkie and Robert L. Millet, eds. *The Man Adam*. Salt Lake City: Bookcraft, 1990. 147–89.

———. "Teaching the Fall and the Atonement: A Comparative Method." In *The Religious Educator: Perspectives on the Restored Gospel*, vol. 5, no. 2. 2004. 101–18.

Kennedy, A. R. S. and James Barr, "Anointing, Anointed." In James Hastings, ed. *Dictionary of the Bible*. Revised edition. New York: Charles Scribner's Sons, 1963. 35.

Kimball, Heber C. Discourse delivered August 23, 1857, in Salt Lake City,

Utah. *Journal of Discourses*. Liverpool: Latter-day Saint's Book Depot, 1859. 5:171–81.

King, Judd. *A Handbook to the Pearl of Great Price*. Unpublished manuscript. 1995.

Kline, Meredith G. "Oath and Ordeal Signs." In *Westminster Theological Journal*. vol. 26. 1967. 115–39.

Klinghardt, Matthias. "Prayer Formularies for Public Recitation—Their Use and Function in Ancient Religion." In *Numen*. vol. 46. no. 1. 1999. 1–52.

Lacheman, Ernest R. "Note on Ruth 4:7–8." In *Journal of Biblical Literature*. vol. 56, no. 1. March 1937. 53–56.

Lawler, Michael G. "Marriage." In Richard P. McBrien, ed. *The Harper Collins Encyclopedia of Catholicism*. San Francisco: Harper San Francisco, 1995. 821–26.

Leeming, David Adams. "Quests." In Mircea Eliade, ed. *The Encyclopedia of Religion*. 16 vols. New York: Macmillian, 1987. 12:146–52.

Lesko, Leonard H. "Egyptian Religion: An Overview." In Mircea Eliade, ed. *The Encyclopedia of Religion*. 16 vols. New York: Macmillian, 1987. 5:37–54.

Leyerle, Blake. "Manichaeism." In Richard P. McBrien, ed. *The Harper Collins Encyclopedia of Catholicism*. San Francisco: Harper San Francisco, 1995. 810–11.

Longenecker, Richard N. "The Acts of the Apostles." In Frank E. Gaebelein, ed. *The Expositor's Bible Commentary*. 12 vols. Grand Rapids: Zondervan, 1976–92. 9:205–573.

Lundquist, John M. "What Is Reality?" In John M. Lundquist and Stephen D. Ricks, eds. *By Study and Also By Faith*. 2 vols. Provo, UT: Foundation for Ancient Research and Mormon Studies, 1990. 1:428–38.

Lundquist, Suzanne E. "Native American Rites of Passage: Implications for Latter-day Saints." In John M. Lundquist and Stephen D. Ricks, eds. *By Study and Also By Faith*. 2 vols. Provo, UT: Foundation for Ancient Research and Mormon Studies, 1990. 1:439–57.

Lyman, J. Rebecca. "Heresy." In John Bowden, ed. *Encyclopedia of Christianity*. New York: Oxford University Press, 2005. 518–24.

Mackey, Albert G. "Pentalpha." In *An Encyclopedia of Freemasonry and its Kindred Sciences*. Philadelphia: Moss and Company, 1879. 569–70.

Madsen, Truman G. " 'Putting on the Names': A Jewish-Christian Legacy." In John M. Lundquist and Stephen D. Ricks, eds. *By Study and Also By Faith*. 2 vols. Provo, UT: Foundation for Ancient Research and Mormon Studies, 1990. 1:458–81.

Marshall, Evelyn T. "Garments." In Daniel H. Ludlow, ed. *The Encyclopedia of Mormonism*. 4 vols. New York: Macmillian, 1992. 2:534–35.

Maxwell, Neal A. "Insights From my Life." In *Ensign*, August 2000, 6–13.

McBrien, Richard P. "Collect." In Richard P. McBrien, ed. *The Harper Collins Encyclopedia of Catholicism*. San Francisco: Harper San Francisco, 1995. 328.

_____. "Corpus Christi, Feast of." In Richard P. McBrien, ed. *The Harper Collins Encyclopedia of Catholicism*. San Francisco: Harper San Francisco, 1995. 369.

_____. "Diptychs." In Richard P. McBrien, ed. *The Harper Collins Encyclopedia of Catholicism*. San Francisco: Harper San Francisco, 1995. 419.

_____. "Gremial." In Richard P. McBrien, ed. *The Harper Collins Encyclopedia of Catholicism*. San Francisco: Harper Collins, 1995. 593.

_____. "Orarion." In Richard P. McBrien, ed. *The Harper Collins Encyclopedia of Catholicism*. San Francisco: Harper San Francisco, 1995. 935.

_____. "Priesthood of all Believers." In Richard P. McBrien, ed. *The Harper Collins Encyclopedia of Catholicism*. San Francisco: Harper San Francisco, 1995. 1051.

_____. "Stole." In *The Harper Collins Encyclopedia of Catholicism*. San Francisco: Harper San Francisco, 1995. 1225.

_____. "Vestments." In *The Harper Collins Encyclopedia of Catholicism*. San Francisco: Harper San Francisco, 1995. 1308.

McConkie, Joseph Fielding. "The Mystery of Eden." In Joseph Fielding McConkie and Robert L. Millet, eds. *The Man Adam*. Salt Lake City: Bookcraft, 1990. 23–35.

_____. "Holy Ghost." In Daniel H. Ludlow, ed. *The Encyclopedia of Mormonism*. 4 vols. New York: Macmillian, 1992. 2:649–51.

McHugh, Michael P. "Jerome." In Everett Ferguson, ed. *Encyclopedia of Early Christianity*. New York: Garland Publishing, 1990. 484–87.

McKechnie, Jean L. "Ceremony." In *Webster's New Twentieth Century Dictionary of the English Language, Unabridged*. Second edition. Collins World, 1978. 296.

_____. "Liturgy." In *Webster's New Twentieth Century Dictionary of the English Language, Unabridged*. Second edition. Collins World, 1978. 1058.

_____. "Rite." In *Webster's New Twentieth Century Dictionary of the English Language, Unabridged*. Second edition. Collins World, 1978. 1565.

_____. "Ritual." In *Webster's New Twentieth Century Dictionary of the*

English Language, Unabridged. Second edition. Collins World, 1978. 1565.

McVey, Kathleen. "Ephraem the Syrian." In Everett Ferguson, ed. *Encyclopedia of Early Christianity.* New York: Garland Publishing, 1990. 304–305.

Martos, Joseph. "Sacraments." In John Bowden, ed. *Encyclopedia of Christianity.* New York: Oxford University Press, 2005. 1060–71.

Meyers, Carol. "Apron," in David Noel Freedman, ed. *The Anchor Bible Dictionary.* New York: Doubleday, 1992, 1:318–19.

_____. "Ephod." In David Noel Freedman, ed. *The Anchor Bible Dictionary.* 6 vols. New York: Doubleday, 1992. 2:550.

Mueller, H. "Baptism." In *New Catholic Encyclopedia.* Second edition. 15 vols. New York: McGraw-Hill, 1967. 2:56–60.

Murphy, Roland E. "Wisdom in the OT." In David Noel Freedman, ed. *The Anchor Bible Dictionary.* 6 vols. New York: Doubleday, 1992. 6:920–31.

Nibley, Hugh. "The Expanding Gospel." In *BYU Studies.* vol 7. no. 1. Autumn 1965. 3–27.

_____. "Facsimile No. 1, By the Figures (Part 8)." In *Improvement Era*, July 1969. 101–11.

_____. "Leaders to Managers: The Fatal Shift." Commencement Address delivered at Brigham Young University, August 19, 1983. In *Brother Brigham Challenges the Saints.* Provo, UT: Foundation for Ancient Research and Mormon Studies, 1994. 491–508.

_____. "Endowment History." Unpublished paper dated February 2, 1990. 67 pages.

_____. "On the Sacred and the Symbolic." In Donald W. Parry, ed. *Temples of the Ancient World: Ritual and Symbolism.* Provo, UT: Foundation for Ancient Research and Mormon Studies, 1994. 535–621.

_____. "Abraham's Temple Drama." In Donald W. Parry and Stephen D. Ricks, eds. *The Temple in Time and Eternity.* Provo, UT: Foundation for Ancient Research and Mormon Studies, 1999. 1–42.

Norris, Frederick W. "Acts of John." In Everett Ferguson, ed. *Encyclopedia of Early Christianity.* New York: Garland Publishing, 1990. 7.

_____. "Epiphanius of Salamis." In Everett Ferguson, ed. *Encyclopedia of Early Christianity.* New York: Garland Publishing, 1990. 307–308.

_____. "Basil of Caesarea." In Everett Ferguson, ed. *Encyclopedia of Early Christianity.* New York: Garland Publishing, 1990. 139–41.

Ostler, Blake. "Clothed Upon: A Unique Aspect of Christian Antiquity." In *BYU Studies.* vol. 22. no. 1. Winter 1982. 31–45.

Parry, Donald W. "Sinai as Sanctuary and Mountain of God." In John M. Lundquist and Stephen D. Ricks, eds. *By Study and Also By Faith*. 2 vols. Provo, UT: Foundation for Ancient Research and Mormon Studies, 1990. 1:482–500.

_____. "Garden of Eden: Prototype Sanctuary." In Donald W. Parry, ed. *Temples of the Ancient World*. Provo, UT: Foundation for Ancient Research and Mormon Studies, 1994. 126–51.

Phelps, W. W. "Pray Without Ceasing." Tuesday, June 15, 1841. In *Times and Seasons*. 6 vols. Commerce and Nauvoo, IL, Nov 1839 through Feb 1846. Photo reprint. Independence, MO: Independence Press, 1986. 2:451.

Pike, Dana M. "Names," in Paul J. Achtemeier, ed. *Harper's Bible Dictionary*. San Francisco: Harper San Francisco, 1985, 682–84.

Porter, Bruce H. and Stephen D. Ricks. "Names in Antiquity: Old, New, and Hidden." In John M. Lundquist and Stephen D. Ricks, ed. *By Study and Also By Faith*. 2 vols. Provo, UT: Foundation for Ancient Research and Mormon Studies, 1990. 1:501–22.

Preston, James J. "Goddess Worship: An Overview." In Mircea Eliade, ed. *The Encyclopedia of Religion*. 16 vols. New York: Macmillan, 1987. 6:35–45.

Pulver, Max. "Jesus' Round Dance and Crucifixion According to the Acts of Saint John." In Joseph Campbell, ed. *The Mysteries: Papers From the Eranos Yearbooks*. New York: Princeton University Press, 1980. 169–93.

Rabikauskas, P. "Popes, Names Of." In *The New Catholic Encyclopedia*. Second edition. 15 vols. Detroit: Gale Group in association with the Catholic University of America, 2003. 11:506–507.

Ricks, Stephen D. "The Garment of Adam." In Donald W. Parry, ed. *Temples of the Ancient World*. Provo, UT: Foundation for Ancient Research and Mormon Studies, 1994. 705–39.

_____. "*Dexiosis and Dextrarum Iunctio*: The Sacred Handclasp in the Classical and Early Christian World." In *The FARMS Review* 18/1 (2006): 431–36.

_____ and John J. Sroka. "King, Coronation, and Temple." In Donald W. Parry. *Temples of the Ancient World*. Provo, UT: Foundation for Ancient Research and Mormon Studies, 1994. 236–71.

Ries, Julien. "Cross." In Mircea Eliade, ed. *The Encyclopedia of Religion*. 16 vols. New York: Macmillian, 1987. 4:155–66.

_____. "The Fall." In Mircea Eliade, ed. *The Encyclopedia of Religion*. 16 vols. New York: Macmillian, 1987. 5:256–67.

Ringgren, Helmer. "Initiation Ceremony of the Bektashis." In *Studies in the History of Religions*. Supplement to no. X. 1956. 202–208.

Roberson, Ronald G. "Maronite Catholic Church." In Richard P. McBrien, ed. *The Harper Collins Encyclopedia of Catholicism*. San Francisco: Harper San Francisco, 1995. 818–19.

———. "Melkite Catholic Church." In Richard P. McBrien, ed. *The Harper Collins Encyclopedia of Catholicism*. San Francisco: Harper San Francisco, 1995. 851–52.

Robinson, Stephen E. "The Book of Adam in Judaism and Early Christianity." In Joseph Fielding McConkie and Robert L. Millet, eds. *The Man Adam*. Salt Lake City: Bookcraft, 1990. 131–50.

———. "God the Father." In Daniel H. Ludlow, ed. *The Encyclopedia of Mormonism*. 4 vols. New York: Macmillian, 1992. 2:548–50.

Rockwood, Jolene Edmunds. "The Redemption of Eve." In Maureen Ursenbach Beecher and Lavina Fielding Anderson, eds. *Sisters In Spirit*. Chicago: University of Illinois Press, 1992. 3–36.

Roundy, Shadrach B. "Record Book." Unpublished manuscript. Salt Lake City: Church Archives, Church of Jesus Christ of Latter-day Saints.

Rudolph, Kurt. "Mystery Religions." In Mircea Eliade, ed. *The Encyclopedia of Religion*. 16 vols. New York: Macmillian, 1987. 10:230–39.

Sailhamer, John H. "Genesis." In Frank E. Gaebelein, ed. *The Expositor's Bible Commentary*. 12 vols. Grand Rapids: Zondervan, 1976–92. 2:1–284.

Sandmel, Samuel. "Parallelomania." In *Journal of Biblical Literature* 81. 1962. 1–13.

Scholem, Gershom. "Kabbalistic Ritual and the Bride of God." In Jerome Rothenberg and Diane Rothenberg. *Symposium of the Whole: A Range of Discourse Toward an Ethnopoetics*. Berkeley, CA: University of California Press, 1983. 303–10.

Sherman, Anthony. "Baptism." In Richard P. McBrien, ed. *The Harper Collins Encyclopedia of Catholicism*. San Francisco: Harper San Francisco, 1995. 133–38.

Smith, Joseph Fielding, Jr. "Fall—Atonement—Resurrection—Sacrament." In *Charge To Religious Educators*. Second edition. Salt Lake City: The Church of Jesus Christ of Latter-day Saints, 1982. 124–28.

Sonne, I. "Synagogue." In *The Interpreter's Dictionary of the Bible*. 4 vols. New York: Abingdon Press, 1962. 4:476–91.

Soyer, Daniel. "Entering the 'Tent of Abraham': Fraternal Ritual and American-Jewish Identity, 1880–1920." In *Religion and American Culture*. vol. 9. no. 2. Summer, 1999. 159–82.

Speiser, E. A. "Of Shoes and Shekels." In *Bulletin of the American Schools of Oriental Research*, 77. 1940. 15–20.

Stinespring, W. F. "Introduction" to "Testament of Isaac—A New Translation and Introduction." In James E. Charlesworth, ed. *The Old Testament Pseudepigrapha*. 2 vols. New York: Doubleday, 1983, 1985. 1:903–904.

Stone, Merlin. "Goddess Worship: Goddess Worship in the Ancient Near East." In Mircea Eliade, ed. *The Encyclopedia of Religion*. 16 vols. New York: Macmillan, 1987. 6:35–59.

Strathearn, Gaye and Brian M. Hauglid. "The Great Mosque and Its Ka) Ba." In Donald W. Parry and Stephen D. Ricks, eds. *The Temple in Time and Eternity*. Provo, UT: Foundation for Ancient Research and Mormon Studies, 1999. 275–302.

Stylianopoulos, Theodore. "Justin Martyr." In Everett Ferguson, ed. *Encyclopedia of Early Christianity*. New York: Garland Publishing, 1990. 514–16.

Tanner, N. Eldon. "Where Art Thou?" In *Ensign*, December 1971. 32–35.

Taylor, John "Name, Names," in James Hastings, ed. *Dictionary of the Bible*. New York: Charles Scribner's Sons, 1963, 687–88.

Tenney, Merrill C. "The Gospel of John," in Frank E. Gaebelein, ed. *The Expositor's Bible Commentary*. 12 vols. Grand Rapids: Zondervan Publishing House, 1976–92, 9:1–203.

Thibodeau, Timothy. "Western Christendom." In Geoffrey Wainwright and Karen B. Westerfield Tucker, eds. *The Oxford History of Christian Worship*. New York: Oxford University Press, 2006. 216–53.

Thomas, M. Catherine. "The Brother of Jared at the Veil." In Donald W. Parry, ed. *Temples of the Ancient World*. Provo, UT: Foundation for Ancient Research and Mormon Studies. 388–98.

Thomasson, Gordon C. "Togetherness is Sharing an Umbrella: Divine Kingship, Gnosis, and Religious Syncretism." In John M. Lundquist and Stephen D. Ricks, eds. *By Study and Also By Faith*. 2 vols. Provo, UT: Foundation for Ancient Research and Mormon Studies, 1990. 1:523–61.

____. "What's in a Name? Book of Mormon Language, Names, and [Metonymic] Naming," in *Journal of Book of Mormon Studies*. vol. 3, no. 1. Spring 1994. 1–27.

Thompson, Thomas and Dorothy. "Some Legal Problems in the Book of Ruth." In *Vetus Testamentum* 18. 1968. 79–99.

Titus, Eric L. "The Identity of the Beloved Disciple," in *Journal of Biblical Literature*. 69. December, 1950. 4:323–28.

Trix, Frances. *"Bektāshīyah."* In John L. Esposito, ed. *The Oxford Encyclopedia of the Modern Islamic World.* 4 vols. New York: Oxford University Press, 1995. 1:213–15.

Tucker, G. M. "Shorter Communications: Witnesses and 'Dates' in Israelite Contracts." In *The Catholic Biblical Quarterly* 28. 1966. 42–45.

Turner, Rodney. "The Doctrine of the Firstborn and Only Begotten" in *The Pearl of Great Price: Revelations From God.* Provo, UT: Religious Studies Center, Brigham Young University, 1989. 91–117.

Tvedtnes, John A. "Priestly Clothing in Bible Times." In Donald W. Parry, ed. *Temples of the Ancient World.* Provo, UT: Foundation for Ancient Research and Mormon Studies, 1994. 649–704.

———. "Temple Prayer in Ancient Times." In Donald W. Parry and Stephen D. Ricks, eds. *The Temple in Time and Eternity.* Provo, UT: Foundation for Ancient Research and Mormon Studies, 1999. 55–98.

Vanderwilt, Jeffrey T. "Altar." In Richard P. McBrien, ed. *The Harper Collins Encyclopedia of Catholicism.* San Francisco: Harper San Francisco, 1995. 36–37.

Von Wellnitz, Marcus. "The Catholic Liturgy and the Mormon Temple." In *BYU Studies.* vol. 21. no. 1. Winter 1981. 3–35.

Young, Brigham. Discourse delivered April 6, 1853. In Richard S. Van Wagoner, ed. *The Complete Discourses of Brigham Young.* 5 vols. Salt Lake City: The Smith-Pettit Foundation, 2009. 2:644–47.

Young, Lorenzo D. Discourse delivered October 25, 1857, in Salt Lake City, Utah. *Journal of Discourses.* Liverpool: Latter-day Saint's Book Depot, 1859. 6:22–226.

Youngblood, Ronald F. "1, 2 Samuel." In Frank E. Gaebelein, ed. *The Expositor's Bible Commentary.* 12 vols. Grand Rapids: Zondervan, 1976–92. 3:551–1104.

Wagner, Walter H. "Clement of Alexandria." In Everett Ferguson, ed. *Encyclopedia of Early Christianity.* New York: Garland Publishing, 1990. 214–16.

Wilkin, Robert. "John Chrysostom." In Everett Ferguson, ed. *Encyclopedia of Early Christianity.* New York: Garland Publishing, 1990. 495–97.

Wilson, E. Jan. "Inside a Sumerian Temple: The Ekishnugal at Ur." In Donald W. Parry and Stephen D. Ricks, eds. *The Temple in Time and Eternity.* Provo, UT: Foundation for Ancient Research and Mormon Studies, 1999. 303–33.

Wintermute, O. S. "Introduction" to "Apocalypse of Zephaniah—A New Translation and Introduction." In James H. Charlesworth, ed. *The*

Old Testament Pseudepigrapha. 2 vols. New York: Doubleday, 1983, 1985. 1:497–507.

Woodruff, Wilford. Discourse delivered March 3, 1889 in Provo, Utah. Recorded in Brian H. Stuy, comp. and ed. *Collected Discourses Delivered by President Wilford Woodruff, His Two Counselors, the Twelve Apostles, and Others.* 5 vols. Burbank, CA: B. H. S. Publishing, 1987–92. 1:215–20.

_____. Discourse delivered October 5, 1895, in Salt Lake City, Utah. Recorded in Brian H. Stuy, comp. and ed. *Collected Discourses Delivered by President Wilford Woodruff, His Two Counselors, the Twelve Apostles, and Others.* 5 vols. Burbank, CA: B. H. S. Publishing, 1987–92. 5:198–201.

_____. Discourse delivered October 19, 1896, in Ogden, Utah. Recorded in Brian H. Stuy, comp. and ed. *Collected Discourses Delivered by President Wilford Woodruff, His Two Counselors, the Twelve Apostles, and Others.* 5 vols. Burbank, CA: B. H. S. Publishing, 1987–92. 5:233–240.

Books

Achtemeier, Paul J., ed. *Harper's Bible Dictionary.* San Francisco: Harper Collins Publishers, 1985.

Ahlstrom, Sidney E. *A Religious History of the American People.* New Haven, CT: Yale University Press, 1972.

Andersen, Francis I. and David Noel Freedman. *The Anchor Bible: Amos.* New York: Doubleday, 1989.

Anderson, Richard Lloyd. *Understanding Paul.* Salt Lake City: Deseret Book, 1983.

Anderson, Robert A. *International Theological Commentary: Daniel—Signs and Wonders.* Grand Rapids: Eerdmans, 1984.

Arrington, Leonard J. and Davis Bitton. *The Mormon Experience: A History of the Latter-day Saints.* Boston: George Allen & Unwin, 1979.

Attridge, Harold W. *Hermeneia—A Critical and Historical Commentary on the Bible: Hebrews.* Philadelphia: Fortress Press, 1998.

Bailey, Betty Jane and J. Martin Bailey. *Who Are The Christians in the Middle East?* Grand Rapids: Eerdmans, 2003.

Barker, Kenneth, ed. *The NIV Study Bible.* Grand Rapids: Zondervan, 1995.

Barker, Margaret. *The Gate of Heaven: The History and Symbolism of the*

Temple in Jerusalem. Sheffield, England: Sheffield Phoenix Press, 2008.

Bayley, Harold. *The Lost Language of Symbolism: An Inquiry Into the Origin of Certain Letters, Words, Names, Fairy-Tales, Folklore, and Mythologies.* 2 vols. New York: Carol Publishing, 1990, 1993.

Beadle, Richard and Pamela M. King, eds. *York Mystery Plays: A Selection in Modern Spelling.* Oxford: Clarendon Press, 1984.

Beckwith, Sarah. *Signifying God: Social Relation and Symbolic Act in the York Corpus Christi Plays.* Chicago: The University of Chicago Press, 2001.

Beer, Robert. *The Handbook of Tibetan Buddhist Symbols.* Chicago: Serindia, 2003.

Benson, Ezra Taft. *Teachings of Ezra Taft Benson.* Salt Lake City: Bookcraft, 1998.

Birge, John Kingsley. *The Bektashi Order of Dervishes.* Hartford: Hartford Seminary Press, 1937.

Blaising, Craig A. and Carmen S. Hardin, eds. *Ancient Christian Commentary on Scripture: Psalms 1–50.* Downers Grove, IL: InterVarsity Press, 2008.

Bloesch, Donald G. *Essentials of Evangelical Theology.* 2 vols. Peabody, MA: Prince Press, 2001.

Bowden, John, ed. *Encyclopedia of Christianity.* New York: Oxford University Press, 2005.

Bowker, John. *World Religions: The Great Faiths Explored & Explained.* New York: DK Publishing, 2006.

Bradshaw, Paul F. *Ordination Rites of the Ancient Churches of the East and West.* New York: Pueblo Publishing Company, 1990.

Bray, Gerald, ed. *Ancient Christian Commentary on Scripture: 1–2 Corinthians.* Downers Grove, IL: InterVarsity Press, 1999.

Bridger, David, ed. *The New Jewish Encyclopedia.* New York: Behrman House, 1962.

Bromiley, Geoffrey W., ed. *The International Standard Bible Encyclopedia.* Revised edition. 4 vols. Grand Rapids: Eerdmans, 1979–88.

Brown, Francis, S. R. Driver, and Charles A. Briggs, eds. *A Hebrew and English Lexicon of the Old Testament.* New York: Oxford, 1968.

Brown, Matthew B. *The Gate of Heaven: Insights on the Doctrines and Symbols of the Temple.* American Fork, UT: Covenant, 1999.

Brown, Raymond E., Joseph A. Fitzmyer, and Roland E. Murphy, eds. *The New Jerome Biblical Commentary.* Englewood Cliffs, NJ: Prentice Hall, 1990.

Brueggermann, Walter. *Genesis: A Bible Commentary for Teaching and*

Preaching. Atlanta: John Knox Press, 1973.

Budge, E. A. Wallis. *Egyptian Religion: Ideas of the Afterlife in Ancient Egypt.* New York: Gramercy Books, 1959.

Buerger, David John. *The Mysteries of Godliness.* San Francisco: Smith Research Associates, 1994.

Bullinger, E. W. *Number in Scripture: Its Supernatural Design and Spiritual Significance.* Grand Rapids: Kregel Publications, 1967.

Burkert, Walter. *Greek Religion.* Cambridge, MA: Harvard University Press, 1985.

Buttrick, George Arthur, ed. *The Interpreter's Bible.* 12 vols. New York: Abingdon Press, 1951–57.

Cairns, Ian. *International Theological Commentary: Deuteronomy—Word and Presence.* Grand Rapids: Eerdmans, 1992.

Calvin, John. *A Commentary on Genesis.* 2 vols. John King, ed. Edinburgh: The Banner of Truth Trust, 1964.

Campbell, Beverly. *Eve and the Choice Made in Eden.* Salt Lake City: Bookcraft, 2003.

Campbell, Edward F., Jr. *The Anchor Bible: Ruth.* New York: Doubleday, 1975.

Campbell, Joseph, ed. *The Mysteries: Papers From the Eranos Yearbooks.* New York: Princeton University Press, 1980.

Constantinides, Evagoras. *Orthodoxy 101: A Bird's Eye View.* Northridge, CA: Narthex Press, 2006.

Carlyon, Richard. *A Guide to the Gods.* New York: Quill, 1982.

Charles, John D. *Endowed From On High: Understanding the Symbols of the Endowment.* Bountiful, UT: Horizon, 1997.

Chrysostomos, Archimandrite. *Orthodox Liturgical Dress: An Historical Treatment.* Brookline, MA, 1981.

Church Educational System. *Old Testament: Genesis-2 Samuel [Religion 301] Student Manual.* Second edition, revised. Salt Lake City: Church of Jesus Christ of Latter-day Saints, 1981.

Church, Leslie F., ed. *The NIV Matthew Henry Commentary in One Volume.* Grand Rapids: Zondervan, 1992.

Cirlot, J. E. *A Dictionary of Symbols.* London: Routledge & Kegan Paul, 1962.

Clark, James R., comp. *Messages of the First Presidency of The Church of Jesus Christ of Latter-day Saints.* 6 vols. Salt Lake City: Bookcraft, 1965–75.

Clarke, Adam. *The Holy Bible containing Old and New Testaments with a Commentary and Critical Notes.* 6 vols. New York: Methodist Book Concern.

Clemen, Carl. *Primitive Christianity and Its Non-Jewish Sources.* Edingburg: Clark, 1912.

Cogan, Mordechai. *The Anchor Bible: 1 Kings.* New York: Doubleday, 2001.

Cole, R. Alan. *Tyndale Old Testament Commentaries: Exodus.* Liecester, England: InterVarsity Press, 1973.

Conner, Kevin J. *Interpreting the Symbols and Types.* Portland, OR: City Bible Publishing, 1992.

Connolly, R. Hugh. *Didascalia Apostolorum.* Oxford: Clarendon Press, 1929.

Coogan, Michael D., ed. *The New Oxford Annotated Bible—New Revised Standard Version.* Third edition. New York: Oxford University Press, 2001.

Cooke, G. A. *The Book of Ruth.* Cambridge, England: Cambridge University Press, 1913.

Cooper, J. C. *An Illustrated Encyclopaedia of Traditional Symbols.* London: Thames and Hudson, 1995.

Cowley, Matthias F. *Cowley's Talks on Doctrine.* Chattanooga, TN: Ben. E. Rich, 1902.

Cross, Frank M. and E. A. Livingstone, eds. *The Oxford Dictionary of the Christian Church.* Second edition. New York: Oxford University Press, 1990.

Cundall, Arthur E. and Leon Morris. *Tyndale Old Testament Commentaries: Judges and Ruth.* Downers Grove, IL: InterVarsity Press, 1968.

Dahl, Larry and Donald Q. Cannon, comps. *The Teachings of Joseph Smith.* Salt Lake City: Bookcraft, 1998.

Davis, John J. *Biblical Numerology.* Grand Rapids: Baker Book House, 2000.

Delitzsch, Franz. *Biblical Commentary on the Prophecies of Isaiah.* 2 vols. Grand Rapids: Eerdmans, 1954.

Douglas, Mary. *Purity and Danger: An Analysis of Concepts of Pollution and Taboo.* Binghampton, New York: Vail-Ballou Press, 1980.

Draper, Richard D. *Opening the Seven Seals.* Salt Lake City: Deseret Book, 1991.

Dummelow, J. R., ed. *The One Volume Bible Commentary.* New York: Macmillian, 1936.

Eakin, Frank E., Jr. *The Religion and Culture of Israel: An Introduction to Old Testament Thought.* Boston: Allyn and Bacon, 1971.

Easton, Burton Scott, trans. *The Apostolic Tradition of Hippolytus.* Ann Arbor, MI: Archon Books, 1962.

Edersheim, Alfred. *The Temple: Its Ministry and Services.* Grand Rapids: Eerdmans, 1963.

Ehat, Andrew F. and Lyndon W. Cook, eds. *The Words of Joseph Smith: The Contemporary Accounts of the Nauvoo Discourses of the Prophet Joseph.* Provo, UT: Religious Studies Center, Brigham Young University, 1980.

Eilberg-Schwartz, H. *The Savage In Judaism.* Bloomington, IN: University of Indiana Press, 1990.

Eliade, Mircea, ed. *The Encyclopedia of Religion.* 16 vols. New York: Macmillian, 1987.

Ellwood, Robert S. *Many Peoples, Many Faiths.* Fourth edition. New Jersey: Prentice Hall, 1992.

Elworthy, Frederick Thomas. *The Evil Eye.* London: John Murray, 1895.

_____. *Horns of Honour.* London: John Murray, 1900.

Eyring, Hernry B. *To Draw Closer to God: A Collection of Discourses.* Salt Lake City: Deseret Book, 1997.

Evans, Craig A. *Noncanonical Writings and New Testament Interpretation.* Peabody, MA: Hendrickson Publishers, 1992.

Fairbairn, Patrick. *The Typology of Scripture.* Grand Rapids: Kregel Publications, 1989.

Farbridge, Maurice. *Studies in Biblical and Semitic Symbolism.* London: Kegan Paul, Trench, Trubner & Co., 1923.

Ferguson, Everett, ed. *Encyclopedia of Early Christianity.* New York: Garland Publishing, 1990.

Ferrell, James L. *The Hidden Christ: Beneath the Surface of the Old Testament.* Salt Lake City: Deseret Book, 2009.

Fisher, J. D. C. *Christian Initiation: Baptism in the Medieval West.* Chicago: Liturgy Training Publications, 2004.

Fitzmyer, Joseph A. *The Anchor Bible: The Acts of the Apostles.* New York: Doubleday, 1998.

Fontana, David. *The Secret Language of Symbols.* San Francisco: Chronicle Books, 1994.

Fox, Robin Lane. *Pagans and Christians.* New York: Alfred A. Knopf, 1987.

Freedman, David Noel, ed. *The Anchor Bible Dictionary.* 6 vols. New York: Doubleday, 1992.

Gaebelein, Frank E., ed. *The Expositor's Bible Commentary.* 12 vols. Grand Rapids: Zondervan, 1976–92.

Gaskill, Alonzo L. *The Lost Language of Symbolism: An Essential Guide to Recognizing and Interpreting the Symbols of the Gospel.* Salt Lake City. Deseret Book, 2003.

Gaster, Theodor H. *Myth, Legend, and Custom in the Old Testament*. New York: Harper and Row, 1969.

Ginzberg, Louis, comp. *The Legends of the Jews*. 7 vols. Philadelphia: Jewish Publication Society of America, 1967–69.

Glassé, Cyril. *A Concise Encyclopedia of Islam*. San Francisco: Harper San Francisco, 1989.

Good News Bible. New York: American Bible Society, 1978.

Goodenough, Erwin R. *Jewish Symbols in the Greco-Roman Period*. 6 vols. New York: Pantheon Books, 1953–56.

Goodspeed, Edgar J. *A History of Early Christian Literature*. Chicago: The University of Chicago Press, 1966.

Green, Mark H., III. *The Scriptural Temple*. Springville, UT: Horizon, 2004.

Greenberg, Moshe. *The Anchor Bible: Ezekiel 1–20*. New York: Doubleday, 1983.

Griggs, C. Wilfred, ed. *Apocryphal Writings and the Latter-day Saints*. Provo, UT: Religious Studies Center, Brigham Young University, 1986.

Gonda, Jan. *Vedic Ritual: The Non-Solemn Rites*. Leiden: Brill, 1980.

Gordon, Cyrus H. *Before the Bible: The Common Background of Greek and Hebrew Civilizations*. New York: Harper, 1962.

Guthrie, Donald. *Tyndale New Testament Commentaries: The Pastoral Epistles*. Revised edition. Grand Rapids: Eerdmans, 1998.

Hafen, Bruce C. *The Broken Heart*. Salt Lake City: Deseret Book, 1989.

Hall, James. *Dictionary of Subjects and Symbols in Art*. New York: Harper and Row, 1979.

Hamilton, Victor P. *Handbook on the Pentateuch*. Grand Rapids: Baker Book House, 1982.

Hamlin, John. *International Theological Commentary: Ruth—Surely There Is A Future*. Grand Rapids: Eerdmans, 1996.

Hansen, Gerald E., Jr. *Sacred Walls: Learning From Temple Symbols*. American Fork, UT: Covenant, 2009.

Hastings, James, ed. *Dictionary of the Bible*. Charles Scribner's Sons: New York, 1963.

Heath, Sidney. *The Romance of Symbolism and Its Relation to Church Ornament and Architecture*. London: Francis Griffiths, 1909.

Heen, Erik M. and Philip D. W. Krey, eds. *Ancient Christian Commentary on Scripture: Hebrews*. Downers Grove, IL: InterVarsity Press, 2005

Hennecke, Edgar and Wilhelm Schneemelcher, eds. *New Testament Apocrypha*. vol. 2. Philadelphia: The Westminster Press, 1965.

Henry, Hugh T. *Catholic Customs and Symbols*. New York: Benziger Brothers, 1925.

Hertz, Joseph. *The Pentateuch and Haftorahs*. London: Soncino Press, 1962.

Hinckley, Gordon B. *Teachings of Gordon B. Hinckley*. Salt Lake City: Deseret Book, 1997.

Holifield, E. Brooks. *Theology in America*. New Haven, CT: Yale University Press, 2003.

Holland, Jeffery R. and Patricia T. Holland, *On Earth As It Is In Heaven*. Salt Lake City: Desert Book, 1989.

Holzapfel, Richard Neitzel and David Roth Seely. *My Father's House: Temple Worship and Symbolism in the New Testament*. Salt Lake City: Bookcraft, 1994.

Hopko, Thomas. *The Orthodox Faith: An Elementary Handbook on the Orthodox Faith—Worship*. 4 vols. New York: The Department of Religious Education, The Orthodox Church of America, 1983.

Hugenberger, Gordon Paul. *Marriage as a Covenant: A Study of Biblical Law and Ethics Governing Marriage Developed from the Perspective of Malachi*. Leiden: E. J. Brill, 1994.

Hunter, Howard W. *The Teachings of Howard W. Hunter*. Clyde J. Williams, ed. Salt Lake City: Bookcraft, 1998.

Hunter, Milton R. *Pearl of Great Price Commentary*. Salt Lake City: Stevens and Wallis, 1951.

Ifrah, Georges. *The Universal History of Numbers: From Prehistory to the Invention of the Computer*. New York: John Wiley and Sons, 2000.

Irwin, Kevin W. and Edmund D. Pellegrino, eds. *Preserving the Creation: Environmental Theology and Ethics*. Washington, DC: Georgetown University Press, 1992.

James, E. O. *Myth and Ritual in the Ancient Near East*. New York: Barnes & Noble, 1958.

James, Montague Rhodes. *The Apocryphal New Testament*. Oxford: Clarendon Press, 1960.

Janzen, J. Gerald. *International Theological Commentary: Genesis 12–50— Abraham and All the Families of the Earth*. Grand Rapids: Eerdmans, 1993.

Johnson, Elizabeth A. *She Who Is: The Mystery of God in Feminist Theological Discourse*. New York: Crossroads, 1994.

Johnson, Luke Timothy. *Sacra Pagina: The Acts of the Apostles*. Collegeville, MN: The Liturgical Press, 1992.

Johnson, Maxwell E. *The Rites of Christian Initiation: Their Evolution and Interpretation.* Revised and expanded edition. Collegeville, MN: Order of Saint Benedict, 2007.

Johnston, Robert D. *Numbers in the Bible: God's Design in Biblical Numerology.* Grand Rapids: Kregel Publications, 1990.

Joranson, Philip N., ed. *Cry of the Environment.* Santa Fe, NM: Bear and Company, 1984.

Julien, Nadia. *The Mammoth Dictionary of Symbols.* New York: Carroll & Graf Publishers, 1996.

Jungmann, Joseph A. *The Mass of the Roman Rite.* Revised and abridged edition. New York: Benzinger Brothers, 1959.

Just, Arthur A., Jr. *Ancient Christian Commentary on Scripture—Luke.* Downers Grove, IL: InterVarsity Press, 2003.

Keil, Carl F. *Biblical Commentary on the Prophecies of Ezekiel.* 2 vols. Grand Rapids: Eerdmans, 1950.

_____ and Franz Delitzsch. *Biblical Commentary on the Old Testament: The Pentateuch.* Grand Rapids: Eerdmans, 1986.

Kenney, Scott G., ed. *Wilford Woodruff's Journal.* 9 vols. Midvale, UT: Signature Books, 1983.

Kertzer, Morris N. and Lawrence A. Hoffman. *What is a Jew?* New York: Collier Books, 1993.

Kidner, Derek. *Tyndale Old Testament Commentaries: Genesis.* Downers Grove, IL: InterVarsity Press, 1967.

Kimball, Spencer W. *Faith Precedes the Miracle.* Salt Lake City: Deseret Book, 1979.

_____. *Teachings of Spencer W. Kimball.* Edward L. Kimball, comp. Salt Lake City: Deseret Book, 1998.

Kittel, Gerhard, ed. *Theological Dictionary of the New Testament.* 10 vols. Grand Rapids: Eerdmans, 1967.

Knight, Thomas C. *The Knights of Columbus—Illustrated.* Chicago: Ezra A. Cook, 1920.

Kraut, Ogden. *The Priesthood Garment.* Salt Lake City: Pioneer Press, 1971.

Kristenesen, W. Brede. *Het leven uit de dood: Studeien over Egyptische en oud-Griekse godsdienst.* Second edition. Haarlem: Bohn, 1949.

Kugel, James L. *Traditions of the Bible: A Guide to the Bible as it Was at the Start of the Common Era.* Cambridge, MA: Harvard University Press, 1998.

Lapidus, Ira M. *A History of Islamic Societies.* New York: Cambridge University Press, 1989.

Larsen, Dean L. *Setting the Record Straight: Mormon Temples.* Orem, UT: Millennial Press, 2007.

LDS Bible Dictionary. Salt Lake City: The Church of Jesus Christ of Latter-day Saints, 1986.

Louth, Andrew, ed. *Ancient Christian Commentary on Scripture: Genesis 1–11.* Downers Grove, IL: InterVarsity Press, 2001.

Ludlow, Daniel H., ed. *The Encyclopedia of Mormonism.* 4 vols. New York: Macmillian, 1992.

Ludlow, Victor L. *Unlocking the Old Testament.* Salt Lake City: Deseret Book, 1981.

Lundquist, John M. and Stephen D. Ricks, eds. *By Study and Also By Faith.* 2 vols. Provo, UT: Foundation for Ancient Research and Mormon Studies, 1990.

Mace, David R. *Hebrew Marriage: A Sociological Study.* New York: Philosophical Library, 1953.

Mackenzie, Donald A. *Egyptian Myths and Legends.* New York: Gramercy Books, 1994.

Mackey, Albert G. *An Encyclopedia of Freemasonry and its Kindred Sciences.* Philadelphia: Moss and Company, 1879.

Madsen, Truman G. *The Temple: Where Heaven Meets Earth.* Salt Lake City: Deseret Book, 2008.

Malan, S. C. *The Book of Adam and Eve also called The Conflict of Adam and Eve with Satan.* London: Williams and Northgate, 1882.

Marcus, Ivan G. *Piety and Society: The Jewish Priests of Medieval Germany.* Leiden, The Netherlands: E. J. Brill, 1981.

Marshall, I. Howard. *Tyndale New Testament Commentaries: Acts.* Grand Rapids: InterVarsity Press, 1998.

Martimort, Aimé Georges. *Deaconesses: An Historical Study.* San Francisco: Ignatius Press, 1986.

Matt, Daniel C. *The Essential Kabbalah—The Heart of Jewish Mysticism.* San Francisco: Harper San Francisco, 1995.

Matthews, Robert J. *A Bible! A Bible!.* Salt Lake City: Bookcraft, 1990.

Maxwell, William D. *An Outline of Christian Worship: Its Development and Forms.* London: Oxford University Press, 1936.

Mayo, Janet. *A History of Ecclesiastical Dress.* London: B. T. Batsford, 1984.

McBrien, Richard P., ed. *The HarperCollins Encyclopedia of Catholicism.* San Francisco: Harper San Francisco, 1995.

McConkie, Bruce R. *The Promised Messiah.* Salt Lake City: Deseret Book, 1978.

_____. *The Mortal Messiah.* 4 vols. Salt Lake City: Deseret Book, 1980–81.

_____. *Doctrinal New Testament Commentary.* 3 vols. Salt Lake City: Bookcraft, 1987–88.

_____. *A New Witness for the Articles of Faith.* Salt Lake City: Deseret Book, 1985.

McConkie, Joseph Fielding. *Gospel Symbolism.* Salt Lake City: Bookcraft, 1985.

_____ and Donald W. Parry. *A Guide to Scriptural Symbols.* Salt Lake City: Bookcraft, 1990.

McCormack, Arthur. *Christian Initiation.* New York: Hawthorn, 1969.

McKechnie, Jean L., ed. *Webster's New Twentieth Century Dictionary of the English Language, Unabridged.* Second edition. Collins World, 1978.

McKenna, Mary Lawrence. *Women of the Church: Role and Renewal.* New York: P. J. Kennedy & Sons, 1967.

McKenzie, John L., ed. *Dictionary of the Bible.* Milwaukee, WI: The Bruce Publishing Company, 1965.

McManners, John, ed. *The Oxford Illustrated History of Christianity.* New York: Oxford University Press, 1990.

Mead, G. R. S. *Pistis Sophia.* London: The Theological Publishing Society, 1896.

Meyers, Carol L. and Eric M. Meyers. *The Anchor Bible: Haggai, Zechariah 1–8.* New York: Doubleday, 1987.

Miller, John H. *Fundamentals of the Liturgy.* Notre Dame, IN: Fides Publishers, 1959.

Milton, John. *A Treatise on Christian Doctrine.* Cambridge: Cambridge University Press, 1825.

Mitchell, Leonel L. *Baptismal Anointing.* South Bend, IN: University of Notre Dame Press, 1978.

Moffatt, James, trans. *A New Translation of The Bible.* New York: Harper & Brothers, 1950.

Morgan, Stephen G. *Hidden Treasures of Knowledge: An Abridgement of Ancient Religious Documents which Support the Revealed Word of God.* Salt Lake City: Deseret Book, 2006.

Morris, Leon. *Tyndale New Testament Commentaries: 1 Corinthians.* Revised edition. Grand Rapids: Eerdmans, 1998.

Myers, Allen C., ed. *The Eerdmans Bible Dictionary.* Grand Rapids: Eerdmans, 1987.

Nachmanides, Raban. *Commentary on the Torah.* 5 vols. New York: Shilo Publishing House, 1971–76.

National Conference of Catholic Bishops. *The Sacramentary.* New York: Catholic Book Publishing Company, 1985.

_____. *Lectionary for Mass.* New Jersey: Catholic Book Publishing Corporation, 1998.

Neusner, Jacob. *Genesis Rabbah: The Judaic Commentary to the Book of Genesis.* Atlanta: Scholars Press, 1985.

_____. *The Enchantments of Judaism.* Atlanta: Scholars Press, 1991.

New Catholic Encyclopedia. 16 vols. New York: McGraw-Hill, 1967.

Nibley, Hugh. *Mormonism and Early Christianity.* Provo, UT: Foundation for Ancient Research and Mormon Studies, 1987.

_____. *Old Testament and Related Studies.* Provo, UT: Foundation for Ancient Research and Mormon Studies, 1987.

_____. *Since Cumorah.* Provo, UT: Foundation for Ancient Research and Mormon Studies, 1988.

_____. *Ancient Documents and the Pearl of Great Price.* Provo, UT: Foundation For Ancient Research and Mormon Studies, 1989.

_____. *Teachings of the Book of Mormon.* Semester 1. Provo, UT: Foundation for Ancient Research and Mormon Studies, 1989–90.

_____. *Temple and Cosmos: Beyond this Ignorant Present.* Provo, UT: Foundation for Ancient Research and Mormon Studies, 1992.

_____. *Brother Brigham Challenges the Saints.* Provo, UT: Foundation for Ancient Research and Mormon Studies, 1994.

_____. *The Message of the Joseph Smith Papyri: An Egyptian Endowment.* Second edition. Salt Lake City: Deseret Book and Foundation for Ancient Research and Mormon Studies, 2005.

_____. *Eloquent Witness: Nibley on Himself, Others, and the Temple.* Provo, UT: Foundation for Ancient Research and Mormon Studies, 2008.

Nicoll, W. Robertson. *Expositor's Greek Testament.* 5 vols. Grand Rapids: Eerdmans, 1983.

Noss, John B. *Man's Religions.* Fifth edition. New York: Macmillan, 1974.

Norris, Herbert. *Church Vestments: Their Origin & Development.* London: J. M. Dent & Sons, 1949.

Noth, Martin. *The Laws In The Pentateuch and Other Studies.* Philadelphia: Fortress Press, 1967.

Ogden, D. Kelly and Andrew C. Skinner. *Verse by Verse: Acts Through Revelation.* Salt Lake City: Deseret Book, 1998.

_____. *Verse by Verse: The Four Gospels.* Salt Lake City: Deseret Book, 2006.

Orr, William F. and James Arthur Walther, *The Anchor Bible: 1 Corinthians.* New York: Doubleday, 1976.

Oxtoby, William G. and Alan F. Segal, eds. *A Concise Introduction to World Religions.* New York: Oxford University Press, 2007.

Pagels, Elaine. *Adam, Eve, and the Serpent.* New York: Vintage Books, 1989.

Papadeas, George L. *Greek Orthodox Holy Week and Easter Services*. New York, 1975.

Parrinder, Geoffrey. *World Religions From Ancient History to the Present*. New York: Facts on File Publications, 1983.

Parry, Donald W. *Temples of the Ancient World*. Provo, UT: Foundation for Ancient Research and Mormon Studies, 1994.

_____ and Jay A. Parry. *Understanding the Book of Revelation*. Salt Lake City: Deseret Book, 1998.

_____ and Stephen D. Ricks, eds. *The Temple in Time and Eternity*. Provo, UT: Foundation for Ancient Research and Mormon Studies, 1999.

_____ and Jay A. Parry. *Symbols & Shadows: Unlocking a Deeper Understanding of the Atonement*. Salt Lake City: Deseret Book, 2009.

Partridge, Christopher, ed. *Introduction to World Religions*. Minneapolis: Fortress Press, 2005.

Pfeiffer, Charles F. and Everrett F. Harrison, eds. *The Wycliffe Bible Commentary*. Chicago: Moody Press, 1975.

Pollock, Robert. *The Everything World's Religions Book*. Avon, MA: Adams Media Corporation, 2002.

Rasmussen, Ellis T. *A Latter-Day Saint Commentary on the Old Testament*. Salt Lake City: Deseret Book, 1993.

Readers Digest, *Great People of the Bible and How they Lived*. Pleasantville, NY: Readers Digest, 1974.

Reed, Michael Glen. *The Development of the LDS Church's Attitude Toward the Cross*. Sacramento, CA: California State University, Sacramento, Masters Thesis, 2009.

Rest, Friedrich. *Our Christian Symbols*. New York: The Pilgrim Press, 1987.

Reynolds, George and Janne M. Sjodahl. *Commentary on the Book of Mormon*. 7 vols. Philip C. Reynolds, ed. and arr. Salt Lake City: Deseret Book, 1955–61.

Ricoeur, Paul. *The Symbolism of Evil*. Boston: Beacon Press, 1967.

Roberts, Alexander and James Donaldson, eds. *Ante-Nicene Fathers*. 10 vols. Peabody, MA: Hendrickson Publishers, 1994.

Robinson, Gnana. *International Theological Commentary: 1 & 2 Samuel: Let Us Be Like The Nations*. Grand Rapids: Eerdmans, 1993.

Robinson, James M., ed. *The Nag Hammadi Library*. Revised edition. San Francisco: Harper and Row, 1988.

Rostovzeff, Mikhail I. *Mystic Italy*. New York: Holt, 1927.

Rothenberg, Jerome and Diane Rothenberg. *Symposium of the Whole: A Range of Discourse Toward an Ethnopoetics*. Berkeley, CA: University of California Press, 1983.

Rudolph, Kurt. *Gnosis: The Nature & History of Gnosticism.* San Francisco: Harper San Francisco, 1987.

Ryken, Leland, James C. Wilhoit, and Tremper Longman, III, eds. *Dictionary of Biblical Imagery.* Downers Grove, IL: InterVarsity Press, 1998.

Rykwert, Joseph. *Church Building.* New York: Hawthorn Books, 1966.

Sailhamer, John H. *The Pentateuch as Narrative.* Grand Rapids: Zondervan, 1992.

Sarna, Nahum M., ed. *The JPS Torah Commentary: Exodus.* Philadelphia: Fortress Press, 1991.

Schaff, Philip, ed. *Nicene and Post-Nicene Fathers—First Series.* 14 vols. Peabody, MA: Hendrickson Publishers, 1994.

Schaff, Philip and Henry Wace, eds. *Nicene and Post-Nicene Fathers—Second Series.* 14 vols. Peabody, MA: Hendrickson Publishers, 1994.

Schimmel, Annemarie. *Mystical Dimensions of Islam.* Chapel Hill, NC: University of North Carolina Press, 1986.

Scott, E. F. *The Moffatt New Testament Commentary: The Epistles of Paul to the Colossians, to Philemon, and to the Ephesians.* London: Hodder and Stoughton, 1952.

_____. *The Moffatt New Testament Commentary: The Pastoral Epistles.* London: Hodder and Stoughton, 1957.

Shariati, Ali. *Hajj.* Ali A. Behzadnia and Najla Denny, translators. Houston: Free Islamic Literatures, 1978.

Shepsut, Asia. *Journey of the Priestess.* San Francisco: Harper Collins, 1993.

Sheridan, Mark, ed. *Ancient Christian Commentary on Scripture: Genesis 12–50.* Downers Grove, IL: InterVarsity Press, 2002.

Simonetti, Manlio, ed. *Ancient Christian Commentary on Scripture—Matthew 1–13.* Downers Grove, IL: InterVarsity Press, 2001.

Skinner, Andrew. *Temple Worship: 20 Truths that will Bless your Life.* Salt Lake City: Deseret Book, 2007.

Slemming, Charles W. *These Are The Garments: A Study of the Garments of the High Priest of Israel.* London: Marshall, Morgan Scott, 1945.

Smith, J. M. Powis and Edgar J. Goodspeed, translators. *The Complete Bible—and American Translation.* Chicago: The University of Chicago Press, 1949.

Smith, Joseph. *Teachings of the Prophet Joseph Smith.* Joseph Fielding Smith, comp. Salt Lake City: Deseret Book, 1976.

Smith, Joseph. *History of the Church of Jesus Christ of Latter-day Saints.* B. H. Roberts, ed. 7 vols. Salt Lake City: Deseret Book, 1978.

Smith, Joseph F. *Gospel Doctrine: Selections from the Sermons and Writings of Joseph F. Smith.* Salt Lake City: Bookcraft, 1998.

Smith, Joseph Fielding, Jr. *Answers to Gospel Questions.* 5 vols. Salt Lake City: Deseret Book, 1993.

_____ *Doctrines of Salvation.* 3 vols. Salt Lake City: Bookcraft, 1998.

Smith, Mick. *The Book of Revelation Plain, Pure, and Simple.* Salt Lake City: Bookcraft, 1998.

Smith, Stelman and Judson Cornwall. *The Exhaustive Dictionary of Bible Names.* New Jersey: Bridge-Logos Publishing, 1998.

Speiser, E. A. *The Anchor Bible: Genesis.* New York: Doubleday, 1962.

Springett, Bernard H. *Secret Sects of Syria and Lebanon.* London: George Allen and Unwin, 1922.

Stone, Merlin. *When God was a Woman.* New York: Harcourt Brace Jovanovich, 1976.

Stuy, Brian H., comp. and ed. *Collected Discourses Delivered by President Wilford Woodruff, His Two Counselors, the Twelve Apostles, and Others.* 5 vols. . Burbank, CA: B. H. S. Publishing, 1987–92.

Talmage, James E. *The House of the Lord.* Salt Lake City: Deseret Book, 1971.

_____. *Jesus the Christ: A Study of the Messiah and His Mission According to Holy Scriptures Both Ancient and Modern.* Salt Lake City: The Church of Jesus Christ of Latter-day Saints, 1981.

Teachings Of Presidents Of The Church: Wilford Woodruff. Salt Lake City: Intellectual Reserve, 2004.

Thayer, Joseph H. *Thayer's Greek-English Lexicon of the New Testament.* Peabody, MA: Hendrickson Publishers, 1999.

The New Catholic Encyclopedia. Second edition. 15 vols. Detroit: Gale Group in association with the Catholic University of America, 2003.

Thompson, Katie. *The Complete Children's Liturgy Book: Liturgies of the Word for Years A, B, C.* Mystic, CT: Twenty-Third Publications, 1995.

Thurston, Herbert. *The Holy Year of Jubilee.* 1980 reprint. Saint Louis: Herder, 1900.

Todeschi, Kevin. *The Encyclopedia of Symbolism.* New York: The Berkley Publishing Group, 1995.

Torjesen, Karen Jo. *When Women Were Priests: Women's Leadership in the Early Church & the Scandal of their Subordination in the Rise of Christianity.* San Francisco: Harper San Francisco, 1993.

Tresidder, Jack. *Symbols and Their Meanings.* London: Duncan Baird Publishers, 2000.

Trimingham, J. Spencer. *The Sufi Orders in Islam.* New York: Oxford University Press, 1998.

Turner, Rodney. *Woman and the Priesthood.* Salt Lake City: Deseret Book, 1972.

Twining, Louisa. *Symbols and Emblems of Early and Mediaeval Christian Art.* New edition. London: John Murray, 1885.

Unger, Merrill F. *Unger's Bible Dictionary.* Chicago: Moody Press, 1966.

Van Gennep, Arnold. *The Rites of Passage.* Monika B. Vizedom and Gabrielle L. Caffee, translators. Chicago: The University of Chicago Press, 1960.

Van Wagoner, Richard S., ed. *The Complete Discourses of Brigham Young.* 5 vols. Salt Lake City: The Smith-Pettit Foundation, 2009.

Vawter, Bruce. *On Genesis: A New Reading.* New York: Doubleday, 1977.

Vellian, Jacob, ed. *Studies on Syrian Baptismal Rites.* Kottayam, India: C.M.S. Press, 1973.

Wainwright, Geoffrey and Karen B. Westerfield Tucker, eds. *The Oxford History of Christian Worship.* New York: Oxford University Press, 2006.

Walker, James D. *Commentator's Lectionary.* Milwaukee: The Bruce Publishing Company, 1965.

Wallace, James A., Robert P. Waznak, and Guerric DeBona. *Lift Up Your Hearts—Homilies for the "A" Cycle.* New York: Paulist Press, 2004.

Weinrich, William C., ed. *Ancient Christian Commentary on Scripture: Revelation.* Downers Grove, IL: InterVarsity Press, 2005.

Wenham, Gordon J. *Word Biblical Commentary: Genesis 1–15.* Waco, TX: Word Books, 1987.

Welch, John W. *The Sermon at the Temple, and the Sermon on the Mount.* Provo, UT: The Foundation for Ancient Research and Mormon Studies, 1990.

West, Fritz. *Scripture and Memory: The Ecumenical Hermeneutic of the Three-Year Lectionaries.* Collegeville, MN: Liturgical Press, 1997.

Westermann, Claus. *Genesis 12–36: A Commentary.* Minneapolis: Augsburg Publishing House, 1981.

Wilcox, S. Michael. *House of Glory: Finding Personal Meaning in the Temple.* Salt Lake City: Deseret Book, 1995.

Wilson, Walter L. *A Dictionary of Bible Types.* Peabody, MA: Hendrickson Publishers, 1999.

Wise, Michael, Martin Abegg, Jr., and Edward Cook, translators. *The Dead Sea Scrolls—A New Translation.* New York: HarperCollins, 1999.

Wiseman, Donald J. *Tyndale Old Testament Commentaries: 1 & 2 Kings.* Downers Grove, IL: InterVarsity Press, 1993.

Woodruff, Wilford. *Leaves from My Journal.* Salt Lake City: Juvenile Instructor Office, 1881.

Yonge, C. D., trans. *The Works of Philo*. Peabody, MA: Hendrickson Publishers, 1997.

Young, Edward J. *The Book of Isaiah*. 3 vols. Grand Rapids: Eerdmans, 1997.

Young, Robert. *Young's Literal Translation of the Bible*. Revised edition. Grand Rapids: Guardian Press, 1976.

Zepp, Ira G., Jr. *A Muslim Primer*. Wesminster, MD: Wakefield Editions, 1992.

About the Author

Brother Gaskill was reared near Independence, Missouri, where he converted to The Church of Jesus Christ of Latter-day Saints in November of 1984. Prior to his conversion he was a practicing Greek Orthodox. One year after his baptism, he served a full-time mission in England.

Professionally, Brother Gaskill taught seminary for four years in southeastern Idaho, after which he was an institute director at Stanford University and at UC Berkeley. He is currently a professor of church history and doctrine at Brigham Young University, where his primary teaching focus is world religions and Christian history.

He is the author of numerous articles and books, including:

- *The Lost Language of Symbolism—An Essential Guide for Recognizing and Interpreting Symbols of the Gospel*
- *Odds Are, You're Going to be Exalted—Evidence that the Plan of Salvation Works!*
- *Know Your Religions Volume 1—A Comparative Look at Mormonism and Catholicism*
- *Paradise Lost—Understanding the Symbolic Message of the Fall*

He and his wife, Lori, are the parents of five children, and reside in Payson, Utah.

0 26575 59650 2